SAUDI ARABIAN HYDROCARBONS
AND WORLD AFFAIRS

Abdulhadi H. Taher
and
Michael Matthews

SAUDI ARABIAN HYDROCARBONS
AND WORLD AFFAIRS

SAQI

ISBN: 978-0-86356-463-5

Copyright © Abdulhadi H. Taher and Michael Matthews, 2011

A full CIP record for this book is available from the British Library

A full CIP record for this book is available from the Library of Congress

Manufactured in Lebanon

SAQI

26 Westbourne Grove, London W2 5RH
www.saqibooks.com

Contents

بسم الله الرحمن الرحيم

Foreword

This book follows an earlier one published almost thirty years ago called *Energy: A Global Outlook*, and subtitled 'The Case for Effective International Co-operation'. However, it is not merely an update of the earlier work, but one with more detail concerning the role of Saudi Arabian hydrocarbons in underpinning the industrialization of the Kingdom's own economy, with indigenous natural gas playing a critically important role in this context. Saudi petroleum exports based on a high level and long duration plateau of production have provided a stable and reliable basis for the world trade in oil and economic growth in numerous oil importing countries. At the same time oil production in some other major oil provinces worldwide has been declining for some years now. New oil discoveries outside OPEC member countries have been relatively modest and many of them concentrated in deep water prospects. Some of these involve prospectively very high development costs and/or hazardous outcomes, as the world witnessed in 2010 with the explosion at the Macondo Well in the Gulf of Mexico.

My recent rereading of the foreword to my earlier book afforded me a good deal of satisfaction. This was not on grounds of complacency but simply because there was nothing included within it which I would now choose to rewrite because of changes in the real world which have occurred in the meantime. The topics discussed in the first few paragraphs in 1981 remain highly relevant in the world of 2011 and, similarly, they remain positive. What were these remarks?

First, the world had historically depended on a sequence of primary energy for its needs: initially, wood had been predominant in the pre-industrial era; it had been superseded by coal; then during the twentieth century oil surpassed coal because of its convenience, versatility and its low comparative cost, until 1973 at least. However, on account of comparatively low proved oil reserves relative to high production, the need to diversify energy sources, both conventional and non-conventional, renewable and non-renewable, was seen as essential thirty years ago.

The three fossil fuels, oil, coal and natural gas, still account for the bulk of world consumption of commercial energy. Growth rates in consumption of energy have been dramatically reduced relative to economic growth, especially during periods of economic recession in the advanced countries.

Secondly, in 1981 we saw significant historical, current and future issues continuing to characterize the international oil market and the global energy industry. Oil and energy-related problems in certain countries, groups of countries and the world as a whole were envisaged. Divergent viewpoints and interests of oil-producing and non-oil-producing developing countries and industrialized countries were foreseen as continuing, as indeed they did. But the urgent need for international recognition to identify areas of cooperation was also identified. The formation of the G20 in 2008 and the stimulus given to it in 2009, along with the role of the International Energy Forum, provides some optimism that more constructive dialogues can be arranged in the future. By 1981 there was already a flood of books from independent authors, oil companies, governments, the International Energy Agency, OPEC, universities and research institutes and these have continued, with problems discussed and solutions proposed. These have continued but their tone has perhaps become less strident with the need for more constructive initiatives more evident in this era.

Among solutions proposed thirty years ago, I suggested reasonable discipline through the adoption of fiscal policies which recognized explicitly the importance of investment for both conservation and substitution in the energy sector, with a genuine willingness to try and understand the preoccupations and problems facing other countries, whether they be exporters or importers of oil or other forms of energy.

I justified the book in 1981 on the basis of its main difference from others being published at a similar time. This was that I examined the energy problem on a global scale but also on a resource-orientation as well as in a political framework. This characteristic remains true of this new book. At the time, too, the players in the international energy market were both national governments, major oil and energy companies, along with the IEA and OPEC. This remains true today. I averred then and do so again that it is essential to approach problems in an integrated manner. It is only through such an approach that one can gain a real appreciation of the magnitude of the problems involved, whether economic, political or otherwise, and hence develop a more comprehensive assessment of the complexity and significance of possible solutions. Decisions to adopt certain solutions need to be made within a more rational atmosphere globally than those taken sometimes in the past.

The emergence of the world's two most populous countries, China, in particular, and India, as major players on the world's political, economic and energy stage has been a major phenomenon of recent years. Though the birth of China's growing dominance can be traced to the reforms introduced by Deng Xiaoping in 1978, the continuing remarkable growth of the Chinese economy and its energy needs was not widely recognized thirty years ago. The continuing uncertainties regarding China's fast-growing energy needs and how they will be met over the next decade, let alone the next twenty to thirty years, remain largely unanswered questions, even if its economic growth and the energy intensity of it falls significantly. The intensity of Chinese energy use per unit of GDP growth has varied considerably over the last forty to fifty years.

Another important uncertainty for the future is the level of oil prices, compounded in our view because of the speculative activity of money invested in spot and futures trading in crude oil and refined products, the growth of which has been an important feature of the last thirty years. Price determination on the basis of marginal markets where crude oil volumes such as North Sea Brent are in long-term decline seems an unstable and volatile foundation not in the best interests of either major oil exporters or oil importers. The experience of 2008 when oil prices overshot then undershot the underlying pressures of oil supply and demand in the world market highlights an essentially undesirable aspect of a major commodity entering world trade.

Other significant features of world energy markets during the last thirty years have included the break-up of the former Soviet Union. During the ten years to 2000, domestic consumption of both oil and gas fell dramatically and more so than production of both. Thus incremental supplies reaching the world market served to relieve potential upward pressure on prices of oil and gas entering world trade during this decade. Similarly, the invasion of Iraq in 2003 and the continuing internal instability in that country have militated against the redevelopment of its oil industry and its capacity to significantly increase its oil export volumes which will surely be required, given the growth of projected worldwide needs and Iraq's ample base of proved reserves.

The financial crisis which started in the advanced industrialized countries in 2007 and led on to the severest economic recession (since 1945) among them in 2008–9 meant that developing countries led by China and India continued to catch up fast in economic terms during this period with the more advanced countries. The question now arises as to whether the developing countries being led by China will be able to sustain significantly faster growth, at least on a per capita basis, than the already more advanced countries. In any event, China's population is stabilizing and its economic growth is expected to slow down significantly.

Now I wish to turn my attention to acknowledge sources used in preparing this book. In the first place we have to recognize the great debt we owe to the prestigious book *A Land Transformed: The Arabian Peninsula, Saudi Arabia and Saudi Aramco*. This is a major work on the Kingdom, published in 2006 by the Saudi Arabian Oil Company (Saudi Aramco), Dhahran, Saudi Arabia. We commend this to anyone wishing to access more detail, history and the modern development of the country and the growth of its indigenous hydrocarbons. These have made Saudi Arabia such an important component of the world oil and gas sector, and of the world economy as a whole.

Two books covering Muhammad and the rise of Islam were useful sources referred to in the preparation of the Introduction: Martin Lings's *Muhammad, his Life* is based on the earliest source documents and Professor Hugh Kennedy's *Great Arab Conquests: How the Spread of Islam Changed the World we Live in.* Other sources used in this context were encyclopedias covering Islam from the universities of Oxford, Cambridge and Harvard, along with several other more specialized books.

Among sources used in the preparation of Parts II–V of this book, an early and reliable update of world energy statistics is the *BP Statistical Review of World Energy 2010* (2009 and earlier from its data bank). This provides a useful base for the examination of the economic recession of 2008–9 and its effect on the energy sector. Secondly, we have to acknowledge our indebtedness to the Secretariats of the Organization of Oil Exporting Countries (OPEC) and the International Energy Agency (IEA), based in Vienna and Paris respectively, for their long-term projections through to 2030 published in 2009. Also in this context the projections through to 2035 from the Energy Information Administration of the US Department of Energy published in 2010 were the first ones we saw to look through to the horizon of twenty-five years hence. Other sources, including newspapers and periodicals, have been used with appropriate references shown in the text. Reference has been made to Communiqués from G20 meetings. Data from the United Nations (UN) International Monetary Fund (IMF) and World Bank also feature in this book.

Finally, I have to thank my co-author Mr Michael Matthews for his sterling and invaluable contribution in preparing much of the draft material for this book. We started working together as long ago as 1978 and cooperated in a number of joint ventures. Collectively, these formed a worthwhile testimony to the need for and achievement of some useful international cooperation: individuals with different national and cultural backgrounds can produce an outcome greater than that which could be accomplished by either of them on their own.

Abdulhadi H. Taher
Jeddah, Saudi Arabia

Introduction

Since 1960 a flood of international visitors has poured into Saudi Arabia. And so far as the petroleum and mineral sectors were concerned, they were primarily interested in having an audience with Sheikh Abdullah A. Al-Turaiki, the first Minister of Petroleum and Mineral Resources. Shortly after he was appointed as Minister, he nominated me to be the first Director General of the Ministry of Petroleum and Mineral Resources.

Some of the international visitors were referred to see me. In my new capacity, as my academic background was in finance and business administration, I had to gather some basic education in the fields of oil and minerals. This was mostly achieved by working with two international petroleum experts, Mr James McPherson, who was previously a Vice President of Amin Oil, and Mr James Prior, a CPA with an office in New York. Mr Frank Hendrex, a lawyer from a law firm in New York, also assisted me.

In the meantime, I assumed all the functions assigned to the position of Director General which meant working directly with the late Sheikh Turaiki, the Minister who dealt with Aramco, and with the late Dr Fadil K. Qabbani (a graduate of the Colorado School of Mines with long experience in mining both inside and outside Saudi Arabia)

I regarded myself as an apprentice working with these world-acknowledged experts. So whatever experience I gained in that position led me to read more and more about this very wide field of knowledge. One of the international visitors referred to see me was a German geologist. As it happened he was personally interested in the prehistoric geology of the Arabian Peninsula. As a souvenir of his visit he gave me a book that dealt with prehistoric geology of the world, when the Arabian Peninsula was part of Africa with no Red Sea to separate the peninsula from the rest of Africa.

I begin with this prehistoric information as an introduction to the time when water sprang between the thighs and hands of Ismail and his mother in Makkah.

Makkah Al-Mukarramah is almost always hot. So, one afternoon Abraham decided to head north to where he came from. He left Hajar and her baby Ismail all alone with some dates and a goat-skin leather container of water. Before saying goodbye he kissed his baby son Ismail and wanted to leave Hajar, with her eyes full of tears and baby Ismail screaming. Before Abraham said his warm goodbye to his son and to his mother, Hajar looked at the dates and water and asked Abraham, 'Did Allah order you to do so?' pointing to Ismail with eyes full of tears. He answered back, 'Yes.' Hajar's response to her husband was, 'If so, Allah will not disappoint us.'

So she was left all alone with Ismail crying, feeling hungry and thirsty. She ran to a nearby hill and kept running back and forth between the two hills called Al-Safa and Al-Marwa. In the middle of this she looked at her baby with unbelieving eyes, saw water springing between his legs and was afraid that the water might drown him. Not knowing what to do, she put her hands between the water and the baby, saying: 'Zummi Zummi'. Hence, ever since, that spring was named Zum Zum.

This fascinating story marks the start of the economic development of the Arabian Peninsula, millennia before oil was discovered. The Arabs began to make their annual pilgrimage to the House of God (al-Ka'bah), answering Abraham's call from one of many mountains around the barren valley of Makkah to Haj.

Since then, hundreds of millions of pilgrims have performed the pilgrimage to Makkah, and with them great quantities of goods, food and other supplies poured into Makkah. The Arabs of that time found a golden opportunity to trade. Other opportunities for cultural activities and annual trade fairs started to be developed. Over the years, it became crowded. The closest word to translate this new development of crowds of people was found in the Arabic word *iktazz*, i.e. became crowded. Hence it became *ukaz*, or *souk ukaz*, with trade, poets and other activities that flourished in such crowds at that time many centuries ago.

The featuring of poetry made a significant impact on the Arabic language. Commercial activity, trade exhibitions, the buying and selling of goods were important. Social, political, military and moral issues were all discussed. Ideals of integrity, benevolence, and wisdom permeated the thoughts of wise Arabs. These gatherings made it possible for an exchange of prisoners of war between the tribes and an ending of hostility between them. A declaration of alliances was made.

Equestrian and racing games took place. Ukaz market was located in a flat plain between Makkah and Taif. These Ukaz markets were maintained for more than two centuries from about 540 until 149 ah and were held in the sacred months.

In the modern era, King Abdul Aziz participated in the festival market Ukaz. There was a symposium of oral history, dealing with the importance of monitoring, documenting and writing of oral history as part of the local history of Saudi Arabia.

Despite the far distances of the Arabian Peninsula, word of mouth travels very fast to various destinations there, and is kept in the memory for centuries. So we listen to the ancient poetry as if it was said yesterday. The Arabs in various parts of the Arabian Peninsula before Islam found time to compose beautiful poems. They held an annual symposium in *Souk Ukaz* to listen to each other's contributions, their best poems were to be hung on the walls of the Ka'bah in Makkah Al-Mukarramah.

Here is a tiny drop of pre-Islamic poetry, by poet Zuhair bin Abi Sulma (*c.* 500–*c.* 609 AD)

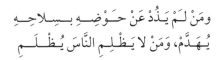

وَمَنْ لَمْ يَذُدْ عَنْ حَوْضِهِ بِسِلاحِهِ
يُهَدَّمْ، وَمَنْ لا يَظْلِمِ النَّاسَ يُظْلَمِ

'He who does not defend his territory with armaments, will be
destroyed and, he who does not deal with his enemies Unjustly,
will be Unjustly treated.'

Let us compare this aggressive pre-Islamic Poem with what the Holy Quran
says:

$$\text{﴿وَقَاتِلُوا فِي سَبِيلِ اللهِ الذِينَ يُقَاتِلُونَكُمْ ولا}$$
$$\text{تَعْتَدُوا إنَّ اللهَ لا يُحِبُّ الْمُعْتَدِين﴾}$$
$$\text{[صـدق الله العظيم]}$$

'Fight in the cause of Allah with those who fight against you,
but do not exceed the limits. Allah does not like transgressors.
[Allah always says the truth]

Here is Imru' Al-Qays (died *c.* 500 AD), describing his horse:

$$\text{مِكَرٍّ مِفَرٍّ مُقبِلٍ مُدْبِرٍ مَعاً}$$
$$\text{كَجُـلْمُـودِ صَخْـرٍ حَطَّـهُ السَّيْلُ مِنْ عَلِ}$$

'Simultaneously, advancing and retracting
as if it was a very large rock throwing from a high mountain.'

After Islam, here is Al-Mutanabbi (915–965 AD), boasting:

$$\text{الخَيْـلُ واللَّيْـلُ والبَيْـدَاءُ تَعْرِفُنِي}$$
$$\text{والسَّيْفُ والرُّمْحُ والقِرْطَاسُ والقَلَمُ}$$

'Horses, Night and Desert Knows me
As well as Sword Dagger Paper and Pen.'

Dr Ghazi Algosaibi – Eastern Saudi Arabia (1950–2010):

آتِيهِ بِالـشِّـعْـرِ... بِالأَبْيَاتِ أَنْحـتُـهَا

مِنَ الضُّـلـوعِ كَـمَـا تُسْتَوْقَدُ النَّارُ

'I offer him my poetry drown out of his rites
Carved as fire burns.'

Hassan Abdalla Al-Qurashi – Western Saudi Arabia (1940–2009):

آمَنْتُ بِالعِـلْـمِ لَكِـنْ لا أُبَارِكُـهُ

إلا إذَا عَـبَّ مِنْـهُ البَدْوُ والحَـضَـرُ

'I believe in science, but I do not give blessings
Until it is spread out to reach bedouins, as well as urbanites.'

The Saudi government recently announced that it will revive *Souk Ukaz* in the same location of the old *Souk Ukaz* with the participation of painters, poets, sportsmen, cultural activities as well as trade.

Although this book focuses on Saudi Arabian hydrocarbons I am including in this introduction a brief discussion of the start of our Islamic civilization and culture as it is a central part of our way of life, with politics and religion intertwined. I start with a quotation from the Quran.

Surah 'Quraish' (the name of the Tribe in Makkah)

'In the name of Allah, the Beneficent, the Merciful'

- For taming (civilizing) of Quraish

- For their taming (we cause) the Quraish Caravans to set forth in winter and in summer.

- So let them worship Allah the Lord of this House (the Ka'bah in Makkah)

- Who hath fed them against hunger

- And hath made them safe from fear'

Allah the greatest said the Truth.

Explanation of Surah Quraish

- Qursh is a monetary unit like pence, riyals, dollars, dinars. In this Surah 106 it conveys that in Makkah, the Qursh was the monetary unit used there since eternity until this day. Hence the name of the tribe Quraish is derived from Qursh.

- So, the Surah Quraish title is derived from the monetary unit Qursh. Also it was (and still) is the name of the most prominent tribe in the Arabian Peninsula.

- The Holy Quran is the most reliable source of historical information because it always says the truth (at least for all Muslim believers). So, the tribe of Quraish is still living in Makkah today.

The Quraish, the most prominent tribe in the Arabian Peninsula, who had for centuries been a trading tribe, had two major camel caravan trips, one in the winter and the other in summer. The trading camel caravans were arranged to travel north (Syria, northeast Iraq, northwest Egypt) year after year for centuries before Islam. The Annual Pilgrimage to Makkah was practised from the time of Abraham and Ismail. To this day it is a religious activity, as well as a great trading event. The Quraish traders reached throughout the known world, trading all the way to Indonesia in the East before the rise of Islam and have continued in one form or another to this day.

A book, *Muhammad, His Life Based on the Earliest Sources*, by Martin Lings, is interesting in throwing early light on the Quraish, the most powerful tribe of Abrahamic descent. About 400 years after Christ, and using ancient Arabic sources, the author traces the leadership of the Quraish through several generations: Qusayy, Abdu Manaf and Abd ad-Dar, Hashim and Shaybah. What is interesting for the modern reader is the way in which the narrative reveals the aspects of meritocracy and compromise reached in determining the succession, thereby ensuring the enduring strength and continuity of the Quraish.

From the time of the Prophet Muhammad, who died in 632, and for the next 120 years or so, his message was disseminated principally by military means. During this comparatively short period there was a rapid expansion of influence from Makkah and Madinah in modern Saudi Arabia to Syria, Iraq and Iran and on into central Asia, Afghanistan and Sind; but also westward, to Egypt, through North Africa to Morocco and into Spain. This remarkable development has been colourfully described with reference to numerous sources, both Muslim and Christian, by Professor Hugh Kennedy in his book *The Great Arab Conquests: How the Spread of Islam Changed the World We Live in*. Belief rather than ethnicity was the driving force of the Muslim advance.

After 750, through the subsequent centuries until about 1500, there was further expansion and consolidation of the influence of Islam. In northern Sudan, Islamization was more or less synonymous with Arab conquests, like the earlier developments. However, elsewhere other means in the dissemination and triumph of Islam were sometimes more important, such as traders and preachers. In West Africa, in regions such as Senegal and Mali, Berber traders seem to have been largely responsible for the spread of Islam. In South Asia, Muslim territory greatly expanded under the Delhi sultans to include most of the subcontinent by 1335, with Sufi advisers to the Mamluks being the main agents in converting a significant part of the subcontinent's population to Islam.

Even before the impetus given to Islam in India by the Turkish conquests and Sufi preaching, sizeable communities of Arab and Persian merchants had established themselves in the coastal towns. Muslim merchants from Gujarat traded in the Malay Peninsula and Sumatra. In the early fifteenth century the ruler of Malacca converted to Islam, followed gradually by the Sumatrans. The Indian and Malacca straits were staging posts in the trade routes to the Spice Islands and to China. With its advanced civilization and huge cities, China was of great importance to the Muslim world. Commercial and intellectual contacts with China dwarfed those with Christendom. Silks and ceramics were China's main exports to the Muslim world. As early as the ninth century, there were alleged to be over 100,000 Arab merchants in Canton. Until about 1250, most Muslims, Arabs and Persians as well as Chinese converts, were found in the ports. Thereafter, the Mongol conquest of 1252–79 brought many Muslim officials, soldiers and merchants into northern China, too. The Mongol ruler Timur (Tamerlane), 1336–1405, was devoted to the idea of universal Mongol supremacy and with this went allegiance to Islam. He had strong support among both the Ulema and Sufis. He was especially careful to protect trade and to punish corrupt commercial practices.

In the sixteenth, seventeenth and eighteenth centuries the Islamic world comprised two major regions. The first was the contiguous territory comprising the Near East, India and Central Asia, where Turko-Mongol forces had established four major states. The second included North Africa, Sudan and Southeast Asia. There it was usually Arabic-speaking merchants, Ulema or Sufis, who founded dynasties or converted local elites to Islam. These two regions were linked by a common body of Islamic scholarship and the pilgrimage to Makkah which Muslims undertook in greater numbers as security and transportation improved. Thus Islam became more broadly diffused from Southeast Asia all the way to West Africa from its centre in the Arabian Peninsula. Subsequently, migration of Muslim populations into Western Europe and North America increased the Muslim presence in these areas during the twentieth century.

In an earlier book, *Energy: A Global Outlook*, prepared in 1980–1 and published in 1982, I made an economic and political evaluation of the world energy scene and went on to produce energy scenarios together with a historical and regional analysis. Projections were included for 1985, 1990 and

2000 for the major components of the world energy sector: for oil, natural gas, coal and other forms of energy. As in any work of this sort, some of my projections, even for the year 2000, proved very accurate and most were within the ranges comprising my three scenarios of co-operation, neutral and confrontation. However, some of my assumptions proved inaccurate. There was a heritage of differences characterizing international relationships in the energy sector, especially oil. This followed the fundamental changes in the prices of petroleum entering world trade in 1973–4. The differences between the Organization of Petroleum Exporting Countries (OPEC) and the International Energy Agency on behalf of the leading oil consuming and importing countries were still quite evident nearly thirty years ago.

Looking back in time now, a number of comments need to be made. The first concerns the oil price assumption. The fact is that the price increases made unilaterally by OPEC in October 1973 and on 1 January 1974 proved sustainable over the five years to 1978, with only moderate annual fluctuations over this period. Nevertheless, an oil price rising by 1.5 per cent in real terms from $46.60 in 1976 would have yielded a price of $73.93 a barrel in 2007, close to the actual prices of more than $72 a barrel for both North Sea Brent and West Texas Intermediate in that year. The price spike in 2008, again brought about by speculative market forces, proved unsustainable with the onset of the financial crisis and economic recession. However, the oil price increase brought about by market forces (discussed in the earlier book and again in this one), during 1979–81, also proved unsustainable by 1986. Again, this occurred through a combination of influences, notably a rise in oil production outside OPEC, economic recession, significant longer term improvement in the efficiency of energy usage and a rising contribution in supplies of other sources of energy.

Another earlier assumption was that the proved oil reserves would not rise as they did, notably in the principal OPEC member countries between 1985 and 1990. Thus by 2000 world oil consumption at 76.4 million b/d proved significantly higher than the 68.5 million b/d we had projected for that year in the most optimistic case.

Part I of this book discusses the evolution of the oil and gas industry in the Kingdom of Saudi Arabia since the founding of the modern state almost eighty years ago, just before the first oil discovery in 1938. After the end of the Second World War there was a series of discoveries of giant oil fields which, in due course, led to Saudi Arabia becoming much the largest holder of proved oil reserves worldwide. I go on to discuss the important role played by the Saudi monarchs over this lengthy period as oil production in the Kingdom increased dramatically from 1949 to 1972. With it there was a rising consciousness of oil as a finite and depletable resource, given the rapid growth in demand.

The Israeli–Arab wars of 1967 and 1973 led on to the first OPEC unilateral oil price increase and again in January 1974. The experience of the next five years to 1978 suggested that these price increases were sustainable. Saudi Arabia played a significant role as the largest producer and exporter of oil within OPEC in these initiatives. We go on to discuss how the largely market-induced and unpremeditated oil price increases of 1979–80 and 2008 proved unsustainable. In this context, it is noteworthy that Saudi Arabia played a critical role in increasing its production and exports when prices rose to higher levels than justified by market fundamentals at these times, in order to bring some measure of stability to the world oil market and, indeed, to the world economy more generally. Similarly, when oil prices fell through in 1986, Saudi Arabia reduced its production and exports sharply for the same reason, to help stabilize the world oil market.

I go on to discuss the future prospects for Saudi Arabian crude oil production through to 2030 and the domestic policy considerations likely to influence the progression. The value of Saudi Arabian petroleum exports reached a new peak in 2008 as did those of other OPEC members, too, but again the world oil price was unsustainable.

The next part of Part I of this book makes a comparative analysis of GDP per capita and oil and gas reserves of Saudi Arabia and other OPEC member countries. I then review the comparatively slow but deliberate move from participation as a concept to the inauguration of Saudi Aramco over the twenty-year period to 1988. I go on analyse important but complementary roles of oil and gas in this process. After this, I discuss the progress of the Saudi Aramco Company over its first twenty years to 2008.

Subsequent chapters in Part I provide readers with details of the population increase in Saudi Arabia associated with its economic growth and infrastructure expansion, along with the immense challenges of vast training programmes associated with it. Schematic diagrams illustrate the operations of the oil and gas industries in Saudi Arabia. Foreign participation involving major companies has been introduced to increase the search for natural gas in previously unexplored areas of the country. There is some discussion of prospects for additional joint venture refinery projects. A classification is made of the five types of Saudi Arabian crude oils, some of which have been discovered only during recent decades. An analysis of the product mix in Saudi oil refineries is followed with a comparison of consumption trends in some leading countries.

The final part of Part I discusses political stability and continuity in the Kingdom of Saudi Arabia along with some of the principal contributions of the country's Ministers of Petroleum and Mineral Resources – only four in number since the 1950s.

Part II discusses the effect of the financial crisis and economic recession from 2007 to 2009 on the world energy sector, with particular reference to the impact on oil and gas. It goes on to consider the initiative to form the Group of Twenty (G-20) leading economies which supersedes the former G-7 or G-8 group of leading advanced industrial countries. The G-20 is a much broader and more representative gathering for the world as a whole, including twelve developing/emerging economies. Among these are the most populous countries, China and India, and thus the G-20 represents a majority of mankind. At the height of the crisis the G-20 met three times, in November 2008, April 2009 and September 2009.

We go on to analyse the leading countries in terms of hydrocarbon reserves and the relationship between the world economy, energy consumption and oil. A comparison of the primary energy mix in the leading consuming countries shows remarkable differences between them.

A comparison was made of proved reserves and production of both oil and gas between OPEC member countries and the rest of the world. This demonstrated much longer prospective life spans for both hydrocarbons characteristic of most OPEC members compared with the rest of the world on the basis of recent past levels of production. A long-period analysis of worldwide oil production from 1965 to 2007 examines the sharp deceleration of growth associated with the oil price rises of 1973–4 and the subsequent effects on both Saudi Arabia and OPEC as a whole.

Subsequent chapters analyse the relationship of oil prices and consumption, together with the progression of international trade in oil. Another reviews gas reserves and production and the increasing competitiveness of gas vis-à-vis oil but with the proportion of worldwide gas production entering international trade being much smaller than for oil. The last decade of the twentieth century in the former Soviet Union and in the emerging giant which is China is discussed, both in terms of its high growth economy and energy sector. The last chapter of Part II is devoted to a justification and rationale for OPEC, pointing to the unsustainability of exponential growth of oil production and consumption beyond the year 2000 if those exponential rates recorded during the years culminating in 1973 had not come to an end at that time.

Part III is concerned with a retrospective analysis of the book *Energy a Global Outlook*. Part I of that book comprised an economic and political evaluation. It included a historical evolution of the international oil industry; the global energy supply and demand balance; a historical review of OPEC's creation and actions and a rationale for it; the Organization of Arab Petroleum Exporting Countries; this was followed by a similar treatment of the International Energy Agency formed by the leading industrial and oil importing countries.

Subsequent chapters in part I of the earlier book discussed the impact of structural changes on the international energy industries; the specific case of Petromin, Saudi Arabian oil policies and industrialization through joint ventures; the international energy dialogue in terms of the so-called north–south debate in the mid-1970s warranted particular attention. New strategies leading towards an international energy development programme were outlined, leading to an epilogue to conclude part 1 of *Energy a Global Outlook*.

The second part of *Energy a Global Outlook* included three energy scenarios with historical and regional analysis for 1985, 1990 and the year 2000 prepared in 1980–1. These were for the world as a whole and for countries/regions as follows: the United States, Western Europe, Japan, OPEC developing countries; non-OPEC developing countries, the Soviet Union, Eastern Europe and China.

Part IV of this book examines population statistics and projections from the United Nations. We regard these as an important basis for the analysis of phenomena such as greenhouse gas emissions on a per capita basis, and similarly GDP, primary energy and oil consumption. This approach yields a quite different insight into current problems such as global warming and climate change associated with energy emissions. This is possibly a more selective and objective way of analysing and solving them than anything based on aggregated data for individual or groups of countries.

I proceed to discuss the short-term effects of the financial crisis and economic recession of 2008/9. This had a dramatic effect on Russia and the advanced industrial countries of the OECD but a comparatively minor adverse impact on China and the economies of most other developing countries' economies.

I continue in Part IV with comparative reviews of statistics and projections included in the most recently published *World Oil Outlook* from OPEC; the *World Energy Outlook* from the IEA; and the *International Energy Outlook* 2010 from the US Department of Energy/Energy Information Administration. The high growth of China over several years to 2009 and its relative importance justify particular comment.

Part V of this book briefly reviews what I consider to be the main conclusions emerging from this discussion of Saudi Arabian hydrocarbons in the context of the evolution of the world economy, both historically and prospectively over the next twenty to twenty-five years. There are some references to political and international relations, the energy sector in general and the roles of oil and natural gas in particular, given the topicality of global warming and climate change relating to greenhouse gas emissions confronting Planet Earth.

Part I

King Abd al-Aziz Al Saʻud: Founder of Modern Saudi Arabia

The King reigned for over fifty years, from 1902 until his death in November 1953. He was its leader and head of a land from which he had been exiled as a youth but later had reunited, pacified and developed. In 1900 when he was a young man, his homeland was one of the least known, poorest and most isolated in the world. At his death it had taken its place on the world stage. His achievement had been to use the creed of his forefathers to harness centrifugal tribal and local elements into a state, and then to set that state on the road to modernization by moderating the potential conflicts within it. Only a person of great courage, formidable intelligence, rare charisma and – above all – a profound faith in God could have accomplished such an undertaking.

The unification of the Kingdom of Saudi Arabia under Abd al-Aziz Al Saʻud took place over some thirty years from 1902, but not without conflict over a number of territories. Abd al-Aziz recognized that he had to make a fundamental change in his own outlook if he was to achieve his vision of uniting the provinces of Arabia into a single state. He drew on his experience of the first Saudi State and the ideas of his grandfather Imam Faysal.

Among the King's many initiatives to develop the country in essential sectors other than the obvious one of hydrocarbons, we can mention education, agriculture and political integration of the various parts into one cohesive whole.

Immediately upon unifying the country in 1926 Abd al-Aziz had founded a new school in Makkah. In 1945 he instituted an extensive programme of school construction and by 1951 there were 226 schools in the Kingdom with 1,217 teachers and a total of 29,887 pupils, all supplied with free books and tuition.

Another pressing need he recognized was agriculture, a reflection of the King's earlier perception that agricultural settlements were vital to a country where less than 1 per cent of the land is arable and where food supply as a result could be problematic. Already in 1942 Abd al-Aziz had invited a US agricultural mission to visit the country and report on its production potential. He also laid the groundwork for pilot projects to be set up which became the nucleus for later government farms and breeding stations. He also strongly backed exploitation of the vast underground water resources in Najd and al-Hasa which were tapped for extensive irrigation projects.

In writing about Saudi Arabia in *World Geography of Petroleum* (1950), Max Steineke contributed the following significant passage including a final quotation from King Abd al-Aziz Al Saʻud himself. This serves to demonstrate the close and effective relationship which had developed at this comparatively early stage.

> While Aramco's mission in Saudi Arabia is essentially commercial – the exploration and development of oil fields – the activities of the company, it has been seen, are widespread, and include various long-range programs that will enable the Arabs to help themselves, and raise their standard of living. The responsibility placed upon Aramco to deserve the trust with which Americans are welcomed into Saudi Arabia – to live and work with the Arabs harmoniously, to understand and respect their traditions, ideas, and feelings – is a vital element in the planning of its enterprises. Human relations must be handled with foresight, sympathy, and wisdom. From the very start the company has conducted its operations on the basis of partnership with the King and his subjects, and great care is exercised to formulate policies that will maintain mutual respect and fair dealing.
>
> Before oil was discovered, the Saudi Arab government's income was derived largely from the annual pilgrimage (Hadj) to the Holy Cities of Mecca and Medina. In the years following Second World War this revenue

has risen to the unprecedented high of seven million dollars, as against two to four million dollars in prewar years. During the war, when the great reduction in revenues from the pilgrim traffic and other sources placed the government in financial difficulty, the company made advances totalling several million dollars.

Today (in 1950) by far the larger part of the governmental revenue is derived from the royalty of twenty-two United States cents per barrel paid to King Ibn Saud by the company. Currently, Aramco's daily production is averaging around 500,000 barrels, and on this basis, His Majesty receives about $40 million per year.

This new source of revenue has enabled the King to import increasing quantities of food for his people, to extend the agricultural project at Al Kharj, and to develop the water resources of the country. Recently he has initiated plans for the establishment of a Ministry of Agriculture, and his dreams of large farms in other sections of the Kingdom are slowly but surely being realized. King Ibn Saud is a wise and just King, who sees clearly the economic development that is necessary. In a recent statement to Aramco officials, His Majesty said: 'We want to teach our people to help themselves to become better and more useful citizens of the modern world. We are very happy that in this enterprise we have as our good partners the representatives of the United States of America.'

In February 1945 King Abd al-Aziz Al Sa'ud met US President Franklin Delano Roosevelt. On returning home the US President reported to Congress: 'Of the problems of Arabia, I learned more about the whole problem, the Muslim problem, the Jewish problem, by talking with Ibn Sa'ud for five minutes than I could have learned in the exchange of two or three dozen letters.' Unfortunately, FDR died two months later and his successor, President Harry S. Truman, apparently felt no obligation to keep Roosevelt's promises on Palestine.

Saudi Arabia and Oil: The Beginnings

Saudi Arabia's Concession Agreement with Standard Oil Company of California to Explore for Oil

This historic agreement took place in Jiddah in May 1933, only some eight months after the Kingdom of Saudi Arabia was officially proclaimed a nation-state. King Abd al-Aziz Al Sa'ud had gathered key aides to approve the Oil Concession Agreement that the Finance Minister Abdullah al-Sulayman had negotiated with Standard Oil of California, Socal. The Minister had read the entire contract out loud. At the silence indicating the end of the recitation, the King sought his advisers' opinions. He had not expected comment or dissent and none was offered. 'All right', he said to al-Sulayman. 'Put your trust in God and sign!'

Thus dawned a new era in the Kingdom's history. Its vast significance can only be appreciated in retrospect. The world economy was still languishing in the Great Depression and the revenues from the pilgrimage to Makkah, the main source of the nation's income, had slumped by 80 per cent since 1930.

Socal agreed to an immediate loan of £30,000 in gold, plus another loan of £20,000 in gold eighteen months later, (equivalent to about $250,000 at that time). Also, it agreed to yearly rentals of £5,000 in gold and royalties of four shillings in gold per ton of oil produced. The company promised to provide the government with an advance of another £50,000 in gold if oil in commercial quantities was found. The agreement called for an immediate start of exploration, for drilling to begin as soon as a suitable structure was found, and for construction of a refinery after oil was discovered. Socal obtained the exclusive right to prospect for and produce oil in eastern Saudi Arabia covering some 829,000 km² for the next sixty years, and preferential rights to explore for oil elsewhere in the Kingdom.

Both Socal and King ibn Sa'ud were taking big risks. The latter needed money to keep the Kingdom solvent. He opened Saudi Arabia to large-scale Western involvement for the first time.

Discovery of Oil in Saudi Arabia in Commercial Quantities, 1938

Oil had been discovered much earlier in Persia (now Iran) across the Gulf in 1909 at Masjid i Suleiman. This was followed by a discovery of oil in nearby Bahrain in 1932. Though the Standard Oil Company of California (Socal) started exploration work in Saudi Arabia in September 1933, only four months after the agreement was signed, it was not until some five years later, in 1938, that the first discovery of oil in commercial quantities was made at Damman No. 7. This followed five years of hard work and thwarted hopes. Finally, the discovery resulted from US geologist Max Steineke deducing that Damman No. 7, now called the Prosperity Well, should be drilled a little deeper.

Some large fields were discovered soon afterwards, notably at Abqaiq in 1940, but major exploration and developments were held up by Second World War. Nevertheless, more than thirty-five years later after its discovery, Abqaiq was the second largest oil-producing field in Saudi Arabia. Texaco had joined Socal and in 1948 these two companies with Exxon and Mobil formed the Arabian American Oil Company, ARAMCO. Much earlier, in November 1933, Socal had formed a subsidiary, California Arabian Standard Oil Company (Casoc) to which its concession had been assigned. It had introduced an advanced new technology in the form of aerial photography to further the search for oil in the Kingdom.

Discovery of Giant Oil Fields After the Second World War

In the post-Second World War period, large-scale exploration programmes started in the Kingdom of Saudi Arabia with Aramco able to draw on the expertise available in its four US partner oil companies. In a prescient contribution on Saudi Arabia in *World Geography of Petroleum* in 1950, Max Steineke, writing with another Aramco geologist, remarked:

> The development of the oil fields has brought the Industrial Revolution to Arabia, and there will be an abundant supply of oil to run the imported machinery. Arabs from the desert and the town are manipulating tools, repairing or operating engines, running tests in laboratories, constructing modern houses, and drilling oil wells. There are unlimited opportunities for advancement, unknown a decade ago, for those Arabs who have the needed ability and skill.

Exploration at the En Nala anticline had begun as early as 1940 when a young geologist named Ernie Berg was mapping in the area of Haradh. His boss Max Steineke agreed on the significance of a huge structural uplift. This later became known as the Ghawar oil field – much the world's largest, and it still is. However, because of the Second World War drilling did not proceed until 1948 and struck oil the next year. But it was not until 1957 after many probes incorporating six previously discovered oil fields that the Company could confirm the size of the Ghawar field, with estimated proved reserves of some 80 billion barrels initially. To put this in perspective, the next largest oil field worldwide discovered prior to 1970 is reportedly Samotlor in Western Siberia with estimated reserves of up to 15 billion barrels. Even today, some sixty years later, Ghawar is quite unique. Later, its estimated reserves were estimated at 140 billion barrels. It extends for more that 280 kilometres (175 miles) and is up to 26 kilometres (16 miles) wide. Like most of Saudi Arabia's principal oil-producing fields, it is situated in the Upper Jurassic zone reservoirs, generally oolitic and dolomitic limestone. By the mid-1970s, the Ghawar field was producing more than 5 million b/d of crude oil and accounted for 65 per cent of Saudi Arabia's production from its principal oil fields. The crude it produces is Arab Light, 34° API gravity. This became the marker crude for OPEC member countries with quality and freight differentials calculated with respect to it.

In addition to Abqaiq, discovered earlier and mentioned above, other very large fields include Berri (part offshore), also located in the Upper Jurassic zone and discovered later, in 1964. The crude oil gravities produced from it cover a comparatively wide range from 32° API (Arab Medium) to lighter crude of 39° for which it is better known. Like Abqaiq, by the mid-1970s, the Berri field was producing over 800,000 b/d – nowhere near the production from Ghawar, but still a very large volume for a single field worldwide.

Safaniyah lies offshore in the Arabian Gulf and differs geologically from the other three principal Saudi Arabian oil fields mentioned above in being located in the Cretaceous horizon. It was discovered in 1951 and produces heavier crude of 27° API gravity (Arab Heavy) with its output volume exceeding 600,000 barrels per day by the mid-1970s. It is the world's largest offshore field. Together with Khafji in the Neutral Zone, its estimated reserves were 25 billion barrels.

Much more recently, in 1998, Saudi Aramco completed a three-year project to bring on stream the large Shaybah field in the Rub' al-Khali desert – a highly inhospitable environment. This is an oil field with estimated reserves of more than 14 billion barrels of Arabian extra light crude oil of a gravity in the range of 36° to 40° API – a highly desirable characteristic as demand has shifted in favour of light and middle distillate products, both in the Kingdom and in export markets. Subsequently, its reserves were revised upwards to 17.6 billion barrels. Its central producing facility sends 500,000 barrels per day to Abqaiq. Expansion to 750,000 b/d capacity is planned. In addition to the field's oil reserves, Shaybah contains some 25 trillion standard cubic feet of gas, equivalent to some 4.6 billion barrels of oil, as of 1998.

Non-associated gas is estimated to account for more that 36 per cent of total Saudi Aramco gas reserves which, in 1998, were estimated at 210.8 trillion standard cubic feet, equivalent to some 39 billion barrels of oil. In fact Saudi Arabia has been producing gas for more than fifty years. The first commercial gas well, Damman No. 43, went into production in December 1956, not associated with oil. It reached Khuff gas at a depth of 2,637 metres and produced more than 12 billion standard cubic feet before being shut down in 1969.

Saudi Arabian Monarchs since 1953 and their Activities

The founder of modern Saudi Arabia, King Abl al-Aziz Al Sa'ud reigned for over fifty years, from 1902 until 1953. He was instrumental in forging a sense of national identity in what had formerly been a land of many disparate tribes. A devout man of great faith and profound vision, it was he who started the Kingdom on the road to transformation and development while retaining the all important traditional attributes of a stable society firmly anchored in deep religious beliefs.

During years since his death, stability has continued to characterize both the monarchy and appointments to the oil ministry. In both cases, just five and four individuals respectively, have held these outstandingly important and responsible positions in the Kingdom of Saudi Arabia over the years to 2010. The kings and their principal contributions are discussed below.

Monarchs

King Sa'ud 1953–1964
Several government ministries were set up during this period, including Petroleum and Mineral Resources in 1960. King Sa'ud broadened Saudi Arabia's relations with its neighbours by undertaking a series of trips and official visits to

friendly states, among them Egypt. Relations with Jordan and Iraq improved and Saudi Arabia supported Kuwait against external threats.

King Faysal 1964–1975

Even before becoming king, in 1958 Faysal was granted full executive powers in financial, internal and foreign affairs. In addressing the financial crisis, he insisted on strict austerity, reducing both government expenditure and that of the royal family, and published a state budget for the first time. He had become Minister of Foreign Affairs as early as 1930 (at age 26) and had a distinguished career thereafter. This included delivering an historic speech at the UN in 1947 opposing the partition of Palestine. Even during his elder brother's reign, Faysal had introduced political and economic reforms, developed a Cabinet system of government through the Council of Ministers and granted greater freedom to the Saudi press.

It was said he detested extravagance and believed in clarity, sound management and establishing clear priorities. He once remarked: 'In one generation we went from riding camels to riding Cadillacs. The way we are wasting money, I fear the next generation will be riding camels again.' The King's guiding vision was that Saudi Arabia could modernize economically by importing technical expertise while maintaining its social traditions and remaining faithful to Islam. As modernization rolled forward, the Kingdom's growing oil revenues were also directed towards a wide range of social welfare programmes. Faysal established the state bureaucracy as the mechanism of distribution of revenues and systematized its budgets, making welfare benefits, health, housing, education and employment available to all Saudi citizens.

Also he recognized the need to keep the religious establishment behind the reforms. This he did by incorporating the *ulama* into the machinery of state, enabling them to participate in government. Later, during Faysal's reign, oil wealth enabled Saudi Arabia to initiate a substantial aid programme to Muslim countries. Likewise, the oil price rises gave a sudden boost to the Kingdom's economy and enabled Faysal to accelerate the modernization programme embodied in the First Five Year Development Plan 1970–4 and subsequently into the Second Five Year Development Plan, designed to expand the industrial infrastructure of the country.

On 25 March 1975, King Faysal was assassinated in his office in Riyadh by a deranged young relative seeking vengeance for the death of his brother in the anti-television riot of 1965. His murder shocked not only the Kingdom and its people, but the world at large, for Faysal had emerged in his last years as a moderating influence politically and economically throughout the Middle East.

King Khaled 1975–1982

He came to power at the start of the Second Five Year Development Plan and his reign coincided with both the first and second peak in Saudi Arabia's oil revenues. By contrast, his government had to contend with four crises which threatened the Kingdom's security. These were the occupation of the Sacred Mosque in Makkah by a group of armed fanatics in 1979; the Iranian Revolution the same year that deposed the Shah and brought the Ayatollah Khomeini to power; the Soviet invasion of Afghanistan; and the outbreak of the Iran–Iraq War in 1980. King Khaled was a modest and frank man of much personal charm and a strong sense of humour who became the focus of the Saudi people's affection and respect.

This was a period of massive infrastructure development. By the mid-1970s the Kingdom's fast growing economy was outstripping its support systems of roads, ports, electricity and some social services. The second development plan began in 1975 and the third launched in 1980, both mounting full-scale attacks on these bottlenecks. Rapidly expanding oil revenues financed this expensive task, with each of these plans funded at more than $200 billion. The effort was a resounding success. For example, over the ten years 1975–85, paved highways quadrupled in length and port tonnage increased by ten times, while power generation grew from less than 2 billion to more than 44 billion kilowatt hours. The number of schools jumped from 5,600 to more than 15,000, with a remarkable average completion rate of more than two schools per day. The number of hospitals nearly doubled to 176. Also, a major start was made on another development phase aimed to diversify the Kingdom's economy through the development of heavy industry – much of it centred on petrochemical production based on the fuel and feedstock supplied by the Kingdom's Master Gas System, or MGS, which was also under construction at this time. Two massive industrial complexes, one at Jubail on the Gulf and one on the Red Sea at Yanbu, were linked to the MGS by pipeline.

King Fahd 1982–2005

Previously he had been appointed the Kingdom's first Minister of Education in 1953 and then in 1962 he became Minister of the Interior. He served in that capacity until he was named Crown Prince and First Deputy Prime Minister in 1975. He served as chairman of a number of high level committees and councils, including the Supreme Council for Petroleum and Minerals, the Supreme Council for Education and the Royal Commission for Jubail and Yanbu. The King served as an inclusive and modernizing man who guided the Kingdom through challenging times – notably during the slump in oil volumes and prices in 1985–6. This led to years of relative austerity, dealing a blow to the Kingdom's programme of economic development, had an adverse effect on GDP growth and caused some major projects to be frozen. Also, demographic pressures accentuated the impact of austerity with a fast growing population of some 23 million Saudis, of whom some 40 per cent were under the age of 40.

However, the government remained determined to proceed with development and was reluctant to cut spending on social welfare programmes and education. As a result, successive budget deficits had to be financed by borrowing and drawing on reserves. Nevertheless, King Fahd's reign saw the completion of the first great wave of large--scale infrastructure construction included in the first two five year plans (1970–9) and the fruition of a number of industrial and other developments dependent on them. Major strides were taken in diversifying the Kingdom's sources of income across a growing industrial base and in achieving self-sufficiency in many primary manufactured and agricultural commodities. To attract private capital, a policy of privatization was introduced at major petrochemical enterprises at Jubail and Yanbu started by Saudi Arabian Basic Industries Corporation (SABIC). These now hold 7 per cent of the world petrochemical market, helping to make the Gulf countries the world's largest exporter of petrochemicals and plastics. Secondary industries use these materials to manufacture consumer goods for the domestic market, too. Among special road projects was the 26 km King Fahd Causeway linking al-Khobar in the Eastern Province with the island kingdom of Bahrain. Abroad, King Fahd was associated with a number of initiatives including the National Reconciliation Accord that brought peace to Lebanon in 1990. By the time King Fahd died in 2005, both Saudi oil export volumes and oil prices were rising following some twenty-three years of weakness in both during his reign.

King Abdullah 2005–

Because of King Fahd's illness from late 1995 onwards, Abdullah assumed major responsibilities in running the day-to-day affairs of the country. In particular, in 2002 he announced a peace plan calling for Israel to withdraw to its pre-1967 borders and the Palestinians to establish their independent state with Jerusalem as its capital. In return the Arab States that had refused to recognize Israel since 1948 would establish normal diplomatic and trade relations with it. To many external observers this plan seemed to have much merit after more than fifty years of no solution to a chronic and fundamental problem. Perhaps the aftermath of '9/11' in the US rendered its timing somewhat inauspicious. By September 2009 the initiatives of the US Obama administration, based on a clearer recognition of this fundamental unresolved problem threatening peace throughout the Middle East, seemed to be moving ahead more constructively than previously.

Influenced by his father, King Abd al-Aziz Al Sa'ud, King Abdullah developed a profound respect for religion, history and the Arab heritage. He also spent years with Bedouin tribes observing, practising and absorbing their traditions. He has taken a prominent role in politics since the 1950s. He was named Commander of the National Guard by King Faysal whose piety and frugality he shares. He was designated Crown Prince when Fahd became King in 1982. He has proven to be cautiously reform-minded, calling for greater participation by women in society. He is keen to combat growing unemployment by accelerating growth. To do this, he favours gradually liberalizing the economy through privatization and by opening Saudi Arabia to foreign investment. He supported the Kingdom's preparations to join the World Trade Organization, efforts that bore fruit late in 2005.

King Abdullah is experienced in international diplomacy and he has worked to strengthen Saudi Arabia's relations with countries around the globe. He has been a strong voice in promoting the Kingdom's defence of Arab and Islamic issues, and in furthering its efforts to achieve world peace, stability and security.

Saudi Oil Production since 1949

Growth in World Oil Consumption and in Saudi Oil Production

Though world oil consumption grew at the very rapid rate of 7.1 per cent p.a. on average over the years from 1949 to 1972, Saudi Arabian oil production grew considerably faster at 11.5 per cent annually over the same period, or more than 12.1 times, to represent 13.8 per cent of worldwide oil consumption in the latter year. By 1973 Saudi Arabia had replaced the United States as the world's swing producer, US output having peaked in 1970 at 9.63 million barrels a day.

The very fast growth rates of both oil supply and demand through the 1960s occurred against a background of falling real oil prices expressed in constant US dollar terms during that decade. The comparatively low price of oil relative to increasingly affluent consumers in the industrialized countries meant that oil was being used to substitute for coal in the post-Second World War period. Oil was not just consumed in the transportation sector, but also to fuel central heating systems in the residential and commercial/public sectors, plus industrial sector uses, including energy intensive ones, for electricity generation and non-energy use as a feedstock in the petrochemical sector in Europe, Japan and the United States.

Hydrocarbon Losses: Flaring of Associated Natural Gas

Large losses of hydrocarbons occurred in Saudi Arabia as a result of the flaring of natural gas produced in association with oil over twenty years or more until the inauguration of the Master Gas System in 1977. The amount of greenhouse gases emitted will have been equivalent to almost 30 per cent of those associated with worldwide consumption of natural gas in that year, 1977, or 719[1] million tonnes of CO_2 with no economic benefit. To put the loss in a contemporary perspective we can say, the loss from the flaring of associated gas in Saudi Arabia amounted to 574 times as much as BP lost from its unrecovered oil from the Macondo oil-spill in the Gulf of Mexico over ninety days between April and July 2010. Saudi Arabia's loss was 7.2 times as much as BP's loss on the same timeframe. Saudi Arabia invested $12 billion in the recovery and economic use of a hydrocarbon resource formerly wasted.

The quantities of associated natural gas lost to flaring over this lengthy period are extremely large, at an estimated 13.17 trillion cubic feet or 13.54 quadrillion Btus. At the price of $0.75 per million Btus for natural gas delivered to customers in Saudi Arabia for many years, this amounts to some $10.16 billion in value over the historic period concluding in 1977.

Over the period of thirty-two years since the Saudi Master Gas System was inaugurated in 1977, the Kingdom produced almost 99 billion barrels of oil, implying almost 574 quadrillion Btus. Some 45.3 quadrillion Btus of associated natural gas produced with it was supplied to the Master Gas System where it is put to many uses: petrochemicals, propane, butane, LPG and for electricity generating stations, desalination plants and other industrial uses. This implies a value of $37 billion input as a basis for Saudi Arabia's industrialization programme. This means a high proportion of the Kingdom's oil production is available for exports as well as for consumption within the country where gas cannot be used, such as in the transport sector.

Rising Consciousness of Oil and Gas as Finite and Depletable Resources

Consciousness of oil and gas as finite and depletable resources was important in fuelling nationalist concerns in several comparatively poor oil-exporting countries. Some such as Mexico, Venezuela and Iran had taken early action to nationalize the former concessions granted mainly to the major oil companies operating in their countries. The trigger for more concerted action on the part of oil-exporting countries were successive reductions in both 1959 and 1960 in the posted prices of crude oil entering world trade as a result of unilateral action by the international major companies – at that time apparently all-powerful in the oil industry. This culminated in the formation of the Organization of Petroleum Exporting Countries (OPEC) in September 1960. Saudi Arabia was one of the five founder members, together with Iran, Iraq, Kuwait and Venezuela.

World Politics and Oil Prices

The Israeli–Arab Wars of 1967 and 1973

The Six-Day War of 1967 initiated by the Israelis had exacerbated unsatisfactory relations between the Arab States and Israel, with the occupation by the latter of Palestinian land, making matters worse than they had been twenty years earlier when the Israeli state was founded. The Arab response was the so-called Yom Kippur War, initiated by the Egyptians and Syrians during the most important Jewish festival of that name, in October 1973.

For the first time OPEC made unilateral increases in oil prices and its Arab member countries introduced a variable embargo on oil shipments to some export destinations. This was followed by further big oil price rises made by OPEC member countries on 1 January 1974. These changes marked a fundamental change in the balance of power between the formerly dominant major international oil companies and the leading oil-exporting countries gathered together in the Organization of Petroleum Exporting Countries.

OPEC Oil Price Increases of 1973–4 Proved Sustainable

The OPEC oil price increases of 1973–4 proved sustainable over the following five years or so in spite of coinciding with and partly contributing to the economic recession of 1974–5 in the industrialized countries. Recessions are in any case a normal feature of the economic cycle, particularly this one which followed a synchronized boom in the OECD countries. There was a strong economic recovery in 1976–7 and world oil consumption reached successive new peaks in 1976, 1977 and 1978, with annual increases of 6.2 per cent, 3.7 per cent and 4.3 per cent respectively. In just three years from the somewhat depressed level of less than 55 million b/d in 1975, world oil consumption rose by 8.23 million b/d to reach 63.2 million b/d in 1978.

This amounted to strong evidence that the world economic system had successfully adjusted to the fundamental change in the real price of oil entering world trade introduced unilaterally by OPEC in 1973–4. Furthermore, big development projects were initiated in the petroleum exporting countries, particularly in Saudi Arabia, based on increased oil export earnings, so the extra revenues provided a strong fillip to world trade growth and exports from the industrial countries. They were not simply stashed away in bank vaults or invested in US Treasury bonds and elsewhere. A vast, active and highly desirable investment programme in infrastructure development in schools, hospitals, communications, port facilities, defence and the oil, gas and petrochemical industries, etc., characterized the second and third Saudi Arabian five year plans over the decade from 1975, for example.

Oil Price Increases of 1979–80 and 2004–8 Not Sustainable

The increases in world oil prices recorded in 1979–80 and 2004–8 were the result of market forces in the widest sense of that phrase. They owed nothing to initiatives of OPEC. In fact, quite the opposite. On both occasions Saudi Arabia increased production and export volumes in order to dampen down unwarranted oil price increases. For example, even the International Energy Agency has recognized that the world's biggest oil field, Saudi Arabia's Ghawar, reached a peak of nearly 5.6 million b/d production in 1980.

The price increases of 1979–80 were brought about by a combination of influences. First, the major international oil companies were guilty of running down operational stocks held in 1978, then having to rebuild stocks more strongly than usual in 1979–80, as revealed in OECD statistics. Secondly, the Iranian Revolution of January 1979 did cause some disruption to world oil supplies, but these were largely made good by increased production and exports from Saudi Arabia and some other OPEC member countries. Thirdly, the outbreak of war between Iraq and Iran in September 1980 gave a further temporary stimulus to spot prices of both crude oil and products and encouraged some oil-exporting countries, but not Saudi Arabia, to add premiums and surcharges to their official prices which were not justified by the fundamental forces of oil supply and demand. When OPEC official prices were finally reunified in late 1981, it was at Saudi Arabia's then preferred price of $34 a barrel for Arab Light crude, with all other OPEC export grades based on quality and freight differentials with respect to this marker crude oil price.

Once again, over the period 2004 to 2008, increases in the price of oil entering world trade were based not on the actions of OPEC but initially, at least, on a bigger than usual increase of 3.4 per cent, or 2.7 million b/d, in world oil consumption in 2004, with China alone rising by just over 1 million b/d in that year. This happened just as oil production in the OECD countries fell below 21 million b/d for the first time in many years, followed by further falls to less than 20 and then to less than 19 million b/d through to 2008, even as worldwide consumption still rose annually, at least until 2007.

In March 1983 the New York Mercantile Exchange added an oil futures crude contract (WTI) to its daily quotations, followed by London, Singapore and Dubai with petroleum products added in, too, in addition to the traditional spot markets for both crude and products. There was thus a ready-made market for traders, whether oil companies or others, to participate in what had been marginal markets with naturally fluctuating prices to balance supply and demand. More recently, fuelled by cheap credit and a plentiful supply of it from 2003 onwards, market participants were able to speculate on a perceived anticipatory shortage of oil supply from 2003–4 onwards, given the strong growth of oil demand in 2004.

Our graph shows the influence of these formerly marginal markets in setting prices for oil entering world trade. Prices for West Texas Intermediate (WTI) light crude from the United States and North Sea Brent crude followed each other closely from the beginning of 2000 until the end of 2003, with the more desirable lighter WTI usually at a slight premium to Brent, but both fluctuating only mildly during this period between about $20 and less than $40 a barrel. Thereafter, a sustained increase in front-month futures prices of both WTI and Brent occurred, leading to an unsustainable overshooting of prices in July 2008 and undershooting reaction by February 2009. This occurred in spite of the big increases in oil production by OPEC, of which Saudi Arabia contributed more than 1.3 million b/d, and the former Soviet Union. Comparing production volumes on average over the five years 2004 to 2008 with those during the four years 2000 to 2003 inclusive, OPEC was up more than 4 million b/d in an effort to dampen the price increases, while production in the former Soviet Union (or CIS countries) rose by over 3 million b/d. These combined rises of more than 7 million b/d were offset to an extent by net falls of more than 1.8 million b/d in the OECD countries, once again on the basis of the same time period comparison.

Oil Price Falls of 1981 to 1986: Challenge to OPEC

Just as the oil price increases of 1979–80 and 2004–8 were largely the result of market forces, the latter were also responsible for the oil price falls of 1981 to 1986. The combination of influences which brought these about were economic recession in the industrialized countries, the Latin American debt crisis, particularly in Mexico, rising efficiency in energy usage (conservation) in the leading consuming countries, increasing supplies of other forms of energy and rising production of oil from sources outside OPEC, notably from the North Sea and the North Slope of Alaska.

Ten countries outside OPEC raised their oil output by more than 1 million b/d (the UK) down to Australia at 0.2 million b/d, by variable amounts in excess of this latter volume, so that total world oil production outside OPEC increased by more than 5 million b/d and by more than 2.9 million b/d in the OECD countries alone from 1980 to 1985. After the UK, Mexico provided the next biggest increase in oil production, 0.78 million b/d, though it, like the UK, has now been in decline for some years.

Worldwide consumption of other forms of energy rose by 700 million tonnes of oil equivalent (o.e.) over the five years 1980 to 1985, i.e. more than 14 million b/d o.e. and more than over the preceding five years from 1974 to 1979. Nuclear energy and natural gas increased their percentage shares of world energy usage at the expense of oil between 1979 and 1985.

Moreover, the energy coefficient (energy growth usage) divided by economic growth fell from 1979 to 1985 to only 0.40 compared with 0.85 over the preceding six years from 1973 to 1979 – a rather dramatic change, indicative of a big improvement in the efficiency of energy usage, and a critically important influence.

In addition to all these other influences, the world economy grew at an annual average rate of only 2.3 per cent over the six years from 1979 to 1985, compared with 3.3 per cent over the preceding six years, based on World Bank Development Indicators, with both periods having incorporated an economic recession.

Undoubtedly, the oil price increases of 1979–80 had some influence in this further depressing of worldwide economic growth. The cumulative effect of all these influences was not merely a dramatic downward adjustment of world oil prices accentuated by the highly visible trading on futures as well as spot markets for both crude oil and refined products, but also a dramatic decline in both exports and production of OPEC oil in general and of those of Saudi Arabia in particular as self-appointed swing producer within OPEC from 1981 upon reunification of prices within the organization. This was done to contribute to stability in the world oil market and to assist fellow OPEC member states with large populations and comparatively low oil export volumes. The consequence was that total OPEC production fell by 10.47 million b/d between 1980 and 1985 in spite of a rise in Iran of 726,000 b/d, post the revolution there. Saudi Arabia bore the brunt of the fall, down 6.67 million b/d from 10.27 million b/d to only 3.6 million b/d in 1985. There were evidently highly adverse effects on oil export earnings as a result.

This combination of events induced a rethink on policy in OPEC and Saudi Arabia to make their oil exports more competitive on the world market and safeguard market volumes in the medium term. The mechanism adopted by

Saudi Arabia to achieve this was netback pricing. Given the relative similarity of delivered product prices as well as crude oil at that moment in the leading oil importing and consuming markets of the USA, Europe and Japan, this was almost guaranteed to bring success in volume terms. Price was to be a function of supply and demand pressures, but also subject to speculative excesses some twenty years later, both upwards and downwards, up to and after July 2008.

A readjustment of the OPEC price to $18 a barrel for Arab Light was achieved in late 1986. The volume of Saudi Arabian production increased by more than 3.5 million b/d between 1985 and 1990 and then by a further 2.39 million b/d from 1990 to 2000. Comparative increases for OPEC as a whole were 8.17 million b/d and 7.47 million b/d respectively, inclusive of Saudi Arabia.

Thus the new lower price was maintained while volumes were restored. Therefore, after all the pressures brought to bear on OPEC and Saudi Arabia over a five to six year period through the early 1980s, the policy change was successful in ensuring the future of Saudi Arabian and OPEC oil exports.

Focus on Saudi Arabian Oil Production

Saudi Arabian Production Response to Sharp Changes in the World Price of Oil

The Kingdom of Saudi Arabia now has an established history of varying its oil production and export volumes in order to make its unique contribution towards stabilizing the world oil markets. The fact of the matter is that commodity markets in general and oil in particular have a long history (some 150 years in the case of oil) during which sharp price fluctuations have occurred.

Of course, it is an economic truism that higher prices are supposed to stimulate increased supply, and vice versa, so Saudi Arabia's actions have been consistent with economic theory.

Even after the unilateral price increases introduced by OPEC in late 1973 and 1 January 1974, Saudi Arabian production reached a new high of 8.62 million b/d in the latter year. It fell back by 1.4 million b/d in 1975 on account of economic recession in the developed countries of the OECD. Both the oil price and Saudi Arabian production stabilized over the three years 1976 to 1978, averaging 8.9 million b/d with a new peak of 9.4 million b/d in 1977.

Thereafter oil prices took off to reach new peaks during the three years 1979 to 1981, as explained elsewhere in this book, while Saudi Arabian production reached new peaks, exceeding 10 million b/d on average during these three years.

After that, a combination of economic recession and market forces contrived to push oil prices down through 1985 and then dramatically so, in 1986. Much more dramatically still, Saudi Arabian oil production fell by almost 65 per cent from 10.26 million b/d on average in 1980–81 to only 3.6 million b/d in 1985. The concomitant price fall was almost 50 per cent from one year to the next, 1985 to 1986, and 58.4 per cent from the price peak reached in 1981.

Thereafter, from 1987 to 1997 there was little change in the nominal price of oil entering world trade which varied between $14 and $22 a barrel before dipping in 1998 to only $12.28, associated with the Russian debt and Far East crises. However, prices quickly picked up, rising more than $15 to $27.60 in 2000 and were comparatively stable for four years as Saudi oil production rose to 10.16 million b/d in 2003.

After that, Saudi Arabian oil production rose further to average 10.78 million b/d over the five years from 2004 to 2008. In spite of this, the oil price rose dramatically every year from $28.10 in 2000 to $94.45 in 2008 on account primarily of speculative pressures in spot and futures markets. This represented an annual average increase of a remarkable 27.4 per cent, even though, unsurprisingly, it proved unsustainable after July 2008. The consequence has been both a significant fall in world oil prices and in Saudi Arabian production in 2009, coupled with the world financial crisis followed by economic recession in 2008–9.

Table 1.1 summarizes the progression of oil prices and Saudi Arabian oil production (inclusive of NGLs) annually from 1970 until 2008.

Year	Saudi Arabian Oil Production*	Nominal Oil Price
1970	3.85	1.67
1971	4.82	2.03
1972	6.07	2.29
1973	7.69	3.05
1974	8.62	10.73
1975	7.22	10.73

1976	8.76	11.51
1977	9.42	12.39
1978	8.55	12.7
1979	9.74	17.25
1980	10.27	28.64
1981	10.26	32.51
1982	6.96	32.38
1983	4.95	29.04
1984	4.53	28.2
1985	3.6	27.01
1986	5.21	13.53
1987	4.6	17.73
1988	5.72	14.24
1989	5.64	17.31
1990	7.11	22.26
1991	8.82	18.62
1992	9.1	18.44
1993	8.96	16.33
1994	9.08	15.53
1995	9.15	16.86
1996	9.3	20.29
1997	9.48	18.68
1998	9.5	12.28
1999	8.85	17.48
2000	9.49	27.6
2001	9.21	23.12
2002	8.93	24.36
2003	10.16	28.1
2004	10.64	36.05

2005	11.11	50.64
2006	10.85	61.08
2007	10.45	69.08
2008	10.85	94.45

Cumulative Saudi Arabian Crude Oil Production and the Future Prospects to 2030

Cumulative production of crude oil production in Saudi Arabia reached 116.4 billion barrels by the end of 2008. The halfway point to this grand total was passed during the first half of 1989, less than twenty years earlier, and shortly after the inauguration of Saudi Aramco. By comparison, the first half of the total had taken more than fifty years. Just maintaining the level of production actually recorded over the last five years to 2008 would mean increasing by 50 per cent Saudi Arabian cumulative crude oil production during early in 2023, without providing for any rise.

Given the official announcement to increase capacity to 12.5 million b/d, a national average annual production of 11 million b/d, if actually achieved, from, say, 2011 onwards, after 8 million b/d in 2009 and assuming 9 million b/d in 2010, could take cumulative Saudi Arabian crude oil production through the 200 billion barrel level in the year 2030.

The Values of Saudi Arabian Petroleum Exports

The implications of what has been discussed above in terms of the changes in oil prices and Saudi Arabian oil production find expression in the remarkable fluctuations annually seen in the values of petroleum exports, the main driver of the Kingdom's balance of payments on current account and of its GDP.

This important aggregate rose from a very low $2.4 billion in 1970 to $111.5 billion in 1981, falling dramatically to less than $18.1 billion in 1985. After this there was a long fairly slow recovery to 2004. Even then, the total amounted to $110.9 billion, slightly below the 1981 peak. However, after that, there was a sharp rise to $162 billion in 2005, $188 billion in 2006, $206 billion in 2007 and $283 billion in 2008. These exceptionally high numbers reflected both the very steep rises in the price of oil entering world trade but also the unprecedented new highs in the volume of Saudi Arabian oil production and exports in these years. This level of Saudi Arabian petroleum export earnings in 2008 represented more than $11,400 per inhabitant of the Kingdom and some 59 per cent of its GDP in that year.

Per Capita GDP and Per Capita Oil and Gas Reserves

We show in Table 1.1 all thirteen OPEC member countries classified into five groups according to their per capita gross domestic product (GDP) and their proved reserves of oil and gas combined, also on a per capita basis. This serves to highlight the enormous disparities in both economic and hydrocarbon wealth among OPEC member countries.

Qatar stands unique on these indices in having a GDP per capita in 2008 of more than $100,000 and per capita proven oil and gas reserves (predominantly gas) of almost 22,500 barrels of oil equivalent among its small population of well under one million people, accounting for 0.14 per cent of the total population of OPEC countries.

The UAE and Kuwait rank next in this per capita hierarchy with a GDP of more than $50,000 and hydrocarbon reserves of more than 30,000 barrels of oil equivalent, but together they account for only a further 1.21 per cent of the total population of OPEC member countries.

The most surprising feature of these statistics is that even among OPEC member countries there are remarkable differences in the per capita oil and gas reserves. Likewise, their proportions of gas as a percentage of both hydrocarbons varies very much from Qatar at one extreme to Ecuador at the other.

Saudi Arabia ranks fourth on both these measures but accounting as it does for a full 4.0 per cent of the total population in OPEC countries, it is perhaps not surprising that its GDP per capita amounts to only 18.2 per cent of that of Qatar and only 5.6 per cent of Qatar's hydrocarbon wealth in terms of proved oil and gas reserves per capita.

Though we have classified Libya and Venezuela along with Saudi Arabia as having medium to high GDP and oil and gas reserves per capita they are significantly lower in both measures than the Kingdom, but significantly higher than the other seven OPEC member countries in 2008. On a GDP per capita basis these are led by Iran, followed by Angola, Algeria, Ecuador and Iraq, all in the range of less than $4,900 down to more than $3,400 per capita. Among them, both Angola and Ecuador have significantly lower oil and gas reserves than the others.

Table 1.2. Per Capita GDP and Hydrocarbon Proved Reserves of Saudi Arabia Compared with Other OPEC Member Countries in 2008.

		Per Capita GDP $	Per Capita Oil and Gas Reserves bbl o.e.	Gas % of Oil and Gas	% of OPEC Population
1.	Super High				
	Qatar	106,610	224,988	87	0.14
2.	High				
	UAE	57,603	30,531	29 }	1.21
	Kuwait	54,050	38,791	11 }	
3.	Medium High				
	Saudi Arabia	19,405	12,652	16}	
	Libya	15,926	8,667	19}	9.63
	Venezuela	11,464	7,347	16}	

4.	Medium Low				
	Iran	4,837	4,671	59}	
	Angola	4,766	646	16}	
	Algeria	4,712	1,238	72}	26.93
	Ecuador	3,808	475	1}	
	Iraq	3,464	4,608	15}	
5.	Low				
	Indonesia	2,242	107	84}	61.95
	Nigeria	1,415	474	48}	
	Total OPEC	4699	2664	38	613.10 millions

Indonesia (still an OPEC member in 2008) and Nigeria, accounting for almost 62 per cent of the total population of OPEC countries, remained relatively poor with GDP per capita in 2008 of little more than $2,200 and $1,400 respectively and comparatively low reserves of hydrocarbon per capita, especially Indonesia. This country has an obvious need to develop its still comparatively bounteous gas reserves further for both domestic consumption and export, given that its reserves to production ratio for gas still stood at more than forty-five years at its level of production in 2008.

Given the concentration of oil and gas reserves worldwide among OPEC member countries and the fact of their total population amounting to well below 10 per cent of the worldwide total does suggest that global reserves of these hydrocarbons are not overgenerous, since the world's population is still increasingly at a rate of 1.2 per cent p.a. to 2025, according to the UN projections, but at an average rate of 1.7 per cent p.a. in OPEC member countries, excluding Indonesia.

The Emergence of Saudi Aramco

From Participation as a Concept (1968) to the Inauguration of Saudi Aramco (1988)

Saudi Arabia's second Minister of Petroleum and Mineral Resources, Ahmad Zaki Yamani, had first discussed the concept of Saudi Arabian participation in the Arabian American Oil Company as long ago as 1968. Its premise was that the government should share not only in the income of the producing company, Aramco, but also in the ownership of its assets and its top level direction.

Participation became a central issue between the oil-exporting countries and the oil companies. By October 1972 a participation agreement was agreed between Aramco and the Saudi government, giving the latter a 25 per cent share. After further lengthy negotiations involving the Saudi Oil Minister and the Aramco partner companies, and following the tumultuous events of 1973–4, in 1976 Saudi Arabia took over all Aramco's assets and rights within the country – effectively the end of the concession agreement. Aramco would continue to be the operator and provide services to Saudi Arabia, for which it would receive 21 cents per barrel. It would market 80 per cent of Saudi production. In 1980 Saudi Arabia paid compensation, based on net book value, for all of Aramco's holdings within the Kingdom.

The fundamental precept of the four Aramco partner companies, Chevron, Texaco, Exxon and Mobil, had always been to preserve access to Saudi oil and the companies resisted breaking those links. However, as world oil prices and demand fell through the first half of the 1980s, access to Saudi crude oil at official prices became uneconomic. As the Aramco director and chairman of Chevron (formerly Socal) remarked, 'It's something we started, developed and in which we played a key role. So it was more of a problem. We had to back away, and ultimately we had to tell Yamani that we couldn't continue to do this.' Thus the Aramco links were significantly reduced and Saudi Arabia was no longer the special provider.

The change in this commercial relationship between the four companies and Saudi Arabia became one of the chief manifestations of how the oil industry was being transformed from integrated multinational companies, with the rise of national oil companies and the increasing importance of the hitherto marginal spot markets and futures trading with the start of the NYMEX crude contract in 1983.

It was not until 1988, just fifty years after Socal had struck oil in Saudi Arabia, that the final stage of change occurred, with the name changing to Saudi Aramco. Its first Saudi chairman was Hisham M. Nazer in April of that year, followed by Ali I. Al-Naimi in November. In his historic open letter to employees Al-Naimi wrote:

> The most important asset that Saudi Arabia will have upon assuming its responsibilities will be the human resources of the current work force, its depth of experiences, its technical competence and its loyalty ... working together, we can preserve the many Aramco accomplishments of the past, ensure the success of Saudi Aramco and continue to contribute to the future prosperity of the Kingdom.

In the past the company had been primarily concerned with exploration and production. Under its new leadership, Saudi Aramco began to expand into an integrated energy company, engaged in every aspect of the industry from exploration to marketing, distribution and sale of petroleum products in the Kingdom and around the world.

The changes made soon began paying off as Saudi Aramco discovered high value Arabian Super Light Crude oil (more than 40° API) and gas at al-Hawtah in central Saudi Arabia, south of Riyadh, in 1989. Many other initiatives followed including the restoration of production capacity to 10 million b/d, as it had been in 1980; investment in a tanker fleet; downstream investments abroad with joint venture partners, among many others.

The Financing of Saudi Infrastructure Development

The Saudi government's annual oil revenues rose dramatically from only $2.63 billion in 1972 to $89.16 billion in 1980. Though the volume of oil production rose sharply from 5.75 million b/d in 1972 to 9.66 million b/d in 1980, the average oil price per barrel increased by some twenty times over this eight-year period. An increase of this magnitude provided the wherewithal to finance the vast investment made in the Master Gas System and the many other infrastructure projects (oil, gas and many others) incorporated in the second and third five year plans over the ten years from 1975.

In February 1975 the Saudi government had unveiled its second five year plan. This plan assigned top priority to construction of a multi-billion Kingdom-wide network of diversified industries. In particular the government asked Aramco to design, develop and operate a gas-gathering and processing system to fuel this vast new industrial network, including new cities in Jubail on the Arabian Gulf and Yanbu on the Red Sea. This was called the Master Gas System (MGS), the keystone of the country's massive new development programme. Aramco called this 'the most ambitious energy project in history'. The new system would capture and process virtually all the gas that came to the surface with crude oil. Instead of being flared, as most of it had been in the past, the gas would be treated at new facilities and pipelined to industrial centres to serve as a fuel or feedstock for domestic petrochemical, fertilizer and steel industries. It would also supply the energy to power water desalination plants and electricity generation, and supply more natural gas liquids (NGLs) for export. When completed in 1982, the MGS harnessed about 3.5 billion standard cubic feet per day, the equivalent of 750,000 barrels of crude oil. In 1984 the system was enlarged to gather non-associated gas, i.e. not produced with crude oil, so that gas consumption increased to more than 9 billion standard cubic feet daily in 2005. As a result Saudi Arabia had become the largest per capita consumer of gas in the world. Demand is expected to nearly double by 2012.

The enlargement of the MGS in 1984 to gather non-associated gas was a boon to the industrial users in the Kingdom because its supply did not depend on fluctuating crude oil production. At that time it was falling quite sharply from the highpoint reached in 1980–1 to the low of 1985. The other big advantage afforded by the MGS was that domestic utilities that provided electric power for industries and homes in Saudi Arabia could switch from crude oil to cleaner-burning gas, freeing more valuable and higher volumes of crude oil for export.

The expanded MGS provides feedstock to industries that produce more than fifty petrochemical products generating international sales of some $10 billion a year. Also, electricity generated by gas-powered plants rose to about 40 per cent of the total generated by 2004. Within the following fifteen years, electricity generating capacity is expected to almost double, so there is plenty of further scope for additional inputs of natural gas supplies in this sector of Saudi Arabian energy consumption.

Other big oil and gas projects featured in these plans included the construction of joint venture export refineries with Mobil in Yanbu on the Red Sea and with Shell at Jubail on the Arabian Gulf; the installation of many gas oil separation plants (GOSPs); the construction of many pipelines, notably the one of 1170 kilometres across Saudi Arabia from the Arabian Gulf to the Red Sea; the expansion of domestic refineries, particularly at Ras Tanura, to 550,000 b/d capacity; the development of a large tanker fleet including ultra large and very large crude carriers (ULCCs and VLCCs); investment in oil refining and downstream investment in the Far East and in the United States. Also, Saudi Arabian Basic Industries Corporation (SABIC), formed at this time, has become a petrochemical producer of world class.

However, after 1980–1, there was a long period of much lower revenues from petroleum exports as both prices and volumes fell. It was not until 2004 that the value of Saudi Arabian petroleum exports again exceeded $100 billion, with the numbers rising annually thereafter to exceed $283 billion in 2008. The figure for OPEC as a whole was just in excess of $1 trillion in 2008. However, the numbers for both will be much lower once again for the year 2009 after oil prices fell dramatically in late 2008 into early 2009. The world financial crisis and economic recession caused oil export volumes to fall quite sharply from the high levels recorded over the years 2004 to 2008. Perhaps the fluctuations in the value of total Saudi Arabian petroleum exports can best be illustrated by reference to the fact that over the ten years 1989 to 1998 (the first full decade in the life of Saudi Aramco) they averaged $41.5 billion, but in the next ten years to 2008 they averaged $127.2 billion annually.

Among the many infrastructure projects related specifically to oil and gas was the Exploration and Petroleum Engineering Center (EXPEC) in Dhahran which opened in 1982. Within a few years the EXPEC and the adjacent Computer Center (ECC) and the associated Laboratory Research and Development Center enabled the Company to nearly eliminate its dependence on the outside sources for technological support in the exploration and production sector. These developments represented a clear manifestation of the Kingdom's determination to take its energy destiny into its own hands. The 250 computer operators, programmers and technicians had available to them advanced reservoir simulators, precision geological map plotters and the largest computers then made.

The juxtaposition of earth scientists, petroleum engineers and computer experts in EXPEC and the ECC brought major benefits. These facilities enabled experts to work together on one site to find the most effective and efficient ways to discover, recover and use the Kingdom's hydrocarbon wealth. They also provided a primary point to transfer advanced technology to Saudi Arabia's oil and gas development programme.

Developments at Saudi Aramco, 1988 to 2008, and 2009

Sensitivity to contemporary environmental issues has been a central concern of Saudi Aramco's management. Long-term tests in whole crude oil desulphurization began in early 2008. Meanwhile, sulphur recovery increased by 41 per cent from 2004 to 2008, when it amounted to 3.1 million tonnes. Another example of this concern is that the Company has deployed bacteria operationally as part of a nitrate treatment in the Hawtah oil field, thereby controlling a sulphide problem in an environmentally friendly fashion.

Domestic refining capacity amounts to almost 1 million b/d, with Ras Tanura being much the largest at 550,000 b/d. Inclusive of the three large export-orientated joint-venture refineries at Yanbu, Rabigh, both on the Red Sea, and Jubail on the Arabian Gulf, the Kingdom's total refining capacity exceeds 2 million b/d.

By 2008, the Far East had become the main focus for Saudi Aramco's exports with the region accounting for more than 50 per cent of both crude oil and refined product exports and 45.6 per cent of NGL exports. The Company's total exports peaked in 2005 when the total exceeded 3.1 billion barrels, or more than 8.53 million b/d, to meet rapidly rising worldwide oil consumption in both 2004 and 2005, just as oil production in the OECD countries had started to decline quite sharply. In that year, crude oil had accounted for 84.2 per cent of exports, NGLs for 9.3 per cent and refined products for the balance of 6.5 per cent.

Saudi Aramco gas reserves had increased by 2008 to 263 trillion cubic feet, an annual rate of net increase of more than 2.2 per cent. This most recent figure is approximately equivalent to 48.6 billion barrels of oil. On the tenth anniversary of the Company's inauguration in 1998, Saudi Aramco reported that it managed eighty-three oil and gas fields across the Kingdom, more than a third of which had been discovered in its first ten years.

The utilization of gas, both associated and non-associated, has for long been an important concern for Saudi Arabia. This gave rise to the plan and construction of the Kingdom's Master Gas System decades ago. In just four years from 2004 to 2008, Saudi Aramco's supply of raw gas to gas plants increased by 13.7 per cent from 7.3 to 8.3 billion of standard cubic feet per day. Over the same period delivered sales of gas increased by 32 per cent from 5.0 to 6.6 trillion Btus per day.

Other more recently announced major projects will involve adding 1.2 million barrels per day of Arabian Light crude oil production capacity at Khurais, plus 80,000 b/d of natural gas liquids (NGL). In addition, this largest integrated oil project in Saudi Aramco's history will dehydrate 320 million standard feet per day of gas. Also, the offshore Manifa project in the Gulf will add 900,000 b/d of Arabian Heavy crude oil production capacity, 90 million standard cubic feet a day of associated gas and 65,000 b/d of condensate.

Thus it can be seen that exploration and development of oil and gas deposits in Saudi Arabia are continuing with successful outcomes in these and other projects demonstrated more than seventy years after the first commercial discovery at Damman No. 7 oil well.

Ali I. Al-Naimi, Minister of Petroleum and Mineral Resources and Chairman of the Board of Directors of Saudi Aramco, remarked in the Annual Review for 2008 that, in his view, 'The basis of Saudi Aramco's leadership lies not in petroleum energy, but in the energy of people, characterized by a culture of continually seeking new levels of creating value.' On its tenth anniversary in 1998, he had remarked that, 'People, of course, form the heart of the Company.'

The Annual Review of Saudi Aramco for 2008 points out that the company is the world's largest exporter of natural gas liquids (more than 775,000 b/d) as well as being in premier position as a crude oil exporter. It goes on to state that:

> to meet future supply challenges, we have embarked on the largest capital program in our history. Part of our project portfolio is the addition of more than 4 million barrels per day (b/d) of oil production capacity and 3.3 billion standard cubic feet per day (scfd) of gas processing capacity. Some of this crude oil production capacity will be utilized to offset the natural decline of oil fields, while the rest will be employed to expand our maximum sustainable production capacity to 12 million b/d by year-end 2009.

This Annual Review of Saudi Aramco, under the heading 'Exploration', goes on to report that the Company's oil and gas reserves are contained in more than 104 fields, only twenty-three of which were in production in 2008, encompassing 354 different reservoirs. Overall, Saudi Arabia has more than 742 billion barrels of discovered oil resources, including proved, probable and possible reserves and contingent resources (oil in place that requires new methods and technologies to be produced). Remaining proved reserves compose roughly 260[2] billion barrels of the total. In 2008 our exploration programme discovered two gas fields and one oil field and also struck six new reservoirs in existing fields. It goes on to state: 'The likelihood of discovering additional reserves is high, with more than half of Saudi Arabia's potential hydrocarbon bearing areas still relatively unexplored. We support an aggressive and wide-ranging exploration program'.

Reaction to the worldwide financial crisis and economic recession causing a significant fall in unsustainably high oil prices of July 2008, attributable to speculative excesses, and of a fall in Saudi Arabian oil production and exports in 2009 have resulted in some projects going ahead but others being delayed or deferred. Saudi Aramco would launch 114 projects in the next five year plan of which eight would be 'giant' and around eighty 'small to medium'.

The Arabiyah offshore non-associated gas project of 1 billion cubic feet a day contains high levels of sulphur but it has been sanctioned in spite of its high cost, estimated at more than $5.50 per million Btus, even though Saudi Aramco sells gas to internal customers at $0.75 per million Btus. The Middle East Economic Survey suggests that in the long run Saudi Arabia will have to adjust prices upwards in order to unlock its geological gas potential. The Karan gas field is thought to have considerable scope to expand beyond its 1.8 billion cubic feet of gas a day, Saudi Arabia's first non-associated offshore gas development with some production coming on stream in October 2011.

However, the offshore Hasbah gas field development of 800 million cubic feet a day has been deferred. Work on the Shaybah oil field expansion to 750,000 b/d is in the process of being completed but development of a major NGL project there has been deferred. Spending on the offshore Maintain Potential programme, which includes the world's largest offshore field, the 1.2 million b/d capacity Safaniyah field, as well as Zuluf and Marjan, has been reduced to about half the level of recent years.

Saudi Aramco has also postponed a decision to proceed with its proposed new 400,000 b/d refinery at Ras Tanura. Work on other projects such as the 900,000 b/d offshore Manifa increment and proposed new joint venture export refineries at Yanbu and Jubail have also been delayed as the company seeks to bring down costs.

Three new oil production capacity increases totalling 1.55 million b/d are proceeding. The first of these is a 100,000 b/d increment at Nuayyim of Arab Super Light crude oil (lighter than 40° API) with commissioning expected to require two months from early May, including a gas oil separation plant and pumping station at Hawtah, the other field producing Arab Super Light crude. Secondly, the 250,000 b/d expansion at Shaybah Arab Extra Light (36° to 40° API) taking its capacity to 750,000 b/d, is also proceeding. Finally the 1.2 million b/d from Khurais, said to be the largest single increment in the oil industry's history, would come on stream in June 2009. This would push Saudi Aramco's capacity up to 12 million b/d and the Kingdom's capacity to 12.5 million b/d. Saudi Aramco CEO Khalid al-Falih reportedly said in May 2009 in Washington that 'Saudi Aramco alone will ultimately account for more than half the grassroots crude oil production capacity brought on stream worldwide this decade.' In addition the 500,000 b/d Khursaniyah field yielding Arab Medium was reportedly on stream in April 2009.

A Land Transformed quotes *Petroleum Intelligence Weekly* as ranking Saudi Aramco as first among the world's petroleum companies for seventeen consecutive years since 1988. It relies on its employees for success. During the last seven decades, the enterprise has grown enormously, discovered huge reserves of oil and gas, and produced billions of barrels of crude oil and trillions of standard cubic feet of gas. It has built and operated world-class petroleum facilities, and become a reliable partner in refining, marketing and distribution joint ventures around the world. Also it has established itself as the reliable source for about 10 per cent of the world's daily oil needs. At the heart of the company's achievements are its people.

Petro Rabigh: Saudi Aramco Joint Venture with Sumitomo

Petro Rabigh has been mentioned as one of three large joint-venture refineries in Saudi Arabia. Here we give some details of it to illustrate its size, scale and future expansion foreseen for it.

- The joint-venture plant is valued at over $10 billion.

- The plant currently employs around 2,000 people.

- The plant is expected to almost double in size in the next few years.

- The Rabigh oil refinery (long established) has a capacity of 400,000 b/d, equal with Yanbu and second largest in Saudi Arabia.

- A conversion plant will provide up to 5,000 additional jobs.

- The offer of shares in this joint-venture enterprise was made in January 2008.

- China is the plant's largest single client.

Population Increase and Training

Over the twenty years between the formation of Saudi Aramco in 1988 and 2008 the population of the Kingdom increased from 13.77 million to 24.82 million people. This represented a remarkable increase, averaging almost 3 per cent per annum.

The value of Saudi Arabian petroleum exports per capita was $1,467 in 1988 rising to $1,670 in 1998 and then sharply increasing over the last five years to $11,411 in 2008. This illustrates the problem of planning and budgeting over a five-year period when the main source of export revenues can fluctuate so much.

In 1985 Aramco had 51,500 employees, 16 per cent less than the 61,227 it had at the peak in 1982 as the export demand for Saudi crude started to decline. In Saudi Aramco's first year of 1988 its workforce had fallen to 43,822 from more than fifty countries at year end. Saudis by then held nearly 100 per cent of management positions, 77 per cent of the supervisory posts and nearly 50 per cent of its 10,900 professional jobs. A total of 1,520 Saudis were recruited during the year, nearly all of them being secondary school or college graduates. Most of the recruits from high school were science students. Under the Apprenticeship Programme launched in August 1988, high school graduates can join the Company upon successful completion of two years of intensive training. The development of the Saudi workforce to its maximum potential remained a chief priority in 1988. At this time the training programme was reportedly one of the largest in the world, with a full-time staff of 880 teachers and trainers and 825 support personnel. A total of 7,500 Saudis undertook academic training in 1988 to acquire the skills to qualify them for specific positions or to advance to higher job levels.

The Annual Report for 1988 also mentions that forty-three students from the King Fahd University of Petroleum and Minerals participated in a four-month cooperative programme in which they received college credit for work assignments at Aramco. A separate programme offered annually provided summer jobs for more than 1,000 Saudi college and high school students. The same source mentioned that 840 Saudi employees, all recent college graduates, were participating in the three-year Professional Development Programme at the end of the year, gaining experience in a series of individually selected jobs to qualify them for professional positions.

The 1998 Annual Review of Saudi Aramco noted that the Company had unveiled new strategies on the eve of the new millennium. By that year's end the workforce had increased to 55,532. This reflected the absorption of the workforce of Samarec numbering more than 11,000 in 1993. This Review also showed some important forward-thinking. The Company expanded enrolment in language and degree programmes in the Far East and sent the first group of ten Saudi high school graduates to Xiamin University in China for eighteen months to study Mandarin Chinese. Saudi Aramco had increased distance learning and company-wide certification for training professionals. The Company also initiated a pilot Career Center programme to provide internal recruitment services to line organizations, and job and career services to employees in the Employee Relations and Training organization.

By the end of 2008 the Saudi Aramco workforce was slightly less than it had been ten years earlier at 54,441 in total, of whom 87.3 per cent were Saudi nationals. This Annual Review gives impressive figures for Saudi Aramco's Development Programmes. For example, 4,897 were serving two-year apprenticeships; 1,298 were on a college degree programme; 346 were on a college preparatory programme; 281 were studying for an advanced degree; 117 were co-op students; 56 were on two-year diploma courses; 52 were on associate degree programmes for non-employees; and 20 were on advanced medical/dental courses.

All of this and many other references seem fully consistent with the frequent and evidently most sincere remarks by board chairman, Ali I. Al-Naimi, about the importance of people as the Company's principal asset.

Oil and Gas Operations

Figures 1.1 and 1.2 show respectively oil operations and gas operations in the Kingdom of Saudi Arabia. They show the principal oil fields and gas plants along with stabilizers, oil refineries, gas-oil separator plants, tanks and other facilities such as the Abqaiq plants, tanks and terminals. The gas diagram shows prominently the Jubail and Yanbu industrial complexes, the Saudi Electric Company and various gas and fractionation plants and terminals.

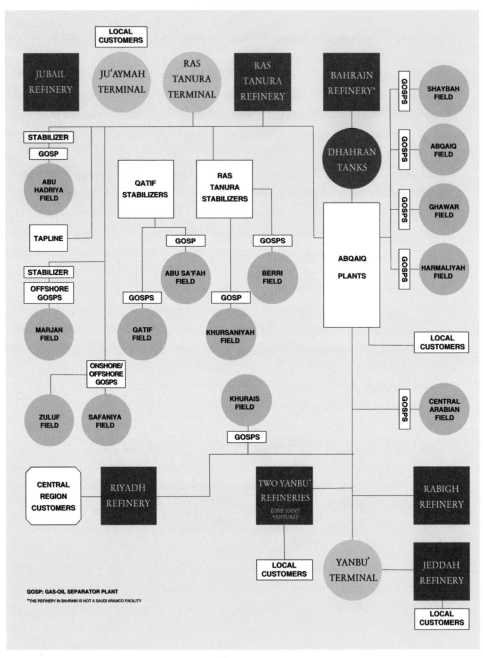

Figure 1.1.

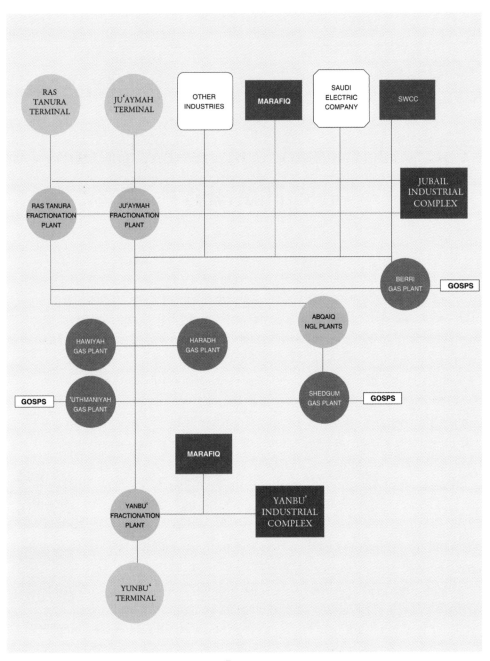

Figure 1.2.

Foreign Participation in Gas Exploration in Saudi Arabia

In 2000 the Kingdom invited major foreign oil companies to bid on gas exploration and development projects in the Rub'al Khali (empty quarter) of Saudi Arabia. Interestingly, this was just fifty years after Max Steineke with an Aramco geologist wrote, in *World Geography of Petroleum* (1950) in a chapter on Saudi Arabia: 'The Rub'al Khali basin may contain oil-bearing strata, but development of the area will be slow and arduous, because of the terrain, the climate and the lack of water. Further improvements of special equipment will undoubtedly overcome these obstacles, and make it possible to explore thoroughly this forbidding area.'

In 2003 Saudi Aramco signed a deal with Royal Dutch/Shell and Total for gas exploration, development and production on more than 200,000 square kilometres of the south-eastern Rub'al Khali. Shell holds a 40 per cent stake and Total and Saudi Aramco each have 30 per cent in the South Rub'al-Khali Co. Ltd (S'RAK).

In 2004 three more gas exploration partnerships were formed, with Saudi Aramco having a 20 per cent in each of them. Lukoil Saudi Arabia Energy Ltd is exploring in a $30,000km^2$ area just south of the Ghawar oil field. Saudi Sinopec Gas Ltd territory covers another $39,000km^2$ just to the south of it. The Italian Spanish consortium of ENI/Repsol YPF received a license to explore for and produce non-associated gas in the northern Rub'al Khali just to the east of the other two over 52,000km².

When work on these projects is finished some 60 per cent of the Rub'al Khali will have been scoured for hydrocarbons. Under the arrangements Saudi Aramco will take over and develop any oil and associated gas discovered. All non-associated gas will be sold to Saudi Aramco.

Additional Joint-Venture Refinery Projects in Prospect in Saudi Arabia

In May 2006 Saudi Aramco signed memoranda of understanding with Total of France and Conoco Phillips of the US to build two export refineries at Jubail and Yanbu respectively. The 400,000 b/d plants are planned to start up in 2011. They will convert heavy grade crude oils into high quality ultra low sulphur products, especially transport and heating fuels that meet all US and European product specifications.

Classification of Saudi Arabian Crude Oils

The classification of Saudi crude oils now incorporates a five-part grouping as shown in Table 1.2. In 2008 Saudi Aramco's exports of crude oil exceeded 2.5 billion barrels, 6.86 million b/d and amounted to 76.8 per cent of the Company's crude oil production. Exports of crude and products together exceeded 2.64 billion barrels, 7.21 million b/d. In addition, total NGL production was almost 1.1 million b/d with 70.6 per cent exported in 2008. Sulphur recovery amounted to more than 3 million tonnes, with 90.6 per cent exported. A significant feature of Saudi Aramco exports is that the Far East accounted for well over 50 per cent of the total for both crude oil and refined products and for almost 46 per cent of exports of natural gas liquids in 2008, too. By this time, the United States and Europe/the Mediterranean accounted for smaller proportions of Saudi Aramco exports than they had done historically. At world level, the Far East, inclusive of Australasia, accounted for 42 per cent of total inter-area oil trade, followed by Europe at 25.5 per cent and the USA at 23.6 per cent. Together these accounted for 90.7 per cent of the worldwide total.

Table 1.3.

Arabian Super Light (ASL)	API > 40°
Arabian Extra Light (AXL)	API 36° to 40°
Arabian Light (AL)	API 32² to 36°

| Arabian Medium (AM) | API 29° to 32° |
| Arabian Heavy (AH) | API < 29° |

Product Mix from Saudi Arabian Refineries

The product mix from Saudi Arabian refineries in 2008 was as shown in Table 1.3. Worldwide, consumption of fuel oil now amounts to only 11.0 per cent of the total. Thus there seems to be scope for further lightening the Saudi barrel from refineries in the Kingdom with the substitution of more natural gas in place of residual fuel oil. However, there remains a big demand for its use for marine in Saudi Arabia, the world's largest oil exporting country.

Table 1.4.

	LPG	Naphtha	Gasoline	Jet Fuel/ Kenosine	Diesel	Fuel Oil	Asphalt & Misc
%	2.1	9.7	15.5	4.1	39.6	24.8	4.1

Worldwide Consumption of Petroleum Products

Worldwide, consumption of light distillates accounted for 31.2 per cent of the total, but a high of 47.5 per cent in the United States. Middle distillates accounted for 36.9 per cent of the total, with a high of 49.3 per cent in Europe where gas oil for heating remains important. For the Asia Pacific region, the world's largest consuming area for petroleum products, light distillates accounted for 28.4 per cent of the total and middle distillates for 37.5 per cent with fuel oil down at 13.4 per cent.

Consumption Trends in Leading Countries

A further analysis of consumption of oil products and growth rates in the major consuming countries/regions is characterized by remarkable differences among them and changes in growth rates among some of them, notably Japan, South Korea, Taiwan, the USA and over the ten years to 2008, as between the first and second five-year periods, reflecting much higher prices during the latter in these countries.

Table 1.5. Consumption of Oil Products and Growth Rates in Major Consuming Countries

	Oil Consumption in 2008 1,000 b/d	% of World	Average % annual growth 1998–2003	2003–2008
Asia/Pacific	25,339	30.0	2.8	2.3
of which				
China	8,293	9.8	6.7	6.5
Japan	4,845	5.6	-0.4	-2.3
India	2,882	3.4	4.1	3.6
S Korea	2,291	2.7	2.4	-0.4
Taiwan	1,074	1.3	5.4	-0.3
USA	19,419	23.0	1.1	-0.6
Europe	16,114	19.1	-0.5	0.5
of which				
Germany	2,505	3.0	-1.7	-1.1
France	1,930	2.3	-0.4	-0.2
UK	1,704	2.0	-0.4	-0.1
Italy	1,691	2.0	-0.6	-2.6
Saudi Arabia	2,224	2.6	5.1	6.6

The disparity in rates of change in oil consumption over the last decade between strong growth in China and a comparatively sharp decline in Japan is noteworthy. China, inclusive of Hong Kong, overtook Japan as the world's second-largest oil consumer in 2002. US oil consumption rose by nearly 1.9 million b/d between 1998 and 2005 but rising prices of products started to affect consumption with a sharp fall of 1.26 million b/d between 2007 and 2008. In Europe a high tax regime on petroleum products acts both as a demand depressant and an important source of revenue (greater than that per barrel for the oil-exporting countries) for the governments of the four leading countries, the UK having the highest tax take among them.

In 2004 to 2008 Saudi Arabia's oil consumption growth rate was marginally greater than that for China. In volume it exceeded that of France, the UK and Italy in 2008, notwithstanding the fact that Saudi gas consumption also grew rapidly at an average rate of 5.4 per cent annually over the five years to 2008.

From its low point in 1998, the real oil price of crude oil rose at an annual rate of 16.6 per cent p.a. through until 2003. In spite of this, worldwide oil consumption continued to grow at an average annual rate of 1.4 per cent. Over the following five years to 2008 the price of crude oil rose considerably faster, at an average rate of 27.8 per cent annually, but worldwide consumption continued to rise, on average at 1.3 per cent p.a., though it did decline by 0.6 per cent in 2008 when a new and unsustainable oil price high was reached after speculative excesses.

As one would expect, growth rates fell back or became more negative than they had done previously over this latest five-year period, except in the three largest European economies of Germany, the UK and France. Among these, there was some deceleration in the rate of decline in consumption. Partly for this reason, but also because, paradoxically, oil consumption growth in most of the rest of Europe was faster from 2003 to 2008 than it had been during the previous five years, total European oil consumption in 2008 was at almost the same level as it had been in 1998.

Political Stability and Continuity
in Saudi Arabia

Over a period of more than fifty years since 1953, Saudi Arabia has been ruled by five monarchs, all sons of the modern founder of the Kingdom, King Abl al-Aziz Al Saʿud who reigned from 1902 until 1953. It was in 1932 that the modern Kingdom was firmly established within its existing boundaries as the dominant nation-state in the Arabian peninsula and then, just some eight months later, set on its modern course towards being a land transformed with the signing of the historic oil prospecting concession agreement with the Standard Oil Company of California (now Chevron).

Another aspect of the political stability existing within the Kingdom of Saudi Arabia is the fact that throughout this lengthy period, it has had just four Ministers of Petroleum and Mineral Resources to control and coordinate its all-important oil policy consistent with the policies made by the King himself and the senior members of the House of Saud.

Abdullah H. Tariki, 1954–1962

In 1949 he was virtually the first of the American educated Saudi technocrats to return to the Kingdom. After a period working in the Finance Ministry he became Director General of Petroleum and Mineral Affairs in 1954 and then first Minister of Petroleum and Mineral Resources on the creation of the Ministry in 1960.

At first he concentrated on trying to gain control over refining and marketing assets. But after BP suddenly cut posted prices of oil in early 1959, he switched his attention to control over prices and production. He was appointed to the board of Aramco in 1959. Abdullah Tariki played a critically important role in the formation of OPEC in September 1960, along with Juan Pablo Perez Alfonso of Venezuela. Its original five members were Iran, Iraq, Kuwait, Saudi Arabia and Venezuela.

Ahmed Zaki Yamani, 1962–1986

He played an important role in the evolution of Saudi Arabian oil policy, particularly as a communicator of it to the world at large. He became legal adviser to Faysal prior to the latter becoming King and was appointed Minister of Petroleum and Mineral Resources in 1962.

Yamani articulated his theory of participation in 1968. It argued in favour of the government sharing in the ownership of oil assets as well as in the oil income of oil-producing countries. Participation became a central issue but Yamani had warned against outright nationalization in 1969. He anticipated that the result would be a dramatic collapse of the price structure, with each of the producing countries trying to maintain budgeted income requirements in the face of declining prices by moving larger quantities of oil to the market. The costs and risks would not only be economic. Financial instability would inevitably lead to political instability. Yamani was put in charge on the OPEC side, in negotiations with the oil companies.

In early 1971, Ahmed Zaki Yamani, together with the Iranian Finance Minister and the Iraqi Oil Minister, forming the OPEC Gulf Committee, met with leading directors of Exxon and BP on behalf of the major oil companies. The negotiations resulted in the establishment of 55 per cent as the minimum government take and raised the price of a barrel of oil by 35 cents. This Tehran Agreement marked a watershed with the initiative in oil policy passing from the major oil companies to the oil-exporting countries.

By October 1972 the participation issue had been resolved in terms of negotiations involving the Gulf oil-producing states and the major oil companies with a 25 per cent initial participation share envisaged as rising to 51 per cent by 1983. The potential problem of valuation of assets was resolved by using updated book values. The Aramco partner companies reached agreement with Saudi Arabia.

By July–September 1973 the situation had changed again. Following a synchronized economic boom in the oil-importing industrial countries, the fundamental balance of supply and demand moved in favour of the oil exporters. Yamani told the oil companies that the Tehran Agreement was dead or dying. He was quoted as saying 'Anyone who knows our regime and how it works realizes that the decision to limit production is made only by one man, i.e. the King, and that he makes that decision without asking for anybody's concurrence.' The King is 'one hundred percent determined to effect a change in US policy (in support of Israel) and use oil for that purpose'. King Faysal had told the oil company executives that simple disavowal of Israeli policies by the United States would help deflect the use of the oil weapon.

On 16 October 1973 OPEC took unilateral action to raise the posted price of oil by 70 per cent to $5.11 a barrel in line with spot market prices. This followed negotiations with the oil companies which the latter had failed to conclude.

The following day Arab oil ministers met to plan an embargo of oil exports to leading oil-importing countries. This involved the prospect of monthly cutbacks and differentiation of export volumes to major oil-consuming countries in order to split them, following the Yom Kippur War, in their policy stances vis-à-vis the Arab countries and Israel. Aramco was to police the embargo on behalf of Saudi Arabia.

Following these developments the spot price of oil entering world trade had increased further in late 1973. Yamani argued against a bigger rise proposed by some within OPEC based on exceptional oil auction prices in the far from normal market conditions then prevailing. Finally a new $11.65 posted price for oil was agreed, based on a consultant's report to Iran, on the cost of alternative energy sources. This was introduced on 1 January 1974.

After years of relative stability in the price of oil entering world trade from

1974 to 1978, Yamani became an advocate of a long-term strategy for OPEC. This proposed regular small increases in real oil prices. This was foreseen as much preferable to and less destabilizing than sudden big increases in oil prices.

Given the disarray in world oil prices which occurred in 1979–80 and into 1981 brought about by market forces, Yamani worked to bring about reunification of prices within OPEC. This was achieved by the end of 1981.

Following the pressures on OPEC and Saudi Arabian oil production volumes from 1981 through 1985 it became apparent that a new policy initiative was needed to restore OPEC and Saudi Arabian competitiveness in the world oil market. For Saudi Arabia Yamani introduced netback pricing for this purpose. This proved successful.

Hisham M Nazer, 1986–1995

He was the former Minister of Planning and thus sensitive to the link between oil export revenues and budgeting for national economic development. He represented Saudi Arabia for the first time at the OPEC Conference in December 1986. This agreed a new price of $18 a barrel for Arab Light and new quotas for OPEC member countries. This outcome proved durable over many years and comparatively successful in achieving fairly stable export volumes and prices fluctuating less than over the 1979 to 1986 period, in spite of spot and futures markets driving world oil prices. In April 1988 Nazer was appointed first Saudi chairman of Aramco.

Ali I. Al-Naimi, 1995–present

He started at the bottom as an Aramco office boy but during the 1970s he rose to become a senior executive in the Company. He became president of Aramco in 1984, chairman in November 1988 as it became Saudi Aramco, then promoted to become Minister of Petroleum and Mineral Resources in 1995.

At a meeting with senior US officials in April 2004 on oil price increases, differing views had been expressed. Naimi pointed out by way of explanation that there had been five unexpected rises in short-term demand forecasts from the IEA and US DOE. Subsequently, statistics revealed an exceptionally high growth of some 3.5 per cent in worldwide oil demand in 2004, with China up almost 1 million b/d and the US demand up by about 0.7 million b/d. In addition, production in OECD countries started declining. Naimi also pointed to the shortage of US refining capacity as another explanation for oil prices rising at this time.

At the same conference Naimi stated that Saudi technical experts had shown that the country could raise output from 10.5 million b/d to 12–15 million b/d and maintain that output for fifty years or more. He asserted that reserve additions would enhance future Saudi production capabilities with none of the booked reserves requiring enhanced recovery techniques.

By April 2009 the Minister was foreseeing production capacity rising to reach 12.5 million b/d during the year. In May 2009 he was addressing G8 energy ministers saying that Saudi Arabia was committed to investing both upstream and downstream to ensure an uninterrupted supply of energy when the global economy recovers. However, he went on to warn that if others did not begin to invest similarly in new capacity expansion projects, we could see within two to three years another price spike similar to or worse than that witnessed in 2008.

At the same time Naimi called for consuming and producing countries to intensify their efforts to better understand the workings of the oil markets and to improve their transparency. Both sides must consider whether an expanded role for governments in regulating the markets is warranted. He said that, in the short term, a low price and a low demand environment discourages substantive investment in petroleum infrastructure. High development costs and tight credit markets were compounding the difficulties.

Also in May 2009, Naimi presented a paper on behalf of Saudi Arabia entitled, 'Energy Strategies to Respond to Global Climate Change'. In this he pointed out that other greenhouse gases have greater global warming potential than CO_2. There was a need to talk about a low emissions economy rather than a low carbon one. Saudi Arabia believed that any new agreement post-2012 should be based on the principles listed in the United Nations Framework Convention on Climate Change and should not be subject for renegotiation.

The four main elements in the energy response to climate change were as follows.

- The specific needs and special circumstances of developing countries had to be taken into account so that they did not have to bear a disproportionate or abnormal burden. Also, measures taken to combat climate change in the energy sector need to avoid disguised restriction on international trade.

- There should be recognition of the fact that fossil fuels will continue to dominate the energy mix for decades to come and that the role of other energy sources, including renewables, will be supplemental only; there is a danger of the wrong message inhibiting future investment in fossil fuels.

- There is a need to emphasize the importance of a level playing field, including R&D in all safe energy technologies; there is a strong need for effective development and transfer of environmentally safe and sound energy technology to developing countries.

- Saudi Arabia is pleased with international efforts in promoting carbon capture and storage to provide a sustainable fossil fuel future; collaboration with the oil industry to provide 'green' fuels is proceeding.

Part II

Geo-Politics and Highlights of Economic and Energy Trends

Introduction

Part II covers developments over the decade to 2008 and back to benchmark years 1965, 1973 and 1979, to the current situation and prospects for the medium-term future. The recession of 2008–9 was concentrated mainly in the advanced economies of the OECD countries and Russia. It started in August 2007 when inter-bank lending froze, causing a 'credit crunch'. Irresponsible US and European bank lending to the housing sector in particular resulted in this becoming the most intense economic downturn since the Great Depression of the early 1930s, nearly eighty years before. It also had a significant depressing effect on worldwide energy usage, especially oil. Energy consumption, including oil, is likely to be well below trend in 2008, 2009 and perhaps in 2010, too. Thus 2007 is likely to be the last trend year for the world economy, primary energy consumption, and oil in particular as the main balancing form of energy for several years, albeit with oil prices being significantly above trend in 2008. These are the reasons for retaining the year 2007 for much of our analyses.

The main long-period analysis of past trends in this book was completed prior to data for the year 2008 becoming available. Though these data have now been analysed with some of the main features being shown in the book, the remarkable rise in the price of oil entering world trade which occurred in 2008, culminating in a price of more than $140 a barrel in July of that year, means that it was a highly untypical year in the major oil and energy consuming countries worldwide.

Over the year of 2008 as a whole, the price of the OPEC reference basket of crudes averaged $94.45 a barrel, an increase of 36.7 per cent from 2007. Of course, the oil price rises were brought about not by OPEC but by the free play of market forces with speculative influences playing a significant role. Thus we open our discussion of the longer-term trends with a review of the changes which occurred in 2008 compared with the situation in 2007. Primary energy consumption worldwide rose 1.4 per cent in 2008 (adjusting for the 366-day leap year) in spite of the financial crisis leading to economic recession. However, oil consumption is estimated to have fallen 0.5 per cent, offset by natural gas consumption rising by 2.5 per cent and coal up 3.2 per cent. Hydro-electricity also rose by 2.9 per cent in 2008, but the nuclear contribution fell by 0.7 per cent, all these numbers adjusted for 2008 being a leap year. The consequence for the world primary energy balance was a fall for oil to below 35 per cent, with coal and natural gas rising to more than 29 per cent and 24 per cent respectively. There is no inclusion of wind, wave, solar or bio-fuel energy or other forms of renewable energy.

Table 11.1. World Primary Energy Balance in 2008 Compared with 2007

	2007 %	2008 %	% Change in Consumption
Oil	35.5	34.8	-0.5
Natural gas	23.9	24.1	+2.5
Coal	28.8	29.2	+3.2
Nuclear	5.6	5.5	-0.7
Hydro-electricity	6.3	6.4	+2.9
Total Primary Energy m.t.o.e	11,104.4	11,294.9	+1.7
Million tonnes oil equivalent per day	30.42	30.86	+1.4

Source: BP *Statistical Review of World Energy.*

Some of the biggest changes on a year-to-year basis occurred in the major energy consuming countries. The swing as between the United States and China amounted to almost 200 million tonnes of oil equivalent from 2007 to 2008, so the difference between these two largest energy consuming countries was reduced to well under 300 million tonnes of oil equivalent. US energy consumption fell 2.8 per cent whereas Chinese energy consumption increased by 7.3 per cent in 2008. Similarly, among the five largest energy consuming countries, there was a big difference between Japan, where energy consumption fell 1.6 per cent, and India where there was an increase of 5.9 per cent. Also, among the top twenty-two energy consuming countries worldwide, there were marked contrasts between rises of 7.0 per cent in Saudi Arabia and 5.5 per cent in Indonesia and falls of 4.0 per cent in Australia and 3.6 per cent in Spain.

Oil consumption fell especially sharply in 2008 by 6.4 per cent in the United States and by 3.5 per cent in Japan, but rose by 2.8 per cent in China and by 4.8 per cent in India, indicating a markedly different response to the oil price increase as between the leading OECD countries and the fast developing populous emerging economies. Figure 11.1 shows the main changes. Similarly, among the fast growing next group of countries, oil consumption rose by 5.3 per cent in Brazil and by 8 per cent in Saudi Arabia, offset in part by significant falls in South Korea and Taiwan.

Natural gas consumption rose especially sharply in China, by 16.2 per cent and the UAE, up 17.8 per cent. There were also rises by more than 11 per cent in both Indonesia and Spain in 2008.

There was a sharp rise in Chinese coal consumption in 2008, up more than 92 million tonnes of oil equivalent, accounting for 84.4 per cent of the worldwide increase. It has now risen at a remarkably high average rate of 8.0 per cent annually between 1998 and 2008. Coal consumption in Brazil, Kazakhstan, the Russian Federation and India rose by more than 8 per cent in 2008, too, in response to the oil price increases.

On the following pages we have analysed the changes between 2007 and 2008 in primary energy, oil and natural gas consumption between the top five, the next six and the following eleven countries in rank order worldwide.

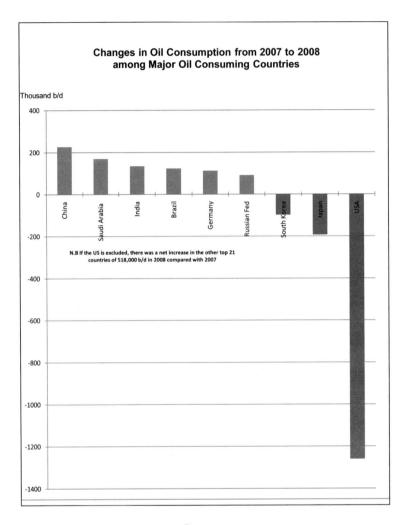

Figure II.I.

These twenty-two countries accounted for more than 80 per cent of world primary energy consumption in 2008, and over 78 per cent of both oil and gas consumption, and thus represent a reasonable cross-section of responses to the oil price increases in that year, induced largely by speculative market forces. All the top eleven countries are among those designated officially as G20 members as of 25 September 2009 in Pittsburgh at the leaders' summit, and seven of the next eleven countries, too. Only Iran, Spain, Ukraine and Taiwan in our listing are not included in the newly constituted G20. Argentina is a G20 country but not featured in our energy and oil lists, though it appears in our list of principal gas consuming countries. There are five other countries with higher energy consumption in 2008 than Argentina. In descending order they are Poland, the Netherlands, Thailand, Venezuela and the UAE. Readers interested in the statistical details are referred to Tables 11.2, 11.3 and 11.4.

Table 11.2. World Consumption of Primary Energy in 2008: Top 22 Countries

	mn m.t.o.e.	Change from 2007	Year on Year % change	% of World total
USA	2,299.0	-60.6	-2.8	20.4
China	2,026.3	+138.0	+7.3	17.9
Russian Federation	684.6	+4.9	+0.4	6.1
Japan	507.5	-8.3	-1.6	4.5
India	433.3	+24.1	+5.6	3.8
Top 5 countries	5,950.7	+98.1	+1.7	52.7
Canada	329.8	+3.7	+1.1	2.9
Germany	311.1	+1.8	+0.6	2.8
France	257.9	+3.1	+1.2	2.3
South Korea	240.1	+4.4	+1.9	2.1
Brazil	228.1	+7.7	+3.5	2.0
UK	211.6	-3.1	-1.4	1.9
Next 6	1,578.6	+17.6	+1.1	14.0
Iran	192.1	+3.7	+2.0	1.7
Italy	176.6	-1.9	-1.1	1.6
Saudi Arabia	174.5	+11.4	+7.0	1.5

Mexico	170.4	+6.7	+4.1	1.5
Spain	143.9	-5.3	-3.6	1.3
Ukraine	131.5	-3.2	-2.4	1.2
South Africa	132.3	+5.2	+4.1	1.2
Australia	118.3	-4.9	-4.0	1.0
Taiwan	112.0	-3.1	-2.7	1.0
Indonesia	124.4	+6.5	+5.5	1.1
Turkey	102.6	+1.5	+1.5	0.9
Next 11	1578.6	+16.6	+1.1	14.0
Total 22 Countries	**9,107.9**	**+132.3**	**+1.5**	**80.7**
Total Middle East	**613.5**	**+35.9**	**+6.2**	**5.4**
European Union	**1,728.2**	**-4.0**	**-0.2**	**15.3**
OECD	**5,508.4**	**-59.9**	**-1.1**	**48.8**
World	**11,294.9**	**+190.5**	**+1.7**	**100.0**

Source: BP *Statistical Review of World Energy* (2009).

Note: All the countries listed are G20 members except for Iran, Spain, Ukraine and Taiwan. The European Union is also a member of the G20 which represents the interests of those 23 EU countries which are not, like the Big 4, represented individually in the G20, as indeed they were in the G7 (i.e. Germany, France, the UK and Italy).

Table 11.3. *World Consumption of Oil in 2008: Top 22 Countries*

	ooos b/d	Change from 2007	Year on Year % change	% of World total
USA	19,419	-1,261	-6.4	22.5
China	8,293	+227	+2.8	9.8
Japan	4,845	-194	-3.5	5.6
India	2,882	+134	+4.8	3.4
Russian Federation	2,797	+91	+3.1	3.3
Top 5	**38,236**	**-1,003**	**-2.6**	**45.3**

Germany	2,505	+112	+4.9	3.0
Brazil	2,397	+123	+5.3	2.7
Canada	2,295	-28	-1.2	2.6
South Korea	2,291	-98	-4.1	2.6
Saudi Arabia	2,224	+170	+8.1	2.6
Mexico	2,039	+12	+0.6	2.3
Next 6	**13,751**	**+291**	**+2.2**	**16.3**
France	1,930	+9	+0.5	2.3
Iran	1,730	+37	+2.2	2.1
UK	1,704	-10	-0.6	2.0
Italy	1,691	-68	-3.9	2.0
Spain	1,574	-43	-2.7	1.9
Indonesia	1,217	+16	+1.3	1.5
Taiwan	1,074	-49	-4.4	1.3
Netherlands	982	+20	+2.1	1.2
Singapore	958	+42	+4.6	1.1
Australia	936	+11	+1.2	1.1
Belgium & Luxemburg	836	+4	+0.5	1.0
Next 11	**14,632**	**-31**	**-0.2**	**17.3**
Top 22 Countries	**66,619**	**-743**	**-1.1**	**78.9**
Total Middle East	**6,423**	**+339**	**+5.6**	**7.8**
European Union	**14,765**	**+19**	**+0.1**	**17.9**
OECD	**47,303**	**-1527**	**-3.1**	**56.0**
World	**84,455**	**-423**	**-0.5**	**100.0**

Source: BP *Statistical Review of World Energy* (2009)

Note: *All the countries listed are G20 members except for Iran, Spain, Taiwan, the Netherlands,*

Singapore, and Belgium/Luxembourg. The European Union represents the interests of Spain, the Netherlands and Belgium/Luxembourg as a member of the G20.

Table 11.4.World Consumption of Natural Gas in 2008: Top 22 Countries

	bn m³	Change from 2007	Year on Year % change	% of World total
USA	657.2	+4.6	0.6	22.0
Russian Federation	420.2	-5.5	-1.6	13.9
Iran	117.6	+4.6	3.8	3.9
Canada	100.0	+3.3	3.2	3.3
UK	93.9	+3.0	3.0	3.1
Top 5 countries	**1,388.9**	**+10.0**	**+0.7**	**46.0**
Japan	93.7	+3.5	+3.9	3.1
China	83.3	+11.6	+16.2	2.8
Germany	82.0	-0.9	-1.1	2.7
Saudi Arabia	78.1	+3.7	+5.0	2.6
Italy	77.7	-0.1	-0.1	2.6
Mexico	67.2	+4.1	6.5	2.2
Next 6	**482.0**	**+21.9**	**+4.8**	**16.0**
Ukraine	59.7	-3.0	-4.8	2.0
UAE	58.1	+8.7	+17.8	1.9
Uzbekistan	48.7	+2.8	+6.1	1.6
Argentina	44.5	+0.6	+1.4	1.5
France	44.2	+1.7	+4.0	1.5
India	41.4	+1.3	+3.2	1.4
Egypt	40.9	+2.5	+6.5	1.3
South Korea	39.7	+4.2	+3.1	1.3

Spain	39.0	+3.9	+11.1	1.3
Netherlands	38.6	+1.6	+4.3	1.3
Indonesia	38.0	+4.0	+11.8	1.3
Next 11	**492.8**	**+25.4**	**+5.4**	**16.3**
Top 22 Countries	**2,363.7**	**+57.3**	**+2.5**	**78.3**
Total Middle East	**327.1**	**+23.8**	**+7.8**	**10.8**
European Union	**490.1**	**+9.2**	**+1.9**	**16.2**
OECD	**1,494.3**	**+27.6**	**+1.9**	**49.7**
World	**3,018.7**	**+80.7**	**+2.7**	**100.0**

Source: BP *Statistical Review of World Energy* (2009).

Note: All the countries listed are G20 members except for Iran, Ukraine, the UAE, Uzbekistan, Egypt, Spain and the Netherlands.

Energy Geo-Politics: The Arrival of G20

The announcement of summit leaders meeting in Pittsburg on 25 September 2009 that 'we designated the G20 to be the premier forum for our international economic cooperation' could prove momentous. This was an historic and potentially most important announcement. Thus we have devoted this chapter to a discussion of the Group of Twenty countries and a profile of them.

The G20 meeting in London on 2 April 2009 immediately followed the two worst quarters in the economic fortunes of the leading OECD countries (i.e. the last quarter of 2008 and the first quarter of 2009) when there were widespread fears of a global financial and economic meltdown. This perception was associated with irresponsible lending by the banks to the real estate sector in particular, the great credit expansion over the preceding five years, then the seizing up of credit markets from August 2007 onwards. These events culminated in the bankruptcy of Lehman Brothers in the United States in September 2008, plus problems at other institutions, too: Fanny Mae, Freddy Mac, AIG, Bear Stearns, Merrill Lynch and Citi Group, and European banks including UBS of Switzerland.

Thus the G20 meeting in London came at a critical time in the evolution of economic policy in the advanced countries. It resulted in a broad consensus among them to introduce fiscal stimulus packages and introduce unprecedentedly loose monetary policies and near-to-zero interest rates.

The communiqué at the conclusion of the G20 meeting in London started:

1. We, the Leaders of the Group of Twenty, met in London on 2 April 2009.

2. We face the greatest challenge to the world economy in modern times; a crisis which has deepened since we last met, which affects the lives of women, men, and children in every country, and which all countries must join together to resolve. A global crisis requires a global solution.

3. We start from the belief that prosperity is indivisible; that growth, to be sustained, has to be shared; and that our global plan for recovery must have at its heart the needs and jobs of hard-working families, not just in developed countries but in emerging markets and the poorest countries of the world too; and must reflect the interests, not just of today's population, but of future generations too. We believe that the only sure foundation for sustainable globalization and rising prosperity for all is an open world economy based on market principles, effective regulation, and strong global institutions.

4. We have today therefore pledged to do whatever is necessary to:

- restore confidence, growth, and jobs;

- repair the financial system to restore lending;

- strengthen financial regulation to rebuild trust;

- fund and reform our international financial institutions to overcome this crisis and prevent future ones;

- promote global trade and investment and reject protectionism, to underpin prosperity; and

- build an inclusive, green, and sustainable recovery.

By acting together to fulfil these pledges we will bring the world economy out of recession and prevent a crisis like this from recurring in the future.

G20: A Potentially Significant International Development

The declaration of the leaders of the former G7, now G20, in Pittsburgh on 25 September 2009 was potentially of great significance for international relations, for political and economic cooperation, and for global dialogue and action in certain key sectors such as energy, finance, agriculture/food production, development and global warming/climate change.

Paragraph 19 read: 'We designated the G20 to be the premier forum for our international economic cooperation. We established the Financial Stability Board to include major emerging economies and welcome its efforts to co-ordinate and monitor progress in strengthening financial regulation.'

As if to ensure that the media and readers did not miss the point, paragraph 50, the final one, under the heading 'The Path from Pittsburgh', repeated the same first sentence, prefacing it with 'Today' (i.e. 25 September 2009) to give emphasis and topicality. The second sentence of this paragraph concluded: 'We have asked our representatives to report back at the next meeting with recommendations on how to maximise the effectiveness of our cooperation.'

This initiative at this point in time is probably attributable to a combination of influences: the severity of the financial crisis and subsequent economic recession in the advanced economies, especially the US and UK, in 2008–9; the marked relative progress of the world's leading developing countries, particularly the most populous ones, China and India, compared with the traditionally more advanced ones over many years now; and the change in the US presidency with the recognition that we are living now in a multi-polar world with many different points of influence and interest around the globe, rather than a small world of just a few countries based on either side of the North Atlantic plus Japan, sharing a history of economic well-being and political purpose since 1945.

The Preamble to the Leaders Statement in Pittsburgh seems worth quoting in full because it is considerably more candid and forthright than is characteristic for statements emanating from such summits in the past.

> We meet in the midst of a critical transition from crisis to recovery to
> turn the page on an era of irresponsibility and to adopt a set of policies,

regulations and reforms to meet the needs of the 21st Century global economy.

When we last gathered in April, we confronted the greatest challenge to the world economy in our generation.

Global output was contracting at a pace not seen since the 1930s. Trade was plummeting. Jobs were disappearing rapidly. Our people worried that the world was on the edge of a depression.

At that time our countries agreed to do everything necessary to ensure recovery, to repair our financial systems and to maintain the global flow of capital.

It worked.

This preamble seemed to reveal palpable relief on the part of the summit leaders that the unprecedented easing of fiscal and monetary policies in late 2008 and early 2009 seemed to be having the desired effects in restricting the duration of the economic downturn, if not its intensity. The IMF in October 2009 projected the fall in economic activity in the advanced economies in 2009 at -3.4 per cent compared with growth of 1.7 per cent in the emerging and developing economies, i.e. a difference in performance of more than five percentage points. This amount of difference is also estimated for 2007 and 2008 by the IMF. The big difference between the years is the extent of the downturn in the advanced economies in 2009 and the lower rate of growth in the group of emerging economies.

Looking back to the early 1970s we can see that an opportunity was not taken at that time to implement more far-reaching global changes, now featured in the G20, involving wider worldwide councils. This followed the partial breakdown of the Bretton Woods system based on the US dollar. This had much to serve the growth of international trade and balance of payments system during the twenty-five years following the Second World War. This was also a period of transition in other respects, too. For example, following the OPEC initiatives of 1973–4, evidence of inflation in some commodity markets, the need for development in many countries worldwide and the need to consider financial affairs at the international level – all of these led to the formation in 1975 of the Conference on International Economic Cooperation. It is of interest to note that fifteen of the current G20 countries were represented on CIEC. The participants agreed the objective for CIEC was to initiate an intensified North–South dialogue on all matters related to energy, raw materials, development and financial affairs, leading to concrete proposals for an equitable and comprehensive programme for international economic cooperation. The four commissions formed to cover these four areas in 1976–7 reached agreement on certain of the topics discussed within each commission but on others they failed to do so.

As one of the co-chairman of the CIEC Energy Commission, I, Abdulhadi H. Taher, remarked that

> Being intimately associated with the CIEC and being a regular participant in numerous energy seminars and conferences since its conclusion, I am quite convinced that the lengthy ongoing dialogue has not been a fruitless exercise after all, as some circles tend to believe. The dialogue has certainly contributed towards a very clear-cut identification of the adverse international trends and their future implications. (*Energy: A Global Outlook*, p. 71)

A possible weakness of CIEC more than thirty years ago was an institutional one. Its twenty-seven member countries were divided into two distinct groups, i.e. the so-called G8 advanced economies and the G19 developing countries, with some within each group regarding their fundamental interests as being opposed to some, if not all, those in the other group. It is perhaps somewhat ironic now that with the passage of time, China and the Russian Federation, formally excluded from CIEC as they were not market economies but centrally planned ones, are now included in the G20 as quite prominent members of it with potentially influential roles as major players within the world economy.

Many other changes of the 1970s and subsequently, e.g. the Club of Rome's Limits to Growth; the Report of the Independent Commission on

International Development Issues *North–South: A Programme for Survival,* under the chairmanship of Willy Brandt; and even the collapse of the former Soviet Union, the ending of the so-called Cold War, failed to bring about the fundamental change in the world economic order which now seems presaged with the replacement of the G7 by the G20.

GDP and Energy Consumption Per Capita in 2008

The differences in GDP per capita among the world's three most populous countries remain remarkably great. In 2008, US GDP per capita averaged more than $46,600, 13.2 times that of China (including Hong Kong and Macao) and 44 times that of India. This makes something of a mockery of the definition in Wikipedia referring to G20 as 'the main economic council of wealthy nations', even if the World Bank estimates of aggregate GDP in 2008 show China ranked third and India twelfth among the 186 countries worldwide for which it shows GDP estimates.

In spite of primary energy consumption having swung almost 200 million tonnes of oil equivalent between USA and China between 2007 and 2008 (US down 60.6 million tonnes, China up 138 million tonnes), per capita GDP and energy consumption in the three most populous countries on the planet remain dramatically different between them.

Table 11.5. GDP and Energy Consumption in the Three Most Populous Countries

	GDP Per Capita $ in 2008	Energy Consumption Per Capita in 2008 metric tonnes o.e.
USA	46,648	7.55
China	3,423	1.53
India	1,059	0.38

Thus US energy consumption was almost five times that of China per capita in 2008 and almost twenty times that of India, with China's per capita consumption already being four times greater than that of India. In aggregate, China's energy consumption surpassed that of the United States in 2009.

We continue this analysis with a profile of some of the main demographic, economic and energy features of the G20 countries in a worldwide context. See Figure 11.2 and Tables 11.6 and 11.7.

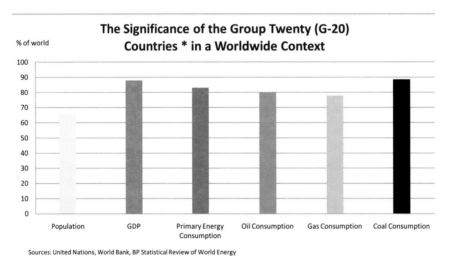

Sources: United Nations, World Bank, BP Statistical Review of World Energy
There are effectively 42 countries represented in the Group of Twenty as 23 EU member countries are represented together by the European Union in addition to 19 countries represented individually , four being EU members.

Figure 11.2.

Table 11.6. Energy Consumption of G20 Countries in 2008

	Population mn	GDP (WB) $ bn	Primary Energy mn m.t.o.e.	Oil m.t. oil	Gas m.t.o.e.	Coal m.t.o.e.
Argentina	39.7	328.4	74.7	24.2	40.1	0.4
Australia	21.3	1,015.2	118.3	42.5	21.7	51.3

Brazil	195.1	1,612.5	228.1	105.3	22.7	14.6
Canada	33.3	1,400.1	329.8	102.0	90.0	33.0
China incl. HK and Macao	1,332.3	4,560.2	2,026.3	390.2	74.1	1413.3
France	62.0	2,853.1	257.9	92.2	39.1	11.9
Germany	82.2	3,652.8	311.1	118.3	73.0	80.9
India	1,149.3	1,217.5	433.3	135.0	37.2	231.4
Indonesia	239.9	514.4	124.4	57.4	34.2	30.2
Italy	59.9	2,293.0	176.6	80.9	69.9	17.0
Japan	127.7	4,909.3	507.5	221.8	84.4	128.7
Mexico	107.7	1,086.0	170.4	90.0	60.5	9.0
Russian Federation	141.9	1,607.8	684.6	130.4	378.2	101.3
Saudi Arabia	28.1	467.6	174.5	104.2	70.3	Nil
South Africa	48.3	276.8	132.3	26.3	Nil	102.8
South Korea	48.6	929.1	240.1	103.3	35.7	66.1
Turkey	74.8	794.2	102.6	32.3	32.4	30.4
United Kingdom	61.3	2,645.6	211.6	78.7	84.5	35.4
United States	304.5	14,204.3	2,299.0	884.5	600.7	565.0
European Union	501.1	18,357.2	1,728.2	702.6	441.1	301.2
Big 4	265.6	11,461.1	957.2	370.1	173.1	145.2

EU net of Big 4 incl. above, 23	235.5	6,896.1	771.0	332.5	268.0	156.0
G20 Total	4,393.4	53,280.6	9,374.1	3,152.0	2,118.4	2922.7
World Total	6,705	60,587.0	11,294.9	3,927.9	2,726.1	3303.7
G20 % of World	65.5	87.9%	83.0%	80.2%	77.7%	88.5%
Former G7 countries: USA, Canada, Japan, Germany, France, Italy and the UK	730.9	31,958.2	4093.5	1578.4	1041.6	871.9
G7 % of World	10.9	52.7	36.2	40.2	38.2	26.4

Sources: *United Nations, World Bank* and BP *Statistical Review of World Energy (2009)*

Table 11.7. GDP in G20 Countries on the Basis of Constant Prices of 2000 and Growth in Real Terms

% of G20 in 2008 at prices of 2000		GDP at constant prices of 2000 in 2008 ($ bn)	Growth % p.a. 2008/2007 2007/2000	
100.0	G20	32,334.3	1.8	2.9
74.8	G7 (as was)	24,195.8	0.6	2.0
20.2	EU Big 4	6,520.7	0.5	1.7
35.9	USA	11,616.9	1.1	2.4
16.0	Japan	5,169.3	-0.7	1.6

2.7	Canada	870.9	0.4	2.6
10.4	EU 23 countries	3,376.6	1.5	3.1
30.6	EU 27 countries	9,897.3	0.8	2.1
25.2	G12	8,156.3	5.9	6.0
	Of which:			
	China	2,602.6	9.0	10.3
	Brazil	853.8	5.1	3.4
	India	825.8	7.1	7.7
	South Korea	750.8	2.2	4.7
	Mexico	701.0	1.8	2.5
	Australia	521.5	3.7	3.1
	Russian Federation	435.8	7.3	6.6
	Argentina	395.4	7.0	3.8
	Turkey	387.3	3.8	4.9
	Saudi Arabia	252.1	4.2	3.6
	Indonesia	233.1	6.0	5.1
	South Africa	183.2	3.0	4.2

Source: World Bank, 23 Oct. 2009.

G20 Countries in a Worldwide Perspective in 2008

Population

The G20 countries accounted for 65.5 per cent of the worldwide population in 2008, based on UN estimates. This is based on the nineteen member countries listed plus the remaining European Union countries (twenty-three in number) not listed individually as G20, or as G7 formerly, i.e. Germany, France, Italy and the UK. The EU outside the Big 4 accounted for 235.5 million in 2008, 3.5 per cent of the world total.

Among all other countries, there are three with populations exceeding 100 million and these account for just under 7 per cent of the world population: Pakistan with 172.8 million, Nigeria with 148.1 million and Bangladesh with 147.3 million population, in total amounting to 468.2 millions.

In addition, there are another fifty-one countries outside the EU with populations of between 10 million and 100 million, with an aggregate population of 1,537.2 million, accounting for just over 22.9 per cent of the worldwide total. Outside the EU only 4.6 per cent of the world's population live in countries with a population of less than 10 million.

Table 11.8. GDP per Person

	Population millions	GDP billions	GDP per person
World	6,705	60,587.0	$9,036
G20	4,393.4	53,280.6	$12,127
All other countries	2,311.6	7,306.4	$3,161

Gross domestic product GDP

The G20 countries accounted for 87.9 per cent of world GDP amounting to $60,587 billion in 2008, the G20 total being $53,280.6 billion, based on World Bank estimates. Thus GDP per person in the G20 countries is more than 3.8 times the average in all other countries worldwide. It should be borne in mind that the G20 member countries are far from a homogeneous group. For example, in India, GDP per person in 2008 averaged only $1,059 and in Indonesia the figure was only $2,144 per person, both well below the average for all non-G20 countries. In China, still the world's most populous country and now third in terms of rank order of total GDP in 2008 (after the USA and Japan), the average GDP per person in 2008 was only $3,423, a mere 8.3 per cent above the average for all non-G20 countries. By 2010, China ranked second in terms of total GDP, above Japan.

Primary energy consumption

The G20 countries accounted for 83.0 per cent of world primary energy consumption, amounting to 9,374.1 million metric tonnes of oil equivalent.

Efficiency of energy use relative to GDP

The important implication of analysing commercial primary energy use relative to GDP is that G20 countries can be seen to be much more efficient than all non-G20 countries collectively, by some 49 per cent, in terms of GDP per metric tonne of primary energy used.

Table 11.9. Commercial Primary Energy Use Relative to GDP

	GDP $ bn	Primary Energy mn metric tonnes	GDP $ per m.t.o.e consumed
World	60,587	11,294.0	5,364
G20	53,280.6	9,374.1	5,684
All other countries	7,306.4	1,920.8	3,804

This rather remarkable difference comes about in spite of the fact that it seems reasonable to suppose that generally less well-off non-G20 countries typically use more non-commercial energy (not recorded), for example, firewood and animal dung, etc, than do the more numerous populations of G20 countries, but this is probably true of G20 member, India, too.

Oil consumption

G20 countries accounted for 80.2 per cent of world oil consumption in 2008, i.e. a lower proportion than the proportion of primary energy as a whole. This is partly due to the fact that several G20 members are comparatively heavily dependent on coal for their energy needs, i.e. China, India, and South Africa, while only two G20 members, oil producers Mexico and Saudi Arabia depended on oil for more than 50 per cent of their total primary energy needs.

Gas consumption

G20 countries accounted for an even lower proportion of natural gas consumption at 77.7 per cent of the worldwide total. In only two G20 member countries was the consumption of natural gas comparatively high at more than 50 per cent of primary energy consumption. These were both gas-producing countries, Argentina and the Russian Federation, the latter being a significant exporter of natural gas. Among other G20 countries, seven of them each consumed at least 70 million tonnes of oil equivalent gas in 2008, with gas consumption rising in G20 countries such as China, Japan and Saudi Arabia. The latter produces gas for domestic use.

Full table of statistics of G20 countries

Table 11.6 is a comparative table of statistics for the nineteen G20 countries plus the European Union twenty-three and the worldwide context.

G20 Further Analysis

As we remarked previously, the year 2008 was a below trend year in the world economy, but not so dramatically low as 2009. The IMF has estimated world output in 2007 at 5.2 per cent growth but significantly lower at 3.0 per cent in 2008 and estimated to be negative at -0.6 per cent in 2009, as reported in July 2010. At this time a return to growth is projected for 2010 at 4.6 per cent.

Perhaps even more significant is the differences among G20 countries. In only six of them, mainly commodity exporters, was GDP growth stronger by half a percentage point or more in 2008 than it had been on average each year from 2000 until 2007. These were Argentina, Brazil, Australia, Indonesia, the Russian Federation and Saudi Arabia. In Germany, GDP growth was 1.3 per cent in 2008 compared with an average of 1.2 per cent annually over the seven years to 2007. For all other G20 countries, growth was lower in 2008 than it had been on average for the seven preceding years in each of them.

Even though the twelve developing countries now included in the G20 account for just over 25 per cent of the combined GDP (expressed in constant prices of 2000, based on World Bank estimates) of all member countries, as of 2008, this proportion is up from only 19.7 per cent in the year 2000. This reflects the much faster growth within the G12 than among the former G7 members, both on average over the seven years to 2007 and again in 2008. The contribution of China was of critical importance in this respect, but India was important too. All the twelve developing countries recorded faster growth than the former G7 countries as a group. The full analysis follows.

Table 11.10. Annual Average Growth (%)

	2008	2000 to 2007
G7	0.6	2.0
12 developing countries	5.9	6.0

Table 11.11. GDP in 2008 for G20 Countries ($ bn)

G20	53,039.0	87.5% of World
G7 (as was)	31,958.2	60.3% of G20
EU Big 4 (Ger., Fr., Italy, UK)	11,444.5	21.6% of G20
USA	14,204.3	26.8% of G20
Japan	4909.3	9.3% of G20
Canada	1400.1	2.6% of G20
EU 23 countries (20th G20 member)	6896.1	13.0% of G20
EU 27 countries (incl. Big 4)	18,340.6	34.6% of G20

G12 Emerging/Developing Countries	14,175.7	26.7% of G20
China	4326.2 (4560.1 incl. HK and Macao)	8.2% of G20 (8.6% of G20)
Brazil	1612.5	3.0% of G20
Russian Federation	1607.8	3.0% of G20
India	1217.5	2.3% of G20
Mexico	1086.0	2.0% of G20
Australia	1015.2	1.9% of G20
South Korea	929.1	1.8% of G20
Turkey	794.2	1.5% of G20
Indonesia	514.4	1.0% of G20
Saudi Arabia	467.6	0.9% of G20
Argentina	328.4	0.6% of G20
South Africa	276.8	0.5% of G20

Source: World Bank, 7 Oct. 2009.

It can be seen that the twelve emerging/developing country members of the G20 collectively almost matched the United States in 2008. In 2009, the US economy fell, while the emerging and developing economies as a group are projected to rise 2.5 per cent (China +9.1 per cent, India +5.7 per cent). This implies that the combined GDP of the twelve emerging and developing economies will overtake the United States in 2009.

Even in the year 2000, all the Big Four European Union member countries had gross domestic products estimated at more than 1 trillion dollars, but in that year China's GDP was estimated to be more than 100 billion dollars above that of Italy. During the intervening years to 2007 China overtook France, the UK and Germany as well. Reports indicate that it surpassed Japan during the second quarter of 2010 and it may challenge the United States for premier position by 2020 if its high rate of growth achieved in recent years can be sustained, even allowing for some deceleration.

In summary, we can highlight the great differences in estimated and prospective growths of GDP through 2008, 2009 and 2010 between the advanced countries and the emerging/developing countries and the principal members in each group, as reported by the IMF in July 2010 (Table 11.12). From this it can be seen that there was a difference of more than five percentage points in growth rates in both 2008 and 2009 between the advanced and emerging/developing economies. In 2009 the Russian Federation suffered more than any other country among those listed here.

Table 11.12. Estimated and Prospective Growth in GDP

	% p.a. change		
	2008	2009	2010
World output	3.0	-0.6	4.6
Advanced economies	0.5	-3.2	2.6
Emerging and developing economies	6.1	2.5	6.8
USA	0.4	-2.4	3.3
Japan	-1.2	-5.2	2.4
Germany	1.2	-4.9	1.4
China	9.6	9.1	10.5
India	6.4	5.7	9.4
Brazil	5.1	-0.2	7.1
Russian Federation	5.6	-7.9	4.3
Oil price $	96.99	61.78	75.27
% change	36.4	-36.3	21.8

Source: IMF July 2010.

Final Comment on G20

The transition from G7 to G20 has evidently given the new group far more credibility worldwide, representing almost two-thirds of humankind, almost 88 per cent of economic activity worldwide and around 80 per cent or more of world commercial energy consumption[3] and each of the three fossil fuels which together account for 88.2 per cent of world energy consumption. Perhaps even more important than these quantitative features is the fact that the G20 membership is more qualitatively reflective of the multi-polar world we all live in today. In spite of pronounced national differences and interests of G20 member countries this could lead to more fruitful international cooperation than the 'them and us' world which tended to be a feature of G7 since its inception in 1975.

World Leaders in Hydrocarbon Reserves and Implications for the EU

World leaders in hydrocarbon reserves are Russia, Iran, Saudi Arabia and Qatar. Only in Saudi Arabia is oil dominant, whereas in the other three countries gas is more important. Because of the unreliability of Russian gas supplies to the EU via Ukraine demonstrated at the beginning of 2006 and 2009, the EU should plan to increase gas storage facilities in the short term and arrange alternative long-distance pipeline supplies from Iran via Turkey and possibly from Qatar, too, perhaps LNG, in the medium term. Alternative gas supply sources for Europe are Algeria and Nigeria, both of which have much longer lifespans for gas than for oil in terms of their current reserves. See Figure 11.3.

Iran: No Need for Nuclear Energy for Decades

As the world's second biggest holder of proven gas and oil reserves, it is quite unrealistic for Iran to plead a need for nuclear energy for 'peaceful' purposes. It seems incredible that the US State Department has not called Iran's bluff on this issue, given the available evidence. At the 2008 volume of production Iran's proven reserves of gas should last 254 years and its oil reserves should last 86 years, as shown in this book. By contrast, for the world's largest reserves holder of gas, i.e. Russia, respective reserves to production ratios in years are only 72 and 21.8 years, respectively for gas and oil, very short compared with

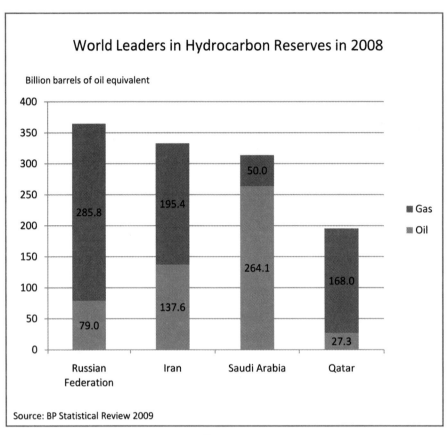

World Leaders in Hydrocarbon Reserves in 2008

Billion barrels of oil equivalent

Figure 11.3.

those of Iran, reflecting Russia's much higher production rates for both oil and gas. Likewise, the proposed doubling of gas production in Qatar in 2009 will bring its lifespan of proved gas reserves down to a level below that of Iran. Prospectively, this will give Iran the longest lifespan for both oil and gas among the world's biggest holders of these hydrocarbon reserves. See Figure 11.4.

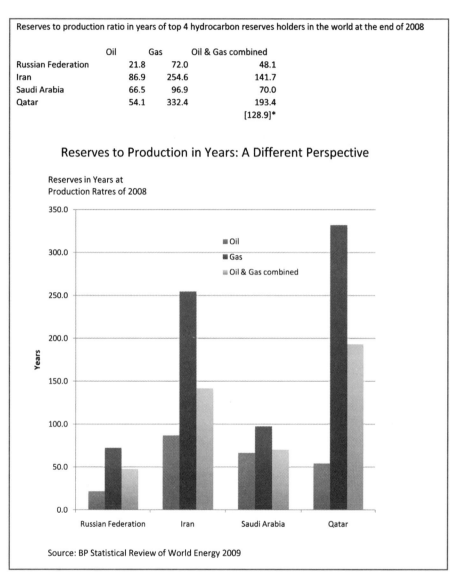

Reserves to production ratio in years of top 4 hydrocarbon reserves holders in the world at the end of 2008			
	Oil	Gas	Oil & Gas combined
Russian Federation	21.8	72.0	48.1
Iran	86.9	254.6	141.7
Saudi Arabia	66.5	96.9	70.0
Qatar	54.1	332.4	193.4
			[128.9]*

Reserves in Years at
Production Ratres of 2008

Source: BP Statistical Review of World Energy 2009

Figure II.4.

GDP of the Leading Economies Worldwide

According to World Bank estimates of gross domestic product for the year 2007, the top five economies in the world accounted for 52.5 per cent of the global total, with the United States alone accounting for 26.4 per cent. The top twenty-two economies worldwide account for 83.5 per cent of worldwide gross national income, with the Kingdom of Saudi Arabia included in the full list. The eleven European countries in the list of twenty-two account for 27.7 per cent of worldwide gross national income, i.e. ahead of the United States. The four so-called BRIC countries; China, Brazil, Russia and India in that economic order, account for 12.2 per cent of the global total with China, third in 2007, pre-eminent among them.

Financial Crisis, Economic Recession of 2008–9

At the late April 2009 meeting of the International Monetary Fund and World Bank, the declines in economic prospects in just three months since January were quite dramatic. By October 2009, the downturn was seen as having abated somewhat, with the recovery in 2010 expected to be similar to the projection made in January 2009. The unprecedented fiscal and monetary stimuli injected in the leading advanced countries and China have to be credited for the improvement in prospects through 2009 projected by the IMF.

Table 11.13. Forecasts for World Output, % Change

For years	Actual	Jan. 2009	April 2009	July 2009	Oct. 2009	July 2010
2007	5.2					
2008	3.0					
2009		+0.5	-1.3	-1.4	-1.1	-0.6
2010		+3.0	+1.9	+2.5	+3.1	+4.6

In its *World Economic Outlook* of April 2009 the IMF said:

> By any measure, this downturn represents by far the deepest global recession since the Great Depression. Even once the crisis is over, there will be a difficult transition period, with output growth appreciably below rates seen in the recent past.

It went on to state that overall credit to the private sector in advanced economies will decline in 2009 and 2010 as banks continue to reel in lending. A protracted slowdown was increasingly likely.

The IMF blamed the worsening prospects on the intensifying 'vicious circle' between the ailing financial sector and the shrinking real economy. As well as fiscal easing, the IMF said the central banks of developed economies should continue to ease monetary policy where possible. Also, it warned that declines in consumer prices and falls in asset prices could foster expectations of deflation. The IMF also updated its estimates of losses to the world's financial sector, at $4,050 billion. This represents almost 7.7 per cent of the World Bank's estimate for gross domestic product worldwide in 2007. The US losses on loans and securities are estimated at $2,700 billion, those in Europe at $1,200 billion and at $150 billion in Japan. The losses on securities amount to about half the total with losses on loans, said to be based on conservative models.

Another important lesson of the IMF's report is that the recession in the real economy is compounding losses that originated in finance: conventional loans, not exotic securities, make up half of the forecast write-downs. It stated that European institutions, less exposed to the securities that brought down US banks, face the biggest losses. The IMF expects US institutions to write down $550 billion in 2009–10 on top of the $510 billion written down already. Losses in the euro area and UK are estimated at $750 billion and $200 billion respectively.

The IMF went on to state that bringing banking systems back to the leverage ratios of the mid-1990s will require massive recapitalization: $500 billion in the US, $725 billion in the euro area and $250 billion in the UK. To make this possible, the authorities have to lay the ground for converting preference stock into common equity and enforcing debt-to-equity swaps, if necessary.

In its October 2009 review of global prospects the IMF estimates that the global bank write-downs could reach $2.8⁴ trillion, of which $1.5 trillion have yet to be recognized. The bulk of these losses are attributable to US, UK and euro area banks which face a wall of maturing debt.

The IMF said that a quick rebound in commodity prices to the record levels of 2007/8 was 'unlikely'. But it also said in April 2009 that oil prices were likely to stabilize at almost $50 a barrel and to 'rise moderately' in the second half of 2009. It warned that supply constraints could emerge sooner than for other non-renewable commodities, given the adverse effect on investment from the financial market crisis and low oil prices. By late October 2009 the oil price had already risen to $80 a barrel, but the IMF projected an average price of $61.53 a barrel for 2009, down 38.6 per cent from 2008, and $76.50 for 2010. By July 2010 these estimates were marginally different at $61.78 for 2009 and $75.27 in 2010.

In its updated *World Economic Outlook* of July 2010 the IMF stated that downside risks have risen sharply amid renewed financial turbulence. Supported by accommodative monetary conditions, fiscal actions should be complemented by financial sector reform and structural reforms to enhance growth and competitiveness.

Growth of Gross Domestic Product at Constant Prices of 2000 (US$) Worldwide and for Each of the Top Twenty-Two Economies (as of 2007)

Worldwide economic growth fell from an average annual rate of 5.4 per cent over the eight years up to 1973 to only 3.3 per cent during the following six years to 1979. The further very significant oil price increases of 1979–80 (brought about not by OPEC but by market forces) contributed to a further fall in worldwide economic growth to just 2.5 per cent on average each year over the next six years to 1985, coinciding with an economic recession in the industrialized countries during the early 1980s. After the OPEC inspired oil price decrease of 1986 world economic growth recovered strongly to average 3.7 per cent annually over the five years to 1990. Over the last decade of the twentieth century growth fell quite sharply to average only 2.8 per cent each year to 2000. This lower rate was attributable in part to the break-up of the former Soviet Union. The decline in gross domestic product of its main erstwhile constituent, the Russian Federation, amounted to an average annual rate of -3.9 per cent. See Table 11.14.

Table 11.14. Growth of GDP at Constant Prices of 2000 (US$): Average Annual rate of Change (%) as at 2007 Table 11.14. Growth of GDP at Constant Prices of 2000 (US$): Average Annual rate of Change (%) as at 2007

	1965-73	1973-9	1979-85	1985-90	1990-00	2000-07	2008
USA	3.8	3.0	2.6	3.3	3.3	2.4	1.1
Japan	9.8	3.5	3.0	4.8	1.2	1.6	-0.7
Germany	N/A	2.6	1.4	3.3	2.1	1.2	1.3
China	6.7	6.0	10.2	7.9	10.4	10.3	9.0
UK	3.2	1.5	1.3	3.3	2.4	2.6	0.7

France	5.4	3.1	1.6	3.3	2.0	1.8	0.4
Italy	5.4	3.7	2.0	3.1	1.6	1.1	-1.1
Spain	6.5	2.3	1.5	4.5	2.8	3.4	1.2
Canada	4.9	3.7	2.6	2.9	2.9	2.6	0.4
Brazil	9.5	6.4	2.4	2.0	2.5	3.3	5.1
Russian Fed	N/A	N/A	N/A	N/A	-3.9	4.6	7.3
India	3.4	3.2	5.4	6.0	5.5	7.7	7.1
Korea Rep	9.7	8.3	6.2	9.6	6.1	4.7	2.2
Mexico	6.4	6.3	3.1	1.7	3.5	2.5	1.8
Australia	4.8	2.7	2.9	3.9	3.3	3.1	3.7
Netherlands	4.9	2.6	1.4	3.5	3.2	1.8	2.1
Turkey	NA	4.5	3.6	5.6	3.6	4.9	3.8
Switzerland	3.9	-0.4	2.0	2.9	1.1	1.8	1.6
Belgium	4.9	2.4	1.5	3.1	2.1	1.9	1.1
Sweden	3.5	1.8	1.8	2.5	2.0	2.8	-0.2
Poland	N/A	N/A	N/A	N/A	3.8	4.0	4.8
Saudi Arabia	N/A	9.9	-2.8	3.4	2.7	3.6	4.2
World as a whole	5.4	3.3	2.5	3.7	2.8	3.1	2.0

Source: World Development Indicators, World Bank, Apr. and Oct. 2009.

Over the same ten years economic growth of the other Communist superpower, China, accelerated to more than 10 per cent on average each year as a result of the enlightened economic policies introduced by Deng Xiaoping in 1978. This has resulted in China becoming the factory for the world and an economic colossus in some thirty years, surpassing Germany as the third most important economic world power during the recent past and even Japan by the second quarter of 2010.

Like some other OPEC countries, the dramatic change in the economic experience of Saudi Arabia emerges clearly in Table 11.14. Following the OPEC oil price increases of October 1973 and 1 January 1974 Saudi Arabian economic growth averaged almost 10 per cent each year to 1979. Subsequently, the fall in world oil prices from 1980 and dramatic fall in Saudi oil production and export volumes over the years to 1985 resulted in Saudi Arabian gross domestic product declining at an average rate of -2.8 per cent annually over this six-year period, but made good over the following five years when growth averaged 3.4 per cent annually.

Table 11.15. The World Economy, Primary Energy and Oil Consumption.

	Annual Average % Changes			Energy coefficients
	GDP	PE	Oil	PE/GDP
1965 to 1973	5.4	5.2	7.6	0.96
1973 to 1979	3.3	2.8	2.0	0.85
1979 to 1985	2.5	1.0	-1.7	0.40
1985 to 1990	3.7	2.5	2.4	0.68
1990 to 2000	2.8	1.4	1.2	0.50
2000 to 2007	3.1	2.6	1.5	0.84
Year 2008	2.0	1.4	-0.4	0.70
Year 2009	-0.6	-1.1	-1.7	-1.83

Sources: World Development Indicators, World Bank, Apr. and Oct. 2009; BP *Statistical Review* (2010) and database; IMF *World Economic Outlook*, July 2010.

The World Economy, Primary Energy and Oil Consumption

Table 11.15 shows the strong growth of worldwide gross domestic product and primary energy demand and very strong growth of oil consumption in the era of cheap oil, culminating in a synchronized economic boom in the industrialized countries in 1973. At this time the growth of primary energy usage was very little less than that of the economy, as can be seen from the energy coefficient in the last column of the table. Figure 11.5 illustrates the progression graphically.

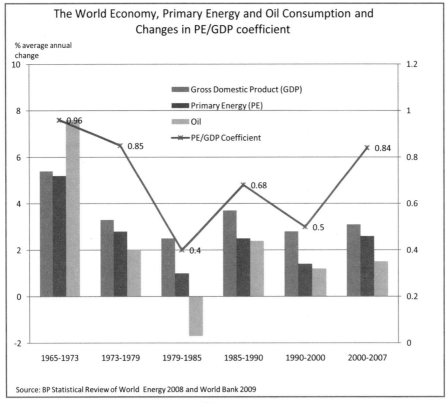

Figure 11.5.

Subsequently, all the average changes were significantly less. Most significant was the change in world oil consumption which became negative during five of the six years 1980 to 1985 inclusive. Also economic activity became much less energy intensive over this period as the energy coefficient dropped to only 0.40. Then, from 1985 to 1990, the growth of the worldwide economy, energy consumption and oil increased, with the energy coefficient also rising.

The last decade of the twentieth century saw a fall in the average rate of economic growth and of primary energy and oil consumption. A major contributor to these declines was the demise of the Soviet Union. Table 11.16 shows the average falls recorded by the Russian Federation from 1990 to 2000. Worldwide economic growth and consumption of both primary energy and oil picked up somewhat in the seven years to 2007, but the financial crisis and economic recession of 2008–9 resulted in significantly lower figures for these years.

Table 11.16. Average Annual Falls in the Russian Federation 1990 to 2000

Gross Domestic Product	Primary Energy Consumption	Oil Consumption
-3.9%	-3.1%	-6.8%

Though the energy coefficient has bounced around somewhat since 1973, the fact is that the world economy has become less energy intensive over the thirty-five years to 2008. Perhaps most significant was the change in the energy coefficient for China which rose from only 0.34 over the 1990 to 2000 decade, below the worldwide average, to 0.93 from 2000 to 2008, well above the global average for these eight years. This has potential implications for the future. Changes in oil consumption have been lower than for primary energy, reflecting its lower share of the worldwide energy mix and a potentially more stable position for it in the future if financial, economic and speculative excesses can be avoided, following the recession of 2008–9.

Primary Energy Consumption Relative to their Gross Domestic Products of the Leading Economies Worldwide

Among these twenty-two leading economies, it can be seen from Table 11.17 that in 2007, they varied widely in terms of their energy intensity. For example, among the top five, China stood out in accounting for only 5.9 per cent of world GDP but for 16.8 per cent of primary energy demand in 2007. The other four leading economies are recorded as all having a bigger share of world GDP than their share of world primary energy demand. They are, in order of GDP, the USA, Japan, Germany and the UK.

Table 11.17. Primary Energy Consumption Relative to their Gross Domestic Products of the Leading Economies Worldwide in 2007

Rank order in GNI		Billions of US$	% of World GDP	% of World PE	Rank Order in PE
1	United States	13,886.5	26.4	21.3	1
2	Japan	4,813.3	9.1	4.7	4
3	Germany	3,197.0	6.1	2.8	7
4	China	3,120.9	5.9	16.8	2
5	United Kingdom	2,608.5	5.0	1.9	11
Top 5		**27,626.2**	**52.5**	**52.6**	
6	France	2,447.1	4.7	2.3	8
7	Italy	1,991.3	3.8	1.6	13
8	Spain	1,321.8	2.5	1.4	16
9	Canada	1,300.0	2.5	2.9	6
10	Brazil	1,133.0	2.2	2.0	10
11	Russian Fed	1,071.0	2.0	6.2	3
Next 6		**9,264.2**	**17.6**	**14.0**	
12	India	1,069.4	2.0	3.6	5

13	Korea Republic	955.8	1.8	2.1	9
14	Mexico	878.0	1.7	1.4	15
15	Australia	755.8	1.4	1.1	19
16	Netherlands	750.5	1.4	0.8	24
17	Turkey	592.9	1.1	0.9	22
18	Switzerland	452.1	0.9	0.3	44
19	Belgium	432.5	0.8	0.7	27
20	Sweden	421.3	0.8	0.5	35
21	Poland	374.6	0.7	0.9	23
22	Saudi Arabia	373.5	0.7	1.5	14
Next 11		7,056.4	13.4	13.8	
Top 22		43,946.8	83.5	80.4	
World as a whole		52,621.4	100.0	100.0	

Sources:Gross Domestic Product estimated by the World Bank (Atlas method);
BP *Statistical Review of World Energy* (June 2008).

Similarly, in the next group of six countries, France, Italy, Spain and Brazil have a larger share of the world's gross domestic product than they do of world primary energy demand. The well-endowed energy resource countries, Canada and the Russian Federation, are in the opposite position, accounting for a higher share of world primary energy demand than of world GDP. In the next group of eleven countries, just four of them, India, South Korea, Poland and Saudi Arabia, account for higher shares of world primary energy demand than of world GDP.

In aggregate, these top twenty-two countries accounted for 83.5 per cent of GDP in the year 2007 and for 80.4 per cent of primary energy demand with the top five of them collectively at almost identical figures of 52.5 per cent and 52.8 per cent respectively, because of the relative imbalance of China compared with the other leading economies.

World Consumption of
Primary Energy in 2007

By 2007 China's consumption of primary energy had reached almost 1.9 billion tonnes of oil equivalent, a total which amounted to 80 per cent of the US energy consumption, still world number one in that year. Moreover, over the ten years to 2007 China's energy usage had grown at an annual average rate of 6.8 per cent compared with the much lower growth of 0.7 annually in the United States.

Expressed another way, China's energy consumption in 2007 exceeded by 17 per cent the total of the next three countries by rank order in the table, the Russian Federation, Japan and India combined. This is surely clear evidence of the need for policy-makers throughout the world to monitor what is happening in the Chinese economy, its future energy needs and how these are being satisfied, both from indigenous sources (coal being predominant) and probably increasingly from imports, notably of oil, gas and perhaps coal, too, in the medium term. See Table 11.18.

Table 11.18. World Consumption of Primary Energy in 2007

	Million tonnes oil equivalent	% of world total	% average annual growth 1997–2007
USA	2361.4	21.3	0.7
China	1889.9	17.0	6.8
Russian Federation	692.0	6.2	1.3
Japan	517.5	4.7	0.2
India	404.4	3.6	4.5
Top 5	5865.2	52.8	
Canada	321.7	2.9	
Germany	311.0	2.8	
France	255.1	2.3	
South Korea	234.0	2.1	
Brazil	216.8	2.0	
UK	215.9	1.9	
Next 6	1554.5	14.0	
Iran	182.9	1.6	
Italy	179.6	1.6	
Saudi Arabia	167.6	1.5	
Mexico	155.5	1.4	
Spain	150.3	1.4	
Ukraine	136.0	1.2	
South Africa	127.8	1.2	

Australia	121.8	1.1	
Taiwan	115.1	1.0	
Indonesia	114.6	1.0	
Turkey	101.7	0.9	
Next 11	1552.9	14.0	
Top 22 countries	8972.6	80.8	
Total Middle East	574.1	5.2	4.6
European Union	1744.5	15.7	0.4
OECD	5566.4	50.2	0.8
World	11099.3	100.0	2.2

Source: BP *Statistical Review of World Energy* (June 2008).

Changes in Primary Energy Use, 1997 to 2007

Figure 11.8 illustrates the increasingly important role of China in dominating the growth of demand for primary energy worldwide over the decade from 1997 to 2007. It accounted for over 41 per cent of the total increase compared with only 40 per cent of the total increase during this period of the next 21 other most important countries on this criterion, Iran and Saudi Arabia being among them. The increment in comparatively large energy consuming countries such as this United States, India and the Russian Federation was dwarfed by the rise in China. Figure 11.8 shows the top eleven countries. Table 11.19 complements this.

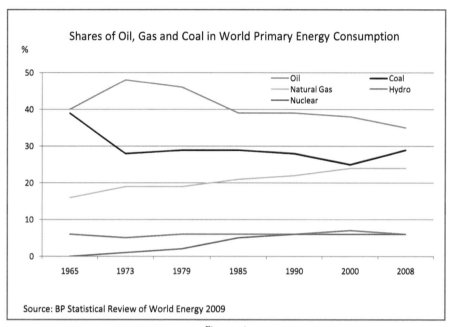

Figure 11.6.

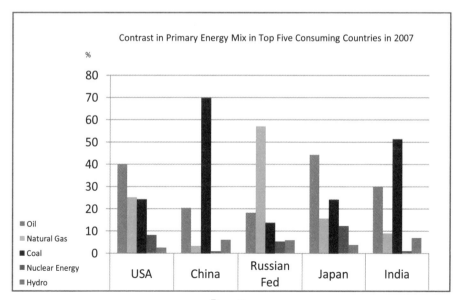

Figure 11.7.

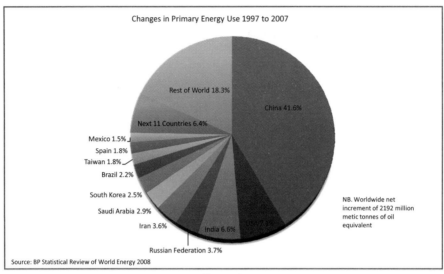

Figure 11.8

Table 11.19. Changes in Primary Energy Use 1997–2007 among Top 22 Countries in 2007

	Million tonnes oil equivalent	% of worldwide increase
China	912.9	41.6 %
USA	156.6	
India	143.8	
Russian Federation	80.3	
Iran	78.4	
Top 5 countries	1372.0	62.6 %
Saudi Arabia	62.8	
South Korea	54.4	
Brazil	49.3	
Taiwan	40.2	
Spain	38.6	
Mexico	33.3	

Next 6 countries	278.6	12.7%
Canada	32.0	
Indonesia	31.8	
Turkey	31.8	
Australia	19.3	
South Africa	18.4	
Italy	15.7	
France	14.1	
Japan	10.9	
Ukraine	-2.9	
United Kingdom	-4.5	
Germany	-26.8	
Next 11 countries	139.8	6.4%
Total Middle East	205.2	9.4%
European Union	66.6	3.0%
OECD	415.3	18.9%
Total World	2192.0	

Source: BP *Statistical Review of World Energy* (June 2008).

Contrast in Primary Energy Mix in Top Five Consuming Countries in 2007

Among the fast developing giant countries of China and India coal remains the dominant fuel in the energy mix, accounting for almost 70 per cent and more than 51 per cent respectively of the total primary energy used, even in 2007, in these two countries, ranked second and fifth largest in the world. In the USA, still the largest energy consuming country, in that year, and Japan ranked fourth, oil is the most important fuel, while in Russia, ranked third, natural gas accounts for 57 per cent of energy consumed. These top five countries used 52.8 per cent of primary energy consumed worldwide in 2007. By contrast, the twenty-seven European Union member countries as a whole accounted for only 15.7 per cent of the total and for a mere 3.0 per cent of the net worldwide increase over the ten years to 2007 (see Tables 11.18–19). See Figure 11.7 along with Table 11.20.

Table 11.20. Contrast in Primary Energy Mix in Top Five Consuming Countries in 2007.

	Oil %	Natural gas %	Coal %	Nuclear energy %	Hydro-electricity %	Total m.t.o.e.
USA	39.9	25.2	24.3	8.1	2.4	2361.4
China	20.4	3.3	69.8	0.8	5.9	1889.9
Russian Federation	18.2	57.1	13.7	5.2	5.8	692.0
Japan	44.2	15.7	24.2	12.2	3.7	517.5
India	29.8	9.0	51.4	1.0	6.8	404.4
Total world	35.6	23.8	28.6	5.6	6.4	11099.3

Source: BP *Statistical Review of World Energy* (June 2008).

Note: These 5 countries alone account for 52.8% of the worldwide total.

Top Twenty-Three Primary Energy-Consuming Countries in 2007 and their Energy Mixes

In 2007 world primary energy consumption reached a new peak exceeding 11 billion tonnes of oil equivalent for the first time. In this year oil's share fell to 35.6 per cent of the global total, followed by coal at 28.6 per cent and natural gas at 23.8 per cent in third place. Hydro-electricity and nuclear accounted for comparatively small shares at 6.4 per cent and 5.6 per cent respectively.

Among the leading consuming countries/regions, the USA still occupied first place with 21.3 per cent of the total, followed by China with 17.0 per cent and the European Union as a whole in third place with 15.7 per cent. These three alone accounted for 54 per cent of the worldwide total.

The former territories of the Soviet Union were less important than they had been in 1989 at the time of its break-up. Nevertheless, it still consumed

9.3 per cent of world energy, with the Russian Federation responsible for 6.2 per cent.

The countries with relatively low oil shares in their energy consumption, i.e. about 20 per cent or less, were China, the former Soviet Union/Russian Federation, the Ukraine and South Africa. Countries with relatively high shares of oil in their energy consumption, i.e. 46 per cent or more, included South Korea, Italy, Spain, Indonesia, Mexico and Saudi Arabia – the latter two for obvious reasons.

Similarly, for natural gas, several countries had very low shares of this resource in their energy consumption, i.e. less than 10 per cent. Most important of these was China with only 3.3 per cent reliance on gas, with India, Brazil, South Africa (nil) and Taiwan also in this category.

Leading coal-using countries were led by China where it accounted for almost 70 per cent of energy consumption, India with 51.4 per cent and in South Africa it was even more dominant, satisfying 76.4 per cent of that country's energy needs. There were, in contrast, ten out of the twenty-three countries where coal represented less than 15 per cent of energy consumption. These were the Russian Federation, Canada, France, Brazil, Iran, Italy, Saudi Arabia (nil), Mexico, Spain and Venezuela.

The only other remarkable features of national energy mixes worthy of comment here concern, in particular, nuclear energy in France, accounting for 39.1 per cent of that country's energy consumption in 2007. This reflects that country's policy initiative in promoting nuclear electricity as a long-term objective after the oil price increases of 1973–4. Other countries with relatively strong nuclear contributions (but much less than France) are the Ukraine, South Korea, Japan and Germany. Six of the listed countries were without any nuclear energy in 2007.

Similarly, hydro-electricity is relatively important in only three of the twenty-three leading energy consuming countries in 2007. It accounted for 38.8 per cent of the total in Brazil, for 26.6 per cent in Venezuela and for 25.9 per cent in Canada. Table 11.21 provides the full detail.

Table 11.21. Top 23 Primary Energy Consuming Countries in 2007 and their Energy Mixes (million tonnes o.e.)

		Total PE	Oil %	Gas %	Coal %	Nuclear %	Hydro %
	World	11,099.3	35.6	23.8	28.6	5.6	6.4
1	USA	2,361.4	39.9	25.2	24.3	8.1	2.4
2	China	1,889.9	20.3	3.3	69.8	0.8	5.8
3	EU	1,744.5	40.3	24.9	18.2	12.1	4.4
4	Former USSR	1,035.2	17.6	54.9	16.1	5.8	5.5
+4	Russian Federation	692.0	18.2	57.1	13.7	5.2	5.9
5	Japan	517.5	44.2	15.7	24.2	12.2	3.7
6	India	404.4	31.8	9.0	51.4	1.0	6.8
7	Canada	321.7	31.8	26.3	9.4	6.6	25.9
8	Germany	311.0	36.2	24.0	27.7	10.2	2.0
9	France	255.1	35.8	14.8	4.7	39.1	5.6
10	South Korea	234.0	46.0	14.2	25.5	13.8	0.5
11	Brazil	216.8	44.5	9.1	6.3	1.3	38.8
12	UK	215.9	36.2	38.1	18.2	6.5	1.0
13	Iran	182.9	42.1	55.1	0.6	-	2.2
14	Italy	179.6	46.4	39.0	9.7	-	4.9
15	Saudi Arabia	167.6	59.2	40.8	-	-	-
16	Mexico	155.5	57.4	31.3	5.9	1.5	3.9
17	Spain	150.3	52.4	21.0	13.4	8.3	4.9
18	Ukraine	136.0	11.3	42.8	28.9	15.4	1.7

19	South Africa	127.8	20.2	-	76.4	2.3	0.9
20	Taiwan	115.1	45.6	9.2	35.7	8.0	1.6
21	Indonesia	114.6	47.5	26.5	24.3	-	1.7
22	Venezuela	107.9	37.5	35.9	0.1	-	26.6
23	Turkey	101.7	30.6	31.1	30.5	-	7.9

Source: BP *Statistical Review of World Energy* (2008).

Note: All the countries listed consumed more than 100 million tonnes o.e. in 2007.

Changes in the Shares of Oil, Gas and Coal in World Primary Energy Consumption 1965 to 2008

The share of oil in world energy consumption rose at a rapid rate of one percentage point annually, on average, over the eight years from 1965 to 1973 to 48.0 per cent in the latter year. Thereafter, as a consequence of the OPEC price increases of 1973–4, the oil share fell slightly to 45.9 per cent in 1979. But, following the further big price increases of 1979 and 1980, dictated by market forces, the oil share fell much more dramatically by 6.8 percentage points in just six years from 1979 to 39.1 per cent in 1985. Figure 11.6 illustrates the progression from 1965 to 2008.

This was attributable to higher than normal stock building in 1979 and into 1980, and to anxieties about shortfalls of oil supplies related to the revolution in Iran and the outbreak of war between Iraq and Iran, along with higher longer term elasticities of demand/conservation of energy use and substitution by other forms of energy.

Thereafter, the oil price fall recorded in 1986 resulted in comparative stabilization of the oil share of energy demand, falling just 0.3 percentage points over the five years to 1990 and a further 0.5 percentage points over the next ten years to 2000. Subsequently, there was a further drop to just 35.6 per cent for oil in the global total of world energy use in 2007, and to 34.8 per cent in 2008, once again associated with significant price increases for oil in 2004 through to 2008. These proved unsustainable once again during the second half of that year and into 2009, associated with the international financial crisis and economic recession in the advanced economies.

Another important but indirect factor depressing world oil supply and demand in 2008 was the rise in Chinese coal consumption which accounted for 48.4 per cent of the total increase in worldwide primary energy consumption in that year.

Thus though OPEC's actions on price in 1973–4 arrested the sharp rise in oil's share of the world energy market, the bigger falls in 1979 to 1985 and from July 2008, resulting from economic recession and market forces in the most general sense, seem to have had/are having a more profound effect on the oil share through unsustainable price increases. These price increases of 1979–80 and 2004–July 2008 were brought about by 'market forces', not by OPEC. Moreover, the OPEC action of 1986 in depressing oil prices through increasing oil export volumes resulted in a more stable long-term plateau for oil prices over the following period of almost twenty years.

Finally, one can remark that in spite of three significant increases in oil prices over the thirty-five years from 1973 to 2008, the oil share of world primary energy consumption has fallen only 13.2 percentage points, in spite of which the volume of consumption increased by 50.4 per cent. The winners in terms of energy market share were natural gas, up 5.6 percentage points; nuclear up 4.7 percentage points, but including a fall from 6.3 per cent in 2000 to 5.5 per cent in 2008; coal up a mere 1.7 percentage points and hydro-electricity just 1.2 per cent higher in 2008 than it had been in 1973. See Table II.22.

Table II.22. Changes in the Shares of Oil, Gas and Coal in World Primary Energy Consumption 1965–2008

	Oil	Natural Gas	Coal	Hydro	Nuclear
1965	40.0	15.6	38.7	5.5	0.2
1973	48.0	18.5	27.5	5.2	0.8
1979	45.9	19.2	29.1	5.6	2.1

1985	39.1	20.9	28.9	6.3	4.7
1990	38.8	22.0	27.5	6.1	5.6
2000	38.3	23.7	25.2	6.6	6.3
2007	35.6	23.8	28.6	6.4	5.6
2008	34.8	24.1	29.2	6.4	5.5

Source: BP *Statistical Review of World Energy* (2009).

World Oil and Gas Reserves

Distribution of World Oil Reserves, Production and Consumption in 2008

Figure 11.9 is a series of pie charts illustrating the differences between the three main categories of OPEC member countries, i.e. Saudi Arabia, other Middle East and other OPEC, compared with six other main areas of the world in terms of oil reserves, oil production and oil consumption. It can be seen that the OPEC countries have a much bigger share of world oil reserves in 2008 than they do of oil production, with their share of oil consumption much lower still, though growing comparatively fast.

Among the other groups of oil reserves holders, the Commonwealth of Independent States (former Soviet Union) can be seen to be much the largest but at its fairly high volume of production in 2008 (12.82 million b/d) the lifespan of these existing proved reserves amounts to only twenty-seven years, and less for the Russian Federation alone. Nevertheless, its oil consumption at little more than 4 million b/d in 2008 remained far less than it had been some twenty years earlier. Thus its surplus of production over consumption had risen remarkably from twenty years previously, by almost 4.65 million b/d, thus alleviating the pressure on world oil supplies very significantly.

Other regions shown as segments in these pie charts are generally in the opposite position to OPEC member countries in accounting for higher shares of world oil consumption than of production, with their shares of reserves being lower still.

Oil Reserves at end 2008 (Billion Barrels)

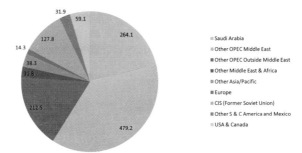

Oil Production (Thousand Barrels/Day)

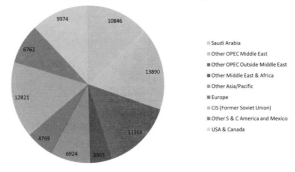

Oil Consumption (Thousand Barrels/Day)

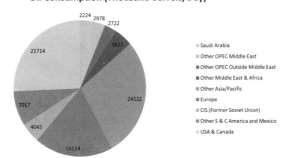

Figure 11.9.

High Degree of Concentration in World Oil and Gas Reserves

There is a high degree of concentration of reserves of gas and oil in relatively few countries worldwide. For the two forms of energy together, the top four countries in rank order are the Russian Federation, Iran, Saudi Arabia and Qatar. See Table 11.23. Together, these account for 49.8 per cent of the world's total of gas and oil reserves combined. The next eleven countries in rank order account for a further 35 per cent of worldwide proven reserves of oil and gas, with the next eleven countries after the top fifteen accounting for an additional 7.1 per cent. Thus, these twenty-six countries account for over 90 per cent of the worldwide total of proved oil and gas reserves.

Table 11.23. High Degree of Concentration in World Oil and Gas Reserves in 2007;

		Billion bbl oe	% Gas
	Gas	283,815	78.1
1. Russian Federation	Oil	79,400	
	Total	363,215	
	Gas	174,862	55.8
2. Iran	Oil	138,400	
	Total	313,262	
	Gas	45,099	14.6
3. Saudi Arabia	Oil	264,200	
	Total	309,299	
	Gas	161,024	85.5
4. Qatar	Oil	27,400	
	Total	188,424	

Source: BP *Statistical Review of World Energy* (June 2008).

Among the world's four leading countries in terms of proven reserves of oil and natural gas, Saudi Arabia stands out as being different from the other three in having much the largest reserves of oil but only comparatively small reserves of natural gas accounting for just 14.6 per cent of its combined total. Some observers, knowing about the concentration of oil and gas reserves in the same countries/areas, might be tempted to speculate that Saudi Arabia could surely increase its proven reserves of natural gas quite significantly, given some reasonable exploration effort to this end. In recent years the search for gas, particularly for gas not associated with oil, has been intensified, with exploration in previously unexplored parts of the Kingdom. Adjacent countries Iraq and Kuwait also have proven gas reserves estimated at only 10 per cent to 15 per cent of their combined oil and gas reserves, like Saudi Arabia.

Top Twenty-Six Countries with Combined Significant Oil and Gas Reserves in 2007

In addition to the top four countries which hold between them almost half the world's combined proved reserves of oil and gas, the next eleven countries account for another 35 per cent of the global total. No less than ten of these fifteen countries high up in the rank order of combined proven reserves of oil and gas are OPEC members. The twelve OPEC members featured in this list of the top twenty-six countries account for 63.2 per cent of the worldwide total between them. Apart from the Russian Federation ranked first, the next largest non-OPEC holder of combined oil and gas reserves is the USA, ranked only in tenth place with comparatively low reserves to production ratios for both oil and gas. See Table 11.24.

Table 11.24. Top 26 Countries with Combined Significant Oil and Gas Reserves in 2007, End Year

	Gas $M^3 \times 10^{12}$	Oil 10^9 bbl	Oil % of Total	Both Oil and Gas bn bbl o.e
Russian Federation	44.65	79.4	22.0	360.3
Iran	27.80	138.4	44.2	313.3
Saudi Arabia	7.17	264.2	85.4	309.3

Qatar	25.60	27.4	14.5	188.4
Top 4 countries have 49.8% of combined world proven reserves of oil and gas				1171.3
UAE	6.09	97.8	71.8	136.2
Iraq	3.17	115.0	85.2	134.9
Venezuela	5.15	87.0	72.9	119.4
Kuwait	1.78	101.5	90.1	112.7
Nigeria	5.30	36.2	52.1	69.5
USA	5.98	29.4	43.9	67.0
Kazakhstan	1.90	39.8	76.8	51.8
Libya	1.50	41.5	96.5	43.0
Algeria	4.52	12.3	30.2	40.7
Canada	1.63	27.7	72.9	38.0
China	1.88	15.5	56.8	27.3
Next 11 countries have 35.7% of combined world proven reserves of oil and gas				840.5
Norway	2.96	8.2	30.6	26.8
Malaysia	3.00	5.4	22.2	24.3
Australia	2.51	4.2	21.0	20.0
Turkmenistan	2.67	0.6	3.4	17.4
Egypt	2.06	4.1	24.0	17.1
Azerbaijan	1.28	7.0	46.4	15.1
Brazil	0.37	12.6	84.6	14.9
Mexico	0.36	12.2	84.1	14.5
Uzbekistan	1.74	0.6	5.2	11.5

Indonesia*	1.08	4.4	39.3	11.2
Angola	Not shown	9.0	100.0	9.0
The next 11 countries in rank order have just 7.7% of combined world proven reserves of oil and gas				181.8
Worldwide total	177.36	1237.9	52.6	2353.5

Source: BP *Statistical Review of World Energy* (June 2008).
*Suspended its membership of OPEC in Dec. 2008.

World Reserves and Production of Oil and Gas

Although world estimated gas reserves are somewhat smaller than for oil, worldwide, the significantly higher production of crude oil than gas means that the reserves to production ratio in years for gas is about 45 per cent longer than for oil. The data in Table 11.25 refer to 2007 for the world as a whole and separately for OPEC and the rest of the world.

Table 11.25. World Reserves and Production of Oil and Gas and Resulting Reserves to Production Ratios in 2007

World	Gas	Oil	Combined oil and gas
Reserves	1115.6 bn.bbl o.e	1237.9 bn.bbl	2353.5 bn.bbl o.e
%	47.4	52.6	100.0
Production	18492.6 mn bbl o.e.	29759.5 mn bbl	48252.1 mn bbl o.e.
%	38.3	61.7	100.0
Reserves to Production Ratios in Years	60.3	41.6	48.8

OPEC			
Reserves	579.2 bn.bbl o.e	934.7 bn.bbl	1513.9 bn.bbl o.e
%	38.3	61.7	100.0
Production	3382.8 mn bbl o.e.	12849.5 mn bbl	16232.3 mn bbl o.e.
%	20.8	79.2	100.0
Reserves to Production Ratios in Years	171.2	72.7	93.3
Non-OPEC			
Reserves	536.4 bn.bbl o.e	303.2 bn.bbl	839.6 bn.bbl o.e
%	63.9	36.1	100.0
Production	15109.8 mn bbl o.e.	16910 mn bbl	32019.8 mn bbl o.e.
%	47.2	52.8	100.0
Reserves to Production Ratios in Years	35.5	17.9	26.2

Source: BP *Statistical Review of World Energy* (June 2008).

Lifespan in Years of Proved Oil and Gas Reserves at Production Levels Reported for 2008

Table 11.26 shows a comparison for both oil and gas in terms of the prospective lifespan at production levels reported for 2008, measured on the basis of reserves to production ratios. Only countries with an R:P ratio of more than forty years have been included in this analysis. Remarkably, Iraq heads the list for both oil and gas, though it has to be pointed out that its level of production of gas was minimal in 2008 as its reserves base has been hardly exploited at all. Given the fact that Iraq's reported gas reserves are almost identical to those of Indonesia, it should be capable of supporting a similar production volume of about 70 billion cubic metres annually, as Indonesia has done for years, while still keeping Iraq's reserves to production ratio above 40, assuming no new discoveries. Of course, prospective big increases in Iraq's production of both oil and gas presuppose peaceful internal conditions within the country, and cooperation and harmonious relations between Iraq and its neighbours and throughout the world in terms of the global market for oil and gas. Evidently, this scenario can only come to fruition if there is a stable government in Baghdad, able to ensure peaceful conditions between Shia, Sunni and Kurdish elements within the country. Also, rapid improvements in economic conditions are needed among a population which has been suffering from extremely low per capita incomes for years, as shown elsewhere in this book, not to mention physical violence and terrorism.

Table 11.26. Lifespan in Years of Proved Oil and Gas Reserves at Production Levels Reported for 2008 Measured by Reserves to Production Ratios

	Oil	Gas
Iraq	129.7	1686.2*
Venezuela	105.8	153.7
Kuwait	99.6	DNQ
UAE	89.7	128.1
Iran	86.9	254.6
Kazakhstan	70.0	DNQ
Saudi Arabia	66.5	96.9
Libya	64.6	DNQ
Qatar	54.1	332.4

Nigeria	45.6	149.1
Russian Federation	DNQ	72.0
Turkmenistan	DNQ	120.1
Indonesia	DNQ	45.7
Former Soviet Union		
Average lifespan in years (unweighted) for qualifying countries	81.3	145.2(excluding Iraq)

Note: Iraq's gas production in 2008 was reported in the *OPEC Statistical Bulletin* as being only 1.88 billion cubic metres with its proved reserves at 3.17 trillion cubic metres. Its highest level of gas production since 1986 was only 6.45 billion cubic metres but in a stable and peaceful local and international environment its production could easily be at least ten times that volume as its gas reserves base is almost the same as that of Indonesia. DNQ = Does not qualify on the criteria adopted for this analysis.
Source: BP *Statistical Review of World Energy* (2009).

Perhaps most important of all in this table of comparative statistics, it can be seen that seven countries feature in both lists for oil and gas. These are Iraq, Venezuela, UAE, Iran, Saudi Arabia, Qatar and Nigeria. The thing they have in common is that at production volumes for oil and gas reported for 2008 all seven of these countries have a larger prospective lifespan for gas than they do for oil – much larger in the case of Iraq, Iran and Qatar. Excepting Iraq, because of very low production of natural gas, it can be seen that the average lifespan for gas at 145 years is some 78 per cent greater than it is for oil with an average of only 81 years, in terms of the reserves to production ratio for these well-endowed countries. The other thing that these seven countries have in common is that all of them are OPEC members.

We suggest this analysis contains important implications for international relations generally and for cooperation between oil and gas importing and exporting countries, probably through existing institutions such as the International Energy Agency and the Organization of Petroleum Exporting Countries, but with other neutral ones such as the United Nations, the World Trade Organization, the International Monetary Fund and the World Bank involved as well. International trade in energy, especially in oil, has for long been an important link in world trade growth, contributing significantly to it and the improvement in economic conditions recorded in so many countries over the past fifty to sixty years.

In addition, the newly enhanced role of the Group of Twenty (G20), discussed earlier in this book, is potentially most important as a forum for dialogue and possible policy action to resolve problems in the energy sector worldwide, not excluding the possible need for increased regulation.

The other important conclusion to be drawn from this analysis is that it suggests that even more national and international efforts need to be made to encourage energy importers and consumers to continue to switch their needs away from oil and into gas, as far as their sector usage allows. A relatively advantageous price and a stable one for gas *vis-à-vis* oil needs to be achieved to ensure this transition over the medium to long term, at least until the reserves to production ratio in years for gas approaches that of oil for these comparatively well-endowed countries.

Though all the analysis presented here is simply a paper exercise, it is suggested that the facts presented could provide a useful basis for meaningful international cooperation and planning among leading oil and gas importing and exporting countries, away from the usual conferences based on prior preoccupations and policy stances, sometimes inadequately prepared or with incomplete understanding of the factors which can come into play in affecting future world energy prospects ten to twenty years on, to 2020 and 2030.

That is effectively the task we are setting ourselves in Part IV of this book, so a critical review of hydrocarbon reserves and production worldwide is an essential base for considering possible scenarios for 2020 and 2030. Such a review, with projections based on available facts and judgements about the probable evolution of the world energy balance and its interaction with the world economy as a whole is seen as a potentially important input to policy-making at the national and international level, either as a part of or as an adjunct to G20-type meetings. The time seems propitious for this purpose, given the evident failures of regulation through 2007 and 2008, not merely in the financial sector, but also in commodity markets, notably with oil prices overshooting both upwards and downwards, within the space of a few months, unsupported by fundamental features of supply and demand. The oil price spike of July 2008 and its subsequent collapse were destabilizing influences, along with over-easy credit creation during several years in the financial sector, resulting in economic recession worldwide.

The hope we express here is that this unfortunate combination of events can be avoided in the future through a proper analysis of what went wrong in 2008 and 2009 and the preceding period with appropriate new policy measures and regulation being introduced.

Countries with Proved Oil Reserves of More than 10 Billion Barrels and an R:P Ratio of More than Eighteen Years at End 2008

Only fourteen countries worldwide have these two characteristics. Ten of these are OPEC members. The other four are Brazil, Canada, Kazakhstan and the Russian Federation. All of these countries have the capacity to increase production, but only Kazakhstan could do so really significantly from its 1.55 million b/d in 2008, with its R:P ratio of 70 years at the end of 2008. Its output could rise to about 5.5 million b/d, or 4 million b/d more than in 2008, and its R:P ratio would fall to about 20 years with no additions to its proved reserves. Figure 11.10 shows on a scatter diagram all these countries, showing the relationships for each of them between total reserves against the reserves to production ratio.

Scope for Potential Oil Production Increases

Saudi Arabia is in a class of its own, as shown on the vertical axis of the diagram, with proved oil reserves of 264 billion barrels. Nevertheless, its reserves to production ratio of only 66.5 years is less than that of Kazakhstan and five other OPEC member countries. Given that Saudi production in 2008 was in excess of 10.8 million b/d its unmatched volume of national proved oil reserves was actually less than half the total of the other five OPEC member countries, i.e. 551 billion barrels of Iran, Iraq, Kuwait, UAE and Venezuela collectively. Yet the total production of these other five OPEC countries in 2008 was only 39 per cent more than that of Saudi Arabia at 15.08 million b/d.

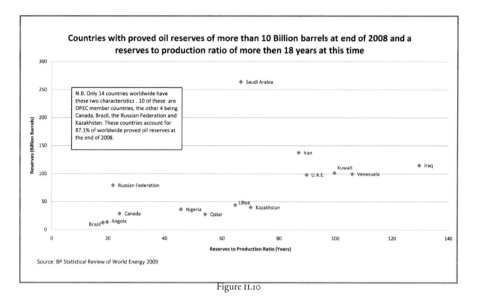

Figure 11.10

Consequently, their collective reserves to production ratio averaged 99.9 years, or 50 per cent more than that of Saudi Arabia. Thus if Saudi Arabia decided, as a matter of policy, that it did not wish to raise its oil production above 12 million b/d, reducing its R:P ratio to sixty years, the burden of meeting a significant increase in worldwide oil demand would fall primarily on its Arabian Gulf neighbours and Venezuela, all of whom are, of course, OPEC member countries.

If all of these were prepared to increase their production volumes consistent with reductions in their reserves to production ratios to sixty years, as suggested for Saudi Arabia, this could mean incremental production from the five of them amounting to 10 million b/d to add to a prospective increase of 1.15 million b/d from Saudi Arabia. This would take oil production worldwide up to about 92 million b/d, if the world demand was there, at whatever price proved necessary to bring onstream such an increase. Undoubtedly, large investments and considerable time would be required for such an increase.

Short of further significant discoveries of giant or large new oil fields, or big increases in the recovery factor, increases in oil production elsewhere are likely to be very modest and may do no more than partially offset declines already evident in the US, the UK, Norway, Mexico and Indonesia, etc. Among net oil-exporting countries outside OPEC, excepting Russia, Canada was the only one worldwide producing more than 3 million b/d p.a. (since 2003) with potential to increase it, but Canada's net surplus of production over domestic consumption has remained less than 1 million b/d over the ten years to 2008.

The former Soviet Union and the Russian Federation in particular remain something of an enigma. Evidently, the latter needs the foreign exchange earnings deriving from its exports of oil and natural gas. However, in spite of the incentive of rising and high world oil prices over the five years 2004 to 2008 inclusive, Russia's production volume has remained at less than 10 million b/d during this period, some 1.5 million b/d or more below the previous peak of 11.48 million b/d reached by Russia in 1987. By contrast oil production in the whole of the former Soviet Union (now the Commonwealth of Independent States) exceeded the previous peak in both 2007 and 2008, by some 150,000 b/d, at 12.8 million b/d in both years. Clearly, the rise in oil production of 1 million b/d in Kazakhstan between 1998 and 2008 was the most important explanation for this difference.

With a reserves to production ratio of 21.8 years, the Russian Federation should be able to increase its production significantly from the 9,886,000 b/d reported for 2008, though this was almost 100,000 b/d less than the year before. The former Soviet Union as a whole has a larger reserves to production ratio of 27.2 years but this was attributable to the inclusion of Kazakhstan with an R:P ratio of seventy years. This trend seems bound to continue for many years to come, thus an important potential source for increasing world oil supplies.

The position of these five OPEC countries plus Saudi Arabia in 2008 and the prospective increases in their production volumes to bring their reserves to production ratios down to sixty years is shown in Table 11.27.

Table 11.27. Position in 2008 and Projected Increase in Production Volumes

Country	Production in 2008 10^6 b/d = mnbbl		Reserves at End 2008 10^9bbl	R:P Ratio in Years	Production Implication to 60 Years R:P mn b/d	Implied Increase in Oil Production from 2008 mn b/d
Iran	4.325	1583.0	137.6	86.9	6.264	1.956
Iraq	2.423	886.8	115.0	129.7	5.238	2.815
Kuwait	2.784	1018.9	101.5	99.6	4.621	1.837
UAE	2.980	1090.7	97.8	89.7	4.455	1.475
Venezuela	2.566	939.2	99.4	105.8	4.525	1.959
Total	15.078	5,518.5	551.3	99.9	25.103	10.042
% more than Saudi Arabia	39.0	39.0	108.7	50.2	108.8	8.55 times more
Saudi Arabia	10.846	3969.6	264.1	66.5	12.020	1.174

Evidently, the implied production volumes consistent with bringing proved reserves to production ratios down to sixty years are large, as are the implied increases in oil production for all five countries, except Saudi Arabia, from the levels reported for 2008, as shown in the last two columns of the table. However, two considerations have to be borne in mind. Comparatively high volumes of oil production were reported in the now fairly distant past by these countries. For example, Iran was producing more than 6 million b/d in 1974, Iraq produced almost 3.5 million b/d in 1979, Kuwait produced more than 3.3 million b/d in 1972 and Venezuela produced more than 3.7 million b/d in 1970. The second point is that all these countries reported very big increases in their proved oil reserves, mostly over the five years from 1985 to 1989 inclusive. Thus between 1980 and 2008 the proved oil reserves of Kuwait increased by 49 per cent and those of Saudi Arabia rose by 57 per cent. For all other countries listed, reported proved oil reserves increased by well over 100 per cent over this period of nearly thirty years.

At the end of the day, decisions as to whether or not to increase oil production consistent with maintaining an oil reserves to production ratio of 60 years, or perhaps less, must be a matter for the national governments of the countries concerned, perhaps in concert with deliberations involving the OPEC Secretariat and delegations from the relevant countries, since all of them are OPEC members.

To put this matter in a global perspective, it can be noted that the increase in oil production of some 11.2 million b/d or a little more among these six countries, including Saudi Arabia, would not even match the worldwide increase of 11.6 million b/d recorded between 1996 and 2006. Over that period world oil production outside these six countries rose by 7.3 million b/d. However, nothing like that can be expected over the next few years, once the world economy emerges from the recession of 2008–9. Net oil production from all other countries worldwide seems to have already fallen from a peak of more than 45.7 million b/d in 2007 by 0.6 million b/d to 45.1 million b/d in 2008 – its lowest annual average total since 2003.

US Reserves, Production and R:P Ratios for Oil and Gas between 1979 and 2008

US proved oil reserves rose by 15.1 per cent between 1979 and 2008 but oil production fell dramatically by 34.3 per cent over this period. As a result, the reserves to production ratio increased quite sharply from 7.1 years in 1979 to 12.4 years in 2008. In the intermediate year of 2000 the R:P ratio had been 10.7 years.

US proved reserves of natural gas over this twenty-nine-year period actually increased by 22.4 per cent from 5.5 to 6.73 trillion cubic metres. Its production in 2008 was 4.6 per cent higher than it had been in 1979; its

R:P ratio also increased from 9.9 years in 1979 to 11.6 years in 2008 but had been lower at only 9.2 years in 2000.

Table 11.28. US Oil and Gas Reserves and Production

		Oil bn bbl	Gas $10^9 m^3$
Reserves	1979	26.5	5500
	2008	30.5	6730
Production	1979	3.750	556.8
	2008	2.465	582.2
R:P ratios in years	1979	7.1	9.9
	2008	12.4	11.6

It is worth noting that the US Geological Survey reported an improvement in the recovery factor of oil in place in the US from 22 per cent on average in 1979 to 35 per cent on average in 1999.

Crude Oil and Natural Gas Reserves for the Leading Countries in 2007

The reserves of both natural gas and crude oil for the United States appear low relative to Russia and the OPEC countries of the Middle East. The same is true of China as far as crude oil is concerned but China's natural gas reserves should permit production to rise at a fairly healthy rate for some years to come. China's gas reserves had increased from a low level but its oil reserves declined by 22.5 per cent or 4.5 billion barrels, implying a reserves to production ratio of only 11.3, marginally below that of the United States. Table 11.29 for oil and gas provide the details.

Table 11.29. Crude Oil and Gas Reserves for the Leading Countries in 2007

Crude Oil

	Reserves bn bbl	Production mn bbl	Reserves/ production ratio (years)
Saudi Arabia	264.2	3801	69.5
Iran	138.4	1606	86.2
Iraq	115.0	783	146.9
Total Middle East	755.3	9189	82.2
Russian Federation	79.4	3642	21.8
USA	29.4	2512	11.7
China	15.5	1366	11.3

Natural Gas

	Reserves trillion m3	Production bn m³	Reserves/ production ratio (years)
Russian Federation	44.65	607.4	73.5
Total Middle East	73.21	355.8	205.76
Iran	27.80	111.9	248.4
Qatar	25.60	59.8	428.1
USA	5.98	545.9	11.0
China	1.88	69.3	27.1
Saudia Arabia	7.07	75.9	93.1

Source: BP *Statistical Review of World Energy* (June 2008).

Net Additions to Proved Reserves of Oil and Gas 1977 to 2007

Over the thirty years to 2007 Middle Eastern countries accounted for two-thirds of the world's net additions to proved reserves of oil but for only half of the net addition of natural gas. The Russian Federation and other former territories of the USSR accounted for 26 trillion cubic metres of the additional gas reserves in the rest of the world, almost half the total. See Table 11.30.

Table 11.30. Net Additions to Proved Reserves of Oil and Gas 1977–2007.

	Oil billion barrels	%	Gas trillion m³	%
Middle East	395.5	67.0	52.81	49.8
Rest of World	194.7	33.0	53.15	50.2
Total World	590.2	100.0	105.96	100.0

Source: BP *Statistical Review of World Energy* (June 2008).

Note: i.e. gross additions to proved reserves over the 30-year period - depletion.

Crude Oil Proved Reserves

as at End 2007

The top five Middle Eastern OPEC countries with proved reserves of crude oil amounted to 717 billion barrels at the end of 2007 dominate the worldwide scene. Along with other OPEC members Venezuela, Libya, Nigeria, Qatar, Algeria and Angola, these eleven countries account for 75.2 per cent of the worldwide total. Moreover, these top five countries along with Venezuela have comfortably large reserves to production ratios in 2007 relative to almost all other countries shown here. Norwegian crude oil production peaked in 2001 and by 2007 its output had fallen by 25.2 per cent. With a reserves to production ratio of only 6.0 the UK's crude production has been in decline for longer, having fallen 43.8 per cent from its peak by 2007. Table 11.31 gives the statistics for twenty countries.

Table 11.31. Crude Oil Proved Reserves as at End 2007

	bn bbl	Share of world total %	R:P ratio in years
1. Saudi Arabia	264.2	21.3	69.5
2. Iran	138.4	11.2	86.2
3. Iraq	115.0	9.3	146.9

4. Kuwait	101.5	8.2	105.9
5. UAE	97.9	7.9	91.9
Top 5	717.0	57.9	87.3
6. Venezuela	87.0	7.0	91.3
7. Russian Federation	79.4	6.4	21.8
8. Libya	41.5	3.3	61.5
9. Kazakhstan	39.4	3.2	73.2
10. Nigeria	36.2	2.9	42.1
Next 5	283.5	22.9	42.5
11. USA	29.4	2.4	11.7
12. Canada	27.7	2.2	22.9
13. Qatar	27.4	2.2	62.8
14. China	15.5	1.3	11.3
15. Brazil	12.6	1.0	18.9
16. Algeria	12.3	1.0	16.8
17. Mexico	12.2	1.0	9.6
18. Angola	9.0	0.7	14.4
19. Norway	8.2	0.7	8.8
20. Azerbaijan	7.0	0.6	22.1
Next 10	161.3	13.0	16.0
NB Total Middle East	755.3	61.0	82.2
Total world	1237.9	100.0	41.6

Source: BP *Statistical Review of World Energy* (June 2008).

World Oil Reserves and Production 1979–2008

World proved oil reserves rose by a remarkable 95 per cent between 1979 and 2007 in spite of oil production rising continuously during the mainly five-year periods analysed in Table 11.32. The total stood at 1,258 billion barrels at the end of 2008.

Table 11.32. World Oil Reserves and Production 1979–2009 (bn barrels)

Year	Reserves at End	Net additions during 5 Years	Production during 5 Years	Implied Gross Additions to Reserves
1979	643.5			
1980–4		+118.1	107.5	225.6
1984	761.6			
1985–9		+244.2	111.7	355.9
1989	1005.8			
1990–4		+13.4	120.4	133.8
1994	1019.2			
1995–9		+69.4	130.1	199.5
1999	1088.6			
2000–4		+122.7	139.4	262.1
2004	1211.3			
2005–9		+121.8	148.3	270.1
2009	1333.1			
Totals during 30 years 1979–2009		689.6	757.4	1447.0

Source: BP *Statistical Review of World Energy* (2010).

The rate of net additions to reserves was very uneven, peaking at 244 billion barrels of oil during 1985–9 followed by a period of comparative drought when the net additions amounted to only 13 billion barrels in 1990–4. In aggregate, over the twenty-nine years, the net additions to reserves were 114 billion barrels less than total world oil production.

World Reserves and Production of Oil and Gas: Resulting Reserves to Production Ratios in 2008

Although world estimated gas reserves are somewhat smaller than for oil, worldwide, the significantly higher production of crude oil than gas means that the reserves to production ratio in years for gas is about 45 per cent longer than for oil.

For OPEC, of course, the ratios in both cases are considerably higher, but the difference is far greater, too, with existing gas reserves having a lifespan of more than 160 years at 2008 production volumes. Exploitation of their gas reserves should be a priority for Iran and Qatar among OPEC countries as their reserves are both very large and bigger than their oil reserves, too.

Worldwide Reserves of Oil and Gas: Disparity between OPEC and Non-OPEC Countries

At the worldwide level, even though reserves of natural gas are somewhat less than for oil, as production of gas is still significantly less, the proven reserves to production ratio for gas at 60.3 years is significantly higher than for oil at 42 years (2008 data). For OPEC as a group, reserves relative to production are higher for both gas and oil but the difference is significantly greater for both than for the non-OPEC average with an R:P ratio of 162.6 years for gas and 71.1 years for oil. The contrast with non-OPEC worldwide is remarkable: for gas it was only 36.7 years in 2008 and for oil it was a mere 18.3 years. OPEC controlled 76 per cent of world proven oil reserves in 2008 and 50.6 per cent of world gas reserves. Over the twenty-four years to 2008 incremental oil reserves of OPEC member countries rose by 421 billion barrels while for the world outside OPEC the net rise was a mere 52 billion barrels. Figure 11.11 illustrates the differences.

Figures 11.12 and 11.13 bring out the remarkable differences between OPEC

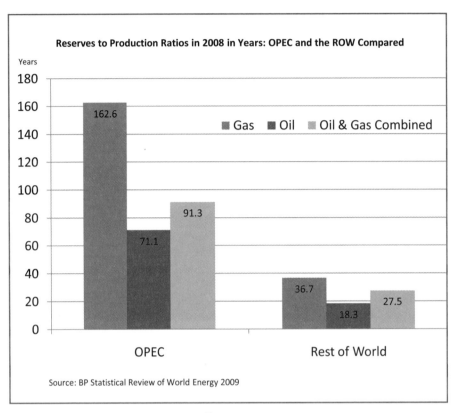

Figure II.II.

member countries and the rest of the world over the period from 1980 to the end of 2008. It can be seen that over the consecutive ten-, ten- and eight-year periods analysed here, OPEC oil production was less than in the rest of the world. Reserves at the end of each period were much higher in OPEC countries than in the rest of the world, as (inferred) new reserves added during each period in the OPEC countries were very much higher than elsewhere, notably from 1985 to 1989. These inferred new reserves' added estimates include improvements in recovery factors for oil in place as well as discoveries of new oil fields.

Estimates of proved reserves at the end of 1979 were 437.5 billion barrels for all OPEC member countries and 206 billion barrels for all other countries worldwide. Thus as a result of the changes over the twenty-nine years to 2008

OPEC's share of the remaining recoverable reserves had increased from 68 per cent of the world total of 643.5 billion barrels at the end of 1979 to 76 per cent of 1,258 billion barrels at the end of 2008.

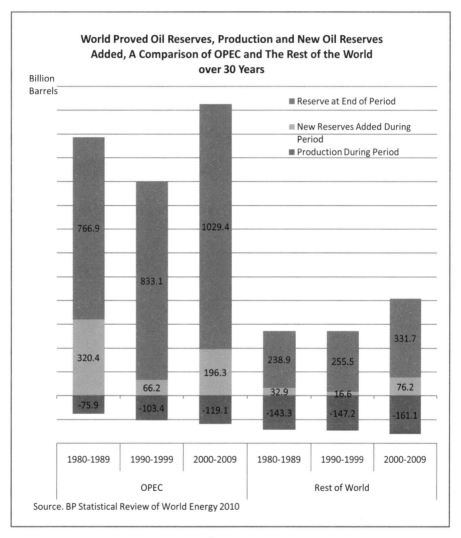

Figure II.12

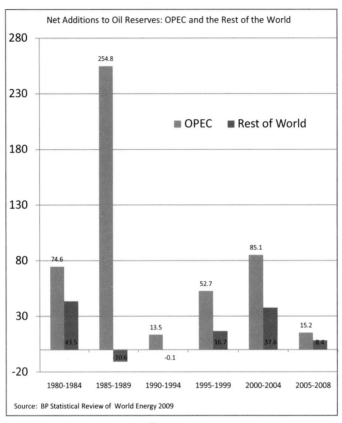

Figure 11.13

Figure 11.14 shows the dramatic differences between Saudi Arabia, all other OPEC members and six other areas of the world in terms of the prospective lifespan of existing proved oil reserves at their rates of production recorded for 2008. The lifespan for Saudi Arabian reserves is a little over sixty-six years but other OPEC member countries collectively have a prospective lifespan of more than seventy-three years. Other regions/areas are considerably less, with only the former Soviet Union and other Middle East/Africa having a current lifespan exceeding twenty years. Three of the other regions have a constraint of little more than sixteen years down to just under thirteen years. Thus barring big new oil discoveries (and some have been announced in 2008) or significant

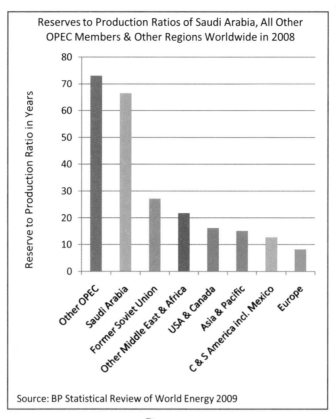

Reserves to Production Ratios of Saudi Arabia, All Other OPEC Members & Other Regions Worldwide in 2008

Source: BP Statistical Review of World Energy 2009

Figure 11.14

improvements in the recovery factor, there appear to be quite low ceilings on the scope for increasing production from 2008 volumes in these areas. The position in Europe looks particularly unpromising with Norwegian and UK production having been declining for some years already and a prospective lifespan for existing reserves of only 8.2 years.

Figure 11.15 shows the prospective lifespan of existing oil reserves in all thirteen OPEC member countries at their production volumes reported for 2008. It may surprise some readers of this book to find Saudi Arabia almost halfway down this list of OPEC member countries. Five of them, ranging from Iran up to Iraq, through the UAE, Kuwait and Venezuela, have RP ratios or lifespans for existing reserves, based on production volumes reported for 2008,

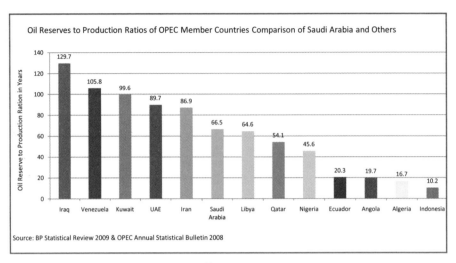

Figure 11.15

of twenty up to sixty-three years greater than Saudi Arabia which stands at 66.5 years. These other OPEC members are those whose reserves base enables them to increase production more than the others. Most of them have produced higher volumes in the past than they did in 2008, mostly during the 1970s. Like Saudi Arabia, Libya, Qatar and Nigeria are all capable of increasing production significantly, but to a lesser extent than the five better endowed with reserves mentioned above. The existing oil reserves suggest that production increases in Ecuador, Angola and Algeria will be quite limited, barring new discoveries. Indonesia is already out of OPEC in 2009 (though a member of G20), with its potential for increasing hydrocarbon exports seemingly being confined to natural gas, like those of Algeria too.

OPEC Oil Reserves and Production

Tables 11.32 and 11.33 show that the big rise in world reserves which occurred from 1985 to 1989 was more than accounted for by OPEC members with net additions of almost 255 billion barrels during that five-year period.

Table 11.33. OPEC Oil Reserves and Production 1979–2007 (bn barrels)

Year	Reserves at End	Net Additions during 5 Years	Production during 5 Years	Implied Gross Additions to Reserves
1979	437.9			
1980–4		+74.6	38.9	113.5
1984	512.1			
1985–9		+254.8	37.0	291.8
1989	766.9			
1990–4		+13.5	48.4	61.9
1994	780.4			
1995–9		+52.7	55.0	107.7
1999	833.1			
2000–4		+85.1	58.3	143.4
2004	918.2			
2005–9		+111.2	63.1	174.3
2009	1029.4			
Totals during 30 years 1979–2009		591.9	300.7	892.6

Source: BP *Statistical Review of World Energy* (2010).

The net additions over the twenty-eight years from end 1979 to end 2007 reported by OPEC members amounted to 497 billion barrels, an increase of 113 per cent. Also, these additional reserves at the end of the period amounted to 80 per cent more than the volume of OPEC production over the twenty-eight years.

Non-OPEC Oil Reserves and Production 1979–2008

Table 11.34 shows that there was an actual fall in oil reserves in the world outside OPEC member countries over the five years to end 1989, precisely when those reserves in OPEC countries increased dramatically. The net additions to reserves increased by 96 billion barrels from end 1979 to end 2008. This represented just 22 per cent of the 438 billion barrels produced during the period. The implied gross additions amounted to just 66 per cent of those achieved by OPEC with its much higher net additions and lower volume of production over the twenty-nine-year period.

Table 11.34. Rest of World (Non-OPEC) Oil Reserves and Production 1979–2008 (bn barrels)

Year	Reserves at End	Net Additions during 5 Years	Production during 5 Years	Implied Gross Additions to Reserves
1979	206.0			
1980–4		+43.5	68.6	112.1
1984	249.5			
1985–9		-10.6	74.7	64.1
1989	238.9			
1990–4		-0.1	72.1	72.0
1994	238.8			
1995–9		+16.7	75.1	91.8
1999	255.5			
2000–4		+37.6	81.2	118.8
2004	293.1			
2005–9		+10.6	85.2	95.8
2009	303.7			
Totals during 30 years 1979–2008		+97.7	456.9	554.6

Source: BP *Statistical Review of World Energy* (2010).

Dramatic Rise in OPEC Oil Reserves 1985–1989

Five OPEC countries increased their proved reserves by around 30 billion barrels each or more during the period, led by Saudi Arabia with a rise of 88 billion barrels followed by UAE with an increase of more than 65 billion barrels. The others were Iraq with a rise of 35 billion barrels, Iran with 34 billion barrels and Venezuela up by 31 billion barrels. The timing of years of the principal increases is shown in Table 11.35: it was Venezuela in 1985, the UAE and Iran in 1986 (when world oil prices fell dramatically) followed by Iraq in 1987 and Saudi Arabia in 1988. Prior to this Kuwait had increased its reserves by 25.7 billion barrels during 1984.

Table 11.35. Dramatic Rise in OPEC Oil Reserves, 1985–1989

	End 1984	1985	1986	1987	1988	1989
Saudi Arabia	171.7	171.5	169.7	169.6	255.0	260.1
UAE	32.5	33.0	97.2	98.1	98.1	98.1
Iraq	65.0	65.0	72.0	100.0	100.0	100.0
Iran	58.9	59.0	92.9	92.9	92.9	92.9
Venezuela	28.0	54.5	55.5	58.1	58.5	59.0

Source: BP *Statistical Review of World Energy* 2008 (database)

Note: It was during this five-year period that the rest of the world (outside OPEC) proven oil reserves actually declined by more than 10 bn barrels, thus increasing OPEC's share of the total very significantly, from 67.2% to 76.2% between the end of 1984 and the end of 1989.

Significant Changes in Worldwide Proved Reserves of Oil during 2008

During 2008 the only countries for which significant increases in proved reserves of oil were recorded were two OPEC member countries; Venezuela at 12.3 billion barrels and Libya at 2.2 billion barrels. Falls in oil reserves were recorded by Iran at -2.25 billion barrels and Mexico at -1.15 billion barrels. The net worldwide increase amounted to 10.5 billion barrels. A total of twelve countries recorded some increases over 2008, with fifteen countries recording decreases. Collectively, OPEC countries as a group increased their oil reserves by a net 12.0 billion barrels during 2007 while all countries outside OPEC collectively suffered a decline in their oil reserves by a net 1.5 billion barrels. See Table 11.36.

Table 11.36. Significant Changes in Worldwide Proved Reserves of Oil during 2008 (in millions of barrels)

Increases +		Decreases -	
OPEC			
Venezuela	12,342	Iran	2,250
Libya	2,196	Indonesia	380
Ecuador	143	Saudi Arabia	41
Angola	5		
Qatar	3		
Increase	14,689	**Decrease**	2,671
OPEC net increase 12,018			
Non-OPEC			
Brazil	442	Mexico	1149
USA	345	Canada	500
Pakistan	50	UK	190
Peru	33	Norway	185
Argentina	29	Colombia	141
Tunisia	25	Denmark	128
New Zealand	5	Germany	91
		Thailand	19
		France	17
		Surinam	8
		Morocco	1
Increase	929	**Decrease**	2429
Non-OPEC net Decrease 1,500			
Total world	+15,618		- 5100
Net increase worldwide 10,518			

Source: *Oil and Gas Journal*, 22 Dec. 2008.

As a result of these changes, OPEC's share of proved reserves of conventional crude oil (i.e. not including oil shale and tar sands) increased to 75.8 per cent of the worldwide total.

Crude Oil Production over Thirty Years to 2007

Conventional crude oil production is clearly on the decline in the USA, Norway and the UK with the reserves to production ratio below ten years in the two latter. Mexico's reserves to production ratio is also below ten, so there appears to be no prospect of a sustained increase in production from that country. Iranian oil production remains below the level achieved more than thirty years ago from 1971 to 1978.

The high reserves to production ratio for Iraq explains the high level of US interest in that country and the scope for it to increase crude production very significantly. However, the continuing internal instability of Iraq, in spite of the enormous sums of money spent in maintaining the US military presence there, mean that crude oil output has remained slightly lower than it was twenty or thirty years ago. The US President has scaled down and withdrawn active US military involvement in Iraq in 2010. However, several other countries in the Gulf plus Venezuela are evidently capable of increasing production of crude oil very significantly from 2007 levels if the political will, economic incentives and market demand are in place. See Table 11.37.

Table 11.37. Crude Oil Production over 30 Years to 2007 (1000 b/d)

	1977	1987	1997	2007	R:P ratio in 2007 in years
Saudi Arabia	9412	4555	9,482	10,413	69.5
Russian Federation	N/A	N/A	6,227	9,978	21.8
USA	9865	9,945	8269	6,879	11.7
Iran	5705	2310	3776	4,401	86.2
China	1880	2675	3211	3,743	11.3

Top 5 countries			30,965 42.9% of world	35,414 43.4% of world	40.8
Mexico	1085	2875	3410	3477	9.6
Canada	1610	1695	2588	3309	22.9
UAE	2015	1650	2567	2915	91.9
Kuwait	2013	1270	2137	2626	105.9
Venezuela	2315	1775	3321	2613	91.3
Next 5	9038	9265	14023	14,940	59.8
countries	14.4%	15.5%	19.4%	18.3%	
Norway	275	1000	3280	2556	8.8
Nigeria	2095	1290	2316	2356	42.1
Iraq	2495	2310	1166	2145	146.9
Algeria	1150	1040	1421	2000	16.8
Libya	2065	1000	1491	1848	61.5
Next 5	8080	6640	9674	10,905	53.6
countries	12.9%	11.1%	13.4%	13.4%	
Brazil	165	600	868	1833	18.9
Angola		350	741	1723	14.4
United Kingdom	765	2555	2702	1636	6.0
Kazakhstan	N/A	N/A	536	1490	73.2
Qatar	435	340	692	1197	62.8
Next 5			5,539	7879	32.0
countries			7.7%	9.7%	
Total world	62,670	59,895	72,231	81,533	41.6

Source: BP *Statistical Review of World Energy* (June 2008).

N/A = Not Available

The sharp rise of some 6 million b/d in non-OPEC crude oil production between 1979 and 1985 noted in the next section was a major reason for the weakening of world oil prices over this period, combined with falls in consumption exceeding 6.5 million b/d in the USA the EU and Japan during the same six years.

World Oil Production 1965–2007: Saudi Arabian and OPEC Share

Cheap oil as the balancing form of world energy rose rapidly with production at 31.8 million barrels per day in 1965 to 58.5 million barrels per day in 1973. The oil price increases of 1973–4 and the economic recession of 1974–5 resulted in a sharp fall in output in 1975, but growth in demand and production resumed in 1976 through to 1979 when stock building accentuated apparent consumption. There was an actual need to rebuild stocks in 1979 but there was another factor at work in that year too, the Iranian Revolution. This induced fears of scarcity of oil supplies, almost certainly also contributing to a rise in demand beyond the actual volume of consumption.

Subsequently, economic recession and a further significant rise in oil prices in 1979 of some 127 per cent associated with the anxieties related to a foreseen shortage of oil supplies (not in fact realized) caused a fall of world oil production of some 9.5 million barrels per day over just four years from the 1979 peak of 66.1 million barrels per day. In 1984 and 1985 there was a slight recovery in oil demand, but it was not until a policy-induced sharp fall in oil prices in 1986 that world oil production rose sharply by 3.0 million barrels per day. The volume did not recover to the level recorded in 1979 until 1993. After that, world oil output rose quite gradually in most years with an aggregate increase of more than 15 million barrels per day over the fourteen years to 2007. Small falls were recorded in only four of those years, more than offset by a sharp rise of 3.3 million barrels per day in just one year – 2004 when oil prices started to rise rapidly.

Consistent with the worldwide fast growth in oil production and demand from 1965 to 1973, Saudi Arabian production rose more dramatically from 2.2 million barrels per day in the earlier year to 7.7 million barrels per day in 1973 – an annual compound rate of increase of some 17 per cent on average. During that period its share of the global total rose from 7.0 per cent to 13.2 per cent.

Over the same eight years, total OPEC production increased from 14.4 million barrels per day to 31.1 million barrels per day with its share of the world total increasing from 45.3 per cent to 53.2 per cent.

In spite of the oil price increases of 1973–4 and economic recession of 1974–5, Saudi Arabian oil production continued to rise in most years, peaking at 10.3 million barrels per day in 1980–1, when its prices remained relatively competitive.

Total OPEC production peaked at 31.4 million barrels per day in both 1977 and 1979, marginally above its previous peak recorded in 1973. While Saudi Arabia's share of the world total continued to rise to a new peak of 17.2 per cent in 1981, that of OPEC countries as a whole fell quite dramatically, from a high of 54.5 per cent in 1974 to only 39.1 per cent in 1981. The Iranian Revolution and the outbreak of war between Iraq and Iran contributed to a fall of over 8 million barrels per day in just two years (1979–81), even as Saudi output rose slightly, as it had a comparative price advantage at this time.

Thereafter, following price reunification within OPEC in 1981, Saudi Arabian oil production fell quite dramatically by 6.7 million barrels per day in just four years from 1981 to 1985, marginally more than that of OPEC as a whole, down a further 6.4 million barrels per day. Figure 11.17 shows this graphically. As a result of these big falls, Saudi Arabia's share of the global total decreased from 17.2 per cent in 1981 to just 6.3 per cent in 1985 while that of OPEC as a whole declined almost commensurately, from 39.1 per cent in 1981 to 29.5 per cent in 1985.

The policy-induced oil price fall of 1986 marked the beginning of a recovery in production in both Saudi Arabia and OPEC as a whole. However, it was much less sharp than the previous fall. Saudi Arabian output did not surpass its earlier peak until more than twenty years later, in 2004, at 10.6 million barrels per day. For OPEC the delay was also more than twenty years, but achieved slightly earlier, in 2000 at 32.2 million barrels per day. For both Saudi Arabia and OPEC as a whole oil production remained higher over the five years 2004 to 2008 than it was previously, but it fell in 2009 and perhaps in 2010 on account of both high spot and futures prices in 2008, plus worldwide financial crisis and economic recession adversely affecting oil demand globally during these years.

At 44.9 per cent of world production in 2008 OPEC's share of the total was

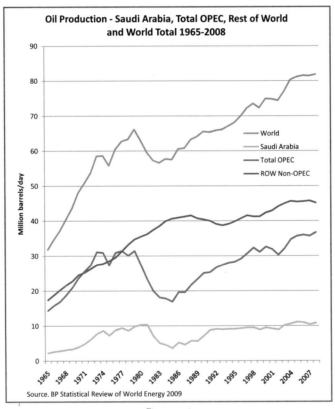

Figure 11.16

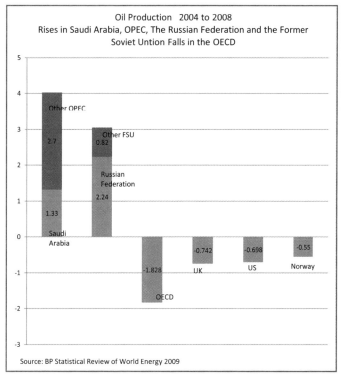

Figure 11.17

higher than it had been in any year since 1979, with its output 17 per cent higher than it had been in that year. Figure 11.16 shows the progression over forty-four years to 2008, together with Table 11.38 providing the relevant statistics.

Table 11.38. World Oil Production and Saudi Arabia's and OPEC's Share 1965–2008

| Year | million barrels per day | | | | % shares | |
	World	Saudi Arabia	Total OPEC	ROW* Non-OPEC	Saudi Arabia	OPEC
1965	31.8	2.2	14.4	17.4	7.0	45.3
1966	34.6	2.6	15.8	18.8	7.6	45.8

1967	37.1	2.8	16.9	20.2	7.6	45.5
1968	40.4	3.1	18.8	21.6	7.6	46.6
1969	43.6	3.3	20.9	22.7	7.5	47.9
1970	48.1	3.9	23.6	24.5	8.0	49.1
1971	50.8	4.8	25.6	25.2	9.5	50.3
1972	53.7	6.1	27.4	26.3	11.3	51.0
1973	58.5	7.7	31.1	27.4	13.2	53.2
1974	58.6	8.6	30.9	27.7	14.7	54.5
1975	55.8	7.2	27.3	28.5	12.9	48.9
1976	60.4	8.8	30.9	29.5	14.5	51.2
1977	62.7	9.4	31.4	31.3	15.0	50.2
1978	63.3	8.6	30.1	33.2	13.5	47.5
1979	66.1	9.8	31.4	34.7	14.9	47.5
1980	62.9	10.3	27.4	35.5	16.3	43.5
1981	59.5	10.3	23.3	36.2	17.2	39.1
1982	57.3	7.0	19.9	37.4	12.1	34.7
1983	56.6	5.0	18.1	38.5	8.7	32.0
1984	57.7	4.5	17.8	39.9	7.9	30.8
1985	57.5	3.6	16.9	40.6	6.3	29.5
1986	60.5	5.2	19.6	40.9	8.6	32.5
1987	60.8	4.6	19.6	41.2	7.6	32.2
1988	63.2	5.7	21.7	41.5	9.1	34.4
1989	64.1	5.6	23.4	40.7	8.8	36.5
1990	65.5	7.1	25.1	40.4	10.8	38.3
1991	65.3	8.8	25.3	40.0	13.5	38.7
1992	65.8	9.1	26.7	39.1	13.8	40.5
1993	66.1	9.0	27.4	38.7	13.6	41.5
1994	67.1	9.1	28.0	39.1	13.5	41.7
1995	68.1	9.1	28.3	39.8	13.4	41.5

1996	69.9	9.3	29.2	40.7	13.3	41.7
1997	72.2	9.5	30.7	41.5	13.1	42.5
1998	73.5	9.5	32.3	41.2	12.9	43.3
1999	72.3	8.9	31.1	41.2	12.2	42.4
2000	74.9	9.5	32.6	42.3	12.7	42.9
2001	74.8	9.2	31.9	42.9	12.3	42.1
2002	74.4	8.9	30.3	44.1	12.0	40.2
2003	77.0	10.2	32.1	44.9	13.2	41.2
2004	80.3	10.6	34.7	45.6	13.2	42.6
2005	81.1	11.1	35.7	45.4	13.7	43.5
2006	81.5	10.9	36.0	45.5	13.2	43.5
2007	81.4	10.4	35.7	45.7	12.8	43.2
2008	81.8	10.8	36.7	45.1	13.2	44.9

Source: BP *Statistical Review of World Energy* (June 2009).

*ROW = Rest of World, including Soviet Union.

World Oil Consumption/Demand

1973–2008

A word of explanation is necessary for this heading. Nobody really knows what the volume of oil consumption is in any one year in the world as a whole, or in any one country, for that matter. The statistics do reflect the underlying level of consumption, but there can be significant changes in stocks from year to year, both on land and at sea. Thus, actual consumption is in fact a less precise number than suggested by statistical reports and subject to margins of error. Thus a better term is really apparent consumption or demand.

By 1977 world oil consumption had reached a new peak of 60.6 million barrels per day, 7.6 per cent higher than it had been at its earlier peak in 1973. US oil demand was 6.5 per cent higher than it had been four years earlier. China and South Korea consumed in 1977 more than 50 per cent more than they had done four years earlier, while Mexico was up almost 47 per cent, Brazil by 23.5 per cent and India by 14 per cent. The exceptions were the European Union, down 4.4 per cent, as the four big member countries all fell by more than this, while Japanese oil consumption fell by 2.6 per cent over these four years.

However, in the two years from 1977 to 1979, world oil apparent consumption had increased by a further 6.2 per cent with new peaks being reached in the European Union and Japan, contributing to a global aggregate of 64.38 million barrels per day in that year. Thus the diversity of experience among leading countries was considerable, but the world as a whole seemed to have assimilated the very significant oil price increases of 1973–4, albeit with oil consumption growth falling back to an annual average rate of only 2.3 per cent from 1973 to 1979 compared with 7.6 per cent over the eight years of cheap oil culminating in 1973. However, the spot price of crude oil increased sharply from $13.08 a barrel in 1978 to $29.75 in 1979 and to $35.69 in 1980, respective annual rises of 12.7 and 20 per cent. These had a fairly dramatic impact on apparent consumption/demand such that the 1979 worldwide peak was not surpassed again until 1989, ten years later. After that, growth resumed globally, up 9.49 million barrels per day between 1990 and 2000 and a further 8.88 million barrels per day over the next seven years to 2007. Nevertheless, worldwide growth in oil consumption rose at an average rate of only 1.0 per cent per annum over the twenty-eight years to 2007, after the fall back through the early 1980s.

Among the leading oil consuming countries over this period, the most remarkable change occurred in the former Soviet Union, where consumption plunged by 4.96 million barrels per day or 57.8 per cent over the decade from 1990 to 2000. Even in the Russian Federation, its main constituent during these Yeltsin years, the fall amounted to 49.6 per cent. Table 11.39 shows this and other statistics.

Table 11.39. World Oil Consumption 1973–2008 (in 000s barrels per day)

	1973	1977	1979	1980	1985	1990	2000	2007	2008
World	56,325	60,604	64,381	61,841	59,391	66,855	76,340	84,878	84,455
USA	17,318	18,443	18,438	17,062	15,726	16,988	19,701	20,680	19,419
EU	15,512	14,836	15,879	14,806	13,114	13,925	14,689	14,746	14,765
Japan	5,324	5,185	5,487	4,936	4,435	5,304	5,577	5,039	4,845
China*	1,162	1,755	1,958	1,821	1,929	2,454	4,973	8,066	8,393
Former Soviet Union	6,119	7,217	8,117	8,494	8,535	8,582	3,623	3,973	4,045

Russian Fed	N/A	N/A	N/A	N/A	5,022	5,129	2,583	2,706	2,797
India	474	541	633	643	895	1,211	2,254	2,748	2,882
South Korea	236	371	480	475	537	1,038	2,229	2,389	2,291
Canada	1,696	1,826	1,947	1,915	1,569	1,762	1,937	2,323	2,295
Brazil	864	1,042	1,231	1,204	1,262	1,476	2,056	2,274	2,397
Mexico	525	771	932	1,034	1,239	1,458	1,910	2,027	2,039
Germany	3,314	3,130	3,380	3,056	2,670	2,708	2,763	2,393	2.505
Saudi Arabia	467	502	656	599	945	1,171	1,536	2,054	2,224
Total Middle East	1,427	1,741	2,096	2,046	2,939	3,484	4,716	6,084	6,423
Rest of world +	5,666	6,876	7,183	7,405	7,211	9,173	12,675	14,579	14,661

Source: BP *Statistical Review of World Energy* (2009).

* Includes Hong Kong.

+ To ensure consistency through time as Russia is included in the former Soviet Union.

N/A Not available

Note: All countries/groups exceeding 2 million barrels per day in 2008 are shown here. Eastern Germany was reunified with Western Germany in 1990 and the eight countries of the former Eastern Europe were incorporated in the EU.

The average annual growth rate over the full twenty-eight-year period varied remarkably. In South Korea, India and China, it exceeded 5 per cent per annum. In Mexico and Brazil it was more than 2 per cent per annum with a small increase in the United States but small average falls in Japan and the EU. But in Germany, its largest member, the annual fall averaged -1.2 per cent per annum with the total volume falling almost 1 million barrels per day over the twenty-eight years from 1979 to 2007.

Aggregate volume increases in China, India, USA, South Korea, Mexico, Brazil and Canada of 14.9 million barrels per day among these leading consuming countries were partially offset by the huge fall in the former Soviet Union/Russia, unlikely to be replicated in the future, and smaller ones in the EU and Japan.

The slow growth of world oil consumption after 1979 was associated with the sharp increase in the oil price in that year, with falling oil prices after 1980, especially in 1986. The 1980 price level was not surpassed, even in current dollars, until 2004.

All of this evidence suggests that the OPEC price increases of 1973–4 were much more sustainable than the subsequent rises of 1979–80 associated with anxieties about supplies from Iran as a result of the revolution there, unusually large rebuilding of stocks in 1979 and the start of the war between Iraq and Iran and economic recession in 1980–2. Other factors operating through the 1980s were the comparative rises in supply of non-OPEC oil and other forms of energy in the global mix and the fact of medium to longer term conservation of oil and energy use starting to have a very significant impact.

Figure 11.17 shows the relationship between nominal or current year-by-year prices from 1970 to 2008 together with Saudi Arabian crude oil production volumes over this period. Over the period from 1970 to 1980 both rose as Saudi Arabia increased production in an attempt to quell high and rising oil prices associated with fears of shortages in 1979–80. Thereafter, Saudi production as the swing producer fell from more than 10 to less than 4 million b/d under a combination of influences from 1981 to 1985: economic recession; big improvements in the efficiency of energy usage; increased supplies of other forms of energy and increased supplies of non-OPEC oil supplies. This culminated in the sharp fall in oil prices in 1986 which, with the introduction of netback pricing for crude oil, enabled Saudi Arabian oil production to rise to more than 6 then to more than 8 million barrels a day as the oil price continued to languish at a comparatively low level for well over ten years. Actually, it was even lower in 1998 than it had been in 1986. After that an almost sustained rise started in 1999 with a slight fall in 2001 before the much more dramatic rise from 2003 to July 2008.

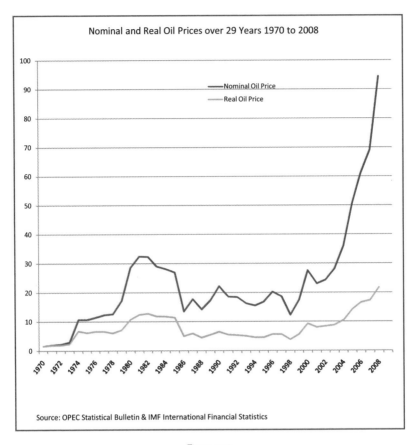

Figure 11.18

Figure 11.18 shows the comparatively modest rise in real oil prices expressed in US dollars of 1970 (taking account of the changes – mostly rises, but sometimes falls) in export unit values of the advanced countries. Against this progression from 1970 to 2008 we have shown the rise in the current or nominal price, year by year, to what looked like an astronomical peak of more than $94 a barrel on average in 2008. On this basis we can say that in money of the day terms, the oil price rose by a factor of 56.6 times from 1970 to 2008 but in real terms, as we have defined it, the increase was only by a factor of 14.7 times.

Relationship between World Oil Prices and Oil Consumption 1970–2008

Figure 11.19 and Table 11.40 provide illustrations and statistics covering the full period from 1970 to 2008. The real oil prices expressed in constant US dollars of 2008 in the table show that they were actually rising slightly before the OPEC initiatives to increase crude export prices substantially in October 1973 and 1 January 1974. Consequently, the big annual increase in oil consumption also came to an end with the economic recession of 1974–5, following a synchronized boom ending in 1973, also having an adverse impact on oil demand.

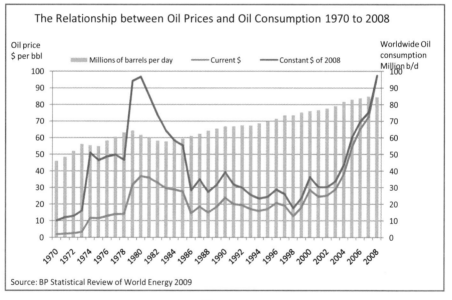

Figure 11.19

Table 11.40. Relationship between Real World Oil Price and Consumption 1970–2008

	Current $	Constant $ of 2008	Millions of barrels per day
1970	1.80	10.02	46.1
1971	2.24	11.97	48.6
1972	2.48	12.83	52.1
1973	3.29	16.01	56.3
1974	11.58	50.78	55.5
1975	11.53	46.34	55.0
1976	12.80	48.62	58.4
1977	13.92	49.65	60.6
1978	14.02	46.47	63.2
1979	31.61	94.13	64.4
1980	36.83	96.62	61.8
1981	35.93	85.38	59.9
1982	32.97	73.78	58.2
1983	29.55	64.08	57.9
1984	28.78	58.27	59.1
1985	27.56	55.23	59.4
1986	14.43	28.25	61.1
1987	18.44	34.92	62.4
1988	14.92	27.24	64.2
1989	18.23	31.63	65.6
1990	23.73	39.26	66.9
1991	20.00	31.73	66.9
1992	19.32	29.74	67.5
1993	16.97	25.45	67.4
1994	15.82	23.23	68.7

1995	17.02	24.29	69.8
1996	20.67	28.59	71.4
1997	19.09	25.91	73.6
1998	12.72	17.32	73.6
1999	17.97	23.60	75.3
2000	28.50	36.24	76.1
2001	24.44	30.14	76.8
2002	25.02	30.16	77.7
2003	28.83	33.75	79.1
2004	38.27	43.61	81.8
2005	54.52	60.10	83.1
2006	65.14	69.58	83.8
2007	72.39	75.14	84.9
2008	97.26	97.26	84.5

Source: BP *Statistical Review of World Energy* (2009) and database.

Nevertheless, oil consumption rose again quite rapidly over the four years 1976–9 to reach a new peak of 64.4 million barrels a day in the latter year. This seemed to imply that the OPEC price increases some years earlier had been sustainable. However, the further big price increases in 1979–80 brought about by unusually large oil company stock building, the Iranian Revolution and the outbreak of war between Iraq and Iran induced market anxiety about oil supplies.

Subsequent experience showed these oil prices to be unsustainable as world oil consumption/demand fell more than 10 per cent from its 1979 peak of 64.4 million b/d to 1983 and the real oil price fell 43 per cent or $41 a barrel in constant dollars of 2008 between 1980 and 1985.

After this an OPEC initiative to increase supplies to the market drove the oil price down to a new low in 1986 of only $28.25 a barrel in prices of 2008. Subsequently the market stabilized at around that level until 2004, being a little above or below it, allowing oil consumption to resume growing by just over 21 million b/d over twenty years from the low of 1983 to a new peak of 79.1 million b/d in 2003. This represented a somewhat uneven annual increase averaging 1.6 per cent p.a.

Thereafter, oil consumption increased over the next four years from 79.1 to 84.9 million b/d but the real oil price increased much more dramatically from over $32 a barrel in 2004 to over $97 on average in 2008. During the first six and a half months of 2008, fuelled by speculative excesses, the mid-July 2008 price collapsed from its then current peak of $147 a barrel, demonstrating once again the unsustainability of a price rise driven by market forces, in spite of Saudi Arabian and OPEC production volumes reaching new high levels over the years 2004 to 2008. We showed this graphically in Part I above.

We can summarize the changes in oil consumption relative to changes in the real oil price expressed in constant dollars of 2008 as in Table 11.41.

Table 11.41. Changes in Oil Consumption Relative to Changes in Real Oil Price

Duration	Years	World Oil Price (constant $ of 2008) % p.a.	World Oil Consumption Change (averages) % p.a.
10 years	1970–80	25.4	3.0
18 years	1980–98	-9.1	1.0
10 years	1998–2008	18.8	1.4
38 years	1970–2008	6.2 11.1 (money of the day)	1.6

Thus we have the comparatively perverse outcome of the longest middle period of eighteen years during which oil prices dropped dramatically for six years then stabilized for the next twelve years, leading to the lowest rate of increase in oil consumption over the full thirty-eight years. At the opposite extreme, oil consumption growth was strongest when the real oil price rose the most, from 1970 to 1980.

Changes in Oil Consumption and Oil Prices 1973–2008

Table 11.42 complements others in showing the changes for the world at large and for the leading economies. This serves to show up very clearly the remarkable change at world level, with oil consumption growing by over 8 million b/d from 1973 to 1979 but falling by almost 5 million b/d over the next six years to 1985. Growth then resumed by between 7.5 and 9.5 million b/d over the subsequent five-, ten- and seven-year periods to 2007 analysed in the table. Over the six years to 1985 the USA, the EU and Japan together accounted for much more than the total fall in oil consumption worldwide, collectively by more than 6.5 million b/d.

Table 11.42. Changes in Oil Consumption and Oil Prices in 16 Main Countries/ Areas, 1973–2007 (in 000s barrels per day)

	1973–9	1979–85	1985–90	1990–2000	2000–7	1979–2007
World	+8,056	-4,990	+7,464	+9,485	+8,880	+20,839
USA	+1,120	-2,712	+1,262	+2,713	+997	+2,260
EU	+367	-2,765	+811	+764	+172	-1,018
Japan	+163	-1,052	+869	+273	-526	-436
China	+796	-29	+525	+2,519	+3,223	+6,238
Former USSR	+1,998	+418	+47	-4,959	+300	-4,194
Russian Fed	N/A	N/A	+107	-2,546	+116	N/A
India	+159	+262	+316	+1,043	+494	+2,115
South Korea	+244	+57	+501	+1,191	+142	+1,891
Canada	+251	-378	+193	+175	+366	+356
Brazil	+367	+31	+214	+580	+136	+961
Mexico	+407	+307	+219	+452	+114	+1,092

Germany	+66	-710	+38	+55	-370	-987
Rest of world	+1,517	+ 28	+1,962	+3,502	+1,975	+7,467
Saudi Arabia	+189	+289	+226	+365	+618	+1,498
Total Middle East	+669	+843	+545	+1,232	+1,487	+4,107

Oil price $ per barrel	1973	1979	1985	1990	2000	2007	2008	% p.a. average change	
								1973–2007	1979–2007
Current $	3.29	31.61	27.56	23.73	28.50	72.39	97.26	9.5	3.0
$ constant of 2008	16.01	94.13	55.23	39.26	36.24	75.14	97.26	4.7	-0.8

Source: BP *Statistical Review of World Energy* (2009).

The other comment to be made here is to draw attention to the dramatic falls between 1990 and 2000 in the volume of oil consumption recorded in the former Soviet Union/Russian Federation. These amounted to almost 5 million b/d and more than 2.5 b/d respectively.

It can be seen that over the twenty-eight years to 2007 increases in oil consumption in Saudi Arabia and the Middle East as a whole have accounted for more than 7 per cent and almost 20 per cent of the worldwide total. Growth in the region amounted to more than 3.4 million b/d. At 6.47 million b/d in 2007 oil consumption in the region amounted to 7.6 per cent of the worldwide total.

Net Oil Importing and Exporting Countries in 2008

Figure 11.20 shows the relative and absolute positions of the leading oil importing and exporting regions and countries for world trade including crude oil, NGLs and refined products. Production peaked in the UK in 1999 and in Norway in 2001 and had fallen by a combined 2.33 million b/d by 2008. In spite of a net fall of 249,000 b/d in oil consumption among the nineteen original European member countries of the OECD from 2000 to 2008, this led to substantial rise in their net imports, exceeding 2 million b/d, to a net total of more than 11.7 million b/d in 2008.

Similarly, in the United States, oil production fell, but by just under 1 million b/d between 2000 and 2008. In Europe too, oil consumption fell by a similar margin, by 282,000 b/d over the same eight years. As a consequence, US net oil imports rose by 0.7 million b/d to 10.9 million b/d in 2008.

Even in 2008 the United States obtained slightly more of its oil from Canada and South and Central America (primarily Venezuela), in excess of 2.4 million b/d from each, than it did from the Middle East at just below that total. Likewise, Europe's oil imports came primarily from the former Soviet Union, over 6.4 million b/d in 2008, with the Middle East being in second place but a long way behind at 2.56 million b/d in 2008.

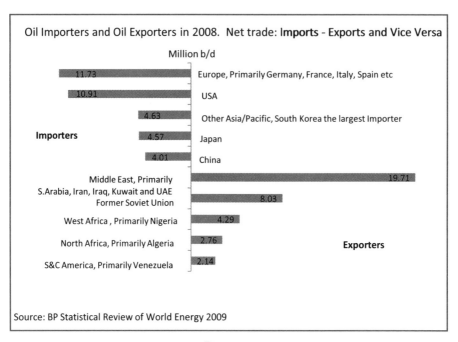

Figure 11.20

By contrast, Eastern destinations had become much the most important for Middle East oil in 2008 with this number one source of world oil trade having become the biggest supplier to India as well as the others shown in the chart, other Asia Pacific, Japan and China. The three latter each imported a total of more than 4 million b/d in 2008, with India at over 3 million b/d.

The Middle East region exported more than 20.13 million b/d of oil in 2008, accounting for 36.8 per cent of the total world trade of 54.6 million b/d. in 2008 89.1 per cent of Middle East oil exports were in the form of crude oil plus NGLs and 10.9 per cent in the form of refined products.

Japan was the country importing more Middle Eastern oil than any other at 3.96 million b/d in 2008 but the 'other Asia/Pacific' region as a whole took 4.8 million b/d, with South Korea being the largest among many countries. Next most important as Eastern destinations for Middle Eastern oil in 2008 were India at 2.17 and China at 1.84 million b/d.

Western destinations for Middle East oil, with Europe and the United States being dominant, were only just over 6 million b/d and 29.9 per cent of the total, with Eastern destinations accounting for 13.95 million b/d in 2008, or 69.3 per cent of all Middle Eastern oil exports, the small balance being unaccounted for in terms of destinations.

Middle East Crude and Product Exports Relative to Crude Spot Price and Exports of Crude and Products from Other Areas over Thirty Years

After the OPEC price increases of October 1973 and 1 January 1974 the spot price rose fairly gradually but seemingly sustainably until late 1978. Thereafter, stock building, the Iranian Revolution and the outbreak of war between Iraq and Iran resulted in a dramatic increase of spot and indeed official prices of crude plus netback values from Rotterdam. Though spot crude prices subsided fairly slowly from 1980 until 1985, the impact on Middle East exports of crude and products was quite dramatic, falling from 20.4 million b/d in 1979 to only 9.3 million b/d in 1985, i.e. more than 54 per cent. There was scarcely any change in crude and product exports from the rest of the world over this period. As a result of the sharp policy-induced fall in spot crude prices in 1986, Middle East exports gradually rose until in 2004–2008 they regained the volumes last seen in 1977–9. However, Middle East exports which had averaged over 58 per cent of worldwide oil exports in 1977–9 lost more than 20 percentage points, falling to a new low of 35.4 per cent in 2007, when the rest of the world's petroleum exports averaged 35.87 million b/d, or 82 per cent more than those from the Middle East. In incremental terms petroleum exports from the Middle East rose just 1.4 million b/d between 1998 and 2008 while those from all other parts of the world increased by 12.1 million b/d. The former Soviet Union contributed the largest increase, 4.62 million b/d over the ten years. The rise in spot crude prices which occurred between 2002 and July 2008 was not accompanied by a really dramatic rise in world oil consumption. Over the ten years to 2007 it varied between rises of 0.7 per cent and 2.2 per cent annually, except for 2004 when the rise was 3.5 per cent, but notably high for China at 16.7 per cent, or 970,000 b/d. Given the absence of a pronounced imbalance and only a marginal tightening in world oil supply and demand, the rise in spot prices through to July 2008 seems to be largely attributable to speculative excesses which fuelled other markets through 2007 and 2008, notably in the USA and UK. Perhaps significantly, 2008 was the first year in a decade that oil exports worldwide excluding the Middle East declined year on year, by the considerable margin of 1.38 million b/d. Exports from the Asia Pacific region were down 612,000 b/d and those from Mexico by 366,000 b/d. Figure 11.21 and Table 11.43 provide the annual details.

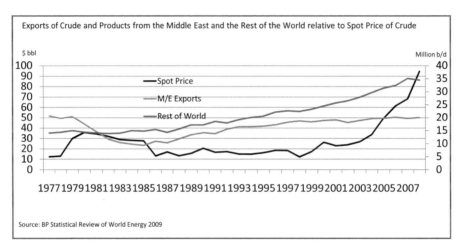

Figure 11.21

Table 11.43. Middle East Crude and Product Exports Relative to Crude Spot Price and Exports of Crude and Products from Other Areas over 30 Years

	Spot Price	Middle East Exports	Middle East % of World	World-Middle East	Total World
	$ bbl	million b/d	%	million b/d	
1977	12.38	20.7	59.6	14.1	34.8
1978	13.03	19.7	57.9	14.4	34.1

1979	29.75	20.4	57.8	15.0	35.4
1980	35.69	17.5	54.8	14.4	31.9
1981	34.32	14.6	51.0	14.1	28.7
1982	31.80	11.7	45.6	13.9	25.6
1983	28.78	10.4	42.5	14.0	24.4
1984	28.06	9.8	39.8	15.0	24.8
1985	27.53	9.3	38.7	14.8	24.1
1986	13.10	10.9	41.4	15.4	26.3
1987	16.95	10.3	41.9	14.3	24.6
1988	13.27	11.8	43.3	15.6	27.4
1989	15.62	13.4	43.8	17.2	30.6
1990	20.45	14.2	45.2	17.2	31.4
1991	16.63	13.8	42.8	18.5	32.3
1992	17.17	15.5	46.3	17.9	33.4
1993	14.93	16.5	46.1	19.2	35.7
1994	14.74	16.5	45.1	20.1	36.6
1995	16.10	16.7	44.7	20.6	37.3
1996	18.52	17.2	43.6	22.2	39.4
1997	18.23	18.2	44.5	22.7	40.9
1998	12.21	18.7	45.5	22.4	41.1
1999	17.25	18.3	44.1	23.3	41.6
2000	26.20	18.9	43.7	24.5	43.4
2001	22.81	19.1	42.6	25.7	44.8
2002	23.74	18.1	40.5	26.5	44.6
2003	26.78	18.9	40.5	27.9	46.8
2004	33.64	19.6	39.8	29.7	49.3
2005	49.35	19.8	38.7	31.4	51.2
2006	61.50	20.2	38.4	32.4	52.6
2007	68.19	19.7	35.9	35.1	54.8
2008	94.45	20.1	36.8	34.5	54.6

Source: BP *Statistical Review of World Energy* (June 2009).

External Trade in Oil: Comparison of USA and Europe 1997 to 2007

Net oil imports (crude + products) declined in both the USA and Western Europe between 1977 and 1987 on account of rising production of crude respectively primarily from the North Slope of Alaska and the North Sea. However, as production from both areas peaked subsequently then started to decline, so net oil imports started to rise to meet gradually increasing oil consumption. See Table 11.44.

Table 11.44. External Trade in Oil: Comparison of USA and Europe 1997–2007

	Net Oil Imports of Crude and Products 1,000 b/d	Net Oil Imports as a % of	
		oil consumption	primary energy consumption
USA			
1977	8,560	48.3	22.7
1987	5,500	35.4	14.6
1997	8,931	52.4	20.2
2007	12,194	63.9	25.5
Increase 1977 to 2007	+3634 +42.5%		
(Western) Europe*			
1977	12815	96.3	54.4
1987	6850	57.6	26.0

		W. Eur. 65.8	W. Eur. 28.8
1997*	8958	Eur. 59.9	Eur. 26.9
2007*	11680	W. Eur. 85.2	W. Eur. 31.9
		Eur. 77.1	Eur. 30.1
Decrease 1977	-1135		
to 2007	-8.9%		

Source: BP *Statistical Review of World Energy* (June 2008).

Note: In 1997 and 2007 Western Europe is now shown as Europe, a larger entity than formerly with the inclusion of the former Communist countries of Eastern Europe.

Over the thirty years the difference between the USA and Europe is quite stark. US net oil imports were more than 3.6 million b/d higher in 2007 than they had been in 1977, a rise of 42.5 per cent, whereas even in the enlarged Europe, they were more than 1.1 million b/d lower, a fall of 8.9 per cent. Similarly, as a proportion of both total oil and total primary energy usage, net oil imports were higher in 2007 than they had been in the United States in 1977 whereas in Europe they were lower.

International Oil Trade since 1980 and as a Proportion of World Oil Production

The international trade in oil since 1980 analysed over five-year periods shows the unique experience of what happened from 1980 to 1985 compared with anything which the world market has seen since. Over that period world exports fell 7.8 million b/d, and as a proportion of world oil production exports fell 8.8 percentage points. During each five-year period since 1985 the growth in world exports has been in the range of 5.9 to 7.8 million b/d. Exports worldwide as a proportion of world oil production rose during each of the four consecutive five-year periods from the low of 42.6 per cent in 1985 to 63.1 per cent in 2005 then further to 64.5 per cent in 2006 and 68.2 per cent in 2007 before falling back to 66.8 per cent in 2008 in response to the high average prices in that year and 66.2 per cent in 2009 associated with the recession. Nevertheless, world oil exports remained higher in volume than in any year up to 2006.

Table 11.45. International Trade in Oil since 1985

	World Oil Exports mn b/d	Exports as % of Production
1980	32.3	51.4
1985	24.5	42.6
1990	31.4	48.0
1995	37.3	54.7
2000	43.4	57.9
2005	51.2	63.1
2006	52.6	64.5
2007	55.6	68.2
2008	54.6	66.8
2009	52.9	66.2

The Concentration
of World Gas Reserves at End 2007

For natural gas alone the same four countries feature as for oil, with Qatar supplanting Saudi Arabia in third place. The four of them together account for 59.3 per cent of worldwide natural gas reserves. The next five countries in rank order account for 15.3 per cent of total reserves and the following eleven countries account for another 14.7 per cent. Thus these twenty countries between them hold almost 90 per cent of worldwide reserves of natural gas. It can also be noted that the four leading reserves countries still have much more bountiful reserves to production ratios in years than those groups of countries with smaller remaining reserves. See Tables 11.46 and 11.48.

Table 11.46. The Concentration of World Gas Reserves at End 2007 in Top 20 Countries

	Trillion Cubic Metres	Share of World Total	R:P Ratio in Years
1. Russian Federation	44.65	25.2%	73.5
2. Iran	27.80	15.7%	248.4
3. Qatar	25.60	14.4%	428.1
4. Saudi Arabia	7.17	4.0%	94.4

Total above 4	105.22	59.3%	123.1
Others with >1.0% of worldwide total			
5. UAE	6.09	3.4%	
6. USA	5.98	3.4%	
7. Nigeria	5.30	3.0%	
8. Venezuala	5.15	2.9%	
9. Algeria	4.52	2.5%	
Total next 5	27.04	15.3%	36.5
10. Iraq	3.17	1.8%	
11. Indonesia	3.0	1.7%	
12. Norway	2.96	1.7%	
13. Turkmenistan	2.67	1.5%	
14. Australia	2.51	1.4%	
15. Malaysia	2.48	1.4%	
16. Egypt	2.06	1.2%	
17. Kazakhstan	1.90	1.1%	
18. China	1.88	1.1%	
19. Kuwait	1.78	1.0%	
20. Uzbekistan	1.74	1.0%	
Total next 11	26.15	14.7%	48.1
Total Middle East	73.21	41.3%	205.8
Total world	177.36	100.0%	60.3

Source: BP *Statistical Review of World Energy* (June 2008).

Proved Gas Reserves: Changes during 2008 in Billions of Cubic Metres

The increases in world gas reserves were led by an OPEC country in 2008, i.e. Iran, with a rise of 1,215 billion cubic metres. In total, eight OPEC member countries increased their gas reserves by a gross 2,173.5 billion cubic metres (14.3 billion barrels of oil equivalent) but in Qatar there was a significant fall of 373.9 billion cubic metres, so that for OPEC as whole there was a net increase of just under 1,800 billion cubic metres.

Non-OPEC countries recorded gross increases of 915 billion cubic metres, led by the USA with a rise of 745.9 billion cubic metres. However, the increases were substantially offset to the extent of falls amounting to 809 billion cubic metres among twelve countries, led by declines of 420 billion cubic metres in reserves in Kazakhstan and 168 billion cubic metres in Turkmenistan. Germany and the UK were also significantly lower.

Thus the net increase of OPEC gas reserves in 2008 amounted to seventeen times as much as the net increase in all other countries worldwide so that by the end of the year OPEC countries accounted for 51.8 per cent of total world gas reserves, having risen from a low of 36.7 per cent in 1985. By contrast, the former Soviet Union accounted for a high of 39.7 per cent of world gas reserves as the dominant world number one when it disappeared as an entity in 1990, falling to 30.2 per cent in 2007 end year. Nevertheless, Russia as the pre-eminent member of the former Soviet Union still accounted for 26.9 per cent of the world's proved reserves at the beginning of 2009, according to the *Oil and Gas Journal*, followed by Iran with 15.9 per cent and Qatar with 14.3 per cent, i.e. together exceeding Russia. See Table 11.47.

Table 11.47. Proved Gas Reserves: Changes during 2008 (in billions of cubic metres)

Increases +		Decreases -	
OPEC			
Iran	1215.0	Qatar	373.9
Indonesia	338.8		
Kuwait	205.6		
Saudi Arabia	150.2		
Venezuela	130.5		
Libya	119.8		
Ecuador	8.8		
Nigeria	4.8		
	2173.5		373.9
OPEC net increase 1799.6			
NON-OPEC			
USA	745.9	Kazakhstan	420.0
Pakistan	91.4	Turkmenistan	168.0
Norway	71.4	Germany	78.4
New Zealand	4.3	UK	68.3
Croatia	2.0	Mexico	19.3
		Colombia	16.9
		Thailand	14.0
		Denmark	9.1

		Canada	8.3
		Argentina	4.2
		Peru	2.4
		France	0.3
	915.0		809.2
Non-OPEC Net Increase	105.8		
Worldwide Total Increase	3088.5	**Total Decrease**	1183.1
Net increase worldwide 1905.4			

Source: *Oil and Gas Journal* (22 Dec. 2008).

Note: 1 billion cubic feet = 0.028 billion cubic metres; 1 billion cubic metres = 6.60 million barrels of oil equivalent (changed from 6.29 in 2008).

Countries with Large[5] Proved Gas Reserves and an R:P Ratio of More than Forty Years at End 2008

This analysis of large holders of natural gas reserves and a reserves to production ratio of more than eighteen years covers only eleven countries worldwide, of which nine were OPEC members in 2008. This was in spite of our relaxation of the criteria for inclusion to only 3 trillion cubic metres of proved reserves of natural gas, equivalent to only some 4.5 billion barrels of oil.

There is a top group of just five countries with proved reserves exceeding 6.6 trillion cubic metres (or 10 billion barrels of oil equivalent) and also very long prospective lifespans exceeding seventy years at rates of production reported for 2008. Of these countries three were OPEC members in 2008: Iran, Qatar and Saudi Arabia. The other two were the Russian Federation and Turkmenistan.

The second group of sixty countries is made up entirely of OPEC members in 2008 having reserves of more than 3, and up to 6.6 trillion cubic metres. In terms of the rank order of their reserves base they were, in 2008, the UAE,

Nigeria, Venezuela, Algeria, Indonesia and Iraq. Indonesia ceased to be an OPEC member at the end of 2008, with its oil production declining to around 1 million b/d in that year and its oil R:P ratio falling to ten years.

In addition to the eleven countries listed above, the USA still had a reserves base of natural gas of 6.73 trillion cubic metres, which puts it into the first category above. But with its high production in 2008 of 582 billion cubic metres (only slightly less than that of the Russian Federation) its reserves to production ratio amounted to only 11.6 years, though its lifespan had increased since 1979 with proved reserves increasing rather more than production. In any event, the United States is never likely to be a net exporter of natural gas, only an importer, as it has been for many years. This is a principal reason for this comparative analysis of prospective as well as actual exporters of both oil and natural gas being limited in a world likely to continue demanding increasing quantities of both hydrocarbons, in spite of the constraining influences of climate change and global warming on rising energy usage. Figure 11.22 is a scatter diagram showing the gas reserves of these eleven countries relative to their reserves to production ratios, as at the end of 2008.

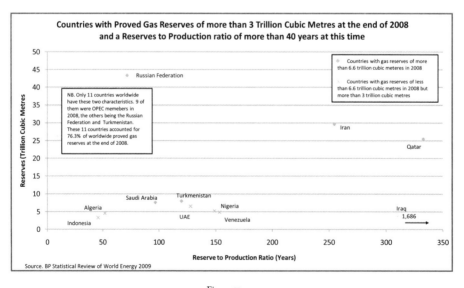

Figure 11.22

Leaving aside the special situation of the United States with still relatively bountiful reserves of conventional natural gas but limited lifespan and its consumption of gas already exceeding production, all the countries featuring in this analysis have a prospective lifespan much exceeding the eighteen years used for oil, in terms of the reserves to production ratio.

Scope for Potential Increases in Natural Gas Production

As we did for oil, for those countries still well-endowed with proved reserves of gas exceeding a sixty-year lifespan at 2008 production rates, we have looked at countries with a reserves to production ratio mostly far exceeding sixty years at the end of 2008. We show in Table 11.48 what the implications are for increased production of natural gas consistent with reducing the R:P ratio to this level and the increment in production from 2008 for each country.

Table 11.48. Leading Holders of Natural Gas Reserves and Production

Country	Production in 2008 $10\ 9m^3 =$ $106bbl$ oe		Reserves at end 2008 $1012m^3$	R:P Ratio in years	Production Implication to 60 years R:P $109m^3$	Implied Increase in Gas Production from 2008 $109m^3$
Russian Fed	601.7	3971.2	43.30	72.0	722.0	120.3
Iran	116.3	767.6	29.61	254.6	493.5	377.2
Qatar	76.6	505.6	25.46	332.4	424.4	347.8
Saudi Arabia	78.1	515.5	7.57	96.9	126.1	48.0
Turkmenistan	66.1	436.3	7.94	120.1	132.3	66.2
Top 5 Reserves > 6.6 × 1012m³ = 10 bn bbl o.e.	**938.8**	**6196.2**	**113.88**	**121.3**	**1898.3**	**959.5**

UAE	50.2	331.3	6.43	128.1	107.2	57.0
Nigeria	35.0	231.0	5.22	149.1	87.0	52.0
Venezuela	31.5	207.9	4.84	153.7	80.7	49.2
Algeria	86.5	570.9	4.50	52.1	Already below	Nil
Indonesia	69.7	460.0	3.18	45.7	Already below	Nil
Iraq	1.88	12.4	3.17	1686.2	52.8	50.9
6 countries with $<6.6\times10_{12}m^3$ but $>3\times10_{12}m^3$	274.8	1813.5	27.34	99.5	327.7	209.1
Total 11 countries	1213.6	8009.7	141.22	116.4	2226.0	1168.6
Former Soviet Union	793.7	5238.4	57.0	71.8	949.8	156.1

Source: BP *Statistical Review of World Energy* (June 2009).

The countries have been divided into two groups: those with proved gas reserves of more than 6.6 trillion cubic metres, of which there are only five worldwide, three being OPEC members: Iran, Qatar and Saudi Arabia. The others are the Russian Federation and Turkmenistan.

Though Russian gas reserves are larger than those of any other country, its reserves to production ratio, at only seventy-two years, reflects Russia's already high production volume exceeding 600 billion cubic metres, equivalent to a little less than 4 billion barrels of oil equivalent or 10.85 million b/d. coincidentally almost exactly equivalent to Saudi Arabia's oil production in 2008.

Because the reserves to production ratios for Iran and Qatar are so much higher than for Russia, given their much lower production volumes in 2008, their scope for increasing production volumes while still maintaining a hypothetical R:P ratio of sixty years is very much greater. The implied increase in gas production from these two countries alone, from 2008 levels, amounts to 725 billion cubic metres or 4785 billion barrels o.e., or 13.11 million b/d. In fact, Qatar increased its production of gas in 2009 by 16 per cent. Its R:P ratio fell to 284 years on the basis of unchanged reserves. The table does not include this assumption.

The second group of six countries with comparatively large gas reserves but less than 6.6 though more than 3 trillion cubic metres is made up wholly of OPEC member countries, as of 2008, i.e. prior to Indonesia leaving the group at the end of that year. All of them except Algeria and Indonesia had R:P ratios far in excess of the sixty years we have chosen as a benchmark. So reducing R:P ratios to this level for the other four OPEC countries in this category, results in another 209 billion cubic metres, i.e. 1380 billion barrels o.e or 3.78 million b/d.

For the eleven countries combined, consistent with a standard R:P ratio of sixty years, gas production could rise by 1,168 billion cubic metres from 2008 levels, i.e. more than 7.7 billion barrels o.e. or 21.13 million b/d o.e.

Of course, this is a comparatively high number compared with the 11.22 million b/d deriving from increased oil production from the six OPEC member countries analysed above if they were prepared to reduce their oil R:P ratios to sixty years from much higher levels for most of them, though less high than for Iran and Qatar for gas.

However, this comparative analysis for oil in Chapter 7 and gas here does serve to demonstrate the much greater potential for increasing gas production and exports than for oil, by about 88 per cent, consistent with an admittedly rather arbitrary choice of reducing reserves to production ratios to sixty years for those countries with higher ratios of either oil and/or gas, as at the end of 2008.

Natural Gas Production over Thirty Years to 2007

The top five countries accounted for 52.3 per cent of worldwide production in 2007 and the next fifteen countries for a further 30.8 per cent, together amounting to more than 83 per cent of the global total. The Russian Federation and the USA continue to dominate the worldwide production of natural gas but over the last twenty to thirty years growth has been rapid in Canada, Iran and Norway. Output is declining in the UK and the Netherlands, but given the low reserves to production ratios the prospects in Canada, Argentina and Mexico are not looking bright for the future production of natural gas in the western hemisphere, Venezuela excepted (R:P ratios of 153). See Table 11.49.

Table 11.49. Natural Gas Production over 30 Years to 2007 (billion cubic metres)

	1977	1987	1997	2007	R:P ratio in 2007 in years
Former Soviet Union	322.8	678.5	627.4	790.2	65.2
Russian Federation	N/A	507.7	532.6	607.4	71.3
USA	543.2	461.4	535.3	545.9	12.3
Canada	80.8	78.5	168.6	183.7	8.9
Iran	21.0	19.0	47.0	111.9	251.4
Norway	2.9	29.7	43.0	89.7	32.1
Top 5 countries in rank order in 2007 **1096.3** **i.e not including Former Soviet Union**			1326.5	1538.6	53.7
% of world production **59.1**	**N/A**		59.3%	52.3%	
Algeria	8.7	41.7	71.8	83.0	54.2
Saudi Arabia	8.0	21.0	45.3	75.9	96.2
United Kingdom	39.1	45.3	85.9	72.4	4.7
China	12.0	13.9	22.7	69.3	32.6
Turkmenistan	N/A	82.2	16.1	67.4	36.1
Indonesia	5.7	32.6	65.7	66.7	45.0
Netherlands	81.4	62.3	67.1	64.5	21.6
Malaysia	–	15.6	38.6	60.5	39.5
Qatar	N/A	5.6	17.4	59.8	425.8
Uzbekistan	N/A	37.1	47.8	58.5	27.2

Next 10 countries	N/A	357.3	478.4	678.0	79.1
% of world production		19.3	21.4%	23.1%	
UAE	3.2	7.6	36.3	49.2	130.9
Egypt	N/A	5.3	11.6	46.5	44.5
Mexico	20.6	27.7	31.7	46.2	11.0
Argentina	7.6	18.7	27.4	44.8	9.8
Australia	9.3	19.2	29.8	40.0	60.3
Next 5 countries	N/A	78.5	136.8	226.7	52.4
% of world production	N/A	4.2	6.1%	7.7%	
Worldwide production	1356.4	1855.7	2235.7	2940.0	

Source: BP *Statistical Review of World Energy* (June 2008).

Among these top twenty gas-producing countries six really stand out from the others in terms of big reserves enabling them to make very large increases in production. In terms of reserves to production ratios, in rank order, they are Qatar, Iran, the UAE, Turkmenistan,[6] Saudi Arabia and the Russian Federation. Among these, Qatar increased its output in 2009, having almost quadrupled its output during the ten years to 2008. Iran has increased its output by a factor of 2.3 times during this period and the UAE has scope to do likewise during the next ten years, if the demand for exports is there. Turkmenistan is now in a similar position. Saudi Arabia is concentrating on utilizing its gas production for domestic purposes in its petrochemical, other industrial and electricity generating sectors in particular, thus maximizing the use of its oil reserves and production for export. The Russian Federation is in the fortunate position of having the existing largest reserves base of natural gas to increase its total exports to East and/or West and to fuel domestic consumption which has still not, in recent years, regained the peak of 431 billion cubic metres it reached in 1991.

Thus in contrast to the western hemisphere, the eastern hemisphere looks potentially well supplied to increase its dependence on natural gas very significantly during the coming decades, inclusive of rising demand in China.

World Natural Gas Production Relative to World Oil Production

The production of natural gas expressed as a proportion of world oil production rose sharply from 37.5 per cent in 1979 to 50 per cent in 1985 as oil output fell during this period. Subsequently, as gas production rose more rapidly than that of crude oil, it became relatively more important, amounting to over 62 per cent of the volume of world oil production in 2007. This was achieved as it became relatively more competitive and economic than oil, as discussed later in this book, particularly as oil prices rose sharply from 2004 to mid-2008. In the latter year, a change in the conversion factor in favour of gas led to a further rise in the volume of gas production worldwide expressed in terms of oil equivalent, as well as gas production rising relative to oil. Thus in 2008 gas represented 67.6 per cent of world oil equivalent in production terms. See Table 11.50.

Table 11.50. World Natural Gas Production Shown Relative to World Oil Production

	Oil million barrels	Natural Gas bu cubic metres = million bbl. o.e.		Gas as % of Oil
1979	24,108	1,439.3 =	9,053	37.6
1985	20,977	1,668.8 =	10,496.8	50.0
1990	23,899	1,992.9 =	12,535	52.5
2000	27,419	2,412.4 =	15,174	55.3
2007	29,726	2,945 =	18,524	62.2
2008	29,946	3,065.6 =	20,233	67.6

Source: BP *Statistical Review of World Energy* (2009).

Note: Change in conversion factor in 2008 gas to oil, 6.60, instead of 6.29 used previously.

The Twelve Largest Gas Consuming Countries in 2007

The United States was the largest gas consumer worldwide in 2007 accounting for 22.3 per cent of the total, followed by the Russian Federation at 15 per cent. However, given its premier position as the largest holder of proven gas reserves it is not surprising that Russia recorded the largest rise in gas consumption over the ten years to 2007 with 13.1 per cent of the worldwide total, followed by Iran in second place at 9.6 per cent, also reflecting its second place in rank order of gas reserves worldwide. China, too, is starting to show an influence in the world gas market in third place, having increased its consumption by 47.6 billion cubic metres over the ten years to 2007, accounting for 7 per cent of the worldwide increase over this period. Evidently, China could become a significant gas importer in the medium to long term, particularly as gas represented only 3.7 per cent of China's energy consumption in 2008, even after quadrupling in volume over the previous ten years. Indeed it would be surprising of China did not move up into third or fourth place among the world's leading gas consuming countries by 2020 from its position as tenth in 2007. See Table 11.51.

Table 11.51. The 12 Largest Gas Consuming Countries in 2007

	Billion m3 in 2007	% of World	Change 1997 to 2007 bn m3	% of World
USA	652.9	22.3	+9.1	1.3
Russian Federation	438.8	15.0	+88.4	13.1
Iran	111.8	3.8	+64.7	9.6
Canada	94.0	3.2	+6.8	1.0
UK	91.4	3.1	+6.9	1.0
Japan	90.2	3.1	+26.1	3.9
Germany	82.7	2.8	+3.5	0.5

Italy	77.8	2.7	+24.7	3.6
Saudi Arabia	75.9	2.6	+30.6	4.5
China	70.3	2.4	+47.6	7.0
Ukraine	64.6	2.2	-9.7	-
Mexico	54.1	1.9	+21.8	3.2
Top 12	1904.5	65.2	320.5	47.4
European Union	481.9	16.5	+81.2	12.0
OECD	1454.3	49.8	+198.8	29.4
Former USSR	631.9	21.6	+112.8	16.7
Total World	2921.9	100.0	+676.8	100.0

Source: BP *Statistical Review of World Energy* (June 2008).

Natural Gas Consumption 1979–2007

World gas consumption more than doubled over the twenty-eight years to 2007, rising at an average annual rate of 2.4 per cent (see Table 11.52). Growth in the USA, the EU and the former Soviet Union was less than this, with consumption in the latter actually falling by 111 billion cubic metres from 1990 to 2000.

Table 11.52. Natural Gas Consumption 1979–2007 (billions of cubic metres)

	World	Former USSR	USA	EU	Japan	Middle East	Rest of World
1979	1438.0	360.3	573.2	270.7	20.3	40.1	173.4
1980	1450.9	371.3	562.9	272.0	24.1	35.3	185.3
1985	1661.9	544.1	489.3	296.5	38.3	60.5	233.2
1990	1980.7	662.9	542.9	326.7	48.1	95.5	304.6

2000	2437.3	551.9	660.7	440.4	72.3	185.4	526.6
2007	2921.9	631.9	652.9	481.9	90.2	299.4	765.6
Change 1979 to 2007	+1483.9	+271.6	+79.7	+211.2	+69.9	+259.3	+592.2
Annual average % change over 28 years	+2.4	+2.0	+0.5	+2.1	+5.5	+7.4	+5.4

Source: BP *Statistical Review of World Energy* (2008).

By contrast, gas consumption rose rapidly by more than 5 per cent on average each year over the twenty-eight years in Japan and the rest of the world. Unsurprisingly, growth in the Middle East was the fastest at 7.4 per cent annually and accounting for 17.5 per cent of worldwide growth over the period. Over the seven years to 2007 growth in gas consumption in the region was accounted for mainly by Iran, Saudi Arabia and the UAE. Gas consumption increased from 42 per cent of primary energy in the Middle East to 48 per cent in 2008.

Comparison of Natural Gas and Crude Oil Prices

Natural gas prices, LNG to Japan and mainly pipeline supplies to Europe and the US, remained comparatively stable over much of the twenty-year period from 1985 to 2003/4. But then, in the latter year, as crude oil prices started to rise quite sharply above the level they were at in 1985 in terms of current dollars per million BTUs, so too did the price of natural gas to some extent, given a linkage between the two. This can be seen in the comparative analysis shown below for the six years 2003 to 2008, with gas market prices in the three major locations expressed as differentials from the crude oil price cif to OECD countries. Perhaps more immediately comprehensible is Table 11.53 which shows the differentials in terms of percentages. As crude oil prices rose continuously and substantially from 2003 onwards, and in spite of the high levels of OPEC oil production from 2004 through 2007, so the percentage differential for LNG delivered to Japan widened as its gas imports became increasingly economic *vis-à-vis* crude oil. For Europe the same was true from 2003 to 2005 but then there was a blip in 2006 before the differential widened to more than 25 per cent again, as it had done in 2004 and 2005. In the United States the differential oscillated remarkably from an advantage in favour of gas of almost 43 per cent in 1990 to a disadvantage of 15 per cent against oil in 2003. However, by 2006, 2007 and 2008 the US price differential in favour of natural gas *vis-à-vis* crude oil became greater than in either Europe or Japan as crude oil prices moved to new high levels. In none of these three major gas markets did gas prices move commensurately, but by 2008 the competitive price of natural gas was much greater in the US than in Europe or Japan, both absolutely and relatively as the volume of gas produced from shale increased.

Table 11.53. Gas Prices Expressed as Differentials from Crude Oil Price cif (US$ per mn BTUs)

	Crude oil pricecif to OECD countries	LNG Japancif	European Unioncif	US Henry Hub
2003	4.89	-0.12	-0.49	+0.74
2004	6.27	-1.09	-1.71	-0.42
2005	8.74	-2.69	-2.79	+0.05
2006	10.66	-3.52	-1.97	-3.90
2007	11.95	-4.22	-3.02	-5.00
2008	16.76	-4.21	-4.15	-7.91
Competitive advantage of natural gas in 2008, % price of gas less than oil		-25.1%	-24.8%	-47.8%

Thus by 2007 the competitive advantage of gas had become very pronounced, accentuated in 2008 in the United States when crude oil prices rose quite dramatically until mid-July of that year, mainly accounted for by speculative pressures by commodity buyers (reviewed elsewhere in this book). Figure 11.23 illustrates the relative position of gas prices in those major markets.

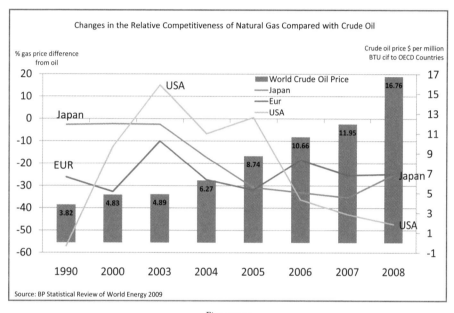

Figure 11.23

We should add that until 2003 the US gas price had consistently been below the price of crude oil to OECD countries, but between 2002 and 2003 the US gas price rose by 69 per cent while the Canadian price in Alberta (on which the US depends for some of its supplies) rose even more dramatically by 88 per cent from one year to the next, while the crude oil price increased by only 17.3 per cent. Another longer period analysis of comparative prices of crude oil and natural gas in 1985, 1990, 2000 and 2007 is shown in Table 11.54.

Table 11.54. Comparison of Natural Gas and Crude Oil Prices

$ per million BTUS	LNG Japan cif	European Union cif	USA Henry Hub	Crude Oil OECD Countries cif
1985	5.23	3.83	N/A	4.75
1990	3.64	2.82	1.64	3.82
2000	4.72	3.25	4.23	4.83
2007	7.73	8.93	6.95	11.95
Lowest prices reported over this 23-year period	3.05 in 1998	1.80 in 1999	1.49 In 1991	2.16 in 1998
Highest prices reported over this 23-year period	7.73 in 2007	8.93 in 2007	8.79 in 2005	11.95 in 2007

Source: BP *Statistical Review of World Energy* (2008).

N/A = Not Available.

Natural Gas Worldwide Production, Exports and Imports in 2008

Worldwide production of natural gas in 2007 was estimated at 2,945 billion cubic metres and 3,065 bcm in 2008. This is equivalent to 18.5 billion barrels of oil equivalent or 50.66 million barrels per day, representing more than 62 per cent of world oil production in 2007. This is a fairly dramatic comparative increase since 1979. This increased to 67.6 per cent in 2008, precisely 30 percentage points more over the twenty-nine years.

Total exports of natural gas in 2007 amounted to 776 billion cubic metres or 26.4 per cent of worldwide production in that year. The principal gas-exporting countries were the Russian Federation, Canada, Norway and the Netherlands, all by pipeline, each with 50 billion cubic metres or more. Qatar led the LNG exporters, followed by Malaysia, Indonesia, Algeria, Nigeria and Australia, in that order. Total exports by pipeline amounted to almost 550 billion cubic metres or 18.7 per cent of worldwide gas production. LNG exports exceeded 226 billion cubic metres in total, or 7.7 per cent of world production. The principal gas-importing countries were the USA, Germany, Italy, France, Turkey and the UK, in that order, while Japan led the LNG-importing countries, followed by South Korea, Spain and the USA. Table 11.55 shows the statistical detail of international gas trade by pipeline and LNG in 2007, together with the principal exporting and importing countries.

Table 11.55. Natural Gas Worldwide Production, Exports and Imports in 2007 (billion cubic metres)

	Production in 2007	Total Exports in 2007		
		By pipeline	By LNG	Total
World	2940.0	549.67	226.41	776.08
% of production		18.7%	7.7%	26.4%
Principal exporters	Russian Federation	147.53		
	Canada	107.30		
	Norway	86.05		
	Netherlands	50.06		
	Algeria	34.03		
	USA	22.01		
	Germany	16.38		
	Qatar		38.48	
	Malaysia		29.79	
	Indonesia		27.74	
	Algeria		24.67	
	Nigeria		21.16	
	Australia		20.04	

	Trinidad & Tobago		18.15	
	Total above	463.36	180.23	
Principal importers	USA	108.90		
	Germany	83.72		
	Italy	72.45		
	France	33.76		
	Turkey	30.59		
	UK	28.00		
	Belgium	19.34		
	Netherlands	18.86		
	Japan		88.82	
	South Korea		34.39	
	Spain		24.18	
	USA		21.82	
	Total above	395.6	169.21	

Source: BP *Statistical Review of World Energy* (2007).

Table II.56. China: Oil, 1997–2008 – A Rising Shortfall (1,000 b/d)

	oil consumption	oil production	Difference: Shortfall Consumption-Production
1997	4371	3211	1160
1998	4413	3212	1201
1999	4671	3213	1458
2000	4974	3252	1722

2001	5116	3306	1810
2002	5556	3346	2210
2003	6073	3401	2672
2004	7088	3481	3607
2005	7271	3627	3644
2006	7687	3684	4003
2007	8066	3743	4323
2008	8293	3795	4498
%p.a. growth avarage 1997-2008	**6.0**	**1.5**	**13.1**

Source: BP *Statistical Review of World Energy (*June 2009*)*.
*Includes Hong Kong

Table 11.57. Annual % Rates of Change in Chinese Primary Energy Consumption over 10 Years to 2008 and Total Consumption

	% change year on year	total consumption mn m.t.o.e
1999	1.9	950.9
2000	3.4	983.4
2001	3.7	1020.0
2002	5.8	1079.1
2003	15.9	1250.5
2004	16.2	1453.4
2005	9.7	1595.1
2006	9.5	1747.1
2007	8.1	1888.3
2008	7.3	2026.3

Source: BP *Statistical Review of World Energy* (June 2009).

By 2008 gas exports by pipeline had risen by 6.8 per cent to 587 billion cubic metres but the trade in LNG was virtually unchanged from the year before. The world trade in natural gas had increased to 814 billion cubic metres, 27 per cent of worldwide production. This proportion seems bound to increase, given the geographical distribution of world gas reserves and areas of potential demand. Also, this estimate of inter-area world gas trade compares with 67 per cent of world oil production moving into international trade. During 2008 the one really significant development was the export by pipeline of 15.4 billion cubic metres from Qatar to its neighbour, the UAE.

The 'Lost Decade'
in the Former Soviet Union

Following the demise of the former Soviet Union the contrast between the falls in economic activity and in the energy sector in both the Russian Federation and the larger ex-USSR or Commonwealth of Independent States (CIS) and the rest of the world over the decade 1990 to 2000 is quite dramatic. In the Russian Federation gross domestic product fell almost 33 per cent while in the rest of the world it rose by 33 per cent. Figure 11.24 gives the full comparative details over the decade.

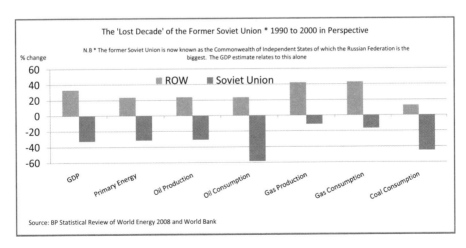

Figure 11.24

In the former Soviet Union primary energy consumption fell by 31.6 per cent while in the rest of the world it increased by almost 24 per cent, reflecting more efficient use of energy in the latter. A similar relationship is in evidence for oil production. The drop in oil consumption in the former Soviet Union was the most remarkable statistic, falling by 58 per cent, almost double the fall of 30.7 per cent recorded for oil production over the ten years, hence releasing more oil supplies for export, by a margin of more than 1.4 million b/d.

In spite of being the biggest holder of proven gas reserves worldwide its production of this resource fell 11 per cent and consumption of it by 16.7 per cent, even as both production and consumption of gas increased by more than 42 per cent in the rest of the world over these ten years.

Coal consumption fell by 45 per cent even as it rose by 13 per cent in the rest of the world. The data are shown in the accompanying chart.

The political, economic and energy sector in the former Soviet Union had a depressing effect on the statistics for the world as a whole. This adverse impact was offset only to an extent by the fast growth of the Chinese economy where growth of gross domestic product averaged 10.4 per cent annually from 1990 to 2000. However, Chinese growth of primary energy was far lower at only 3.5 per cent p.a. on average during this decade, an increase of only 286.5 million tonnes of oil equivalent compared with a reduction in the former Soviet Union of 483.9 million tonnes of oil equivalent.

China: The Emerging Colossus

A Special Case for Rising Energy, Oil and Gas Demand, with Worldwide Implications for the Future

China represents a special case in terms of primary energy and incremental use of it, in particular, during recent years. The same is true of its remarkable economic growth average of more than 10 per cent p.a., while coal remains dominant in the Chinese energy mix. The slow growth of its oil production, averaging only 1.7 per cent p.a. from 1998 to 2008, has fallen a long way behind the average growth of oil consumption in China which averaged 6.5 per cent p.a. over the same period. Thus the shortfall in Chinese oil production relative to its oil consumption increased from 1.16 million b/d in 1997 to almost 4.5 million b/d, in 2008, a rise of more than 3.3 million b/d or an annual rate of increase of 13.1 per cent. If this annual rate of increase were to continue until 2018, Chinese oil imports would rise to 16.8 million b/d in that year, assuming worldwide supply availability. The economic downturn of 2008–9 had little effect on China.

In fact, its oil production actually fell by 2.3 per cent in 2009 and oil consumption rose 6.3 per cent. Its deficit in terms of oil consumption outstripping oil production increased by 642,000 b/d, or 14.3 per cent between 2008 and 2009, with its oil imports actually rising by 734,000 b/d or 16.7 per cent between these two years. At 5.13 million b/d in 2009, Chinese oil imports already represented 9.7 per cent of the total volume of oil entering world trade in that year.

While Chinese production of natural gas has risen at the comparatively fast pace of 12.6 per cent p.a. from 1998 to 2008 and its reserves to production ratio of 32.3 years represents no short-term constraint, the fact is that natural gas still accounts for only 3.7 per cent of Chinese energy consumption. Also, Chinese gas consumption has risen even faster, at an average rate of 13.6 per cent annually over the ten years to 2008, with consumption exceeding production every year since 2002, with the shortfall being 9.5 per cent by 2008. Potential long-pipeline supplies of gas from the Russian Federation, and perhaps Turkmenistan, Kazakhstan and Uzbekistan too, to China, could alleviate the evident medium- to long-term upward pressure on world oil supplies within a ten-year time horizon, given the scenario outlined above. Gas rather than oil or coal contributing to rising Chinese energy needs could also contribute to that country's contribution to confronting the threat of global warming and climate change. Likewise, the rise in the share of hydro-electricity at the expense of coal is a move in the right direction, given the international pressures on China related to climate change and energy related CO_2 emissions.

Whatever improvements in CO_2 emissions can be achieved through the introduction of cleaner coal burning technology could alleviate such problems and enable China to continue its relatively heavy reliance on the burning of coal for electricity generation and other uses.

The two truly exceptional years were 2003 and 2004. Annual increments in Chinese coal consumption have fallen every year since 2003. It can be seen that the annual gas increment in Chinese energy consumption increased each year from 2002 until 2007 and seems as if it may match that of oil soon. Hydro-electricity has become quite important, accounting for 7.8 per cent of the rise in Chinese energy consumption over the ten years to 2008, but is subject to considerable annual fluctuations, with implications for the alternative fossil fuels used to generate Chinese electricity. The increasing dominance in the growth of both Chinese coal and Chinese primary energy consumption as a whole since 2000 is illustrated in Figure IV.6, relative to the worldwide increase in primary energy consumption. Tables II.56–8 provide the main statistical detail.

Table 11.58. Annual Changes in Chinese Energy over 10 Years to 2008 (million tonnes o.e.)

	Coal	Oil	Gas	Hydro	Nuclear	Total PE
1999	+3.8	+13.0	+1.4	-1.0	+0.2	+17.5
2000	+11.0	+14.4	+2.5	+4.2	+0.4	+32.5
2001	+15.1	+6.4	+2.6	+12.5	+0.2	+36.6
2002	+33.0	+20.6	+1.5	+2.4	+1.7	+59.1
2003	+140.5	+24.4	+3.3	-1.0	+4.1	+171.4
2004	+129.9	+49.6	+5.9	+15.8	+1.6	+202.9
2005	+117.6	+7.4	+6.4	+9.8	+0.6	+141.7
2006	+114.8	+19.3	+8.6	+8.8	+0.4	+152.0
2007	+99.1	+17.8	+11.5	+11.2	+1.7	+141.2
2008	+92.2	+11.4	+10.3	+22.6	+1.4	+138.0
Total over 10 years	+757.0	+184.3	+54.0	+85.3	+12.3	+1092.9
Net % of total	69.3	16.9	4.9	7.8	1.1	100.0

China: Natural Gas 1997 to 2008

Chinese production of natural gas has risen at a comparatively fast pace of 11.8 per cent p.a. average in recent years but the reserves to production ratio of only 32.3 years suggests it may not be possible to sustain this over a long period unless substantial additions to reserves are proven. Though Chinese gas reserves rose over the ten years to 2008 their lifespan was reduced as production increased more rapidly. Its R:P ratio fell from 58.8 in 1998. See Table 11.59.

Table 11.59. China: Natural Gas 1997–2008

	Reserves bn m³	Production bn m³ x
1997		22.7
1998		23.3
1999		25.2
2000		27.2
2001		30.3
2002		32.7
2003		35.0
2004		41.5
2005		49.3
2006		58.6
2007		69.2
2008	2460	76.1

Source: BP *Statistical Review of World Energy* (June 2008).

Reserves:production ratio = 32.3.

Coal in China: Reserves, Production and Consumption 1997–2007

China's 62.2 billion tonnes of hard coal reserves is approximately equivalent to 41.5 billion tonnes of oil. Thus at the rate of Chinese production in 2008 its reserves to production ratio for hard coal amounts to 29.3 years, theoretically adequate to permit production to continue to increase quite rapidly for some years to come. This is based on the probably unrealistic assumption that all Chinese coal production and consumption currently is of anthracite and bituminous hard coal, which may mean the following text presents an unduly pessimistic picture of prospects for Chinese coal over the period to 2020.[7] However, if Chinese coal production continued to rise at an average annual rate of 10 per cent, as it has since 2000, then production over the ten years to 2018 would amount to 24.8 billion tonnes o.e. over the decade and more than 3.6 billion tonnes o.e. in 2018. If no additional reserves were proven in the meantime, the ratio of Chinese reserves of hard coal to this volume of production would fall to less than five years. This suggests that Chinese coal production rising at 10 per cent p.a. may be unsustainable for as long as ten years. Evidently, this has implications for a range of possible options or some combination of them: use of lower grade Chinese sub-bituminous coal and lignite; hard coal imports from the US West Coast, eastern Russia, Australia and South Africa; or oil and/or gas imports from the Middle East and Russia via Siberia or from Southeast Asia and substantial improvements in the efficiency of coal use in China; or lower economic growth. Even in 2009, Chinese coal consumption rose by 9.3 per cent, or 132 million tonnes of oil equivalent. In spite of Chinese coal production continuing to exceed consumption by a small margin in 2009, there are reports of substantial Chinese coal imports in 2010.

Chinese coal production in 2008 was 1,414.5 million tonnes of oil equivalent, representing 42.5 per cent of the worldwide total, up from 28.2 per cent in 1998. Also, the implication of the 10 per cent p.a. growth of Chinese coal production is that it would exceed the worldwide total as of 2008 as early as 2017. See Table 11.60.

Table 11.60. Coal in China: Reserves, Production and Consumption 1998–2008

Reserves	Anthracite & bituminous bn tonnes	Sub-bituminous & lignite bn tonnes
China	62.2	52.3
% of world	15.1	12.6
Ref. USA	109.0	129.4
Russian Federation	49.1	107.9
India	54.0	4.6
South Africa	30.4	-
Australia	36.8	39.4
	411.3	414.7

Chinese Coal	Production mn tonnes o,e.	Consumption* mn tonnes o,e
1998	628.7	656.3
1999	645.9	660.1
2000	656.7	671.1
2001	697.6	686.2
2002	733.7	719.2
2003	868.4	859.7
2004	1012.1	989.6
2005	1120.0	1107.2
2006	1205.1	1222.0
2007	1282.4	1321.1
2008	1414.5	1413.3
% p.a. growth average over 10 years	8.4	8.0
	10.1% p.a. since 2000	9.8%

Source: BP *Statistical Review of World Energy* (June 2009).
*included Hong Kong.

China: the longer term historical perspective

The Chinese economy in general and the energy sector in particular are rapidly becoming dominant in the world at large. Figures 11.25 and 11.26 illustrate this by reference to the remarkable Chinese growth rates.

Its gross domestic product (GDP) in constant US dollars of 2000 grew at relatively modest rates of only 6.7 per cent on average each year from 1965 to 1973 from a very low base and then by 6.0 per cent annually from 1973 to 1979. In both 1965 and still in 1973 Chinese GDP had represented only 0.8 per cent of worldwide GDP to the nearest one decimal place (actually 0.75 to 0.84).

By 1979 the first full year after Deng Xiaoping assumed power in China and

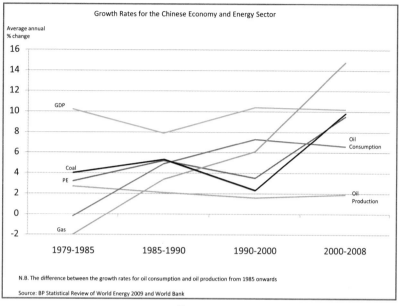

Figure 11.25

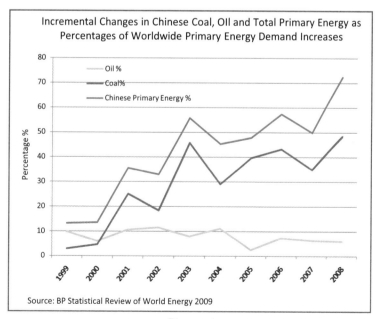

Figure 11.26

started to introduce economic reforms, Chinese GDP represented a full 1.0 per cent of the worldwide total. Subsequently Chinese GDP represented 1.5 per cent of the worldwide total in 1985, 1.8 per cent in 1990, 3.7 per cent in the year 2000 and 7.5 per cent in 2008.[8] This rapid advance reflected an average annual growth rate of 10.2 per cent over the full twenty-nine years from 1979 to 2008 with annual average growth over the four periods within it being as in Table 11.61.

Table 11.61. Growth in Chinese GDP (% p.a.)

1979–85	1985–90	1990–2000	2000–8
10.2	7.9	10.4	10.2
			(9.6, incl. Hong Kong & Macao)

Expressed another way we can say that while the world economy expanded by 4.2 times in real terms, with GDP expressed in constant US dollars of the year 2000, the Chinese economy expanded by a multiple of 36.3 times from 1965 to 2008, a forty-three-year period (based on World Bank data). Based on World Bank estimates, we can say that China accounted for 8.3 per cent of the growth in the world economy from 1979 to 2000 but this proportion rose remarkably to 17.8 per cent of world economic growth in real terms over the eight years to 2008 compared with 22.2 per cent of the increase accounted for by the United States over this most recent period. At this point in time the US economy remained much larger than the Chinese economy.

Chinese consumption of primary energy has grown more erratically than its gross domestic product. From 1965 to 1973 it grew at 6.3 per cent on average each year, then 6.9 per cent annually over the next six years to 1979. Then, following the large oil price increases of 1979–80, the Chinese managed to reduce the growth rate of primary energy consumption in total to an annual average rate of only 3.2 per cent over the next six years to 1985, followed by an average rise to 5.2 per cent over the five years to 1990. The average rate then fell back again to only 3.5 per cent each year to 2000 but then rose quite dramatically to 9.5 per cent annually over the next eight years to 2008, more than doubling from less than one to more than 2 billion tonnes of oil equivalent. The consequence of these changes can be seen in the energy coefficients for China (see Table 11.62).

Table 11.62. Chinese Energy Efficiency (PE/GDP)

1965–73	1973–9	1979–85	1985–90	1990–2000	2000–8
0.94	1.15	0.31	0.66	0.34	0.93

The Chinese share of worldwide primary energy consumption rose consistently over the thirty-five years to 2000 but then rose quite dramatically over the eight years to 2008, as can be seen in Table 11.63.

Table 11.63. Chinese % Share of Worldwide Primary Energy Consumption

1965	1973	1979	1985	1990	2000	2007	2008	2009
4.8	5.2	6.6	7.6	8.6	10.6	17.0	17.9	19.7

Thus China's share of worldwide primary energy consumption at 17.9 per cent far exceeds its share of world gross domestic product at only 7.5 per cent in 2008. Even over the twenty-nine years from 1979 its energy consumption mix had not changed dramatically while the total had increased by 4.5 times.

Table 11.64. % Shares of Each Type of Energy in Chinese Consumption Mix

	Oil	Gas	Coal	Hydro	Nuclear
1979	21.7	2.9	73.0	2.5	Nil
2008	19.3	3.7	69.7	6.5	0.8

Change in % points	-2.4	+0.8	-3.3	+4.0	+0.8

Coal remains China's predominant form of energy, its slight fall of 3.3 percentage points over this lengthy period fully offset by the large comparative rise in hydro-electricity. An actual fall in oil's share was partially offset by a small percentage rise in natural gas use and an initial contribution from nuclear electricity during this long period.

Even though oil's share of Chinese energy consumption fell, as noted above, the volume of oil consumption increased by more than seven times between 1973 and 2008, increasing at an uneven annual average rate of 5.8 per cent over the thirty-five years.

The significant point is that China's oil consumption growth has accelerated to 6.5 per cent p.a. during the ten years to 2008 while its growth in production has averaged only 1.7 per cent annually during this period. This has given rise to a rapidly increasing shortfall between the two, averaging 13.1 per cent annually. China's proven crude oil reserves at end 2008 represent only 11.2 times that year's production, falling from 17.2 years in 1988 and 14.2 years in 1998. This is a quite significant rate of decline, given the rather modest rate of increase in China oil production (see graph), followed by a fall of -2.8 per cent in 2009.

OPEC: Justification and Rationale

OPEC has often been criticized and lampooned in Western media with cartoons and text portraying it as a monopoly or oligopoly operating to increase oil prices by controlling oil production or supplies to the detriment of the interests of oil-importing countries and worldwide economic growth. What are the facts, as we observed the fiftieth anniversary of OPEC's foundation in September 2010?

During its first ten years, export prices of oil entering world trade remained very low and falling in real terms while the oil industry continued to be dominated by the major transnational oil companies, popularly known as the Seven Sisters. Yet oil-exporting countries generally were and remained heavily dependent on income from their exports of 'black gold' for generating economic growth. Many of the OPEC member countries have few natural resources other than oil and gas with which to improve the living standards of their people. Yet many oil-importing countries were already levying comparatively heavy taxes on oil products,[9] notably for gasoline, as long ago as the 1960s. In spite of these facts, we demonstrate in this book that growth in worldwide oil consumption was proceeding at a rapid pace of more than 7.6 per cent annually from 1965 to 1973, implying a more than doubling every ten years.

If that rate of increase had persisted until 2007 it would have implied worldwide oil consumption of more than 689 million barrels per day in that year, a multiple of more than 12.2 times the worldwide level of 1973. Had that

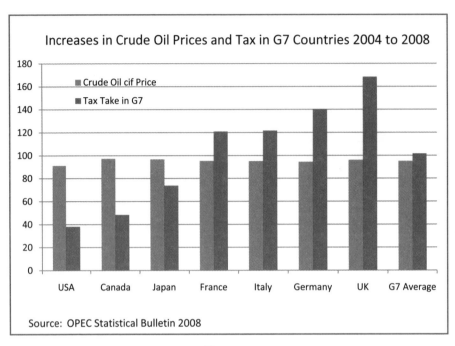

Figure 11.27

actually happened, the worldwide oil reserves would have fallen to zero in the millennium year of 2000 on the basis of the difference between actual world oil production from 1974 to 2000 and a theoretical growth rate of more than 7.6 per cent p.a. The difference is 1,196 billion barrels in the year 2000 compared with proved reserves reported at the end of that year of 1,104.5 billion barrels. Thus market forces based on the world supply and demand balance working through the price mechanism would have dictated a fundamental change anyway, long before 2007, had OPEC not existed.

Thus we turn to what actually happened over the thirty-five years to 2008 and OPEC's role in it during this period. Worldwide oil consumption continued growing rapidly from 1970 to 1973. The OPEC price increases of October 1973 and January 1974, coupled with an economic recession in 1974–5 resulted in a slight fall in oil consumption, followed by a gently rising plateau. In other words, those OPEC price increases, also associated with a short-term Arab embargo, for political reasons, associated with the Yom Kippur War, seemed to indicate the sustainability of those price increases, initiated by OPEC, over the subsequent years 1976 to 1979.

The big price increases of 1979–80 were brought about by market forces, not by OPEC. These included unusually large rebuilding of stocks by the major oil companies; a fear but not the reality of a shortage of oil supplies, with the revolution in Iran; and the outbreak of war between Iraq and Iran, two of the five OPEC founder member states.

Subsequently, worldwide oil consumption dropped quite sharply from 1979 to 1983, with oil prices, too, falling through to 1985. As a result of these turnarounds in both oil volumes and prices, there was a highly adverse impact on the economies of OPEC countries. For example, these two factors had the effect of reducing the gross domestic product of Saudi Arabia, OPEC's leading member, by 15.6 per cent between 1979 and 1985.

So in 1986 OPEC made a rather dramatic move to secure its position in the market with netback pricing and a consequent much sharper drop in oil prices than that which occurred from 1980 to 1985, again illustrated in Figures 11.17, 11.18 and 11.19. The result was that the market regained some sort of equilibrium through to 2003 in terms of both current and constant dollar prices, albeit with some comparatively minor fluctuations seen in terms of highs in both 1990 and 2000 and lows in 1998.

Thereafter, oil prices started rising again quite rapidly between 2003 and 2004 and this continued until July 2008 when the oil spot price peaked at a remarkable $147 a barrel. This happened in spite of the fact that OPEC oil production, having averaged 31.3 million barrels per day over the five years, 1999 to 2003, rose 13.2 per cent over the 5 years 2004 to 2008 to average an unprecedented high of 35.76 million barrels per day in an attempt both to meet rising demand and to dampen the evidently increasingly unsustainable oil spot and futures markets price rises. These were being fuelled increasingly by speculators causing a commodity boom and based on cheap money, especially manifest in the USA and UK, through the period, and most markedly in 2007 and 2008.

Thus we can say that the unsustainable rapid oil price booms of both 1979–80 and 2004–8 were the result of market forces in the widest sense, resting on sentiment and speculative behaviour of market participants, especially during the latter period. OPEC had no responsibility for them. On the contrary, its production volumes were particularly high in both periods and should have served to quell the market-dictated price increases.

By contrast, these oil price increases of 1973–4 were the result of premeditated decisions by OPEC which sought to right what it saw as a long-standing wrong of unfairly low prices for its fast depleting and non-renewable natural resource and, indeed, its principal one on which its members depended for their economic development.

Its oil policy of increasing oil supplies to the world market in 1986 and inducing a sharp fall in prices was clearly successful in leading to a new rough equilibrium in oil prices which lasted some sixteen years until 2003, enabling oil consumption to continue growing at a quite reasonable and predictable pace with fairly limited year-to-year fluctuations.

Table 11.65. Comparison of Crude Prices, cif and Tax on Petroleum Production in G7 Countries ($ per barrel)

	2004		2008	
	Crude Price cif	Tax	Crude Price cif	Tax
United States	32.8	18.4	91.1	38.1
Canada	35.1	21.9	97.3	48.4
Japan	33.3	38.0	96.7	73.7
France	35.0	70.4	95.2	120.8
Italy	34.2	66.0	95.0	121.6
Germany	34.1	61.7	94.3	140.3
UK	34.9	96.4	96.1	168.4
G7	34.2	53.3	95.1	101.6

We conclude our comments on OPEC member countries with a few comparisons with the world as a whole. The population of the thirteen member countries of OPEC in 2008 amounted to 613.1 million, 9.1 per cent of the worldwide population. The GDP of OPEC member countries aggregated $2,880.7 billion, or 4.75 per cent of the worldwide aggregate. GDP per capita averaged only $4,699, compared with $9,036 on average for the world as a whole, thus the average for OPEC countries amounted to 52 per cent of the global average. Four member countries accounting for 69.0 per cent of the total OPEC population had a GDP per capita below the OPEC average and another 19.8 per cent in three countries were less than 3 per cent above it. A further 9.6 per cent in another three member countries had a GDP per capita around double the worldwide average, and a mere 1.4 per cent in the three wealthiest OPEC countries with very small populations had a GDP per capita above $50,000 and higher than in the United States in 2008. Even with petroleum exports in 2008 of OPEC members above $1 trillion this represented just 35 per cent of their combined GDPs and less than 1.7 per cent of worldwide aggregate GDP.

Part III

Introduction to Retrospective View of
Energy: A Global Outlook

Energy: A Global Outlook was prepared in 1980–1 and published in 1982. This critical review of it is included here as it is considered that some salutary lessons might be learned from this vantage point of hindsight. It is suggested that in spite of or perhaps because of the deep and probably protracted worldwide recession in progress during 2009 as this book is being prepared, the analysis of longer term trends over the past thirty years and more in Part II, can provide a useful basis for evaluating the earlier book. Then Part IV provides projections of where world energy is heading through 2015, 2020 and 2030. Particular attention is paid to the likely roles foreseen for oil and natural gas supply and demand among all forms of primary energy in Part IV.

Part 1 of *Energy: A Global Outlook* covered an economic and political evaluation of the energy sector. Part 2 contained energy scenarios for the years 1985, 1990 and 2000, with regional analysis and reviews of the energy situation in important countries and groups of countries. These were the United States, Western Europe, Japan, the OPEC developing countries, non-OPEC developing countries, the USSR (as it then was, now the Commonwealth of Independent States), Eastern Europe and the People's Republic of China.

There were eighteen illustrations covering these topics, along with figures showing the relationship between GDP per capita and oil reserves to production ratios among OPEC member countries; world oil trade in terms of exports from Saudi Arabia, total OPEC and the rest of the world; the official and spot market prices of Arabian Light crude oil; world proved oil reserves, production and new reserves added over four five-year periods, from 1960 to 1979; energy consumption per capita was illustrated for the base year 1979 and in terms of projections for the year 2000 in three scenario cases for OPEC countries, other developing countries, OECD countries and the Centrally Planned Economies; similarly, world economic growth was projected for the three scenario cases for the time periods 1979 to 1985, 1985 to 1990 and 1990 to 2000.

A total of fifty-nine statistical tables provided an important basis of evidence for the historical analysis and projections along with other appendices covering OPEC, the IEA and the Conference on International Economic Cooperation. This latter is once again an important topic of international economic and political concern, as illustrated by the worldwide G20 economic summits held in London and Pittsburgh in 2009, in Toronto and Seoul in 2010, the latest *World Economic Outlook* published by the International Monetary Fund, plus estimates from the World Bank of GDP in the major economies and growth rates for them.

The energy scenarios used in *Energy: A Global Outlook* were described in some detail in chapters 14 and 15 of that book and are reviewed in this section. In the very first paragraph of the introduction to *Energy: A Global Outlook*, I mentioned that in the 1960s the world began to believe in the wishful dream of endless cheap oil supplies. We have shown in Part II of this book what could have happened if worldwide growth of oil consumption had continued at the rate it did until 1973 during the subsequent period until 2007. World oil demand would have increased to an incredible 689 million barrels per day. This would have been the consequence of a high compound growth rate continuing over a thirty-four-year period. But in fact this was not feasible as our calculations show that world production rising at this rate would have overtaken world proved oil reserves in the year 2000.

Secondly, in talking with the Japanese in 1971 about their then rapidly rising oil demand, their Institute of Energy revealed that they expected to obtain their incremental needs from the Middle East, of course. Now, nearly forty years on, the big potential increase in oil demand worldwide seems most likely to come from China, as discussed in this book.

One incorrect assumption contained in the introduction to *Energy: A Global Outlook* was that the future availability of crude oil could hardly meet demand, even at mid-1981 prices, unless serious steps were taken by various countries to develop additional oil supplies as well as alternative sources of energy, and to improve the efficiency of energy use. In fact, those mid-1981 prices proved unsustainable because of a combination of influences: recession and comparatively weak economic growth; additional oil supplies becoming available from non-OPEC countries and the efficiency of energy and oil use improving significantly. The policy-induced fall in oil prices in 1986 did result in a rough new equilibrium being reached which lasted beyond the millennium year of 2000 and was consistent with the earlier equilibrium level seen over the five years 1974 to 1978 following those price increases set by OPEC in October 1973 and January 1974.

The remarks made all those years ago about oil supply and demand always being more or less in balance, subject to unusual stock changes as a caveat, are subject to another qualification. This is that any fairly limited imbalances, or perhaps even more importantly, expectations of imbalances, find rapid expression in volatile spot or futures prices of oil and other commodities. In the case of oil, these marginal markets have increasingly driven the underlying physical volume of world trade ever since the NYMEX started the contract for West Texas Intermediate crude oil in 1983, followed by North Sea Brent a little later, with the Singapore market and a spot market price for Dubai Fateh crude following subsequently. Of course, spot prices for crude oil and the gross product worth for Rotterdam were clearly driving the volume market earlier in 1979 and 1980, as we illustrated in figure 5 in *Energy: A Global Outlook*.

Another incorrect assumption made in the introduction to *Energy: A Global Outlook* was the reference to the decreasing probability of finding large hydrocarbon reserves with the present technology. In fact, there was an unexpectedly big spurt in the finding of new oil reserves in OPEC member countries over the five years from the end of 1984, even as proven oil reserves declined in the rest of the world. Improvements in the recovery factor of the oil reserves in place have contributed to this, as evidence from the US Geological Survey shows. We have discussed and illustrated this phenomenon in Part II above. As a result of these very fundamental changes, OPEC member countries have increased their share of world oil reserves to some 76 per cent of the total. Their dominance in the field of gas reserves has also risen but remains less, at some 52 per cent. Another factor contributing to this has been the faster depletion of reserves among non-OPEC countries than OPEC members, through rising production over the lengthy period since 1979.

Also touched upon in the introduction to *Energy: A Global Outlook* was the relationship between the traditional major transnational oil companies and the oil-producing countries, particularly their national oil companies. The power, control and influence of these latter have become increasingly important over the last twenty to thirty years or so.

Another important development since the earlier book was published is the emergence of the so-called BRIC countries, i.e. Brazil, Russia, India and China, as significant players in the world economy but even more relatively important in the energy sector. China is by far the most important among them, with the probability of rising further in both relative and absolute terms, following the economic reforms introduced by Deng Xiaoping in 1978. Since then China's growth in national income has averaged about 10 per cent annually, just as that of Japan did many years earlier, as discussed in Part II above.

Review of Part 1 of the Book

The first chapter was 'Historical Evolution of the International Oil Industry'. There is really little to add in terms of further structural changes which have occurred over the last twenty-five to thirty years, except to emphasize the further growth in control and power over their reserves of oil and gas of the national oil companies of the resource-rich countries, at the expense of the traditional transnational companies. Nevertheless, these latter continue to thrive in the world oil market with the biggest of them, Exxon Mobil, earning a record $45 billion in 2008, more than any other company in history, in or outside the oil industry. Of course, mergers have occurred among these traditional Seven Sisters long-established major oil companies, most notably that involving Exxon and Mobil under the pressure of cost savings and the manifest advantages of large-scale operations in our industry.

'Global Energy Supply and Demand Balance' was the title of chapter 2 in *Energy: A Global Outlook*. The long-run evolution of this topic up to 2007 was the subject of Part II above, from the base year of 1979, which formed the foundation for the projections to 1985, 1990 and 2000 found in three scenario cases. In fact, as we have shown in Part II, 1979 was an unfortunate choice of year as it subsequently became clear that oil prices reached a level that year way above the trend established over the five years 1974 to 1978, following the OPEC-initiated oil price increases of October 1973 and January 1974. A central thesis of this book is that this OPEC initiative led to a sustainable world oil market over those five years, as did the downward correction induced in 1986, followed by years beyond the year 2000 with a rough equilibrium for oil prices being established. In contrast, the oil price rises of 1979–80 and 2004 to a peak in July 2008, brought about by market forces (in the widest sense) and speculators, proved unsustainable, given the influence of the financial crisis, economic recessions and the role of oil as the balancing form of energy in the world system. In other words, when growth in world energy demand is weak, demand for oil is weaker still. When growth in energy demand is strong, growth in oil demand is also strong, but not necessarily stronger than for all forms of primary energy, as in 2004. This is unlike the situation which prevailed up to 1973 when strong demand for energy was accompanied, typically, by significantly stronger growth in oil demand from year to year.

In this same second chapter of *Energy: A Global Outlook* it was emphasized, in 1980–1, that there were then serious concerns about the life-expectancy of the remaining proven reserves if the then-present trends continued, i.e. declining finding rate of new reserves (figure 6 shows this clearly in the earlier book) and growth in oil demand, or apparent consumption, which still averaged 2.3 per cent per annum from 1973 to 1979.

The fact is that things have changed since that basis for our expectations was set down. World proven oil reserves rose very significantly and unexpectedly as of 1980, over the five years 1985 to 1989, albeit concentrated entirely in OPEC member countries, as discussed and illustrated in Part II of this book. By 2007 this meant OPEC controlled 75 per cent of the worldwide total while the 180 or so countries outside OPEC had a proven oil reserves to production ratio average of only 17.9 years, with non-OPEC oil production still rising at an average rate of 1.2 per cent annually, on average, over the seven years to 2007. The prospect is that, barring significant new additions to reserves or big further improvements in recovery rates for oil in place, then world oil production outside OPEC will peak and then start declining during the period 2020 to 2030 at the latest. It has already done so in certain important countries such as the USA, Mexico, the UK and Norway.

The second significant change which has occurred since 1979 is the lower rate of growth in world oil consumption, which averaged only 1.0 per cent annually over the twenty-eight years to 2007. However, this included the sharp decline of some 6.5 million barrels per day over the four years from 1979 to 1983, implying an average fall of -2.6 per cent per annum over this period. From the 1983 low point over the twenty-four years to 2007 world oil consumption increased at a variable rate but averaged 1.6 per cent annually over this long period. Once again, the economic recession years of 2008–9 saw an absolute fall in world oil demand in the latter with a reduction in the long-term average rate to something closer to 1.0 per cent annually over the period to 2020.

Thus the pressure on the world oil supply and demand system should not be too great over the next decade, barring unexpected untoward events occurring on the world stage. The greatest uncertainty probably relates to the rate of growth of Chinese oil imports.

In *Energy: A Global Outlook*, we suggested that the finding and proving rate for new oil reserves might fall from the level of 14 to 15 billion barrels of the years up to 1979, to less than 10 billion barrels and perhaps as little as 5 billion barrels by the year 2000. In fact, after the extraordinary additions averaging 51 billion barrels annually in OPEC member countries over the period 1985 to 1989 (discussed and illustrated in Part II), the finding rate fell to only 2.7 billion barrels annually worldwide over the five years from 1990 to 1994 but then rose to 13.9 billion barrels per annum in 1995 to 1999 and then increased again to 24.5 billion barrels p.a. from 2000 to 2004. In the five years to 2009, the annual rate was almost identical at 24.4 billion barrels.

In all of these time periods, the finding and proving rate for new oil reserves was higher for OPEC member countries than for the whole of the rest of the world. Net additions outside OPEC amounted to zero, 3.4, 7.5 and 2.1 billion barrels annually, respectively over these five-year time periods, from 1990 to 2009. To put these estimates in perspective, we can remark that worldwide oil production outside OPEC over the twenty years from 1990 to 2009 averaged 15.7 billion barrels per year, i.e. a much higher figure and seemingly unsustainable in the long run, barring big new discoveries and/or big improvements in the recovery factor of oil in place. This was a central thesis of

Energy: A Global Outlook. The one thing which has changed is the time period when an unsustainable situation could arise, much longer than anticipated thirty years ago, given the rise in the recovery factor already achieved over this period.

Tables 11.33 and 11.34 illustrate the dramatic differences over the thirty years to 2009 between OPEC and the rest of the world. Proved oil reserves in OPEC countries increased by 592 billion barrels while those in the rest of the world increased by only 98 billion barrels. Over the same period OPEC oil production amounted to 301 billion barrels while the rest of the world produced 457 billion barrels.

Increased dependence on OPEC oil supplies already increased over the period 2004 to 2008 and this trend seems bound to continue once the recession of 2009 ends and economic recovery gets under way, as it surely will – the short-term uncertainty relates to the depth and duration of the recession. The recovery is under way: the IMF in July 2010 saw world output growing at a rate of 4.6 per cent in 2010, with China in the lead at 10.5 per cent but the advanced economies at only 2.6 per cent.

This same chapter in the earlier book made the point that 'history may yet record that the timeliness and extent of OPEC moves led to a less cataclysmic change in the world's energy mix over the long-term than if the initiatives of the 1970s had never been undertaken'. We believe the course of events through until 2008, as illustrated and discussed in several sections of Part 11 of this book, have vindicated this view.

Chapter 3 made a historical review of OPEC's creation and actions. The fiftieth anniversary of OPEC's creation in September 2010 seems an appropriate time to review what was written about it in the earlier book and make some updated comments about both its composition and actions since 1980–1. By the beginning of 2009 both Gabon and Indonesia had left OPEC but Angola had joined it. Ecuador had left OPEC but rejoined OPEC in 1997 after an absence of some fifteen years.

Though there were indisputable differences in the interests of OPEC members, these have not been sufficient to preclude a relatively effective working relationship among the quite diverse group of member countries, in spite of the sometimes quite strong pressures among them, given the varied political and economic difficulties they have faced. The convictions among the major transnational oil companies had been that OPEC would not prove to be an enduring organization, simply because of their divergent interests. That proved incorrect.

The critically important stage in OPEC's evolution occurred in October 1973. This was fully explained in *Energy: A Global Outlook* (p. 15) under the subheading 'Events Leading to OPEC Becoming the Sole Price Administrator'. In retrospect, it seems quite remarkable that the two big OPEC oil price increases of October 1973 and 1 January 1974 proved sustainable over the next five years, in spite of a recession hitting economic activity in the industrialized countries following a synchronized boom among them. In Saudi Arabia the full takeover of Aramco finally took place in 1988 with the Company's name being changed to Saudi Aramco.

The fourth chapter of *Energy: A Global Outlook* was 'The Rationale for OPEC'. In figure 3 it showed in a scatter diagram that only five OPEC member countries had a GDP per capita in 1979 of more than $5,000 while another six had a GDP per capita of between a meagre $1,000 and $5,000, while Nigeria and Indonesia were still genuinely poor and very populous countries with GDP per inhabitant of well below $1,000 per year, in spite of the OPEC price increases of six years earlier. Against GDP per capita we showed proved reserves to production ratios in years for all OPEC member countries to position them in this scatter diagram. In 1979 Kuwait was in a uniquely favorable position in having a GDP per capita already well exceeding $15,000 per year and an oil reserves to production ratio in excess of seventy-five years.

At that time only Saudi Arabia and Iran among other OPEC member countries had R:P ratios exceeding forty-five years, while as many as eight had R:P ratios of less than twenty-five years, including Nigeria and Indonesia which, between them, accounted for 67.9 per cent of the total population of OPEC member countries. This sort of comparative analysis illustrates the great diversity among OPEC member countries and serves as a testimony to its durability.

Later in this chapter, we remarked that the essential requirement was that member governments were willing to agree and sustain their agreement in spite of adverse changes in the market place. Of course, that was especially true from 1980 to 1985, with OPEC having survived perhaps its greatest test in 1986. This resulted in increasing oil supplies for exports while suffering large falls in prices but thereby securing its volume position in the market over the next twenty years or so. During this period non-OPEC oil-producing countries were depleting their significantly smaller reserves comparatively rapidly. Thus by 2004, when worldwide oil production and consumption increased more than usual, UK and Norwegian oil output had already passed their peaks in the hostile North Sea environment.

Also in this chapter of *Energy: A Global Outlook* we emphasized the need to move towards a more balanced energy mix in both the industrialized and developing countries for economic as well as for political reasons, which we made clear in that book. We believe that readers of Part II will recognize that that has been achieved over the twenty-nine years from 1979 to 2008. A rather dramatic fall occurred in oil's share of world primary energy consumption from 45.9 per cent in 1979 to only 39.1 per cent in 1985, a period of just six years. This resulted from the sharp oil price increases of 1979 and 1980 driven by anxieties rather than any real shortage of oil supplies in the market, and in spite of Saudi Arabia's enlightened policies of increasing its production and export volumes on into 1981, with its production rising from about 8.6 million barrels per day in 1978 to 9.8 in 1979, and 10.3 million barrels per day in both 1980 and 1981. Other circumstances discussed in Part II also contributed to this sharp fall in oil's share at this time, including economic recession, which is, once again in 2009, depressing oil's share of the world energy market, as it already did in 2008, to 35.0 per cent and 34.8 per cent respectively.

From 1985 through 1990 to 2000, oil's share of world primary energy consumption fell much more gradually from 39.1 per cent to 38.8 per cent and 38.3 per cent respectively. After 2000 oil's share fell more sharply once again to only 35.6 per cent in 2007. Thus over the twenty-eight-year period oil's share of world primary energy consumption fell by more than 10 percentage points while that of natural gas increased by more than 4 percentage points. Coal's share was actually less in 2007 than it had been in 1979 but after declining by almost 4 percentage points between 1979 and 2000 this long-ago dominant fossil fuel recovered strongly by 3.4 percentage points during the first seven years of the twenty-first century to 28.6 per cent in 2007; just 7 percentage points behind oil. Nuclear and hydro-electricity together increased their share of world primary energy consumption by 4.3 percentage points over the twenty-eight-year period, with nuclear accounting for 3.5 percentage points, though actually falling back between 2000 and 2007. Part II of this book includes some updates for the off-trend year of 2008 with oil's share declining to 35 per cent with coal and natural gas rising to more than 29 per cent and 24 per cent respectively.

All of this serves to underline a cautionary note appearing in the same paragraph in chapter 4 of *Energy: A Global Outlook*. This was to the effect that unreliable oil supplies and uncompetitive prices for oil entering the world market would lead to accelerated and perhaps uncontrollable erosion of exported oil's share of the world energy market. This can now be seen as directly relevant to what was going on as this earlier book was being prepared, and also, in all probability, to the still current course of events from 2004 through to 2008, with unsustainable price rises dictated by market forces, not by OPEC, on both occasions.

In the earlier book, we went on to point out that if international economic relations moved towards a cooperation scenario, there would be net advantages for OPEC member countries as a whole – otherwise the relatively short run of the next twenty years (to 2000) might witness the virtual death of the international oil market, as some exporters sought unrealistically high prices and came to experience economic lessons at first hand: namely, the laws of supply and demand and, in particular, the effect on those with the highest prices.

We went on to point out that oil reserves and other parameters suggested that this would be too short a time scale for oil's demise and a far from optimal path for the evolution of the world economy. We quoted His Excellency Shaikh Ahmed Zaki Yamani, already then in 1981, Saudi Arabia's Minister of Petroleum and Mineral Resources for the past twenty years, responding to a question about the country producing more oil than its economy needed and selling at lower prices than other oil exporters.

> As the price rises, consumption falls and capital is invested in searching for alternate sources of energy ... raising prices excessively and without restrictions or limits, will not be in the interest of certain OPEC members including Saudi Arabia and Iraq ... the study indicates that we have reached a crucial point, and that going beyond it would jeopardize the interests of Iraq, Saudi Arabia and the UAE.

We pointed out that by the summer of 1981 the combination of a weak international economy, low seasonal demand, a strong dollar and some evidence of a stock drawdown rather than the usual stock build-up by the major oil companies demonstrated the specific weakness of demand for OPEC oil as the balancing contributor to world energy needs.

We went on to say that the medium-term prospect for OPEC production and exports in 1985, say, was much more important than any temporary weakness of demand, driving OPEC production down to something in the region of 20 million barrels per day. In fact, it fell to a new low of 16.9 million barrels per day in precisely that year, 1985, a volume last seen as long ago as 1967. Saudi production was down to 3.6 million barrels per day, 21 per cent of the OPEC total. Our following paragraph pointed out that if there was to be a realistic price regime envisaged by the OPEC Long Term Strategy Committee, it was also necessary that price be responsive in order to maintain reasonable worldwide energy market equilibrium and to ensure that OPEC oil exports could be sold in acceptable volumes, having regard to the competitive challenge from other sources of energy and non-OPEC oil supplies. If OPEC prices were too high over a prolonged period, development of alternative energy sources would be artificially stimulated, as would improvements in the efficiency of energy use.

In another passage a little later (p. 36) we stated that since Saudi Arabian crude prices ($32 a barrel for Arab Light) were actually quite close to those suggested by a formula derived by OPEC's Long Term Strategy Committee, the implication was that the average price of other OPEC members considered as a whole was more than 15 per cent above the proposed level (in 1981). To the extent that actual rises (in prices) were larger than recommended rises over the medium term, world economic growth was likely to be lower, and so too would be the demand for OPEC oil.

Similarly, we said that, assuming Saudi Arabian oil production was maintained at the preferred official ceiling of 8.5 million barrels per day, OPEC oil prices which were too high on average would make it difficult for other OPEC members to rebuild their export volumes to desired levels on a sustained basis. Also, the medium and longer term export volumes of all OPEC members were certainly likely to be less than their desired levels.

Further evidence we produced at that time showed the dramatic deterioration in the balance of payments external trade account of five leading developing countries and five leading industrialized countries, all of them being oil importers. For the first group, in just two years from 1978 to 1980, during which the price of oil entering world trade had risen dramatically, their external deficit had increased by $7.4 billion. For the industrialized countries there was a huge turnaround of $62.7 billion from a surplus of $18.4 billion in 1978 to a collective deficit of $44.3 billion in 1980.

It seems to us that what we stated in the last two paragraphs of chapter 4 in *Energy: A Global Outlook* are worth quoting again here in full because of their relevance to the run-up of oil prices through to July 2008, the so-called credit crunch which started in August 2007 and the worldwide economic recession now abundantly evident to all concerned, perhaps most of all to the International Monetary Fund whose *World Economic Outlook* of April 2009 has warned of the dangers of a worldwide synchronized recession related to a financial crisis being both deep and protracted, compared with all other recessions which have occurred since the Great Depression.

From p. 31 of *Energy: A Global Outlook*:

> The problems of adjustment in the financial sector must be kept within
> manageable proportions, just like the inevitable adjustments in the real

energy sector. Otherwise the policies of enlightened international creditors, whether countries or banks, are bound to come under increasing strain. If the credibility of the world economic and financial system were called into question because it was thought that intolerable strains were developing, then an unprecedented economic and financial collapse could ensue.

It seems to me that this is a prospect which OPEC members must avoid at all costs if they are to consolidate over the next two decades the progress made in the past. Just like any other countries on the face of God's earth, OPEC members have to live within the existing system whilst hopefully working to transform it for the better. A proper balance between political and economic pressures will ensure not merely the survival of OPEC and the world economic system upon which it must inevitably depend, but also an enhanced place in the world community of nations for OPEC members.

Chapter 5 of *Energy: A Global Outlook* discussed the Organization of Arab Petroleum Exporting Countries. It reviewed the formation of OAPEC; its membership; its purpose and objectives; the various constituents of it; its specialized joint companies; and the proved oil and gas reserves of OAPEC member countries. We pointed out that the antecedents of OAPEC could be traced back to the Arab League which was formed in 1945. The Arab States recognized the problems and potentialities of oil as early as 1951 and formed a Committee of Arab Oil experts charged with the task of submitting recommendations for the planning of an Arab oil policy. Consequently an Arab Department for Oil was created inside the Arab League.

It seems timely now to compare the proved reserves of oil and gas of OAPEC member countries as reported by the *Oil and Gas Journal* at the beginning of 2009 with those shown in *Energy: A Global Outlook*, twenty-nine years earlier from the same source.

Table III.1. Proved Reserves of OAPEC

Crude Oil (billion barrels)	Natural Gas (trillion cubic feet)

OAPEC members	1.1.1980	1.1.2009	Change over 29 years	1.1.1980	1.1.2009	Change over 29 years
Algeria	8.4	12.2	+3.8	132.0	159.0	+27.0
Bahrain	0.2	0.1	-0.1	9.0	3.3	-5.7
Iraq	31.0	115.0	+84.0	27.5	111.9	+84.4
Kuwait	68.5	104.0	+35.5	33.5	63.4	+29.9
Libya	23.5	43.7	+20.2	24.0	54.4	+30.4
Qatar	3.8	15.2	+11.4	60.0	891.9	+831.9
Saudi Arabia	168.4	266.7	+98.3	95.7	258.5	+162.8
Syria	2.0	2.5	+0.5	1.5	8.5	+7.0
UAE	29.4	97.8	+68.4	20.5	214.4	+193.9
Total	335.3	657.2	+322.0	403.7 = 72.7 bn bbl o.e.	1765.3 = 317.8 bn bbl o.e.	+1361.6 = 245.1 bn bbl o.e.

Thus with the exception of Bahrain, all OAPEC member countries increased their proved reserves of both oil and gas by significant margins over this lengthy twenty-nine-year period. It is worth noting that the enormous increases of natural gas, as well as oil, aggregate to a combined addition of 567 billion barrels of oil equivalent of which natural gas accounts for 43.2 per cent of the total. In Saudi Arabia, this has enabled the country to initiate and expand its Master Gas System to support its industrialization programme, while Qatar is proceeding with LNG exports based on production increasing by 16.3 per cent in 2009 alone with great potential to rise further.

Chapter 6 of *Energy: A Global Outlook* made a historical review and rationale of the International Energy Agency's (IEA) creation, policies and action. As we pointed out in our introduction to this topic, the emergence of the IEA could be traced to initiatives taken by OPEC and OAPEC respectively in October 1973 in raising oil prices and introducing a partial and limited embargo of oil supplies in the wake of the Arab–Israeli war.

The first initiative for action was taken by the US Secretary of State, Dr Henry Kissinger, in a speech in London in December 1973. This was followed by an Energy Conference in Washington in February 1974. Then in November 1974 the OECD Council decided to establish the International Energy Agency with six aims. These included the promotion of cooperative relations with oil-producing countries and with other oil-consuming countries, particularly those of the developing world. Following the lack of success with the conclusion of the Conference on International Economic Co-operation, in October 1977, IEA Ministers adopted twelve Principles of Energy Policy. These were listed fully in *Energy: A Global Outlook* (pp. 43–5).

By mid-1980 the IEA included twenty-one of the twenty-four then existing OECD countries but somewhat ironically this did not include France where the IEA office was based (Paris). Following some eighteen months of sharply rising spot market prices for crude oil and products (see especially figure 5 in the earlier book), the Governing Board of the IEA met in May 1980 and issued a communiqué (appendix 11.3 in *Energy: A Global Outlook*).

In the earlier book I reflected on the nature of the IEA and its performance. I remarked that the fact that the attempt to broaden the dialogue in the Conference on International Co-operation did not achieve effective progress could be represented as an attempt on the part of the industrialized countries to contain the spread of bargaining strength demonstrated by the developing countries in the oil sector to other important parts of the international economy.

By June 1980, Dr Kissinger's thinking seemed to have undergone a rather fundamental change under a new set of pressures. The *us* and *them* mentality was crystallized in a sentence from his address to the Conference on 'The Energy Emergency: Oil and Money', 1980.

> We in the West agree that economic development automatically produces political stability but the fact is that economic development substantially produces in developing countries political instability because it is bound to

undermine the traditional patterns of authority in which so many of these countries have operated for centuries.

A most important feature seemingly not recognized by people such as the former US Secretary of State and other influential voices in the advanced countries was the enormous disparity in economic well-being of ordinary citizens in the OECD countries and their counterparts in most OPEC countries, in spite of the oil price increases of 1973–4. In 1979 the average GDP per capita of people living in the United States, Japan, the German Federal Republic, Canada and Australia was $10,287. It was more than $10,000 in eight other OECD European countries, i.e. a majority of all of them. This was more than twenty times the average GDP per capita of the two most populous OPEC countries, Indonesia and Nigeria, where almost 68 per cent of the total population in all OPEC countries lived. At the other extreme, again illustrating the remarkable diversity of OPEC member countries, just 0.7 per cent of their total population living in just three of them enjoyed a GDP per capita above that of any OECD country in 1979. These were Kuwait, Qatar and the UAE. The GDP per capita of Saudi Arabia at $7,370 was significantly below that of the OECD average which exceeded $10,000 in 1979.

I concluded that the reluctance of the industrialized countries to come to terms with their dependence on OPEC oil and make the necessary accommodations in economic and political terms seemed to be leading them more in the direction of confrontation than of cooperation.

In its first real test in 1979 the IEA was shown to be a body without effective power to bring discipline to bear on the demand end of the oil market. The reality of increases in worldwide supply running well ahead of growth in demand should have proved quite manageable.

There seemed to have been no recognition on the part of the IEA or member governments of the responsibility of themselves and the companies for the damaging effects of competitive bidding for spot market supplies. OPEC played no role in this. Moreover, the competitive bidding was not even indulged in to ensure that unconstrained demand could be met, but simply in order to build up stocks. Throughout 1979 and during the first three-quarters of 1980, as spot market prices were rising rapidly, the stock changes, rather than the Iranian Revolution, contributed to a tighter oil market than the corresponding quarterly changes during 1978.

The purpose of reiterating these points here and now is that a similar explosion of oil market prices took place much more recently, from 2004 (when demand growth was strong) all the way through to July 2008. The spot and futures markets had become much more important by this time and speculators rather than bona fide oil traders had become much more significant 'players' in the oil market following years of 'easy money' and cheap credit in the world's financial markets. Yet with a longer lead time in which to identify the growing problem and the benefit of hindsight from the experiences of twenty-five years earlier, the IEA once again seemed not to take any effective action to try and keep some sort of lid on oil price rises. I pointed out in the earlier book that only in June 1980 did the IEA recognize that stock building had to be controlled as a contra-cyclical activity, after the unhappy lessons of 1979 had made this evident for all to see. There is still no clear evidence that the concept of stock building in soft markets and stock drawdown in tight markets is being put into practical effect.

Another parallel between 1979–80 and 2004–8 (to July) was the big increase in OPEC oil supply to the market, in spite of which spot and futures market prices took off quickly and to a remarkable extent on both occasions without a genuinely fundamental cause in terms of consumption exceeding production for a prolonged period. I pointed out that the recommendations of OPEC's Long Term Strategy Committee deserved serious consideration by the world community generally and by the IEA in particular, as a reasoned basis for strategic planning.

Another aspect of policy regarding oil stocks seemingly unresolved when *Energy: A Global Outlook* was prepared and still with us in 2009, apparently, is the dilemma between security of supply considerations, which are of paramount importance for the IEA, and short-term financial criteria and expectations of changes in the oil supply and demand balance which have a major influence on the stock policies of the transnational oil companies and oil traders. Furthermore, expectations of change in the world oil supply and demand balance have been the underlying cause for the enormous growth of over the counter (OTC) derivatives and futures trading in crude oil and refined products during the last thirty years or so. Apart from their legitimate use for hedging risk, the rise in speculative trading has contributed significantly to the big annual fluctuations in real oil prices characterizing this period and thus disturbing the smooth evolution of the world economy in consequence. We discuss this topic further in Part IV below.

Chapter 7 of *Energy: A Global Outlook,* 'Impact of Structural Changes on the International Energy Industries', covered the emergence of new development criteria; conservation; elimination of wasteful practices; diversification of the economic base; energy transportation; exploration for oil and gas and development of alternative sources of energy; position of foreign companies in the new situation; possible modes of cooperation between oil exporting countries and the foreign companies. I still believe that what I asserted at the beginning of this chapter remains true after the passing of almost another thirty years, namely that the then recent changes in the international petroleum industry signified a crucial turning point in its long history. The transfer of effective control over petroleum resources from the traditionally dominant transnational oil companies to the newly emerging national petroleum enterprises of the producing countries has become an irreversible evolutionary process. This would inevitably lead to significant changes in the traditional policy-making criteria in the international petroleum industry.

In spite of these foreseen changes, the major transnational oil companies have mostly made record profits/net income in 2008. This was true of companies operating in many other economic sectors in the world economy, at least through 2007.

One important concern of the oil producing and exporting countries was the former wasteful practice of flaring or reinjecting associated natural gas and NGLs in the cheap oil era prior to 1973. When a country is heavily dependent on one or two major non-renewable and depletable natural resources such as oil and gas for generations still to come, it behoves them to plan ahead for one hundred years or more to avoid wasting their resources and optimize use of them, even when heavy capital investment is a prerequisite. A good example of this is the Saudi Arabian Master Gas System discussed in Part I above.

In the earlier book I discussed three forms of international cooperation between sovereign oil-exporting countries and the major foreign oil companies, given that the former confrontational relationship had been amicably settled.

Chapter 8 was 'Petromin, Saudi Arabian Oil Policies and Industrialization through Joint Ventures'. Our follow-up to this constitutes Part I above. It is based on generally available published sources of information and covers an important updating of what appeared in this chapter in *Energy: A Global Outlook*. 'North–South: An International Energy Dialogue' was the title of chapter 9. The central part of this was the Conference on International Economic Co-operation (CIEC). It was convened in Paris in December 1975. The Group of 19 represented seventy-seven developing countries, while the Group of 8 represented all developed countries. Saudi Arabia was among seven OPEC members in the Group of 19. Four commissions were set up covering energy, raw materials, development and financial affairs. Representatives from Saudi Arabia and the USA were elected as the co-chairmen of the Energy Commission.

The objective agreed for the CIEC was to initiate an intensified North–South dialogue on all matters covered by the four commissions. This was intended to lead to concrete proposals for an equitable and comprehensive programme for international economic cooperation, including agreements, decisions, commitments and recommendations. This, it was agreed, should constitute a significant advance in international economic cooperation and make a substantial contribution to the economic development of the developing countries.

Some thirteen inter-governmental functional organizations, including OPEC, OAPEC and the IEA, participated in the four commissions as permanent and *ad hoc* observers. Working sessions of the four commissions took place between February 1976 and May 1977. A number of proposals and studies were made with an assessment of the world energy situation. However, members of the Group of 19 and the Group of 8 could not agree on a uniform assessment and interpretation of the energy situation on certain issues and arrived at different conclusions and recommendations.

The concept of international economic cooperation has recently come back as an important topic for discussion among the world's leading politicians under the pressure of what has become recognized as the worst recession in some eighty years. Meetings took place in Washington in November 2008 with the G20 (actually 22 including Saudi Arabia) of the leading economies worldwide convening in London in April 2009. The culmination was reached at the Pittsburgh summit in September 2009. We have discussed this fully in Part 11 above. The credit crunch started in August 2007 with a major banking crisis involving enormous write-offs of loans, especially to the housing sector, mergers and actual bank failures, culminating in the bankruptcy of Lehman Brothers in September 2008. This has had worldwide ramifications with an adverse effect on the energy sector, particularly oil and gas.

The leading economies have already taken unprecedented steps in the form of stimulus via fiscal policies and remarkable easing of monetary policies in a new desperate attempt to avert financial meltdown. This was a real fear during the fourth quarter of 2008 and the first quarter of 2009. In April 2009 the IMF's *World Economic Outlook* produced a particularly gloomy short-term forecast for the world economy in 2009, emphasizing that this would be the worst year since the Great Depression. The economic recession would be both deep and protracted as it was both centred on the financial sector and synchronized in its timing across the world. Happily, by October 2009 the economic outlook seemed rather less gloomy then it had done six months earlier.

The purpose of discussing these events here is to remark that because of the threats they pose to populations around the globe, they should lead to a more genuine effort for effective and constructive international economic and financial cooperation than those seen in CIEC and elsewhere over the last thirty to forty years. The comparatively fast growth of the big developing country economies such as China, especially, India and Brazil, as well as others including

Saudi Arabia, really do mean that the world is a fast-changing economy as the position of these developing countries becomes more important relative to the more mature industrialized economies of the OECD countries. In these latter nations, GDP per capita is growing more slowly with the additional problems among many of them associated with high healthcare costs inevitably linked to ageing populations. These burdens will simply exacerbate the extraordinary costs of the unprecedented fiscal stimuli introduced in late 2008 and early 2009 in most of them, with the effects likely to be felt for years to come.

The fact of the matter is that unsustainable price rises for oil such as those resulting from market forces in both 1979–80 and 2004–2008 (July) are not in the long-term interest of either OPEC members or other countries worldwide in the medium to long term. The same is true of other commodities too. Moderate fluctuations are inevitable, but not those which cause diseconomies and major disturbances to the normal evolution of economic activity worldwide. This is why initiatives such as the OPEC Long Term Strategy Committee, CIEC, and the recent G20 meetings should be welcomed, with realistic policy proposals being implemented internationally to avoid or mitigate future shocks to the system, whether they are sourced in the energy sector, banking and finance, or elsewhere. The announcement in Pittsburgh of the G20 replacing the former G7 looks particularly encouraging for the developing countries.

Chapter 10 of *Energy: A Global Outlook* was 'Structural Changes and New Strategies'. The thoughts expressed above were implicit in this chapter of the earlier book. We pointed out that thirty years ago many buyers found that recourse to the spot market was necessary to ensure adequate oil supplies. We had seen that during 1979 and 1980 the prime factor behind the increasing oil prices was the spot market. Within a few years futures markets had developed, with the NYMEX being the first for West Texas Intermediate light crude, followed by North Sea Brent, Singapore and Dubai. Collectively, these offer oil traders a twenty-four-hour continuous real-time monitor as to what is going on in the world's markets for crude oil and refined products. They became price setters for the market as a whole. In due course long-running time series data for Arab Light (OPEC's marker crude, against which differentials for other crudes were calculated) gave rise to alternatives such as North Sea Brent, even though the probable lifespan for crudes such as this must be much shorter than for Arab Light, given the comparative reserves and resource base of all those crudes which serve as a benchmark for the spot and futures markets.

In contrast to this state of affairs which resulted in the unsustainable rise in oil prices from 2004 to mid-2008, we pointed out that in this chapter of the earlier book that it could be reasonably assumed that OPEC would follow a predictable path in its pricing and supply strategies. This was derived directly from the recommendations of the OPEC Long Term Strategy Committee in 1981. The fact is that the rise in Saudi Arabian and OPEC crude oil production to hitherto unprecedently high levels over the period 2004 to 2008 in an attempt to cap the runaway rise in spot and futures market prices amount to powerful evidence in support of what we wrote nearly thirty years ago.

Also in the earlier book we said that:

> If it is assumed that the developed industrialized countries could achieve a greater than predicted change from oil and gas to alternative sources of energy as well as greater than predicted energy conservation rates, it would certainly make it possible to free more oil for export to the developing countries, while having the added benefit of alleviating the pressure on oil prices.

This has been achieved to some extent, but after OECD countries' gas consumption fell by 3.8 per cent between 1979 and 1985, it rose at an average rate of 2.3 per cent annually over the twenty-two years to 2007, with an aggregate increase over this period of 574 billion cubic metres. Similarly, oil consumption fell by a remarkable 15.4 per cent over the years from 1979 to 1985 in OECD countries as a whole, i.e. 6.79 million barrels per day, but after that growth resumed at an average rate of 1.3 per cent annually to 2007, amounting to an aggregate increase of 11.72 million barrels per day.

We also remarked that the industrialized countries would continue to account for the bulk of world oil imports for many years to come. That remained true in 2007 when US, European and Japanese oil imports together accounted for 59.5 per cent of the worldwide total, though this marked a significant fall from the 63.7 per cent recorded ten years earlier. Only Japanese oil imports among the three major OECD constituents fell in volume during this period, by 0.7 million barrels per day. US oil imports rose by 3.73 million barrels per day and European imports by a similar amount, 3.53 million barrels per day from 1997 to 2007. Oil imports into all other countries worldwide rose 7.38 million barrels per day over this decade, only marginally more than the combined total for the USA and Europe.

Another point made in *Energy: A Global Outlook* was vindicated by subsequent events in the 1980s. That was to the effect that a spot market related strategy almost develops by default. We went on to point out that the spot market for petroleum derivatives, i.e. products, would still be affected by the spot market for crude oil. Both markets react to each other to a certain degree, although in the past, the basic influence had usually been derived from the spot market for derivatives, as shown in figure 5 of *Energy: A Global Outlook*.

I wrote that a relatively small percentage of total supply was still sold as spot cargoes (in regard to products). There were those who thought in terms of higher percentages to be sold in the spot market. But with increasing volumes expected from producing countries' export refineries, and new gas systems, this seemed most unlikely, I said at that time. I concluded that under the circumstances and assumptions described, I supposed that the market strategies for petroleum products and gas liquids would be more uniform than the market strategy for crude oil.

I went on to remark that notional gaps in supply and demand balances are not a feature of the real world. Therefore, what in fact will happen will be lower economic growth and higher oil prices, in some combination, subject to change through time at whatever levels of conservation and substitution by other forms of energy are actually achieved.

In going on to consider possible different policy positions of oil production among oil-exporting countries, I concluded that oil producers generally were likely to be reluctant to over-produce in relation to their financial needs, unless their accumulated surplus financial assets maintained their value in real terms, and yielded a positive rate of interest after allowing for inflation (and currency depreciation, if relevant, one might have added).

I suggested that if consumers limited their demand for oil to the available supply and the OPEC long-term strategy had been implemented, a highly complex system would be greatly simplified. But I concluded that the probability that something like this happening on a sustained basis would not seem to be high. Hence we had to face a potentially explosive situation which might affect the world economic system adversely, with serious consequences for both the developed and developing countries.

I continued by observing that although we had seen double digit inflation and wild monetary fluctuations, the system had survived and the doomsday forecasts had still not been realized. I believed then, and still do now, almost thirty years down the road, that the world economy has the intrinsic strength to adapt to changes in the long term, in spite of the recent alarm in the financial sector which could and should have been avoided.

I believe it is still worth quoting the final conclusion reached by the Energy Commission of the Conference on International Economic Co-operation, which appeared in *Energy: A Global Outlook*:

> The world community requires an international energy co-operation and development program within the overall framework of an international economic co-operation program that would, recognizing relevant constraints, encourage and accelerate energy conservation and the development of additional energy supplies through, inter alia, facilitating and improving access to energy-related technology, expanding energy research and development and increasing investment flows into energy exploration and development. Without such a comprehensive program the world risks significant shortages of energy in the medium term and rapid depletion of oil and gas that will seriously jeopardize the economic progress of all countries. This comprehensive program would address financial aspects of energy development problems, energy conservation, exploration and development for non-renewable energy resources and technological research and development efforts related to both renewable and non-

renewable energy sources. There is need to initiate measures promptly and simultaneously that will produce results in the short, medium and long term.

'Plus ça change, plus c'est la même chose', as the French say.

Later in this chapter, I remarked that in Saudi Arabia we believe firmly in the contribution of international cooperation and trade as the basis for development of the oil and energy sector, albeit in a changing environment. For example, there was our participation in CIEC quoted above, delivery of papers to many international conferences over the years, right up to our participation in the G20 economic summits in April and September 2009 and two more in 2010.

With respect to my remarks about the transnational companies, I am pleased to note that they have been engaged in developing other sources of energy to reduce the burden on oil in fuelling growth of the world economy and in maintaining their own corporate development. For example BP and Shell have been advertising their endeavours in this field in 2009.

I remarked that we entered the energy transition era rather uncertainly in 1974 from an oil industry based on historic costs to one based on the replacement cost of oil in terms of other forms of energy. I pointed out that that had been formalized in the proposal recommended by the OPEC Long Term Strategy Committee. Unfortunately, like many potentially useful initiatives, this was not implemented in the rather exceptional oil market conditions which prevailed from 1980 to 1985 and then on into 1986.

I concluded that the oil price increases of the 1970s combined with the publicized intention of OPEC to increase the real price of oil in the future acted to dispel the illusions about abundant supplies of oil at low prices. I went on to say that those price increases held out the promise of providing the basis for a reasonable equilibrium between oil supply and demand in the coming years, particularly in view of the significant improvements already then evident in the energy/GDP ratio in most industrialized countries.

I noted that remarkable investment programmes would be needed to sustain rising energy demand and to satisfy GDP growth rising at an average of say 5 per cent annually in the developing countries and near 3 per cent in the industrialized countries, even allowing for generous and continuing improvements in the energy/GDP relationship.

Of course, these matters and relationships have now been analyzed and discussed in Part II above for the world as a whole and for the leading economies and energy-consuming countries which constitute over 80 per cent of the worldwide total. There are some remarkable differences between them, as we have shown.

To provide some insight into the investments foreseen for oil in particular and for energy in general, I quoted the then President of Royal Dutch Shell in a paper presented to the World Petroleum Congress in 1979 and another paper presented by staff at Dresdner Bank to the World Energy Conference in 1980. Both of them covered the period from 1980 to 2000. As I said, the investment requirements looked formidable by any standard.

In the final part of this chapter I said that cooperation rather than confrontation should be a happy consequence of the so-called second oil crisis. But I went on to state that this was likely to happen only if the industrialized countries recognized more explicitly than they had done so far the fragile basis for OPEC aspirations. This was the heavy dependence of oil exporters on making maximum use of this unique, finite and non-replaceable natural resource for their own economic development. The purpose of *Energy: A Global Outlook* was to concentrate on the supply and demand for oil and other forms of energy, and to show how the changing balance of economic forces made OPEC so much more powerful in the 1970s than in the 1960s. I discussed how OPEC members were able increasingly to assert their sovereign rights over their precious natural resources in dealing with the world's most powerful companies, organized in a highly integrated oligopolistic industry.

To end this chapter, I had to mention a critically important political issue. I make no apology for including that very same final paragraph in this book because it remains unresolved and the situation has actually worsened in some respects.

In spite of my preoccupation with economic influences in the oil market, this chapter on Structural Changes and New Strategies would be incomplete without brief reference to a major political determinant of Arab and, indeed, of Islamic oil policies. The continuing lack of decisive action on the return of Arab lands, and particularly Jerusalem, to the dispossessed Palestinians, will bring inevitable consequences, not only on the Zionists, but for those who are in a position to influence them and fail to do so. While Arab oil production rose dramatically to make up for the shortfalls in exports from elsewhere in 1979, in spite of lack of satisfactory progress on the Palestinian question, it is inevitable that the recent Israeli initiatives must bring retribution in terms of significantly lower Arab oil production and exports if such initiatives go unchecked. The political dimension of the medium term oil supply scenarios cannot be ignored. Oil importing countries will do so at their peril.

In the event of senior politicians and statesmen around the world becoming complacent because of the lack of action by Arabs in general and Saudis in particular, I conclude by drawing their attention to an important article in a leading newspaper entitled 'Saudi Arabia's Patience is Running Out' by Prince Turki al-Faisal. He points out that to preserve its leadership role in the Middle East, the US must revise drastically its policies on Israel and Palestine. It is significant that this article was published immediately after President Barack Obama's inauguration. The new US President's early comments on this most important issue suggest, at least, a more even-handed view of the problem than that prevailing for so long in Washington, DC, in the past. Subsequently, the US President's speech in Cairo on 4 June 2009 was potentially a most important event, marking his watchword change.

Chapter 11 of *Energy: A Global Outlook* was 'Towards an International Energy Development Programme'. Ever optimistic, we believe this concept could still be realized during the next few years. It is likely to become important some time during the next twenty years. The global recession of 2008 through 2009, following the financial crisis of 2007–8, with depressed demand for energy, like all other sectors of the world economy, should not delude policy-makers into a sense of complacency just because there is no immediate problem, with no insurmountable ones having occurred during the last thirty years or so.

One principal reason for the comparative lack of concern hitherto about this problem and lack of real international progress during this lengthy period is the enormous and unforeseen growth of proven oil reserves in several OPEC member countries during the period 1985 to 1989. This has been discussed and illustrated in Part II. But the experience of finding and proving of new oil reserves outside OPEC countries, i.e. in the whole of the rest of the world, has been very different, once again discussed in Part II. Another factor also mentioned in this first paragraph of the earlier book was the fact of certain OPEC countries, particularly those in the Arabian Gulf region, being potentially discretionary oil producers and exporters, if called upon by the world market for larger volumes of oil than those required to meet their budgetary needs.

Likewise, one might conclude at this point in time that the financial crisis of 2007 and 2008 had the potential to cause concern for policy-makers responsible for the sovereign wealth funds, not only of countries in the Arabian Gulf, but also of others such as China, Norway and Singapore, for example. For such asset holders, as indeed for big insurance companies, banks, holders of large pension funds and so on, there is the hazard of currency fluctuations as well as inflation potentially acting to erode their reserves of wealth upon which the world financial system has come increasingly to depend for its smooth functioning and the reconciliation of imbalances within major economies (in particular in the United States) and between those with surpluses and those with long-running deficits on both capital and/or current external accounts.

Once again, I find it worthwhile to refer back to what I wrote almost thirty years ago. I referred to the possibility of it being technically feasible to mine enough coal, to generate sufficient nuclear power and develop hydro and solar energy to fill in a notional gap that conventional oil and gas were unlikely to fill. To these other sources we can now add biomass, wind and wave energy, much talked about by politicians, but along with solar still accounting for comparatively negligible contributions to the world's primary energy balance.

Meanwhile, considerable concerns have been expressed in the agricultural sector already about the effect on prices associated with these relatively small volumes of biomass used as a fuel.

As we showed in Part II, oil's percentage share of the world primary energy balance fell fairly sharply between 1979 and 1985, then more or less stabilized for some fifteen years, but fell again from 2000 to 2007. But if we look at the combined share of both oil and gas we find it, too, fell quite sharply from 65.1 per cent of total primary energy in 1979 to 60.0 per cent in 1985. Over the next twenty-two years to 2007 the further fall was negligible to 59.4 per cent in this latter year. If we put these figures into the context of others shown in Part II above, i.e. the reserves to production ratios for oil and gas worldwide for countries outside OPEC, the concept of potential shortages of these key hydrocarbons in coming decades, becomes clearer, with production and consumption of both of them rising year on year, except during periods of recession. In 2007 the reserves to production ratio for conventional oil was only 17.9 years while for natural gas it was 35.5 years for all countries on average outside OPEC, with a combined estimate for oil and gas together of 26.2 years.

One major caveat entered in the original text in *Energy: A Global Outlook* turned out to be unfounded. In spite of the incentive of comparatively high oil prices the additions to worldwide oil reserves over the five years 1975 to 1979 had been much less than during each of the three previous five-year periods, with the result that the estimate of total oil reserves remaining was lower at the end of 1979 than at the end of 1974. However, because of the enormous increase in reserves in several OPEC countries (aggregating 255 billion barrels) over the five years 1985 to 1989 the total proven reserves did not continue to fall, as it turned out. In fact, OPEC's proven reserves in 2007 at 171 years for gas and 72 years for oil, in terms of the reserves to production ratio, indicate that a more rapid exploitation of gas rather than oil reserves would be appropriate. Even as this text is being prepared, that is already being realized in 2009 with Qatar increasing its natural gas production by more than 16 per cent this year on its huge reserves base. On the basis of the estimates for 2007 OPEC's oil and gas reserves combined are sufficient to last for ninety-three years.

Thus the short- to medium-term anxieties we expressed about production of oil possibly declining as soon as the late 1980s or early 1990s, associated with a continuing decline in new additions to reserves, was not realized. World oil production continued to rise at a modest pace with OPEC production averaging over 35 million barrels per day during the four years 2004 to 2007, a new peak volume. Natural gas production worldwide rose more quickly at an average rate of 2.8 per cent over the decade to 2007.

Nevertheless, given the tendency of senior policy-makers and politicians to be unduly preoccupied with short-term problems, especially those concerning financial crises and economic recessions, there is a continuing need for a longer term perspective in the energy sector in particular. Another point made in this chapter of *Energy: A Global Outlook* is probably even more relevant today. It is that countries are highly interdependent and far from self-sufficient in respect of oil and gas in particular, excepting OPEC countries, in the main.

In terms of the necessary cooperation we foresaw as being desirable, we identified the United Nations, the World Bank and UNCTAD as being the appropriate institutions to assist individual countries and groups of countries to make energy studies, moving on to the financing, engineering, construction and operation of new energy projects in the fullness of time. In this context, the potential needs of China spring to mind as the giant among developing countries and seemingly the emerging Goliath on the world energy stage over the coming decade or more. We have discussed China at some length in Part II because of its growing dominance on the world energy stage.

The existing and continuing heavy dependence of the fast-growing economies of China and India on coal means that their reliance on oil and gas has been comparatively modest until now. However, the very real threat of global warming and climate change represent a new worldwide danger hardly discerned and identified thirty years ago. This new problem has obvious application to the need for clean coal-burning technologies and possibly on-site gasification to mitigate future problems in such big countries as these important players in the world energy scene.

In this context of the threat of global warming, backed by the fast-growing evidence to support it, the need for the development of all forms of renewable energy deserves more urgent attention at the international level. The estimates of costs associated with the economies of scale and technological improvements, along with financing arrangements, seem to justify international study and policy recommendations, the like of which have yet to be seen.

Political and Economic Issues

I remarked at the beginning of chapter 12 of *Energy: A Global Outlook*, that I had left out certain issues of a political and economic nature relating to international energy cooperation during the transition period away from the world's heavy dependence on those key hydrocarbons, oil and gas. As we have seen, nearly thirty years later, these continue to dominate the world's energy balance, between them still accounting for almost 60 per cent of the total.

I still believe that effective cooperation in the critically important energy sector is likely to be achieved only in proportion to the degree of agreement on the broader economic and political issues. Again, as I remarked before, there is a latent conflict between energy exporters and energy importers, but that should not preclude constructive dialogue and effective cooperation if an effort is made on both sides to understand and respect the legitimate aspirations of the other party.

In particular, I referred to the wishes for economic growth leading to a better standard of living for people across the great swathe of developing countries. In terms of energy consumption per capita alone (a good proxy for economic well-being) I showed in figure 7 of *Energy: A Global Outlook* just how far behind the OECD industrialized countries were the OPEC countries and all other developing countries in 1979, but also in terms of projections for the year 2000 in all three scenario cases prepared in 1980–1. An update showing the actual figures for the year 2000 indicates that a substantially similar relative position was seen in that year, too.

Improvements in economic welfare introduced in such a way as to not conflict with religious beliefs and established traditions are generally welcomed by hitherto comparatively poor people who yearn for a better material standard of life. Progress of this sort is beginning to be seen now in China, the most populous country on earth, with a thirty-year history of economic growth averaging almost 10 per cent per year already behind it.

As I remarked that long ago, leave each country to decide its own social and economic policies and accept economic development as one of our major policy guidelines in international cooperation. I believe it remains true that it is difficult for citizens and even senior policy-makers in the industrialized countries to comprehend just how far in advance they are of the masses, i.e. billions of people, in the developing countries. I quoted at that time a senior UN official writing in *Newsweek* magazine under the provocative but thought-provoking title 'Is Altruism in Retreat?' I repeat the last part of that quotation now because I believe it still to be apposite: 'It seems to me there is only one answer to the question of why we should care about another person's hunger; illness or homelessness: we are all humans. That has always been the answer and always will be.'

I went on to discuss options in the Middle East and this continues to have a certain resonance even now, in spite of the fundamental change in US/Russian relationships. The same could be said about my next topic in the earlier book, the Soviet offensive in Asia and Africa.

Then I considered Israeli expansionism. After the events of 2008 and many others in the intervening period, this remains a running sore in the Arab world with constructive Saudi proposals in 2002 on behalf of the Palestinians provoking no adequate response from the United States or the EU. It remains to be seen what well-meaning characters such as George Mitchell and Tony Blair will be able to achieve in their comparatively new roles in this powder-keg situation, which has been festering for more than forty or more than sixty years already, depending on one's choice of dates when the untenable became the unacceptable.

In my discussion of sovereignty over their natural resources, I mentioned the UN support for this, but also the fact that OPEC in general and Saudi Arabia in particular had been taking initiatives to stabilize oil prices and bring an element of predictability into the world oil market, with a particular recognition for the problems faced by oil-importing developing countries.

At the same time, I mentioned the income accruing to the people in oil-exporting countries, countries such as Saudi Arabia, as compared with what I called the staggering profits realized by the major oil companies. In this respect, and in spite of the change in the balance of power between them and the national companies of oil-producing countries, these traditional major companies continue to make unprecedentedly large profits of $45 billion for Exxon-Mobil in 2008 and $35 billion for Royal Dutch Shell, thanks in part to the volatility in oil prices dictated by market forces up to a peak of $147 a barrel followed by a subsequent collapse on account of its unsustainability, fuelled by speculation.

Review of Energy Scenarios

Part III next examines chapters 13 to 23 of the earlier book in a critical way and reviews the energy scenarios, historical and regional analysis with the benefit of hindsight. It is designed to complement Part II which sought to simply identify the main developments occurring from 1979 to 2007 whereas this part reviews the projections made for 1985, 1990 and 2000 in the three scenarios discussed in *Energy: A Global Outlook.*

Oil Reserves and Discoveries

I discussed the fall in the world's proved oil reserves which occurred between 1974 and 1979 and the prospect that a continuation of this trend would have been incompatible with the strong growth of oil demand, doubling every ten years or so, seen in the period of low oil prices which prevailed during the 1960s.

In practice, readers of Part II of this book will be aware that world proved oil reserves increased quite sharply after 1979, especially among some OPEC member countries over the five years 1985 to 1989. In the earlier book I discussed the phenomenon that a high proportion of all the oil discovered in the world so far had been located in so-called giant fields, and these giant fields tend to have been concentrated in relatively few, and geographically limited, areas of the world's surface. I went on to say that these considerations weighed heavily in the relatively pessimistic outlook regarding future oil discoveries among the best informed of the world's petroleum geologists and engineers.

In spite of these somewhat pessimistic views, there were unexpectedly big new finds of oil, but consistent with the above remarks these additional big oil finds occurred mainly in the existing area of the Arabian Gulf where a preponderance of existing world oil reserves had been found previously. Middle East oil reserves had accounted for 55.7 per cent of the worldwide total in 1979 and this had increased to 61.0 per cent by 2007.

Similarly, the share of all thirteen OPEC member countries increased from 68.0 per cent of the worldwide total in 1979 to 75.5 per cent in 2007. Even more dramatically, if one compares the net addition to reserves of the thirteen OPEC member countries with all other countries worldwide and relates these to the statistics of oil production over the same twenty-eight-year period, one finds a remarkable contrast. Not only was the increase in net additions to reserves among OPEC countries much greater than among non-OPEC countries, but the volume of oil production over this long period to 2007 was considerably less for OPEC member countries than for non-OPEC countries worldwide, as can be seen from the statistics below.

A comparison between OPEC and the rest of the world is shown in bar chart form for the periods 1980 to 1989, 1990 to 1999 and 2000 to 2007, indicating for each of them the reserves of oil at the end of each period, new reserves added during each period and oil produced during each period expressed in billions of barrels. Figure II.12 along with the statistical table (Table III.2) brings out the rather stark difference between OPEC and the rest of the world.

Table III.2. The Comparative Experience 1979 to 2007 (billion barrels)

	OPEC	All Other Countries	Worldwide
Increase in proved oil reserves	497.2	97.2	594.5
Oil production during 28 years	276.3	422.2	698.5
Increase in reserves relative to production expressed as %	180	23	85

Non-OPEC proved oil reserves actually increased at an annual average rate of less than 3.5 billion barrels over these twenty-eight years compared with more than 17.7 billion barrels annually for OPEC member countries, aggregating more than 21 billion barrels annually for the world as a whole. Worldwide oil production over this lengthy period averaged more than 24.9 billion barrels annually. This comparison would have been considerably less comfortable than it now seems had it not been for the unexpectedly big rise in OPEC reserves averaging 51 billion barrels annually over the five years 1985 to 1989 inclusive.

In spite of the modest rate of increase of non-OPEC oil reserves, given that they did increase by 47.2 per cent over the twenty-eight years to 2007 with non-OPEC oil production rising by 33.6 per cent, the reserves to production ratio for non-OPEC countries as a whole did rise slightly from 16.3 years in 1979 to 17.9 years in 2007. Over the same period OPEC oil reserves increased from 38.2 to 72.7 years. In other words, the lifespan of OPEC reserves in 2007 was more than four times those of all other countries worldwide, whereas in 1979 the multiple was only 2.3 times.

Changes in Oil and Energy Demand

This topic was discussed briefly on p. 94 of *Energy: A Global Outlook* for the qualitatively very different periods up to 1973 and subsequently to 1979. What has happened since, i.e. from 1979 to 2007, has been comprehensively analysed and discussed in Part II above, with the relevant four time subdivisions within this twenty-eight-year period being a feature of it. The first three of them cover the same time periods up to 2000 which formed the basis for our critical evaluation of *Energy: A Global Outlook*.

Comparative growth rates for the world economy, primary energy and oil: scenario projections in *Energy: A Global Outlook* compared with actual estimates

Table III.3 provides an overall perspective of some of the main features of the projections prepared in 1980–1 compared with actuals recorded in the prior periods of 1965 to 1973 and 1973 to 1979, along the three periods included in the earlier book, together with actuals for 2000 to 2007. In order to facilitate comparisons these numbers are expressed in terms of percentage annual average compound growth rates and percentage shares of totals, except for the primary energy/GDP coefficients.

Table III.3. Comparative Growth Rates: Actuals vs Scenario Projections for World as a Whole (% p.a.)

	1965–73	1973–9	1979–85	1985–90	1990–2000	2000–7
*GDP Actual	5.4	3.3	2.5	3.7	2.8 [2.9]	3.1
Cooperation	N/A	N/A	4.7	3.5	4.1	N/A
Neutral	N/A	N/A	3.2	2.6	3.3	N/A
Confrontation	N/A	N/A	1.0	1.0	2.1	N/A
PE Actual	5.2	2.8	1.0	2.5	1.3 [2.2]	2.6
Cooperation	N/A	N/A	3.5	<3.0	2.8	N/A
Neutral	N/A	N/A	2.5	2.0	2.0	N/A
Confrontation	N/A	N/A	1.0	1.0	1.2	N/A
PE/GDP Actual	0.96	0.85	0.40	0.68	0.46 [0.76]	0.84
Cooperation	N/A	N/A	0.74	0.86	0.68	N/A
Neutral	N/A	N/A	0.78	0.77	0.61	N/A
Confrontation	N/A	N/A	1.0	1.0	0.57	N/A
Oil % PE Actual	40.0 (in 1965)	48.0 (in 1973)	45.9 (in 1979)	39.1 (in 1985)	38.8 (in 1990)	38.3 (in 2000)	35.6 (in 2007)
Cooperation	N/A	N/A	N/A	42.0	35	23	N/A
Neutral	N/A	N/A	N/A	40.0	34	22	N/A
Confrontation	N/A	N/A	N/A	<40.0	32	19	N/A

OPEC % of World oil production Actual	45.3 (in 1965)	53.1 (in 1973)	47.5 (in 1979)	29.5 (in 1985)	38.3 (in 1990)	43.5 (in 2000)	43.9 (in 2007)
Cooperation	N/A	N/A	N/A	46.4	45.1	48.4	N/A
Neutral	N/A	N/A	N/A	44.4	40.5	43.8	N/A
Confrontation	N/A	N/A	N/A	40.3	34.7	35.3	N/A

Numbers in brackets represent worldwide averages omitting the Russian Federation for GDP and the whole of the former Soviet Union for primary energy.

*World Bank.

It can be seen that, at the level of the world as a whole, the six years from 1979 to 1985 were the most exceptional throughout the more than forty years covered in this analysis. World economic growth and the growth of primary energy consumption were both actually lower than during any of the other periods, as was the energy coefficient. This latter was especially significant. Oil's share of world energy dropped more sharply than at any other time, by 6.8 percentage points, and OPECs share as the balancing form of world energy fell much more dramatically, by 18 percentage points between 1979 and 1985.

The comparatively low growth rates for both the world economy and primary energy consumption in the decade from 1990 to 2000 can be attributed in part to the demise of the former Soviet Union. This has been discussed in more detail in Part II, with further treatment of it to follow later in this Part III.

The exceptionally low growth rates recorded for the 1979 to 1985 period can be attributed to the two influences of economic recession and market forces induced big oil price increases in 1979 and 1980, discussed earlier in *Energy: A Global Outlook*. Contributor influences to the oil price increases were changes in market sentiment involving pro-cyclical stock building by the major oil companies, the Iranian Revolution and the outbreak of war between Iraq and Iran, all of which were discussed in the earlier book.

This long-run historical perspective can be used to suggest that the OPEC oil price increases of 1973–4 were sustainable and effective in contributing to lower growth of the world economy and the start of a transition in the energy sector involving a lesser dependence on oil in economic activity, with conservation savings and more efficient use of it. The non-sustainability of the 1979–80 oil price increase was finally proven after five years of decline, rising output by non-OPEC producers, 34.7 million b/d in 1979, up to 40.6 million b/d in 1985, while OPEC output fell by 14.5 million b/d over the same period in response to declining world oil consumption. This combination of events led to an OPEC decision to increase oil supplies to the market, accelerating the fall in prices in 1986. Thus the spot price of crude in 1986 at $13.10 a barrel was almost identical to what it had been in 1978 ($13.03), as shown in Part II.

Similarly, the unsustainability of spot and futures market prices of crude oil rising to more than $140 a barrel in mid-July 2008 after a long but much more gradual increase from 2004 through 2007 (compared with 1979–80) were associated with speculative pressures linked to too-easy credit over a long period of irresponsible bank lending. This led to the credit crunch and the loss of confidence within the financial sector of the world economy, culminating in the failure of Lehman Brothers in September 2008. This was shortly after the oil market bubble burst in July, with the oil price falling to less than $40 a barrel within seven to eight months, more sharply than it had risen, a clear example of market overshoot in both directions and symptomatic of speculation rather than market fundamentals being the primary influence at work. This was illustrated in Part I showing the close relationship of prices for both West Texas Intermediate and Brent Crude Oil. Other crude oil prices are closely aligned to them, too, having regard to both quality and freight cost differentials.

In 1979 to 1985 the world economy grew at a rate less than in our neutral scenario projection but well above the confrontation case. Primary energy consumption grew at an average but uneven rate of 1.0 per cent annually, precisely the same as in our confrontation scenario. As a result, the actual energy coefficient was down at 0.4, much less than our projections in all three scenarios. Likewise, the oil share of worldwide primary energy usage fell to 39.1 per cent, i.e. less than in all three of our scenarios. Most significant of all was the fall in OPEC's share of world oil production which was much greater than in the three scenarios included in *Energy: A Global Outlook*.

During the period 1985 to 1990 the position was quite different. Global economic growth actually exceeded our scenario projections, but only by marginally more than in our cooperation case. Undoubtedly this economic revival was assisted by the low oil prices prevailing from 1986 onwards and no widespread economic recession during this period. Primary energy consumption growth rebounded to 2.5 per cent p.a., between our cooperation and neutral scenarios. Although the energy coefficient rose from the previous six-year-period average, it was still below those implicit in our three scenarios. Comparatively low oil prices during the period also meant that oil's share of world energy consumption was only marginally less than during 1979–85 and in fact considerably above our scenario projections hypothesized on more limited worldwide oil availability and rising real oil prices which did not occur during this period. OPEC's share of world oil production rose nearly 9 percentage points between 1985 and 1990 as a result of the policy decision taken in 1986, but at 39.3 per cent it was still below our projections in the cooperation and neutral scenarios.

In the decade from 1990 to 2000, world economic growth actually fell back to average only 2.8 per cent p.a. and world energy consumption to only 1.3 per cent annually, with the energy coefficient falling back to 0.46. This was largely attributable to the demise of the former Soviet Union – not provided for in our scenario projections. Excluding only the Russian Federation from World Bank estimates of world gross domestic product, the worldwide average would have been 2.9 per cent p.a. rather than the 2.8 per cent shown in the table. For primary energy consumption the exclusion of the whole of the former Soviet Union is more dramatic, with average worldwide growth over the decade at 2.2 per cent p.a. and the energy coefficient increasing sharply to 0.76. The average fall in energy consumption in the former Soviet Union amounted to 4.2 per cent annually over the decade to 2000, or even more sharply from its former peak in 1990 by 36.6 per cent to the trough in 1998.

Our scenario projections for economic growth were too optimistic in the cooperation and neutral scenarios but too pessimistic in the confrontation case. The same can be said for primary energy consumption inclusive of the extraordinary numbers for the former Soviet Union. Our energy coefficients were all between the two extremes inclusive and exclusive of the former Soviet Union.

With relatively low real oil prices continuing to prevail through 2000, the oil share of primary energy demand showed a fall of less than a percentage point between 1985 and 2000. This was in contrast to our three scenarios predicated on tighter oil supplies and significantly rising real oil prices which were not realized during this period.

Our projections for the OPEC share of world oil production were too optimistic in the cooperation scenarios which envisaged a much lower total volume of 62 million b/d than the 74.9 million b/d actually recorded for the year 2000. Our projections for world oil production were much lower still in the neutral scenario and dramatically so in the confrontation case. However, the OPEC percentage share in the neutral scenario at 43.8 per cent, albeit on a very different volume base, was very similar to the 43.5 per cent actually recorded.

Future Prospects

Under this subheading of chapter 13 in *Energy: A Global Outlook* we discussed the then current issues of the impact on the global oil industry of both the Iranian Revolution of 1979 and the conflict between Iran and Iraq which began in 1980 and continued until 1988. In practice, both of these events seem to have been noteworthy mostly for anticipations of possible shortfalls in oil supplies to the world market rather than any actual shortages, as discussed above. However, they both did significantly contribute to previously unanticipated oil price increases. These were exacerbated by precautionary practices of stock building by the major oil companies. Almost certainly, these developments would not have occurred if there had been no Iranian Revolution or no outbreak of conflict between Iraq and Iran.

Figure 8 in *Energy: A Global Outlook* showed growth rates for the world economy for three time periods, 1979 to 1985, 1985 to 1990 and 1990 to 2000, under three scenario headings which we termed cooperation, neutral and confrontation. These were discussed in some detail on pp. 104–7 of that earlier book. We also pointed out that the economic growth projections compared with the historical backdrop seemed consistent with our energy supply and demand projections, together with conservation savings and improvements in the efficiency of energy use which seemed possible at that time.

For comparative purposes we show below the actual progress of the world economy in terms of constant US dollar prices relative to our projections made in 1980–1. For this purpose we have used World Bank estimates of gross domestic product. For the historical period of 1965 to 1973 the estimate of 5.4 per cent p.a. compound growth was unchanged for the cheap oil era. The earlier estimate of 3.5 per cent p.a. for 1973 to 1979 was superseded by a somewhat lower figure of 3.3 per cent for this period.

Table III.4. World Economic Growth 1979–2000 (% p.a.)

		Scenario Case Projections		
	Actual outcome	Cooperation	Neutral	Confrontation
1979 to 1985	2.5	4.7	3.2	1.6
1985 to 1990	3.7	3.5	2.6	1.6
1990 to 2000	2.8	4.1	3.3	2.1
Average over 21 years to 2000	2.9	4.1	3.1	1.8
2000 to 2007	3.1	No projections made		

Thus it can be seen that our earlier projections for economic growth in the 1979 to 1985 period tended to be too optimistic, with the actual outcome falling below our neutral scenario but well above our worst case confrontation scenario. The low average economic growth rate over this period was attributable in large measure to the quite severe recession in the leading industrialized countries during the early 1980s. This contributed to the gradual decline in world oil prices from 1980 to 1985 with a sharp fall in the worldwide energy coefficient to only 0.40 energy use/GDP compared with 0.85 during the preceding five years. Also, with primary energy growing at an average rate of only 1.0 per cent annually and oil consumption as the balancing form of energy falling at -1.7 per cent on average each year, there was marked pressure on oil producers, as noted in Part II above. This meant a fall of 5 million barrels per day in world oil consumption. As we showed there, oil's share of the world energy consumption fell quite dramatically during these six years from 45.9 per cent in 1979 to only 39.1 per cent in 1985. Worse still, as the balancing source of world oil supplies, OPEC's share of the total fell from 47.5 per cent in 1979 to only 29.5 per cent in 1985, as shown in Part II. Saudi Arabia's share fell by 11 percentage points in the four years from 1981 (when its prices were relatively competitive within OPEC) to 1985. Thus as far as Saudi Arabia and OPEC were concerned, this six-year period was both unprecedented and bordering on the confrontation scenario, significantly below the neutral case.

By contrast, the five years from 1985 to 1990 associated with lower oil prices were far more satisfactory, with economic growth actually just exceeding our cooperation scenario. Primary energy consumption rebounded to average 2.5 per cent annually, with oil being marginally less at 2.4 per cent. Also, the energy/GDP coefficient moved up to 0.68 as it normally does over a period of years when economic growth is higher.

Over the last decade of the twentieth century GDP growth slipped back again to average only 2.8 per cent annually with primary energy consumption at half that, i.e. only 1.4 per cent p.a. and oil at marginally less, 1.2 per cent annually on average. Once again, this average growth achieved in the world economy was less than the 3.3 per cent projection annually in our neutral scenario which can be attributed in part to the break-up of the former Soviet Union and the subsequent debt crisis there and in the Far East late in this decade.

Overall, the average growth of the world economy over the twenty-one years to 2000 was marginally inferior to our projection in the neutral scenario. This can be attributed to the adverse influences of economic recession in the industrialized countries along with a debt crisis in Latin America in the early 1980s and the major disruption following the break-up of the former Soviet Union with a weakening economy there and falling production of both oil and gas and consumption there through much of the 1990s.

Our suggestion that the so-called centrally planned economies might account for about 47 per cent of the growth in worldwide primary energy consumption between 1979 and 2000 proved to be completely wrong. They accounted for 37 per cent of worldwide growth from 1979 to 1990 but thereafter primary energy consumption in the former Soviet Union fell by 35 per cent between 1990 and 2000 because of political and economic disruption. China on its own accounted for 21 per cent of worldwide growth in energy demand between 1979 and 2000, an indication of its growing importance over this period, which continued beyond the millennium, of course, and accelerated. Between 2000 and 2009 China accounted for 50.9 per cent of the worldwide growth in primary energy consumption.

These numbers show how political disruption in the former Soviet Union and dramatic economic stimulus in China can disrupt any projections, even though such changes might counterbalance one another to some extent.

Growth in energy consumption among OPEC member countries (or, at least in nine of them for which data are readily accessible) for the twenty-one years to 2000 averaged 4.8 per cent p.a., significantly less than the 8.3 per cent we had projected. In *Energy: A Global Outlook* I also discussed the influence of political and economic factors on the extent to which OPEC members were prepared to produce at what was likely to be near their maximum capacity of about 32 million barrels per day in the year 2000. In fact, OPEC output that year was 32.16 million barrels per day, so that this particular long-term forecast made almost twenty years previously turned out to be remarkably accurate. However, an alternative projection of only 23.5 million barrels per day in 2000 proved to be much too low.

Energy Scenarios for 1985 and 1990

The next chapter of *Energy: A Global Outlook* discussed energy scenarios for 1985 and 1990 with a qualitative description of what these three cases involved. Looking back at these now leads one to conclude that many of the features described were both valid over the time periods to which they related and are still relevant at the end of the first decade of the twenty-first century.

Having regard to the financial turmoil in international credit markets and the banking sector in 2007, 2008 and on into 2009, together with the unsustainable rises seen in oil prices in both 1979–80 and in more recent years through to July 2008, I consider it appropriate to reiterate here what I said under both these headings for the cooperation and confrontation scenarios written nearly thirty years ago.

Cooperation scenario features

A more stable and predictable international financial climate likely to favour saving and investment relative to current consumption. This is likely to be particularly important for ensuring that there is an adequate real transfer of resources to the energy sector where long lead times tend to be characteristic. It is also important to protect surplus revenues generated from higher than necessary oil production and exports.

Implementation by OPEC of a long term strategy (after re-unification of the price structure) which makes oil production and price levels more predictable in the medium term. This is likely to include an element of flexibility to cover deviations from likely medium term trends, whether originating at the supply or demand end of the oil equation. Modest and predictable rises in real oil prices would be a stimulus to change in the energy mix.

Confrontation scenario features

An unstable and unpredictable international financial climate in terms of sharp fluctuations in exchange rates and security of funds invested abroad. The climate will militate against major international investment in capital projects as an increasing number of countries show signs of political instability and/or problems of credit-worthiness.

Lack of any long term strategy for oil prices or production among major exporters with diverse interests, time scales and objectives, leading to contradictions in policies, with the international oil market suffering from periodic crises. The outcome is likely to be sharp fluctuations in the volume of production and exports either side of a significantly more sharply rising trend than in the co-operation scenario. Uncertainty would be the fundamentally important characteristic of the international oil market with rather sharp swings between tight and slack conditions.

Oil prices

Two fundamental shortcomings in *Energy: A Global Outlook* related to the unforeseen and unexpectedly large additions to oil reserves in several leading OPEC countries during the five years from 1985 to 1990; and, secondly, that by mid-1981, it had not become apparent that the oil price increases dictated by market forces in 1979 and 1980 would not be sustainable. Thus the basis of the price projections shown on p. 108 was shown to be invalid by the subsequent evolution of world oil market prices over a long period.

Instead, what does seem to be a relevant base is the average price prevailing over the five years 1974 to 1978 inclusive, subsequent to those mandated by OPEC in October 1973 and 1 January 1974. Expressed in terms of constant US dollars at prices of 2007 the average price for 1974–8 amounts to $46.60 a barrel. This compares with an average price in 2007 of $72.39 a barrel, as reported in Part II of this book. However, to illustrate the volatility of oil prices, even on a constant dollar basis, we can note that the lowest annual average price recorded since 1973 was only $16.69 a barrel in 1998, followed by an unsustainable high of $97.26 in 2008. Prior to the sharp price increases which had started in 2004, the price as recently as 2003 averaged only $32.51 a barrel expressed in constant dollar terms of 2007.

Before entering more caveats concerning oil price volatility and the hazards of making projections for only ten years ahead or even less, in fact, this text would be less than honest and comprehensive if we did not now show what it would have looked like in 1990. To be fair, we have to say we did warn readers (in our 1980–1 text): 'It does not seem reasonable to attach a high level of confidence to these figures (as shown below), having regard to the many factors which can have a significant impact on them either in a relative moment of time or progressively over ten years.' Using our proposed alternative base period of 1974–8 instead (actually 1976) with the price in constant dollars of 2007, i.e. $46.60, Table III.5 shows our low level of confidence not to have been misplaced.

Table III.5. Trend Rate of Change in Real Oil Prices 1981–1990

Scenario	% per year	$ a barrel in 1990 expressed in $ of 2007
Cooperation	Up to 3, say 1.5%	57.40
Neutral	3 to 6, say 4.5%	86.30
Confrontation	> 6, say 7.5%	128.26
Actual price in 1990 in terms of $ of 2007		37.82

In our 1981 text we went on to make a further caveat or qualification for the longer term towards the millennium year of 2000. Of course, once again, with the benefit of long-distance time hindsight, we should have referred too to the early 1980s recession having an adverse effect on the world oil market, even before our earlier book was published.

> To hazard a guess as to how oil prices might move through the 1990s seems unreasonable at this point in time bearing in mind the uncertainties relating to technological change, new oil discoveries, supply of other forms of energy and developments in the energy/GDP growth relationship. It seems sufficient to remark that in qualitative terms they will be similar to the pattern observable in the table above. That is to say that they will be softest or lowest in the co-operation scenario and hardest or highest in real terms in the confrontation scenario.

In theory, we can say that the price rise from $46.60 a barrel to $72.39 in 2007 represents a real increase of 1.4 per cent p.a. on average over the thirty-one years from 1976. However, that is evidently something of a nonsense when the oil price expressed in constant dollars was below its starting point in twenty of those thirty-one years when it rose. Moreover, there were nine years when the oil price fell by more than 10 per cent from one year to the next but eleven years when it rose by more than 10 per cent in consecutive years, i.e. almost two-thirds of all years when the oil price in constant dollars rose or fell by more than 10 per cent in consecutive years. In three of the years oil prices fell by more than 20 per cent and in another seven, it rose consecutively by more than 20 per cent, i.e. almost a third of all cases taking falls and rises together.

These measures of volatility over a thirty-one-year period suggest that deviations from any trend must be considered the norm rather than an abnormality, the dominance of spot markets and the innovation of future markets for crude oil and products fuelled by cheap credit and speculative trading on a vast scale have served to undermine the former system of fixed price contracts. The figure illustrates the four and a half years run-up to the unsustainable peak of July 2008 and the sudden subsequent collapse to less than $40 a barrel in February 2009, nevertheless followed by another rise to more than $70 a barrel by June 2009.

In this context we believe there is once again a strong case for more effective cooperation between OPEC countries holding 76 per cent of the world's proved oil reserves and major oil-importing countries, which must now include China. All of these surely have a common interest in relatively more stable and predictable oil prices in order to ensure that over-exaggerated swings both upwards and downwards do not exacerbate changes not justified by oil market fundamentals, but which are probably inevitably associated with the economic cycle to some extent. Nevertheless, incalculable damage has been done politically, economically and to public confidence as a result of the sharp and unpredictable changes in the prices of oil entering world trade, particularly when apparently unsupported by the fundamentals of supply and demand.

In this context, we can discuss a number of initiatives designed to support international cooperation over a lengthy period since the mid-1970s. The first of these was the Conference on International Economic Co-operation (CIEC) held in Paris from late 1975 to mid-1977. That was reviewed at some length in *Energy: A Global Outlook,* or at least the Energy Commission Report (appendix III.2) forming one of four parts of it. Unfortunately, there was no successful marrying-up of the separate proposals submitted respectively by the Group of 19 and G8 countries. This was followed by the Report of the Independent Commission on International Development Issues, popularly called 'North–South: A Programme for Survival' under the Chairmanship of the former West German Chancellor, Willy Brandt, in 1980.

Then in 1981 OPEC prepared and published a report emanating from its Long Term Strategy Committee aimed precisely at resolving some of the problems outlined above and which now clearly need to be addressed, perhaps more than at any time during the past thirty to thirty-five years.

After that, there was a long quiescent period on account of oil price weakness through the mid-1980s, and effectively for more than twenty years, attributable to a number of influences discussed earlier in this book. Thus by the second quarter of 2008 the G8 countries were becoming quite alarmed by the extent of the oil price rises which seemed not to be justified by oil market fundamentals in terms of a mismatch between supply and demand. Thus they requested the IMF to examine this problem and to report back by October 2008.

Following the problems associated with the unprecedented spike in oil prices running up over several years to the peak of more than $140 a barrel in July 2008, there is surely a strong case for a new conference of all the major oil importing and exporting countries worldwide. The objective should be to explore the potentialities of international cooperation to provide the means for producing a route for more predictable and more gradually changing oil prices for volumes of crude and refined products moving into world trade. An appropriate mechanism would need to reflect first and foremost the underlying influences of supply and demand and be sensitive, above all, to the normal rhythm of the worldwide economic cycle. While there should always be scope for spot and futures markets to respond to exceptional and unexpected events, their economically justified role is really to operate as marginal market safety valves. It should not be to provide well-informed speculators with bountiful profit opportunities for themselves at minimum cost but at a significant cost to consumers and to the world economy generally, given the interdependence of the oil, gas and energy sectors and the other sectors of economic activity worldwide.

The list of potential participants to such a conference should be limited to twenty in number to ensure that proceedings are manageable, with pre-conference position papers desirable in advance in order to pinpoint potential areas of conflict or difficulty. Clearly it would be useful if these could be drawn up and coordinated by appropriate organizations such as the IEA on behalf of oil-importing countries and OPEC on behalf of oil-exporting countries with consultation in advance among each of the two groups to ensure reasonably unanimous positions in advance of formal negotiations being arranged between the two groups. In this context, given the announcement in Pittsburgh on 25 September 2009, there is a potentially important role for the G20 countries, too. China has to be included, given the rapid rise in its oil imports. The proposed participants and their positions in world oil trade are listed in Table III.6.

Table III.6. Oil Trade in 2008

Leading Oil Importers mn b/d			Leading Oil Exporters mn b/d		
	gross	net		gross	net
Europe*	13.75	11.73	Middle East	20.13	19.71
USA	12.87	10.91	Former USSR	8.18	8.03
Japan	4.93	4.57	W Africa	4.59	4.29
China	4.39	4.01	S and C America	3.62	2.14
India	3.02	2.30	N Africa	3.26	2.76

All EU	Saudi Arabia)
* say Germany	Iran)
France	Iraq) to represent Middle East
Italy	Kuwait)
Spain	UAE)
EU Commission	
Other Asia/Pacific 7.02 4.63	Russian Federation the largest oil exporter
South Korea	in the Former USSR
the largest oil	Nigeria to represent W Africa
consumer 2.29 mn b/d in	Algeria to represent N Africa
2008)	Venezuela to represent S and C America
Total 9 countries and EU	Total 9 countries + OPEC Secretariat
Commission and the IEA, too.	
NB UK is now a very small net	
oil importer as consumption	
exceeds declining production	

The International Energy forum should also have a role, comprising as it does with oil importing and exporting countries as well as leading oil companies.

Possible IMF, World Bank and WTO participation as observers to assist in negotiations related to the world economy, the financial sector and world trade and investment in the energy sector

The principal oil importing and exporting countries are more or less automatic selections for any new international group which might be formed to enter a hopefully effective dialogue on possible means to bring about a more stable and predictable course for prices of oil (crude, NGLs and refined products) entering world trade than the disturbances arising in 1979–80 and 2004 through to July 2008. Such incidents/events have a tendency to interact with and contribute to relatively severe downturns in the world economy witnessed in the early 1980s and again from 2007 through 2009 and probably into 2010, too, linked to financial sector turmoil, i.e. irresponsible bank lending.

In spite of my personal disappointment with the outcome of the Conference on International Economic Co-operation in which I participated more than thirty years ago, I believe, more than ever before, that the time is now ripe for a conference of the type described above, if the world is to learn from past mistakes with both oil importers and exporters involved. I do not suggest that the road for oil in the future will be fast, smooth and easy, but rather that it should be less rocky, hazardous and difficult to negotiate if the conference proposed was to have a successful outcome and followed up with the institution of a semi-permanent organization comprising at least the key participants from both sides. I believe the newly enhanced role of the G20 means that it must play an important role, as its member countries are major economies, are major energy importers or exporters and account for almost two-thirds of the world population. An annual review of the world oil market in retrospect and prospect for the coming twelve months or so seems desirable, to be followed by an annual conference of participants to review and hopefully agree on short-term market prospects and appropriate action by the major players, perhaps including new regulatory procedures designed to eliminate markets overshooting as oil prices did in 2008.

In the remaining part of this chapter on energy scenarios for 1985 and 1990 in *Energy: A Global Outlook* I discussed the prospects for the world as a whole in the three scenario cases, for the non-Communist countries collectively, the industrialized countries and the Communist bloc countries. Here I discuss the actual outcome in the world as a whole through to 1985 and 1990 in reference to these three scenarios.

The actual outcome is shown in Table III.7 for the two time periods of six and five years respectively compared with our projections for the cooperation, neutral and confrontation scenarios.

Table III.7. Worldwide % p.a. Growth

	1979 to 1985				1985 to 1990			
	Actual	Coop.	Neutral	Conf.	Actual	Coop	Neutral	Conf.
GDP	2.5	4.7	3.2	1.0	3.7	3.5	2.6	1.0
PE	1.0	3.5	2.5	1.0	2.5	<3.0	2.0	1.0

PE/GDP coefficient	0.40	0.74	0.78	1.0	0.68	0.86	0.77	1.0
Oil % of PE	39.1%	42% in 1985	40%	<40%	38.8%	35% in 1990	34%	32%

These outcomes are interesting in several respects. For 1979 to 1985 world economic growth was below our neutral scenario on average, largely due to the economic recession in the industrialized countries in the early 1980s combined with the contractionary effect on economic activity of the high oil prices of 1979 and 1980 which continued into 1981. By contrast, world economic growth was marginally higher than we had foreseen even in the cooperation scenario from 1985 to 1990.

Primary energy consumption growth actually recorded at only 1.0 per cent p.a. from 1979 to 1985 was a function of both low economic growth, a low energy coefficient relative to GDP of only 0.4 for this period (the coefficient tends to be lower still when economic growth is low). It was in line with our projection in the confrontation scenario for this period, also 1.0 per cent p.a.; likewise, the oil share of primary energy which fell to 39.1 per cent in 1985 compared with 45.9 per cent only six years earlier. We had said less than 40 per cent by 1985 in the confrontation scenario. The low energy/GDP coefficient reflected the high oil prices of 1979–80 which stimulated energy conservation and improvements in the efficiency of energy use, especially oil.

Primary energy consumption worldwide grew at an average rate of 2.5 per cent annually between 1985 and 1990. This was below our cooperation scenario but above our neutral scenario for this period. We can also remark that the energy coefficient was lower than we had projected, implying continuing conservation savings and improvements in energy use. However, oil's share of the energy mix showed little fall between 1985 and 1990 and less than we had projected in all scenario cases. This was almost certainly attributable to the soft oil market, particularly in 1986, when OPEC engineered a real oil price fall of almost 49 per cent from the year before by increasing oil supplies to the market in order to safeguard its medium- to long-term position, following the deterioration in its fortunes over the period from 1979 to 1985, as discussed earlier in this book.

By this means, the previous sharp fall in oil's share of the energy market was brought not quite to a halt but to a much slower rate of decline which persisted for many years subsequently. Our scenario cases for oil's declining share of the world energy market thus proved to be significantly too pessimistic for 1990. Also, our projection for oil's share to fall to only 35 per cent even in the cooperation scenario by 1990 proved too pessimistic, as this level was actually reached only in 2007.

Our discussion of the seven qualitative features of what could happen in our confrontation scenario was realized in fact in only two of them: the endemic conflict between Israel and the Arab states, explicitly the Palestinians, and direct Western military intervention in the Gulf region. Of course, this latter occurred simply because of the provocation of Saddam Hussein's invasion of Kuwait in 1990. Happily, the subsequent pull-out was more satisfactorily arranged than the aftermath of the invasion of Iraq by coalition forces in March 2003.

Energy Scenarios for 2000

Energy scenarios for the year 2000 formed the subject of the next chapter of *Energy: A Global Outlook*. Once again, we refer to the earlier book simply because our discussion of uncertainties arising from many sources proved to be well-founded. We summarized that anticipation by remarking that: 'Actual experience over the next 20 years may well follow a composite mosaic of the scenarios discussed in this book, because that is the way the real world tends to progress over time.' We have already shown how this remark was justified by actual experience through to 1985 and 1990 by comparing this with our three scenario projections for those years. We backed up the quotation with the following remarks in the text prepared in 1981. We believe these worthy of reiteration now, even though surprisingly large new oil discoveries were made and exploited over the period to the year 2000 and subsequently with OPEC production rising to more than 37 million barrels per day in late 2007 and early 2008.

The means that something such as the profile of world oil production may follow a fairly erratic course over an extended period, as indeed it has done during the last ten years, yet remain explicable in politico-economic terms. This should serve to reinforce the central message of this book: namely, that a constructive international dialogue leading to harmonious international relations should facilitate an orderly rather than disorderly transition away from oil dependence. This is inevitable sooner or later, even if surprisingly large new oil discoveries should be made and exploited during the course of the next twenty years or so, including further big rises in the recovery factor for oil in place.

These considerations should make everyone engaged in looking at the misty 'energy 2000' horizon very chary of making strong claims for his own estimate or series of projections.

It is in the light of these cautionary remarks that we now proceed to review our projections made for the period 1990 to 2000 in the light of actual experience during that decade.

Table III.8. Worldwide % p.a Growth 1990 to 2000

	Actual	Cooperation	Neutral	Confrontation
GDP	2.8	4.1	3.3	2.1
PE	1.4	2.8	2.0	1.2
PE/GDP coefficient	0.50	0.68	0.61	0.57
Oil % of PE	38.3	23	24	21
Incl. non-conventional oils mn b/d		+6	+4.5	+3.2
Coal/other solids	25.2%	34%	Coal >36%	Coal 37%

Thus once again we find that the world economy and the energy sector actually followed a composite mosaic of the three scenario projections.

Economic growth was below our neutral scenario but well above the confrontation scenario, but primary energy growth at only 1.4 per cent p.a. was also below our neutral scenario and only marginally above our confrontation scenario case. This comparatively low growth record for the world as a whole reflects the poor performance of the former Soviet Union. Here we can simply note that in 1990 the former Soviet Union accounted for 17.5 per cent of world primary energy consumption but by the year 2000 it was just under 10 per cent, having fallen by an average of 4.2 per cent annually over the decade or 35 per cent for the period. Even more dramatically, its oil consumption accounted for 12.8 per cent of the worldwide total in 1990 but for only 4.8 per cent in 2000, after falling at an average annual rate of 8.3 per cent or 58 per cent from 1990 to 2000.

Once again too, in spite of oil prices declining then remaining fairly stable, the energy coefficient was lower than was implicit in our projections and the elasticity of energy demand higher than we had expected. Mainly for the reason of comparatively soft oil prices, oil's share of the world energy mix declined by only 0.5 percentage points over the decade from 38.8 per cent in 1990 to 38.3 per cent in the year 2000. The shares of other sources of energy rose by 1.7 percentage points for natural gas, by 0.7 percentage points for nuclear and 0.5 percentage points for hydro-electricity but coal's share fell to a new low of only 25.2 per cent of worldwide energy use in 2000, down 2.3 per cent percentage points from ten years earlier. This was in sharp contrast to our scenario projections in *Energy: A Global Outlook* for the year 2000, in all of which we had expected coal to increase its share of the world energy market to as much as 37 per cent in our confrontation scenario.

The comparative weakness of oil prices from 1990 to 2000 helps to explain both the lack of much erosion in oil's share of the world energy market between 1990 and 2000 and the further decline in coal's share during this decade. Another function of oil price weakness at this time was the lack of progress we had foreseen in the growth of non-conventional oils during this period, synthetic shale and tar sands, which we had expected to contribute 7 million barrels per day down to 4 million barrels per day by 2000, in the three scenario cases.

Just as our projections for coal and other solid fuels were much too optimistic, so our projections for oil's share were much too pessimistic, as can be seen from Table III.8. Of course, these projections were predicated on both oil supply constraints and higher real oil prices than those which actually prevailed through the decade from 1990 to 2000 and for several years subsequently.

There was another relevant influence on the lack of progress of not only coal but nuclear and hydro-electricity too, in not increasing their shares of world energy consumption in the way we had anticipated in preparing our energy scenarios. This explanation was the comparatively low growth of primary energy consumption, which averaged only 1.5 per cent annually over the twenty-one years from 1979 to 2000, i.e. below our neutral scenario and only slightly higher than in our confrontation scenario.

Table III.9. Scenario Projections Made in 1981 for Primary Energy Demand Worldwide for 2000 Relative to Actual Estimates for That Year

	Scenario			
	Actuals %	Cooperation %	Neutral %	Confrontation %
Oil (incl. synthetics etc)	38.3	26.1	24.1	21.4
Natural gas	23.7	20.9	20.8	22.1
Solid fuels (incl. biomass)	25.2	34.4	36.3	36.9
Nuclear	6.3	11.0	10.7	10.2
Hydro (incl. geothermal, solar and other renewables)	6.6	7.6	8.1	9.4
Total primary energy	100.0	100.0	100.0	100.0

Average % p.a. growth	1.5	3.0	2.2	1.1
Incremental world primary energy consumption 1979– 2000 mn b/d o.e.	53.4	121.7	80.3	37.6

To put these statistics into context it has to be remembered that after the OPEC oil price increases of October 1973 and 1 January 1974, the average annual growth rate of world energy consumption was 2.8 per cent over the six years from 1973 to 1979 in spite, too, of the economic recession in the industrialized countries. In consequence, the primary energy demand of the OECD countries fell by 1.7 per cent in 1974 and by 2.1 per cent in 1975, yet rebounded in 1976 to average 3.1 per cent annually over the four years to 1979.

Our overview of this analysis leads us to conclude that energy conservation savings and improvements in energy use over the twenty-one years from 1979 to 2000 were rather greater than implied in our scenario projections. However, the substitution of oil by other forms of energy was less than we had expected, with the exception of natural gas which in 2000 accounted for a slightly higher share of world energy consumption than provided for in our three scenario cases.

We conclude this chapter with another excerpt from that earlier book:

> One of the encouraging features of the experience since 1973 in the industrialized countries has been the very significant reduction in the rate of growth in energy demand in relation to economic growth. In the USA and Japan the coefficient averaged about 0.3:1 over the six years to 1979, whilst in Europe the average was about 0.4:1. Even though these encouraging experiences include the once-and-for–all elimination of wastage in 1974-75, there is much scope for technological change facilitating big improvements in the efficiency of energy use through the 1990s. Therefore, growth averaging 2 per cent annually in energy consumption worldwide might be

associated with significant per capita growth of GDP in a way which seemed improbable a few years ago. By contrast, the experience of recent years in terms of the incremental contribution from alternative forms of energy does not give one too much encouragement for the future. Perhaps particularly disappointing has been the political/ecological/technological slow-down in the nuclear sector. Even at mid-1981 oil prices there are few signs that more exotic and renewable energy forms are becoming competitive with petroleum and its derivatives. However, it does seem reasonable to assume that with increasing resources being devoted to the energy sector there will be some technological and economic breakthroughs during the next ten years which could start to have some effect in terms of commercial energy availability and prices during the 1990s. Some provision has been made for this in the projections, though it is not possible to be more than speculative about the prospects at this stage.

Regional Analysis

The remainder of *Energy: A Global Outlook* was concerned with country and regional analysis of the major discrete groups of energy and oil-producing and consuming areas around the world, as they were in 1980–1. We examined the energy situation and prospects for the United States, Western Europe, Japan, the OPEC developing countries, the non-OPEC developing countries, the USSR, Eastern Europe and China. There was a fairly comprehensive analysis and review of each of these, though some warranted more space than others on account of the background material available.

- The section headings within each chapter followed a fairly standard format which for the United States was:

- The US energy problem summarized

- Reserve base

- Supply and demand

- Evolution of a comprehensive national energy policy

- Energy projections for each of the three scenarios (consistent for those for the world as a whole)

Cross-references were made to the numerous statistical tables (fifty-nine in number) and diagrams illustrating growth in each of the scenarios for each of the countries/groups of countries listed above.

Table III.10. Scenario Projections for the USA Relative to Actual Estimates

Consumption	Actual Estimates	Scenarios		
		Cooperation	Neutral	Confrontation
	%	%	%	%
Oil (incl. synthetics etc)				
1979	46.4			
1985	40.8	43.3	42.3	39.6
1990	39.8	34.9	32.8	28.5
2000	38.9	22.1	21.4	18.7
Natural gas 1979	25.9			
1985	25.3	22.6	23.1	24.7
1990	25.2	22.2	23.5	26.3
2000	26.0	17.5	17.4	16.4
Solid fuels (incl. biomass)				
1979	19.9			
1985	25.0	24.2	24.9	26.3
1990	24.6	29.8	30.9	32.7
2000	24.6	39.4	41.1	45.7
Nuclear 1979	3.6			
1985	5.2	5.9	5.5	4.9
1990	7.0	8.9	8.4	7.5
2000	7.8	16.6	15.5	13.9
Hydro (incl. geothermal, solar and other renewables) 1979	4.1			
1985	3.7	4.0	4.2	4.6
1990	3.4	4.1	4.1	5.0

	2000	2.7	4.4	4.7	5.3
		mn m.t.o.e.	mn barrels per day o.e.		
Total primary energy	1979	1893.3			
	1985	1763.1	42.5	40.2	36.9
	1990	1963.3	43.6	40.5	35.8
	2000	2309.5	47.5	42.6	35.9
Average % p.a. growth of PE	1979–85	-1.2	1.6	0.7	-0.7
	1985–90	2.2	0.5	0.1	-0.6
	1990–2000	1.6	0.9	0.5	NC
	1979–2000	1.0	1.0	0.5	-0.3
		mn m.t.o.e.	mn barrels per day o.e.		
Incremental primary consumption	1979–2000	416.2	8.9	4.0	-2.7

Our purpose here is to make a more selective review of what was said in *Energy: A Global Outlook* in the light of actual experience subsequently of the same geographical/political/economic entities, except that Eastern Europe which is now integrated with Western Europe and China (Peoples Republic) is deserving of special treatment as the fastest rising dominant star in the energy firmament. New projections for each country/area will be a feature of Part IV.

The United States

We highlighted the mismatch between the large base of US reserves of coal and the relatively small reserves base for both oil and gas compared with the relatively limited consumption of coal *vis-à-vis* oil and gas. A comprehensive survey was made of what happened to US energy supply and demand over the period 1973 to 1979 following the peaking of indigenous oil production in 1970 and of gas production in 1973. In this context, the strong growth of US oil imports associated with strong growth of the US economy in 1976 and 1977 (following the recession of 1974–5) was recognized as bringing about sudden pressure on the world oil balance at that time.

Under 'Evolution of a Comprehensive National Energy Policy', we discussed the following topics: price controls on natural gas and oil; environmental regulations and health and safety controls; energy policy, basic issues; energy legislation; principles (ten of them in the national energy program of President Carter, 20 April 1977): strategy; national energy goals; latest developments (following President Reagan's inauguration in January 1981, immediate decontrol of oil prices).

Both the initial Carter initiative and his Plan II of July 1979 seemed to have much to commend them, to an external observer, as did some early Reagan initiatives to open up Federal lands and the outer continental shelf to exploration and production. The objective was to bring additional resources to the energy market place while simultaneously protecting the environment. However, in practice, the Carter Plan II to reduce US oil imports by 4.5 million barrels per day and the most recent (at that time of writing in 1981) official document indicated US oil imports were projected at 6 million barrels per day in 1985, 5 million barrels per day in 1990 and only 1.5 million barrels per day by the year 2000, a quite incredible and unrealistic progression, seemingly.

We show in Table III.10 the actual outcomes for the US energy economy in 1985, 1990 and 2000 relative to the three scenarios prepared in 1980–1. First, we pinpoint the accuracy of one of our projections: growth of US primary energy consumption over the full period of twenty-one years from 1979 to 2000. In fact, it actually averaged 1.0 per cent annually, as did our projection in the cooperation scenario. However, the progression through the periods was very different: US energy consumption fell on average by 1.2 per cent p.a. from 1979 to 1985 compared with our expectation of 1.6 per cent p.a. growth. From 1985 to 1990 average growth rebounded to 2.2 per cent annually on the basis of lower oil prices, whereas we had expected a deceleration to 0.5 per cent p.a. Finally, in the decade from 1990 to 2000 growth in US energy consumption averaged 1.6 per cent annually whereas our projection in this cooperation scenario was for growth of 0.9 per cent p.a. Our projections for the full period of twenty-one years were too pessimistic in both the neutral and confrontation scenarios for US energy consumption.

As regards the US energy mix, our projections for nuclear, hydro-electricity and coal were much too optimistic for 1990 and 2000 in all scenario cases. In contrast our projections for US natural gas consumption were too pessimistic for 2000 in particular. As oil's share of the US energy mix fell by some 6 percentage points after 1979 our projections for 1985 in the cooperation and neutral scenarios were too optimistic. However, after that, our expectation of rising coal, nuclear and hydro-electricity/other renewables leading to the backing out of oil to a remarkable extent (plus improvements in fuel economy in the transport sector over a twenty-year period) proved inaccurate as these other energy forms significantly underperformed relative to our expectations. Nuclear growth was weak, coal fell back a little from 1985 onwards and hydro lost 1.4 percentage points over the twenty-one years to 2000.

Western Europe

The comparative analysis is somewhat complicated by the political changes which occurred following the break-up of the former Soviet Union (USSR) in 1989–91 and much of the former Eastern Europe eventually joining the EU, with German reunification having been achieved early, following the demolition of the Berlin Wall between East and West Germany.

Since data are not readily available for all the countries of Eastern Europe, most of the comparative analysis appearing here is based on the nineteen countries of (OECD) Western Europe for which data are readily available for the period reviewed here. This is from 1979 to 2000, including the intermediate years of 1985 and 1990 for which projections appeared under our three scenario headings (cooperation, neutral and confrontation), compared with actual estimates for each of the above years. The data for Eastern Europe will be discussed briefly at the end of this section.

Table III.11. Scenario Projections for Western Europe Relative to Actual Estimates

Consumption	Actual Estimates	Scenarios		
		Cooperation	Neutral	Confrontation
	%	%	%	%
Oil (incl. synthetics etc)				
1979	53.4			
1985	43.1	50.2	48.9	47.6
1990	43.4	41.6	39.1	36.5
2000	42.7	28.2	25.0	16.6
Natural gas 1979	14.0			
1985	14.9	15.6	15.2	15.7
1990	16.0	16.1	17.2	18.9
2000	22.3	15.7	16.9	19.8
Solid fuels (incl. biomass)				
1979	22.2			
1985	24.0	19.7	20.7	22.1
1990	21.7	22.0	23.3	24.1
2000	14.9	26.1	27.0	31.2
Nuclear 1979	3.2			
1985	10.1	7.1	7.2	5.9
1990	11.7	12.1	11.8	11.2
2000	12.5	21.4	21.6	21.7
Hydro (incl. geothermal, solar and other renewables) 1979	7.2			
1985	7.6	7.5	8.0	8.7
1990	7.2	8.2	8.6	9.2
2000	7.6	8.6	9.5	10.7
	mn m.t.o.e.	mn barrels per day o.e.		

	mn m.t.o.e.	mn barrels per day o.e.		
Total primary energy 1979	1369.0			
1985	1339.9	29.5	27.6	25.4
1990	1439.9	30.5	27.9	24.9
2000	1611.6	33.7	29.6	25.3
Average % p.a. growth of PE				
1979–85	-0.4	2.1	1.0	-0.4
1985–90	1.5	0.7	0.2	-0.4
1990–2000	1.1	1.0	0.6	0.2
1979–2000	0.8	1.2	0.6	-0.1
Incremental primary consumption 1979–2000	242.6	7.7	3.6	-0.7
Incremental indigenous production 1979–2000	mn b/d o.e.	+ nuclear 157.9		
oil	4.41	i.e. 288.5		
natural gas	1.59	mn tonnes = 446.4		
total	6.00			

Note: Western Europe was formerly OECD Europe in 1979.

In *Energy: A Global Outlook* we pointed out that Western Europe imported more oil than any other region of the world, more than 13 million barrels a day in 1979, or 37 per cent of inter-regional world trade in oil at that time. Oil accounted for 55 per cent of Western Europe's primary energy consumption in 1979, with locally produced oil already accounting for 16 per cent of total consumption.

Moreover, there had been some significant changes between 1973 and 1979, with European net demand on world oil supplies falling by 6.5 percentage points. This was attributable to its increasing share of world oil production and its falling share of world consumption. The use of other forms of energy had grown at over 3 per cent annually and the energy coefficient had declined.

The oil and gas reserves beneath the North Sea, both UK and Norwegian sectors, were destined to play an important role in the period from 1979 to 2000 in reducing Western Europe's dependence on oil supplies from OPEC, whose oil price increases of 1973–4 had contributed immeasurably to making feasible the relatively high cost development of deep water reserves in the North Sea.

Under the heading of 'Evolution of a Comprehensive Energy Policy' we discussed in the work of the Commission of the European Economic Community (now the EU – at that time consisting of just ten members) in putting forward a number of policy guidelines designed to alleviate the short-, medium- and long-term problems of member countries. We remarked then that the areas where the Commission had achieved some measure of success were the setting up of common targets for energy conservation, for reducing dependence on oil and for developing alternative sources of energy. We noted at the time that there was a general tendency to use taxes (on petroleum products) and prices to encourage energy conservation. We went on to make an analysis of the European economic, energy and oil perspective of the four leading countries, West Germany, France, the UK and Italy, the other six EEC countries and the remaining nine other countries which form collectively the group of nineteen countries the actual performance of which we analyse below over the period 1979 to 2000, together with the three scenario projections for 1985 and 1990 as well as the horizon year.

West European primary energy consumption fell at an average rate of 0.4 per cent annually between 1979 and 1985 on account of economic recession and high oil prices in 1979–80. This was less than the fall of 1.2 per cent p.a. in the US, discussed above, but the recovery of growth in primary energy demand in Europe was lower than in the US between 1985 and 1990 and from 1990 to 2000.

Another very important difference between these two major energy consuming regions was the rise in indigenous production of oil and gas in Europe compared with a fall in production of both hydrocarbons in the United

States between 1979 and 2000. The rise in Europe amounted to 6 million barrels per day for oil and gas combined, or some 288 million tonnes of oil equivalent compared with a fall of 238 million tonnes in the United States over this twenty-one-year period. However, it should be noted that the main growth in European hydrocarbon production came from the UK and Norway sectors of the North Sea. In the UK, oil production peaked in 1999 and gas production just one year later, while Norwegian oil production peaked in 2001 though gas has yet to peak.

Another difference between Western Europe and the United States is the bigger growth of nuclear in the former at 158 million tonnes of oil equivalent compared with 119 million tonnes in the latter, over the twenty-one years from 1979. France alone accounted for 85 million tonnes o.e. of the European nuclear increment. All of these factors had a considerable influence in the greater backing out of more OPEC oil from the European energy economy than in its US counterpart over the twenty-one years to 2000.

One factor working in the opposite direction, however, was a fall in West European coal consumption of some 64 million tonnes o.e. between 1979 and 2000, compared with a rise of 190 million tonnes o.e. in the United States with coal production there rising similarly.

An exceptional improvement was achieved by the largest energy consuming country, i.e. Germany, in reducing its energy consumption by 11.3 per cent between 1979 and 2000 and a further 6.1 per cent to 2007. In 1979 Germany had accounted for 27.1 per cent of West Europe's energy consumption but this had fallen to 20.4 per cent in 2000 and to 18.8 per cent in 2007, even after adding in the former East Germany.

The actual fall in West European primary energy consumption of -0.4 per cent p.a. between 1979 and 1985 was precisely matched by our projection shown in the table for our confrontation scenario. All our scenarios were too pessimistic for the 1985 to 1990 period when actual growth of 1.5 per cent p.a. on average occurred. For 1990 to 2000 when 1.1 per cent annually was recorded, our cooperation scenario was very close at 1.0 per cent p.a. Over the period 1979 to 2000 the 0.8 per cent p.a. actually recorded was between our cooperation scenario of 1.2 per cent and the neutral scenario projection of 0.6 per cent p.a. on average, as can be seen in the table.

As was true in the United States, oil's share of the energy mix in Europe dropped more sharply than we had anticipated between 1979 and 1985 and more sharply than the relative fall in the United States. However, after 1985, there was little movement in oil's share of the energy balance in Europe, probably accounted for by comparatively soft oil prices. By contrast, all our scenario cases projected declining oil shares based on tighter oil supplies and rising real oil prices through the year 2000 than we actually experienced.

Our projections for natural gas in our cooperation scenario were not too far wide of the actual outcome for 1985 and 1990, but we did not anticipate the sharp increase of gas at the expense of coal which actually occurred between 1990 and 2000, respectively up 6.3 and down 6.8 percentage points during this decade.

Coal's share of European energy consumption rose between 1979 and 1985 but then fell, whereas we had expected it to rise. It did not do so as oil's share more or less stabilized instead of falling, as in our scenarios.

In Eastern Europe energy consumption fell sharply, by 24.7 per cent or an average rate of -2.8 per cent p.a. following the collapse of the former Soviet Union and its former policy of supplying these neighbours with energy at subsidized prices. Falls occurred in all of them between 1990 and 2000. Taking West and East Europe together energy consumption grew at an average rate of 0.5 per cent but the Eastern European countries accounted for only 12.6 per cent of the total in the millennium year.

Japan

In *Energy: A Global Outlook* we remarked that Japan had already achieved by 1979 a rather remarkable readjustment in response to the oil price increases of 1973–4 and made its economy less energy intensive. The energy coefficient had fallen from about 1.0 prior to 1974 to below 0.5.

In that earlier book too, there was some discussion of the various energy policy plans then being studied in Japan by MITI and various agencies. We reviewed the three scenario cases in a Japanese context and the expectation of oil's share in the energy mix coming down to about 56 per cent by 1985, which indeed it did, precisely.

Remarkably, Japanese consumption of primary energy fell by almost 9 per cent between 1979 and 1982 but then recovered to show little change by 1985 from six years earlier, in line with our projection in the confrontation scenario. From 1985 to 1990 total Japanese energy consumption rose at an average rate of 3.2 per cent p.a., similar to the rate recorded from 1982 to 1985 and faster than in our three scenarios, as can be seen from the comparative table. Over the full twenty-one years from 1979 to 2000 Japanese energy consumption grew at an average annual rate of 1.6 per cent, precisely the same as in our cooperation scenario projection. However, in both cases the progression was both varied and different through this lengthy period, as can be seen from the table.

After 1985 oil's share of Japanese energy consumption increased slightly by 1990 before falling back to 50 per cent in 2000. The scenario projections showed a much sharper fall in oil's share, predicated on tightening world oil supply and rising real oil prices (from a high base in 1979–80), neither of which came to fruition through all the years up to the millennium. For these reasons, as for the United States and Western Europe too, the energy transition away from oil in Japan occurred much more slowly than projected after 1985 in our three scenarios.

In the case of natural gas, our cooperation scenario projection for 1985 was close to the increase which actually occurred, as was the projection for the year 2000 in the confrontation scenario.

Solid fuel's share of Japanese energy did increase by more than 6 percentage points from 1979 to 1985 but thereafter, unlike natural gas, it fell back a little, probably reflecting the plentiful availability and weak prices of oil throughout the period to 2000 and beyond.

The nuclear share of Japanese energy consumption rose sharply from 1979 to 1985 but then decelerated to 1990 before rising to more than 14 per cent in 2000, a bigger share than natural gas at that time. The scenario projections for Japanese nuclear were too pessimistic for 1985 and 1990 but slightly too optimistic for the year 2000.

Given the rather full exploitation of Japanese hydro-electricity potential already by 1979 our projections showed relatively modest increases in its share of Japanese energy consumption. In fact, however, it fell back after 1985 with its actual contribution in 2000 being 1.3 million tonnes o.e. less in that year than fifteen years earlier, probably on account of poor hydraulic (i.e. weather) conditions that year. For example between 2004 and 2005 alone there was a fall of 3.8 million tonnes o.e. in the contribution of hydro-electricity to the Japanese energy mix.

Table III.12. Scenario Projections for Japan Relative to Actual Estimates

Consumption	Actual Estimates	Scenarios		
		Cooperation	Neutral	Confrontation
	%	%	%	%
Oil (incl. synthetics etc)				
1979	72.3			
1985	56.0	56.3	55.3	55.1
1990	57.3	45.0	41.4	41.6
2000	50.1	23.9	18.9	12.7
Natural gas 1979	5.0			
1985	9.3	9.4	8.2	7.7
1990	10.0	12.0	12.6	13.0
2000	12.8	13.3	13.7	12.7
Solid fuels (incl. biomass)				
1979	13.7			
1985	20.0	21.9	23.5	24.4
1990	17.6	27.0	28.7	28.6
2000	19.4	38.9	42.1	48.1
Nuclear 1979	3.8			
1985	9.3	6.3	5.9	5.1

	1990	10.2	9.0	9.2	7.8
	2000	14.2	15.9	15.8	15.2
Hydro (incl. geothermal, solar and other renewables) 1979		5.2			
	1985	5.4	6.3	7.1	7.7
	1990	4.9	7.0	8.0	9.1
	2000	3.6	8.0	9.5	11.4
		mn m.t.o.e.	mn barrels per day o.e.		
Total primary energy 1979		366.7			
	1985	368.7	9.6	8.5	7.8
	1990	432.5	10.0	8.7	7.7
	2000	510.2	11.3	9.5	7.9
Average % p.a. growth of PE					
	1979–85	0.1	3.5	1.4	Nc
	1985–90	3.2	0.8	0.5	-0.3
	1990–2000	1.7	1.2	0.9	0.3
	1979 to 2000	1.6	1.6	0.9	0.1
		mn m.t.o.e.	mn barrels per day o.e.		
Incremental primary consumption 1979–2000		143.5	3.5	1.7	0.1

Canada, Australia and New Zealand

As of 1979 these were the remaining OECD member countries not covered in the text. They were included in table 49 of *Energy: A Global Outlook*. We bring the combined estimates for the three countries up to date through to the year 2000 with estimated actuals for intermediate years 1985 and 1990.

By the year 2000 Canada was already more than self-sufficient in both oil and gas, being an exporter of both to the United States. Australia produced almost as much oil as it consumed and was an exporter of LNG. New Zealand was self-sufficient in natural gas. These features put these three countries in a different category from virtually all other OECD member countries.

Canada is the dominant energy consumer among the three countries, accounting for 70.8 per cent of the total in 2000, for 66.8 per cent of oil consumption, for 78.0 per cent of the natural gas, for 40.1 per cent of the coal (Australia for 58.6 per cent of it), for all the nuclear and for 89.9 per cent of the hydro-electricity of the total in the three countries.

Consumption of primary energy grew at an average annual rate of 1.5 per cent between 1979 and 1985. This was between the growth rates projected in our neutral and confrontation scenarios. Our projections for growth between 1985 and 1990 and 1990 to 2000 were below the 1.9 per cent p.a. actually recorded in all three scenarios but the average of 1.8 per cent p.a. from 1979 to 2000 was virtually midway between our cooperation and neutral scenarios at 2.1 per cent and 1.4 per cent for this twenty-one-year period.

Table III.13. Scenario Projections for Canada, Australia and New Zealand Relative to Actual Estimates

Consumption	Actual	Scenarios		
	Estimates	Cooperation	Natural	Confrontation
	%	%	%	%
Oil (incl. synthetics etc)				
1979	43.6			
1985	31.9	40.5	35.2	30.8

	1990	33.2	33.3	27.0	23.9
	2000	31.0	21.6	17.9	17.3
Natural gas 1979		19.5			
	1985	21.1	20.3	21.1	21.5
	1990	22.7	19.0	21.6	23.9
	2000	25.2	15.5	15.5	16.0
Solid fuels (incl. biomass)					
	1979	15.2			
	1985	18.7	16.5	18.3	20.0
	1990	17.8	19.0	20.3	20.9
	2000	18.7	21.6	23.8	25.3
Nuclear 1979		2.6			
	1985	4.3	3.8	4.2	4.6
	1990	4.7	6.0	6.8	6.0
	2000	3.9	11.3	11.9	10.7
Hydro (incl. geothermal, solar and renewables) 1979		19.1			
	1985	24.0	19.0	21.1	23.1
	1990	21.7	22.6	24.3	25.4
	2000	21.2	29.9	31.0	30.7

	mn m.t.o.e.	mn barrels per day o.e.		
Total primary energy 1979	291.4			
1985	319.2	7.9	7.1	6.5
1990	350.4	8.4	7.4	6.7
2000	424.9	9.7	8.4	7.5
Average % p.a growth of PE 1979-85	1.5	3.8	2.0	0.5
1985-90	1.9	1.2	0.8	0.6
1990-200	1.9	1.4	1.3	1.1
1979-2000	1.8	2.1	1.4	0.8
	mn m.t.o.e.	mn barrels per day o.e		
Incermental primary con-sumption 1979- 2000	133.5			

Six 'New' OECD Countries

Six countries have been designated OECD members, in addition to the original twenty-four, since *Energy: A Global Outlook* was prepared in 1980–1. They are a disparate group consisting of Mexico, South Korea, the Czech Republic, Hungary, Poland and Slovakia. Mexico has for long been a net oil-exporting country. South Korea has for long been a fast-growing free market economy in East Asia and one of the so-called 'tigers' in that region. The other four are former satellites of the Soviet Union which, along with East Germany, Romania and Bulgaria, were analysed as Eastern Europe and for which scenario projections were included in the earlier book. In the absence of comparable date now we show data for these six new OECD countries in two tables accompanying this text. One shows consolidated data for the six countries, in spite of the big qualitative differences between them. Table III.14 shows their collective primary energy consumption for each of the four years 1979, 1985, 1990 and 2000, as we have done for the other groups of countries analysed in this part of the new book. Also, the growth rates for energy consumption are shown for these six countries together and similarly the progression of their energy mix over the twenty-one years to 2000. Table III.15 shows the data for each of the six countries for each of the same key years by type of energy in millions of tonnes of oil equivalent.

The consolidated data for the six countries shows that in 1979 coal had been the most important source of energy but it declined sharply from almost 50 per cent to only 27 per cent in 2000. The share of oil increased by 10 percentage points and that of gas rose by 5 percentage points and nuclear energy by 7 percentage points. Primary energy consumption grew at an average annual rate of 2.0 per cent from 1979 to 2000 but there were big differences between the countries, as indicated below.

Table III.14. Energy Mix for 6 'New' OECD Countries in 2000

Consumption		Actual Estimates for 2000
		%
Oil (incl. synthetics etc)		
	1979	35.3
	1985	34.3
	1990	39.4
	2000	45.6
Natural gas	1979	12.6
	1985	13.4
	1990	14.0
	2000	17.7
Solid fuels (incl. biomass)		

1979	49.8
1985	47.9
1990	39.0
2000	27.1
Nuclear	
1979	0.4
1985	2.1
1990	5.4
2000	7.4
Hydro (incl. geothermal, solar and other renewables)	
1979	1.8
1985	2.3
1990	2.1
2000	2.2
	mn m.t.o.e.
Total primary energy	
1979	331.2
1985	371.7
1990	394.7
2000	496.7
Average % p.a. growth of PE	
1979–85	1.9
1985–90	1.2
1990–2000	2.3
1979–2000	2.0
Incremental primary consumption	
1979–2000	166.4

Note: 'New' OECD countries were Mexico, S. Korea, Czech Republic, Hungary, Poland and Slovakia.

Table III.15. Average Annual Growth in Primary Energy Consumption

	% p.a. Growth 1979–2000	Million Tonnes o.e.	% of Total
Mexico	3.1	137.4	27.6
South Korea	8.1	190.7	38.3
Czech Republic	-1.5	40.0	8.0
Hungary	-0.7	23.0	4.6
Poland	-1.5	88.4	17.8
Slovakia	-0.1	18.1	3.6
		497.6	100.0

There is a dramatic difference between South Korea on the one side and the four former Soviet satellites of Eastern Europe, all of which suffered even sharper falls in their energy consumption between 1990 and 2000 than the averages from 1979 onwards, as a result of the break-up of the Soviet Union and their loss of access to subsidized energy supplies.

In terms of their energy mix, Mexico and South Korea were mainly dependent on oil in 2000, with oil consumption having grown at an average annual rate of 7.1 per cent in the latter. Natural gas was the pre-eminent energy source in Hungary and Slovakia, with coal being the most important in the Czech Republic and Poland.

Table III.16. Energy Use by Type among 6 'New' OECD Countries (mn tonnes o.e.)

	1979	1985	1990	2000
Oil				
Mexico	43.9	57.8	67.7	85.7
South Korea	24.4	26.1	49.5	103.2
Czech Republic	12.5	10.6	8.4	7.9

Hungary	11.6	10.3	9.3	6.8
Poland	17.4	16.4	15.8	20.0
Slovakia	7.2	6.2	5.0	3.4
	117.0	**127.4**	**155.7**	**227.0**
Natural gas				
Mexico	21.5	24.3	24.5	36.2
South Korea	NIL	NIL	3.0	18.9
Czech Republic	2.6	3.7	4.9	7.5
Hungary	6.5	8.6	8.7	9.7
Poland	8.6	8.9	8.9	10.0
Slovakia	2.6	4.2	5.3	5.8
	41.8	**49.7**	**55.3**	**88.1**
Coal				
Mexico	2.3	3.1	3.4	**6.2**
South Korea	11.8	22.0	24.4	43.0
Czech Republic	39.7	38.2	33.5	21.0
Hungary	8.2	7.6	5.6	3.2
Poland	96.0	99.9	80.2	57.6
Slovakia	7.1	7.2	6.9	4.0
	165.1	**178.0**	**154.0**	**135.0**
Nuclear				
Mexico	NIL	NIL	0.7	1.9
South Korea	0.7	3.8	12.0	24.7
Czech Republic	NIL	0.5	2.8	3.1
Hungary	NIL	1.5	3.1	3.2
Poland	NIL	NIL	NIL	NIL
Slovakia	0.5	2.1	2.7	3.7
	1.2	**7.9**	**21.3**	**36.6**
Hydro				

Mexico	4.1	5.9	5.3	7.5
South Korea	0.5	0.8	1.4	0.9
Czech Republic	0.5	0.4	0.3	0.5
Hungary	NIL	NIL	NIL	θ
Poland	0.6	0.9	0.8	0.9
Slovakia	0.4	0.6	0.6	1.1
	6.1	**8.6**	**8.4**	**10.9**

Table III.17. Scenario Projections for the OPEC Countries Relative to Actual Estimates

Consumption	Actual Estimates %	Scenarios		
		Cooperation %	Neutral %	Confrontation %
Oil (incl. synthetics etc)				
1979	65.4			
1985	61.4	65.2	61.7	65.4
1990	55.5	61.1	58.7	61.1
2000	48.5	61.9	57.6	52.9
Natural gas 1979	31.4			
1985	34.6	29.9	30.0	25.0
1990	39.0	33.6	34.8	30.6
2000	44.5	30.4	35.9	38.7
Solid fuels (incl. biomass)				
1979	0.5			
1985	1.0	4.5	5.0	5.8
1990	1.8	3.5	4.3	5.6
2000	3.1	2.2	3.3	5.0
Nuclear 1979	NIL	NIL	NIL	NIL

1985	NIL	NIL	NIL	NIL
1990	NIL	NIL	NIL	NIL
2000	NIL	NIL	NIL	NIL
Hydro (incl. geothermal, solar and other renewables) 1979	2.7			
1985	3.0	3.0	3.3	3.8
1990	3.7	3.5	2.2	2.8
2000	3.9	3.7	2.2	3.4
	mn m.t.o.e.	mn barrels per day o.e.		
Total primary energy 1979	183.7			
1985	257.7	6.7	6.0	5.2
1990	329.7	11.3	9.2	7.2
2000	488.4	27.0	18.4	11.9
Average % p.a. growth of PE 1979–85	5.8	12.0	9.9	7.3
1985–90	5.1	11.0	8.9	6.7
1990–2000	4.0	9.1	7.2	5.2
1979–2000	4.8	10.4	8.4	6.1
Incremental primary consumption 1979–2000	mn m.t.o.e. 304.7			

Note: Data were available for only 9 of 13 OPEC countries so Iraq, Libya, Nigeria and Gabon have been omitted from this table.

OPEC Developing Countries

The estimates for growth in energy consumption in OPEC developing countries were comparatively modest, amounting to 5.8 per cent p.a. on average from 1979 to 1985, falling back to 5.1 per cent annually from 1985 to 1990 then to only 4.0 per cent each year from 1990 to 2000. These were much lower than our scenario projections and of course far lower than the high rates of around 10 per cent annually achieved by Japan in the distant past of the late 1960s and early 1970s and by China in the much more recent past, as discussed in Part II.

This lower than anticipated growth of energy demand in OPEC member countries can be attributed to a combination of weaker than expected price of exported oil together with comparatively low export volumes from OPEC attributable to a combination of influences: modest world economic growth; a low energy to GDP growth coefficient, reflecting conservation savings and improvements in energy use; rising substitution of oil by other forms of energy; and rising oil output from the North Sea and other sources in the rest of the world outside OPEC.

Similarly, we did not anticipate such a dramatic change in the rise in the share of natural gas consumption at the expense of oil in OPEC member countries. The gas share of OPEC energy consumption rose by some 13 percentage points between 1979 and 2000 while the share of oil in the consumption mix fell by some 17 percentage points, with both coal and hydro-electricity rising a little to make up the difference.

In *Energy: A Global Outlook* (chapter 19) I discussed the energy situation in the OPEC developing countries in some detail and the considerable diversity among them. A few statistics in Table III.18 serves to illustrate and bring up to date the comparative picture in some essentials. This indicates both some of the fundamental differences between them and the fact the great majority of the more than 600 million population living in OPEC member countries still have a relatively low income in relation to the larger population in the OECD member countries.

The population of the thirty member countries of the OECD is almost twice as large as that of the thirteen OPEC member countries. The GDP per capita was

8.9 times as large in the OECD countries as it was in OPEC countries in 2007, with the total value of the OECD economy being 17.5 times that of OPEC.

Table III.18. Economic Diversity of OPEC Countries and Comparison with OECD

			Value $ billions	
In 2007 GDP per capita	Population mllions	GDP at market price $ billions	Petroleum exports	Total Imports
Low Income	402.74	655.90	11.90	155.93
< $2000 per capita Indonesia, Iraq and Nigeria	66.8% of OPEC	29.5% of OPEC	15.2% of OPEC	26.9% of OPEC
Middle Income	168.10	823.33	250.68	167.64
$3000–$10,000 Per capita Al- geria, Angola, Ecuador, Iran, Libya, Venezuela	27.9% of OPEC	37.0% of OPEC	34.3% of OPEC	28.9% of OPEC
Saudi Arabia	24.29	360.3	206.48	88.04
$15,478 per capita	4.0% of OPEC	16.9% of OPEC	28.3% of OPEC	15.2% of OPEC
High Income Kuwait, Qatar and UAE	8.11	367.81	162.37	168.45
>$30,000 per capita	1.3% of OPEC	16.5% of OPEC	22.2% of OPEC	29.0% of OPEC

Total OPEC $3,685 per capita	603.23	2223.07	730.43	580.05
Total OECD $32,747 per capita	1185.72	38,828.96		

Table III.19. Estimates for the Three Leading Non-OPEC Developing Countries for the Year 2000

	India	Brazil	South Africa
% shares of primary energy consumption			
Oil	36.0	32.4	20.9
Natural gas	8.0	4.6	Nil
Solid fuels	48.9	6.8	75.9
Nuclear	1.2	0.8	2.9
Hydro-electricity	5.9	37.7	0.3
Total primary energy mn m.t.o.e.	295.1	182.9	107.9
Average % p.a. growth of primary energy consumption 1979–2000	5.3	3.4	3.6
Incremental primary energy consumption over this 21 year period: mn m.t.o.e.	195.6	93.0	56.3

Note: The growth of primary energy consumption in these three countries in total was equivalent to only 64.5% of the growth in China alone over the same period. As explained in the text, China is treated separately on .account of its great size as an energy consumer and fast growth

Table III.20. Scenario Projections for Developing Countries Outside OPEC (EMEs) Relative to Actual Estimates

Consumption	Actual Estimates	Scenarios		
		Cooperation	Neutral	Confrontation
	%	%	%	%
Oil (incl. synthetics etc)				
1979	52.7			
1985	45.4	53.2	52.8	51.4
1990	46.6	47.5	47.5	47.8
2000	46.6	26.8	26.8	25.0
Natural gas 1979	10.3			
1985	13.3	8.3	8.6	8.9
1990	14.2	9.4	10.0	10.8
2000	16.5	11.9	13.2	14.7
Solid fuels (incl. biomass)				
1979	25.2			
1985	28.4	26.4	25.4	25.1
1990	26.1	29.0	27.1	24.6
2000	23.6	39.7	37.9	35.7
Nuclear 1979	0.5			
1985	1.7	1.4	1.5	1.7
1990	1.5	2.5	2.9	3.0
2000	1.7	6.3	6.3	6.3

	mn m.t.o.e.	mn barrels per day o.e.		
Hydro (incl. geothermal, solar and other renewables) 1979	10.8			
1985	11.6	10.6	11.7	12.8
1990	11.6	11.6	12.5	13.8
2000	11.9	15.2	15.8	18.3
	mn m.t.o.e.	mn barrels per day o.e.		
Total primary energy 1979	721.3			
1985	958.4	21.6	19.7	17.9
1990	1148.1	27.6	24.0	20.3
2000	1526.2	39.5	31.7	25.2
Average % p.a. growth of PE 1979–85	4.9	5.8	4.2	2.5
1985–90	3.7	5.0	4.0	2.5
1990–2000	2.9	3.6	2.8	2.2
1979–2000	3.6	4.6	3.5	2.4
		mn barrels per day o.e.		
Incremental primary consumption 1979–2000	804.9	24.1	16.3	9.8

Source: BP *Statistical Review of World Energy* (2008).

Note: Four OPEC countries should be included in this category of EMEs as no consumption data for Iraq, Libya, Nigeria and Gabon are shown separately.

Non-OPEC Developing Countries: Emerging Market Economies (EMEs)

In *Energy: A Global Outlook* we presented China separately from non-OPEC developing countries as it was already important in the world energy scene and has grown enormously in relative importance during the last thirty years, thus justifying even more separate analysis of it. Though it is also shown separately in the BP *Statistical Review of World Energy 2009*, the numbers for China are also included in the catch-all category of 'Emerging Market Economies' in that source document.

As we said of this group in the earlier book, these total more than 100 countries, excluding all worldwide other than the thirty OECD countries, the fifteen former Soviet Union countries and the thirteen OPEC countries (or four of them at least, as the BP *Statistical Review* does not show consumption data for Iraq, Nigeria, Libya, Angola and Gabon, the latter an OPEC member only until 1 January 1995; Angola joined OPEC only in 2007).

Among this large group of non-OPEC developing countries (or emerging market economies) we choose to identify the three most important ones in terms of their primary energy consumption in the year 2000 and their shares of the total for all this large category of countries. It should be noted that all of them, India, Brazil and South Africa, are G20 member countries.

This shows that Indian energy consumption grew more rapidly than that of either Brazil or South Africa over the twenty-one years to 2000 and by this year it was greater than that in the other two countries combined. Coal was much the most important energy source in South Africa and it was also the main source in India, too. Brazil is most unusual in that hydro-electricity is the most important source of energy, followed by oil.

For the full group of all non-OPEC developing countries inclusive of these three, the usual comparative table included in this book indicates that growth in primary energy demand between 1979 and 1985 was actually between our cooperation and neutral scenarios. Subsequently, it was quite close to our neutral scenario.

Between 1979 and 1985 there was a sharp drop of more than 7 percentage points in oil's share of the energy mix, reflecting high oil prices in 1979–80, but this was followed subsequently by relative stability in the oil share. All our scenario projections showed big falls in oil's share especially between 1990 and 2000 and rising real oil prices, neither of which occurred. The share of natural gas rose more than we had expected. The share of solid fuels actually fell after 1985 but we had projected a rise at the expense of oil. Our projections for both nuclear and hydro-electricity were too optimistic for the horizon year, 2000.

Table III.21. Scenario Projections for the former Soviet Union (CIS) Relative to Actual Estimates

Consumption		Actual Estimates	Scenarios		
			Cooperation	Neutral	Confrontation
		%	%	%	%
Oil (incl. synthetics etc)	1979	34.5			
	1985	31.7	35.2	35.6	36.2
	1990	29.4	30.7	32.2	34.3
	2000	18.7	22.3	22.3	26.5
Natural gas	1979	27.9			
	1985	42.1	30.2	30.4	30.8
	1990	41.9	33.4	32.8	32.7
	2000	52.1	34.8	33.3	36.7
Solid fuels (incl. biomass)	1979	33.0			
	1985	24.5	27.2	27.0	26.1
	1990	21.6	26.6	26.3	24.5
	2000	18.3	26.2	26.7	22.7

Nuclear	1979	1.2			
	1985	2.9	2.7	2.1	1.8
	1990	3.4	4.1	3.6	3.3
	2000	5.3	11.7	10.2	8.3
Hydro (incl. geothermal, solar and other renewables)	1979	3.5			
	1985	3.7	4.7	4.8	5.1
	1990	3.7	5.2	5.0	5.2
	2000	5.6	5.0	5.1	5.8
		mn m.t.o.e.	mn barrels per day o.e.		
Total primary energy	1979	1164.1			
	1985	1315.2	30.1	28.9	27.6
	1990	1424.4	36.5	33.8	30.6
	2000	925.7	49.7	43.0	36.2
Average % p.a. growth of primary energy					
1979–85		2.1	4.7	4.0	3.2
1985–90		1.6	3.9	3.2	2.1
1990–2000		-4.2	3.1	2.4	1.7
1979–2000		-1.1	3.8	3.0	2.2
		mn m.t.o.e.	mn barrels per day o.e.		

Decrease in primary consumption	1979– 2000	-238.4	+26.8	+20.1	+13.3

The Former Soviet Union, now the CIS[10]

The USSR broke up in 1990 with dramatic results for the downturn in energy demand through to 2000 already discussed in Part II above. Nevertheless, it seems useful to retain this unit as an entity for comparative analysis relative to the projections made in 1980–1 and the importance of the former Soviet Union in terms of oil and gas production and consumption and its contribution to the world oil and gas balances, following the downturn noted above.

The discussion below complements that appearing in Part II but relates specifically to the statistical table accompanying this text. We can start by remarking that consumption of primary energy in the former Soviet Union (now the Commonwealth of Independent States, officially) *fell* by almost 500 million tonnes of oil equivalent between the peak of 1,424 million tonnes in 1990 and 926 million tonnes in the year 2000. By contrast, the increase projected in our three scenario cases based on *normal* expectations over this decade were 13.2 million barrels per day oil equivalent in the cooperation scenario, 10.8 million barrels per day in the neutral scenario and 5.6 million barrels per day in the confrontation scenario. These three cases correspond very roughly with, respectively, *increases* in terms of million metric tonnes of oil equivalent of 616, 504 and 262. In other words the *swing* from a fall of 500 million tonnes o.e. to an increase of a similar amount in our neutral scenario, or either rather more or quite a bit less, in the other two scenarios amounted to about 1 billion tonnes of oil equivalent, or 21.5 million barrels per day, or the same amount of total primary energy as the former Soviet Union consumed in total in 1975. Nothing like this quite dramatic transformation had occurred in the world energy economy at any time previously; it was quite unprecedented, in fact.

As a result of the political turmoil in the former Soviet Union, its oil exports dropped from a pre-crisis peak of 3.51 million barrels per day in 1988 to only 1.86 million barrels per day in 1991. There was a fairly sharp recovery afterwards though, with oil exports rising at an average rate of 9.7 per cent p.a., up to 2000, during which oil exports from the Middle East rose by an annual average rate of only 3.6 per cent. After 2000, oil exports from the former Soviet Union continued to rise rapidly at an average rate of 10.0 per cent annually until 2007 when they reached 8.33 million b/d. This turnaround of 6.47 million b/d in exports over the sixteen years from 1991 represents a significant change in the world oil balance over this period to 2007.

Over this same period, exports of oil from the Middle East rose at a very modest but somewhat erratic rate of only 0.5 per cent annually. As a consequence, the volume of oil exports from the former Soviet Union reached 42.3 per cent of those from the whole of the Middle East by 2007.

Moreover, if one analyses what happened to oil in the Soviet Union (specifically in the Russian Federation) during this decade of the oligarchs under President Yeltsin one finds that production fell from 11.6 million barrels per day in 1990 to 8.0 million barrels per day in 2000, an average annual rate of decline of 3.6 per cent. Oil consumption over the same period fell from 8.6 to 3.6 million barrels per day, a much steeper rate of decline averaging 8.3 per cent annually. Thus the difference between the two increased at 3.9 per cent annually in spite of the fact that this difference fell sharply from 1990 to 1992 as production initially fell more rapidly than oil consumption.

For natural gas a similar picture emerges as production fell at an annual average rate of 1.5 per cent but consumption declined at 2.1 per cent over this decade so that the difference between the two, i.e. surplus of production over consumption, increased considerably. It is in this context of extraordinary political events in the former Soviet Union having a profound effect on its economy, estimated by the World Bank at an annual average rate of -3.9 per cent through the 1990s, and such an unprecedented effect on its energy sector, that we analyse the detail of the latter in the table of statistics.

Oil's share of the primary energy consumption fell from 34.5 per cent in 1979 to 29.4 per cent in 1990 but then much more dramatically to only 18.7 per cent in 2000 in what only thirteen years earlier had been the world's biggest oil producer at 12.655 million barrels per day. This big change meant that this was the only country/region worldwide where the backing out of oil consumption by 2000 was greater than in any of our three scenario projections.

In spite of the fall in gas consumption noted above, the rise in the share of gas in the former Soviet Union's energy mix of more than 10 percentage points between 1990 and 2000 almost matched the fall in oil's share. Though we had foreseen an increase in the share of gas in our three scenario cases, it was actually much greater than implicit in our projections, between 1979 and 1985, as well as from 1990 to 2000. Though nuclear and hydro-electricity increased their shares – the latter much as we had anticipated – our nuclear projections were much too optimistic, probably on account of the disaster in Chernobyl in 1986 and its consequences.

The Peoples' Republic of China

Just as the former Soviet Union showed the capacity to shock the world during the near twenty-year review we made of forward prospects through to 2000 in *Energy: A Global Outlook,* so China did too, but in the opposite direction, once again subject to particular investigation in Part II above.

It seems worth pointing out here that China's primary energy consumption more than doubled from 2000 to 2008, an increase averaging 7.5 per cent annually, even heading into a worldwide recession when growth in Chinese energy consumption slipped back marginally to 7.3 per cent growth. This is quite remarkable, since Chinese energy consumption grew at an annual average rate of only 3.8 per cent over the twenty-one years to 2000. In just the eight years afterwards it increased from less than 1 billion tonnes o.e. to more than 2 billion tonnes o.e. So exceptionally, compared with all other countries/regions, we show this at the foot of our table of statistics.

Perhaps most remarkable of all, if the relative average annual rates of change in the United States (-0.5 per cent p.a.) and China recorded over the eight years to 2008 persisted, then Chinese energy consumption would exceed that of the USA in 2010. In fact, it did so in 2009. By 2015, if high growth continued, it would amount to 3.36 billion tonnes o.e., representing almost 30 per cent of the actual worldwide total reported for 2008.

Coal remains king in the Chinese energy mix and even rose between 1979 and 1990 to reach a remarkable 76.8 per cent of total energy consumption, but then fell back to 68.2 per cent in 2000, and increased slightly to 69.7 per cent in 2008. Chinese coal production rose at an average rate of 8.4 per cent p.a. over the ten years to 2008, with the rise in consumption slightly less at 8.0 per cent. By this time they were almost at the same level, more than 1.41 billion tonnes o.e., accounting for more than 42 per cent of worldwide coal production and consumption and 12.5 per cent of global primary energy consumption. Chinese coal reserves account for 46.2 per cent of the worldwide total of reserves with higher grade anthracite and bituminous coal accounting for 54 per cent of the Chinese total. Its reserves to production ratio currently stands at forty-one years. For both grades of coal, production in 2008 alone represented 2.4 per cent of the recoverable reserve basis. Thus growth of coal consumption of 8 per cent p.a. will bring the total up to more than 3 billion tonnes in 2018 if this rate of increase can be maintained, by which time the R:P ratio would be down to only 13.6 years, if no additions to reserves are made, not to mention the prospective using up of 22 billion tonnes of oil equivalent coal in the meantime if Chinese coal production continues to increase at 8 per cent p.a. to 2018. Given this enormous Chinese appetite for coal, perhaps it is not surprising that China is reportedly importing large quantities of coal in 2010.

Table III.22. Scenario Projections for China Relative to Actual Estimates

	Actual	Scenarios		
Consumption	Estimates	Cooperation	Neutral	Confrontation
	%	%	%	%

Oil (incl. synthetics etc)				
1979	21.7			
1985	17.5	15.3	15.2	13.8
1990	17.1	12.2	12.8	11.9
2000	23.7	8.8	8.4	8.4
Natural gas 1979	2.9			
1985	2.1	9.0	8.7	8.9
1990	2.0	11.7	10.4	9.6
2000	2.5	12.0	9.3	7.0
Solid fuels (incl. biomass) 1979	73.0			
1985	76.4	72.2	72.5	73.2
1990	76.8	71.1	72.0	72.6
2000	68.2	70.4	73.5	70.1
Nuclear 1979	Nil			
1985	Nil	Nil	Nil	Nil
1990	Nil	Nil	Nil	Nil
2000	0.4	0.2	0.1	Nil
Hydro (incl. geothermal, solar and other renewables) 1979	2.5			
1985	3.9	3.5	3.6	4.1
1990	4.1	5.0	4.9	5.9

	mn m.t.o.e.	mn barrels per day o.e.		
2000	5.1	7.2	7.9	10.4
Total primary energy 1979	448.9			
1985	541.7	14.4	13.8	12.3
1990	696.9	18.0	16.4	13.5
2000	983.4	25.0	21.5	15.4
Average % p.a. growth of primary energy				
1979–1985	3.2	4.6	3.9	1.9
1985–90	5.2	4.6	3.5	1.9
1990–2000	3.5	3.3	2.7	1.3
1979–2000	3.8	4.0	3.2	1.6
		mn barrels per day o.e.		
Incremental primary consumption				
1979–2000	534.5	14.0	10.5	4.4
2000–8	1042.9	no projections		

It is worth noting that when the coal share of the Chinese energy mix fell by more than 8 percentage points between 1990 and 2000, oil's share rose by more than 6 percentage points. Hydro-electricity contributed 1 percentage point more, natural gas 0.5 and nuclear 0.4 percentage points more, too. The real implication of this big fall in coal's share is that, if there is any repetition of it in the coming years, a huge extra burden is likely to fall on world oil supplies as the main balancing form of energy to sustain the growth of the Chinese economy. That can be seen from the table of numbers. Given that Chinese foreign exchange reserves were reported at $2.65 trillion, at the end of September 2010, the financing of a big increase in Chinese oil imports would present no problem for the Chinese authorities. In any event annual increases of 0.75 to 1 million b/d or more in Chinese oil imports seem quite likely at an annually increasing cost of $20 to $30 billion per year while supplies remain available at about $75 a barrel.

Our analysis here shows our cooperation scenario projection tracked the actual outcome of growth in demand for Chinese energy fairly closely, though actual growth was more volatile between 1979 and 1990 than we had anticipated, rising from only 3.2 per cent p.a. during the first six years to 1985, but 5.2 per cent p.a. over the next five years. The probability is that high world oil prices during the first period may have inhibited Chinese energy consumption growth, with coal's share of the energy mix rising by 3.4 percentage points from 1979 to 1985 providing circumstantial evidence for this hypothesis. Also, consistent with this, is the fall of 4.2 percentage points in oil's share over the same period. During the comparatively cheap oil decade of the 1990s oil's share of Chinese energy more than rebounded by 4.6 percentage points.

The share of natural gas was projected to rise in all three scenarios. However, this did not materialize as the share of gas remained between 2 and 3 per cent of Chinese energy consumption throughout the period from 1979 to 2000. However, in the fast growth Chinese environment this should not be allowed to disguise the fact that Chinese natural gas consumption increased at an average annual rate of 13.6 per cent from 1998 to 2008, accelerating to 18.4 per cent p.a. during the most recent five years to 2008.

Our projections in all scenarios for oil's share to decline considerably, as projected in the rest of the world, was not realized, with world oil supplies being freely available at comparatively low real prices throughout the period from the early 1980s until 2000.

Part IV

Population Statistics and Projections from the United Nations

The United Nations is the leading authority for estimates of populations worldwide by country and region and demographic projections from mid-2008 through to mid-year estimates for the year 2025 and 2050. Here we concentrate on 2008 and the projections through to 2025, the earlier time horizon and a seventeen-year period.

Also, we concentrate our analysis here on the G20 countries, an important group identified in the world economic summits held in London in April and in Pittsburgh in September 2009. This larger grouping of countries supplanted the former G7 of developed industrial countries which had been meeting regularly since 1975. The effect of the financial crisis and economic recession of 2008 and 2009 had given an impetus to the widening of worldwide economic councils to the G20 countries, but the underlying reason was that the faster growing developing countries, with China pre-eminent among them, were increasingly making their presence felt in world trade and global economic growth.

These G20 countries accounted for 65.6 per cent of the worldwide population in 2008 but the proportion is projected to fall to 62.3 per cent in 2025 at just under 5 billion out of the global total projected at 8 billion in that year, compared with just over 6.7 billion in mid-2008.

This reflects the fact the population of the G20 countries on average is projected to rise at only 0.7 per cent p.a. compared with an average rate of 1.6 per cent annually of all other countries worldwide. In fact, in none of the G20 countries is the population projected to rise this fast. Among the G20 countries the fastest rate of population growth projected by the United Nations over the seventeen years to 2025 is the 1.4 per cent p.a. for Saudi Arabia, with India and Indonesia the next fastest at 1.2 per cent annually in both cases. In all other G20 countries projected population growth is projected at less than 1 per cent per annum. In three of the leading ones, Russia, Japan and Germany, the population is expected to decline over this period. The same is true among eleven of the other twenty-three European Union countries, led by Spain, Poland and Romania, the three most populous of this group. These declines more than offset small rises in most of the other EU states in this 'other EU' category, plus France, Italy and the UK where modest increases are projected.

China and India are the dominant countries in terms of population among the G20, accounting for 56.4 per cent of the total in 2008, rising to 58.0 per cent in 2025. While China's population is projected to remain larger than that of India in 2025, between 2025 and 2050 China's population is projected to decline at an average rate of -0.1 per cent p.a., while that of India continues to rise at an average projected rate of nearly 0.9 per cent p.a., so that by mid-century, it is likely to exceed China by more than 300 million people, or by 21 per cent.

In the abbreviated statistical table, we have grouped the nine leading G20 countries in terms of their rank order by population in 2008 and projected for 2025. All twenty-seven members of the European Union are grouped together here, thus ranking third after China and India and followed by the United States. Projected population growth in France, Italy and the UK more than offsets an expected decline in Germany among the four leading EU member countries. It can be seen that the rises projected for India and Indonesia more than offset the declines projected for Russia and Japan over this seventeen-year period. Thus even among G20 countries, there is considerable diversity in terms of expected changes in population.

Table IV.1. UN Population Estimates and Projections for G20 Member Countries with More than 100 Million Inhabitants

	2008	2025	Average % p.a. change
China	1332.3	1484.6	0.6
India	1149.3	1407.7	1.2
EU 27	504.3	512.7	0.1
USA	304.5	355.7	0.9
Indonesia	239.9	291.9	1.2
Brazil	195.1	228.9	0.9
Russia	141.9	129.3	-0.5
Mexico	107.7	123.8	0.8
Japan	127.7	119.3	-0.4

More detailed statistics for all G20 countries and for the rest of the world are shown in Tables IV.2 and IV.3. Among non-G20 countries the UN Population Projections show large increases in some of the most populous countries: Pakistan, Nigeria and Bangladesh (Table IV.4).

Table IV.2. Population in Millions of All G20 Countries as of 2009

	Population mid-2008	Projected 2025	% p.a Change
USA	304.5	355.7	0.9
Argentina	39.7	46.3	0.9
Australia	21.3	24.7	0.9
Brazil	195.1	228.9	0.9
Canada	33.3	37.6	0.7
China inc HK & Goa	1332.3	1484.6	0.6
France	62.0	66.1	0.4
Germany	82.2	79.6	-0.2
India	1149.3	1407.7	1.2

Indonesia	239.9	291.9	1.2
Italy	59.9	62.0	0.2
Japan	127.7	119.3	-0.4
Mexico	107.7	123.8	0.8
Russia	141.9	129.3	-0.5
Saudi Arabia	28.1	35.7	1.4
South Africa	48.3	51.5	0.4
South Korea	48.6	49.1	0.1
Turkey	74.8	87.8	0.9
UK	61.5	69.0	0.7
Other EU (23 countries)	238.7	236.0	-0.1
Total G20	**4396.8 65.6%***	**4986.6 62.3%***	**0.7**
Rest of World	2308.2	3013.4	1.6
Total World	6705	8000	1.0
NB China and India alone account for	2481.6% of G20 56.4%	2892.3 58.0%	

*% of worldwide population.

Table IV.3. Other EU G20 Countries: Population in Millions

	2008	2025
Austria	8.4	8.8
Belgium	10.7	10.8
Luxembourg	0.5	0.5
Denmark	5.5	5.6
Finland	5.3	5.6
Greece	11.2	11.3

Iceland	0.3	0.4
Ireland	4.5	4.9
Netherlands	16.4	16.9
Portugal	10.6	10.5
Spain	46.5	46.2
Sweden	9.2	9.9
Switzerland	7.6	8.1
Bulgaria	7.6	6.6
Czech Republic	10.4	10.2
Hungary	10.0	9.6
Poland	38.1	36.7
Romania	21.5	19.7
Slovakia	5.4	5.2
Estonia	1.3	1.2
Latvia	2.3	2.1
Lithuania	3.4	3.1
Slovenia	2.0	2.1
23 other EU Total	238.7	236.0

Note: 11 of the 23 countries are projected to have a lower population in 2025 than in 2008, including the three most populous ones: Spain, Poland and Romania.

Table IV.4. Most Populous Countries outside of G20

	2008	2025	Average % p.a.change
Pakistan	172.8	228.9	1.7
Nigeria	148.1	205.4	1.9
Bangladesh	147.3	180.1	1.2

However, among the UN's classification of the least developed countries worldwide, the population was estimated at 797 millions in 2008, rising to 1,139 millions in 2025, an average rate of increase of 2.1 per cent p.a. It seems probable that the great majority of these, representing one in seven of the worldwide population in 2025, will continue to live in abject poverty in that year, with their proportion of the global total increasing to 17.8 per cent by 2050, even though the growth in their numbers falls back to a projected 1.5 per cent annually during the second quarter of this century.

Added point is given to the importance of population projections for individual countries and groups of countries because of the high degree of variability among them in terms of energy-related greenhouse gas emissions. In reference to projections published by the International Energy Agency in its *World Energy Outlook* of November 2009 and the US Energy Information Administration's *International Energy Outlook* of 2010 for energy-related CO_2 emissions we have examined the data and projections on a per capita basis. By eliminating populations in countries projected to emit about 3 tonnes of CO_2 per capita in 2030 or 2035 almost 60 per cent of the worldwide population could be exempt from any international agreement in the medium term and enhance the chances of agreement among countries/regions projected to have high or medium levels of energy-related CO_2 emissions in twenty or twenty-five years time – primarily G20 member countries.

Effects of the Financial Crisis
and Economic Recession of 2008–9

In July 2010 we now have a reasonable view of the effect of the financial crisis (which started in 2007) and the economic recession of 2008–9 on the world oil market through these two years. The fall in economic activity was particularly deep through the fourth quarter of 2008 and the first quarter of 2009 in the developed market economies. As the IMF and others have pointed out, this was the worst recession in the post-1945 period.

Table IV.5. Overview of World Economic Outlook Projections

	Estimates		Projections	
% p.a. change	2008	2009	2010	2011
World output	3.0	-0.6	4.6	4.3
Advanced economics	0.5	-3.2	2.6	2.4
All emerging and developing economies	6.1	2.5	6.8	6.4
China	9.6	8.7	10.5	9.6
Oil price	36.4	-36.3	21.8	3.0

Source: IMF *World Economic Outlook*, July 2010.

This reveals that China came through the recession virtually unscathed, losing less than 1 percentage point of its high trend rate of growth in 2009. This compares with the loss of some 4 to 5 percentage points of growth over the two years 2008–9 if the trend rate is in the order of 2 per cent p.a. in the advanced economies.

There has been a profound effect on OECD oil demand which the International Energy Agency estimates as falling by 4 million barrels per day from 49.5 million b/d in 2006 to 45.5 million b/d in 2009, with a further slight fall of 0.1 million b/d projected for 2010. At the same time, oil production in the OECD countries is estimated to have fallen from 20.1 million b/d in 2006 to 19.4 million b/d in 2009.

However, in the principal areas of non-OECD oil demand – China, other Asia, Latin America and the Middle East (including OPEC countries there) – growth in demand has continued, aggregating 5.0 million b/d for these four components. Offsetting this growth in demand from 2006 to 2010, as foreseen by the IEA, production increases are foreseen for China and Latin America totalling 1.0 million b/d over the same period.

The other major component outside OPEC in the world oil supply/demand balance over this economically disturbed period is the territories of the former Soviet Union (FSU, or CIS). Total oil demand there shows only small changes with a net rise of 0.1mn b/d but oil supply from them is seen as rising from 12.3 million b/d in 2006 to an estimated 13.6 million b/d in 2010. This makes a significant depressing impact on the need for OPEC oil supply of crude and NGLs combined in this year. This is in spite of economic recovery now being under way, somewhat uncertainly in the OECD countries, given the threat of sovereign debt crises in some European countries, and some uncertainty about the economic recovery even in the United States in mid-2010.

The fact is that oil demand in the former territories of the Soviet Union, at around 4 million b/d, remains some 5 million b/d less than it was in the early 1980s when it exceeded 9 million b/d, thus representing the major contributor to the softening of the world oil market (or alleviating pressure within it) over the past thirty years or so, as the surplus available for export has increased quite dramatically.

The IEA *Oil Market Report* for May 2010 foresees a significant growth of OPEC NGL production through the year 2010. Thus taking account of the other changes in supply and demand discussed above and noted in this document, and assuming no big changes in worldwide stocks through 2010 beyond those estimated for the first quarter, then demand for OPEC crude should average about 29.0 million b/d, 0.3 million b/d above the level reported for 2009.

The average price of crude oil entering world trade in 2010 seems likely to settle in the range of $70 to $80 a barrel. In real terms,[11] this is compatible with an oil price increasing on average at 1.5 per cent p.a. over the past thirty-five years for a depleting natural resource in spite of new discoveries and improvements in the recovery factor over this period. This is consistent with the comparatively stable price which prevailed over the five years 1974–8 period, following the fundamental changes unilaterally introduced by OPEC in October 1973 and 1 January 1974. The speculative price rise to more than $140 a barrel in July 2008 was evidently unsustainable, but so too was the even more subsequent dramatic fall to less than $40 a barrel in February 2009, almost at the pit of the economic recession.

Barring sovereign debt defaults or major concerns emerging related to the creditworthiness of banks possibly provoking a 'double-dip' recession, we believe this sort of price bracket for oil entering world trade should prevail for some years. This should serve to underpin the worldwide recovery with countries such as China, India and those in the Middle East, rather than the existing developed countries, leading the way. At this price there remains a strong incentive both to achieve continuing improvements in the efficiency of energy usage worldwide, and to introduce more comparatively high-cost alternative energy sources, particularly renewables not giving rise to greenhouse gas emissions. Energy demand growth should resume in 2010 after a fall in 2009, albeit at a modest pace, in relation to growth in the world economy as the recovery becomes stronger and the G20 starts to have some influence on some desirable measures of regulation to limit the excesses seen in certain countries in recent years, both in the financial sector and the oil market, as well as for some other commodities. This prospect is supported by the OPEC member countries having a substantial reserve production capacity of some 5.4 million b/d, as estimated by the IEA in May 2010.

Another important component of the world energy scene is the financial position of OPEC which should be quite tolerable for its member developing countries. The very high average prices in 2008, combined with exports of crude and products together still exceeding 28.4 million b/d, meant that the value of their petroleum exports in that year was just over one trillion dollars, with those of Saudi Arabia being over $283 billion. Thus a period of both lower prices and lower volumes for OPEC countries' exports should be quite tolerable as China, India and other developing countries continue to grow rapidly.

Thus unlike the period from 1981 to 1986 when an oil price bubble burst following an economic recession, strong growth in non-OPEC oil supply, improvements in the efficiency of oil use and the growth in the supply of other forms of energy, it now seems that the world oil and energy market should evolve in a more manageable way over the next five years. Adequate agreement among the principal exporters and importers, perhaps through the meetings of the G20, seems essential. Perhaps more effective regulation of world oil prices may be necessary to mitigate the extent of fluctuations in annual changes in real oil prices seen not just in 2008, but characteristically over most of the last thirty years. These we have analysed elsewhere in this book. The fact of real oil prices fluctuating annually by more than 20 per cent in a third of years in the past three decades and by more than 10 per cent in two-thirds of these years must have contributed significantly to the destabilization of the world economy and the volume of trade in such an important commodity. We suggest this destabilizing phenomenon is contrary to the interests of both oil-exporting and oil-importing countries.

Thus in mid-2010, the world oil market seems to have weathered the financial crisis and economic downturn, sharper than that of almost thirty years ago, with rather less instability and disruption than seen from 1981 through 1986. This is particularly true of OPEC supply where a fall in crude oil production has been and continues to be substantially offset by a rise in output of natural gas liquids (NGLs), as well as growth in oil imports into China, India and some other developing countries.

Table iv.6. Oil Demand and Supply (million b/d)

	2006	2007	2008	2009	2010 prospect	Change 2010 from 2006
Demand						
OECD	49.5	49.2	47.6	45.5	45.4	-4.1
ROW	35.6	37.2	38.4	39.3	40.9	+5.3
Total world	85.1	86.4	86.0	84.8	86.4	+1.3
Supply						
OECD	20.1	19.9	19.3	19.4	19.4	-0.7
ROW (ex OPEC)	28.1	28.6	28.8	29.4	30.2	+2.1
	48.2	48.5	48.1	48.8	49.6	+1.4
Processing gain	2.1	2.2	2.2	2.3	2.2	+0.1
Bio fuels*	0.2	0.3	0.4	0.4	0.5	+0.3
	50.5	50.9	50.8	51.5	52.2	+1.7
OPEC crudes	30.7	30.3	31.2	28.7	28.8	-1.9
OPEC NGLs	4.3	4.3	4.4	4.7	5.4	+1.1
OPEC total	35.0	34.6	35.6	33.3	34.2	-0.8
Stock change	0.3	-0.2	0.4	0.0	0.0	
Deficiency -						
Surplus +						
Former Soviet Union	8.3	8.3	8.7	9.4	9.5	1.2
OECD	-29.4	-29.3	-28.3	-26.1	-26.0	-3.4
China	-3.5	-3.9	-4.1	-4.7	-5.2	-1.7
Other Asia	-5.3	-5.8	-6.0	-6.3	-6.4	-1.1
Latin America	-1.5	-1.7	-1.8	-1.7	-1.6	-0.1

ROW = Rest of World. * Outside Brazil and USA.

Source: IEA *Oil Market Report*, 12 May 2010.

It can be seen from the table that the fall in OECD demand has been more than offset by the rise in the rest of the world led by China, with a prospective rise of 2.0 million b/d in demand over the four years, accompanied by rises of 1.1 million b/d each in both other Asia and the Middle East. Growth in Chinese oil demand seems likely to continue to be strong with the economy rising by almost 12 per cent during the first quarter of 2010 and naphtha demand soaring. China's aggressive petrochemical capacity expansion involved the addition of 3 naphtha crackers totalling almost 2.3 million tonnes in 2009 with another three units each with a capacity of 1 million tonnes p.a. due to come on stream in 2010. Dramatic developments of this scale are quite unknown in the OECD countries during the recent recession years.

One way of expressing the growing dominance of China is to note the changes in primary energy demand and its main component parts in China compared with those in the whole of the rest of the world between 2006 and 2009. Of course, this rather dramatic comparison also encapsulates the effect of the economic recession in the OECD countries.

Table IV.7. Changes 2006–2009 (milllion tonnes o.e.)

	China	The Whole of the Rest of the World
Oil	+ 56.0	- 90.1
Gas	+ 29.0	+ 70.2
Coal	+ 323.0	- 83.8
Nuclear	+ 3.5	- 27.9
Hydro	+ 40.7	+ 15.3
Total primary energy	+ 452.2	- 116.4

Source: BP *Statistical Review of World Energy* (2010).

This serves to bring out the unprecedented changes in the dramatic growth in Chinese energy demand, growing at 8.0 per cent p.a. on average over the three years to 2009 with coal accounting for over 71 per cent of the increase. As a result of the financial crisis and economic recession in the OECD countries primary energy consumption in the whole of the rest of the world continued growing until 2008, but then fell by 3.5 per cent in 2009, or 3.2 per cent on a per day basis (leap year in 2008).

This contrast serves to emphasize the need for energy analysts and forecasters to concentrate on what is happening and likely to happen in China if they wish to make anything like accurate projections of future world energy needs. Until now, it has only been in the natural gas market that China has yet to become a major player, as it still accounted for only 3.7 per cent of total Chinese primary energy consumption in 2009 in spite of having grown at an average rate of 13.9 per cent p.a. over the decade from 1999. Given the potential challenges from climate change policies, with gas emitting fewer greenhouse emissions than coal or oil, it seems probable that natural gas use in China will continue to rise rapidly from the level of more than 91 billion cubic metres (82.1 million tonnes of oil equivalent) reported for 2009.

This comparative analysis of what has happened in the world energy economy during recent years, characterized by the sharpest economic downturn in the leading developed countries in more than sixty years, provides a basis for the remainder of Part IV. This examines the analysis of leading features of projections from the Secretariat of the Organization of Petroleum Exporting Countries, the International Energy Agency and the US DOE's Energy Information Administration, all covering the world market.

Initially, each of these is treated separately in terms of the main points we see emerging from them. We then go on to make some comparisons between them as far as the projections allow, and then conclude with some comments of our own.

Aftermath of the Financial Crisis

After the so-called Basel III agreement on 12 September 2010, one major report included the following observations on 15 and 16 September 2010.

> There is a pretty powerful precedent for the theory that a 'shadow' banking system can cause or compound a crisis. The fall of Lehman, Bear Stearns and other banks around the world in 2008 was made possible because the financial risk that stemmed from the US sub-prime mortgage lending

was being recycled around the market via shadow banking structures. These entities, from money market funds to investment products such as collateralized debt obligations hid the real risk because they were not properly regulated.

Later it goes on as follows:

> Nervousness also exists about the volumes of trading being done within energy companies and other commodity trading houses. Oil companies and trading houses have been steadily extending their reach beyond the traditional focus on physical commodities into exotic over-the-counter derivatives to serve customers, a trend that some expect to accelerate now that their capital advantage over banks is widening sharply.
>
> Oil companies such as Total and BP and traders including Cargill and Vitol are in effect shadow banks for the commodities industry, replicating the services that the likes of Goldman Sachs and Morgan Stanley monopolized for years.

It goes on:

> But some analysts say the activities, which are largely unregulated, bring big risks to the system. Without the capital requirements imposed on banks, a default becomes more dangerous, they say. The shift also awakens unwelcome memories of Enron, the failed US energy company whose traders severely disrupted the California energy markets in 2000-01 as well as costing investors billions of dollars.

In the *Financial Times* of 16 September, the EU internal market commissioner was quoted as follows:

> No financial market can afford to maintain a single 'wild west' territory. The absence of any regulatory framework for OTC (over the counter) derivatives contributed to the financial crisis and the tremendous consequences.
>
> Today we are proposing rules which will bring more transparency and

responsibility to derivatives markets so we know who is doing what and who owes what to whom.

The *Financial Times* went on to remark that the proposals follow an agreement by G20 leaders the previous year to standardize derivatives trading and move them on to exchanges on electronic trading platforms where appropriate. The proposals will closely align the EU with the new regime which is coming into force in the US. It went on to say the rules will require standard OTC derivatives to be processed through clearing houses, a move aimed at reducing systemic risk arising from a default of one party in an OTC deal. They will also require OTC contracts – the bilateral agreement between buyers and sellers to be reported to trade depositories, or databanks, and for this information to be available to regulators.

The report goes on to say that there will be exemptions from the clearing obligation for non-financial institutions – such as manufacturing companies – who are using OTC derivatives to hedge business risks. Evidently this exemption could include still-integrated oil companies; however, this report went on to say that Brussels, HQ of EU Commission, also plans to make it more expensive for firms to deal in non-cleared contracts, by requiring them to hold more capital against these – although that measure was to be introduced in separate legislation shortly.

The report concludes that the rules being proposed by the EU commission will need approval both from EU member states and the European Parliament. Evidently, this is the main reason for the aim being to have them in force only by mid to late 2012. Another *FT* article on 16 September quoted a partner at a large law firm, Allen & Overy, as saying: 'It is clear that consensus and showing a consistent regulatory face globally is a key measure they want to send.'

These reports were complemented by an important article on 17 September, also in the *Financial Times*, by Mario Draghi, chairman of the Financial Stability Board and Governor of the Bank of Italy, who has an influential role in the aftermath of the financial crisis. His contribution appeared under the title 'Next Steps on the Road to Financial Stability' – clearly seen as a necessary ongoing process. He emphasizes that the systemically important institutions must have loss-absorbing capacity beyond the minimum agreed on 12 September 2010.

The chairman of the FSB goes on to identify two main driving forces at work. The first is a different perception of risk. He asserts that the optimistic view that the level of risk in the system could be offset by dispersion was wiped out by the crisis. The result has been a repricing of risk of all sorts. Justifiably, in our view, he remarks that markets no longer reward instruments for complexity and opacity. Yet the changes offer no assurance against a return of complacency, he states. That is why we also need a stronger regulatory framework and that is the second major source of change.

He states that the public will not, and should not, accept more such bailouts (as occurred during the financial crisis). Addressing the problem of 'too big to fail' is therefore the next critical step in the reform programme. In addition to the point made at the end of the last paragraph but one, Draghi goes on to list four others in the work under way. National resolution regimes must enable the authorities to resolve crises without systemic disruptions or taxpayer losses. Next, we need to improve cross-border resolution capacity as national regimes alone are ill-suited to dealing with global banks. The effectiveness and intensity of supervision needs to be strengthened, for banks in general and for systemically important institutions in particular. The financial market infrastructures should be strengthened to reduce contagion risks and to ensure that they do not themselves become a source of systemic risk. Central clearing arrangements, particularly for over-the-counter derivatives, can simply and greatly reduce the risk associated with complex networks of counterparty exposures. FSB and its members are developing measures in all the above areas and were to report on progress and present recommendations to the November 2010 G20 summit in Seoul.

Lastly, the central lesson of this crisis was the lack of system-wide oversight. One of the blind spots, and an important contributor to the crisis, was the regulatory arbitrage that developed in the shadow banking sector. Mario Draghi concluded that as we strengthen the requirements for banks, we must make sure that we also capture within the regulatory perimeter the source of systemic risk presently outside it. That will be a priority for the FSB's work in 2011, Draghi wrote.

In the aftermath of the financial crisis this article by Mario Draghi affords the authors of this book a good deal of satisfaction and reassurance in terms of the progress being made, even if much more remains to be done, perhaps especially in over the counter derivatives, with particular reference to oil and other commodity markets.

All these reports were followed by another quoting the chairman of the US Securities and Exchange Commission. Ms Shapiro reportedly told a Securities Traders Association conference on 22 September 2010 that derivatives rules should reflect the virtues of the current equities market: competition, access, liquidity and transparency.

Under US Dodd-Frank financial reform, the privately traded or over the counter derivatives markets will come under explicit regulatory oversight. The SEC will be the watchdog for securities-based swaps which are expected to include credit defaults swaps, and the Commodity Futures Trading Commission (CFTC) will oversee the rest of the swaps market which includes interest rate swaps. The chairman of the SEC went on to remark that 'Real-time post trade transparency as well as pre-trade transparency helps coordinate markets'.

OPEC *World Oil Outlook* 2009

This *World Oil Outlook* (*WOO*) was published in early July 2009. The next one was expected only in November 2010. The OPEC *World Oil Outlook* 2009 consists of three scenarios not defined in detail in the report as such but which we can summarize in Table IV.8.

Table IV.8. OPEC World Oil Outlook 2009

Reference case	2009 to 2030*	
GDP	3% p.a.	
Primary energy	1.5% p.a.	
PE/GDP coefficient	0.5% p.a.	
Oil supply (crude only)	1.1% p.a.	
Years	2008*	2030
Crude oil only**	71mn b/d	77 mn b/d
Growth	0.4% p.a	
Oil price	$70 to $100 per barrel	

Protracted Recession/ Low Growth	2009	2010	2011	2012	2013	2015	2020	2030
GDP	-2.3	0.1	1.5	2.5	3.0		2.5	
Oil demand mn b/d	83.9	83.8	84.3	85.1	85.4	85.9	88.5	92.7
High Growth								
GDP						–	3.5	–
Oil demand mn b/d						92.1	99.1	113.9

* Different base years.

**The growth of world crude oil production at only 6 million b/d over 22 years to 2030 represents only 30% of the increase in total oil supply which includes rising NGLs, non-conventional oil and oil from biomass discussed in the text.

We concentrate our attention here on points made in the July 2009 *WOO* from OPEC which seem to us important, followed by some illustrations and tables based on data in this source. We applaud the statement by the OPEC Secretary General in the Foreword that OPEC continues to stress the importance of a positive and constructive dialogue between producers and consumers, prompted by the assertion that the *WOO* 2009 points at increasing interdependencies among all stakeholders (in the world oil market).

The review correctly points out that the period from mid-2008 to mid-2009 was a period of unprecedented turbulence in the world oil market. OPEC assumes an oil price in the range of $70 to $100 a barrel in constant prices for the projection period through to 2030 but cautions that this is simply an assumption and does not reflect or imply any projection of whether such a price path is likely or desirable. Another assumption in the reference case is that economic growth will be back to normal in 2012. It points out that using purchasing power parities for measurement of GDP reduces the weight of China and India. It expects GDP growth over the period 2009 to 2030 to average 6.3 per cent in China and 4.7 per cent in South Asia, with global growth averaging 3.0 per cent p.a.

Growth of total energy use in this reference case is projected at 42 per cent over the twenty-three years from 2007 to 2030, implying an average growth rate of 1.5 per cent p.a. Oil demand has been hit by the recession and lower GDP growth. The *WOO* expects OECD oil demand to be 45.5 million b/d by 2010, remaining at this level until 2013, representing 5.7 million b/d less than expected one year earlier, with a difference of more than 4 million b/d already seen in 2009. Also, the efficiency of energy improvement had been greater than previously assumed, OPEC states. From the figures quoted above, the energy coefficient, PE/GDP stands at 0.50 at world level, on average from 2007to 2030. Oil demand in 2030 is projected at less than 106 million b/d compared with 113 million b/d foreseen one year earlier. Almost 80 per cent of the net growth in world oil demand is foreseen as taking place in developing Asian countries, plus 23 million b/d from 2008, to take the total for all developing countries to 56 million b/d in the horizon year, 2030. In spite of the fact that OECD oil demand is falling over the entire projection period, having peaked in 2005, this OPEC report points out that oil use per person in North America will still be more than ten times that of South Asia in 2030.

Complementing this, it expects that the transportation sector will account for over 60 per cent of the increase in oil demand to 2030 with the world stock of cars rising from less than 800 million in 2007 to well over 1.3 billion by 2030. Three-quarters of the increase occurs in developing countries, rising from a low base of 31 cars per 1,000 people in 2007 to 87 per 1,000 in 2030. Nevertheless, this remains at only 16 per cent of the level of 530 per 1,000 for the OECD projected for 2030, demonstrating the scope for further big increases in developing countries, especially in fast growing populous countries, China and India.

Almost 60 per cent of the growth in oil demand is for middle distillates in this OPEC *World Oil Outlook* to 2030.

Over the period from 2008 to 2013 non-OPEC oil supply rises just over 1 million b/d while it envisages demand for OPEC crude oil returning to the 2008 level by 2013. Maintaining spare OPEC upstream capacity at comfortable levels requires investment of around $110 to $120 billion over the five years.

In the longer term total non-OPEC oil supply continues to rise as the increase in non-crude is stronger than the slight decline foreseen in non-OPEC crude supply. Up to 2020 crude production continues to increase in Russia, the Caspian and Brazil to compensate for declines in the OECD. Non-conventional oil supply (excluding bio fuels), mainly from Canadian oil sands, rises by 4 million b/d from 2008 to 2030. But there is also strong growth in bio fuels outside OPEC, as well as NGLs. In addition, OPEC crude that will be needed to balance the world system is seen as rising to just over 41 million b/d in 2030.

In the reference case global crude oil supply is seen as 71 million b/d in 2013, the same as in 2008. By 2030 there is only a need for this to increase to 77 million b/d. OPEC states that the resource base of both conventional crude and non-conventional oil is more than sufficient to meet future demand. There remain uncertainties surrounding the extent to which increases in the demand for crude will actually materialize.

It goes on to state that the issue of investments along the entire supply chain is crucial to both producers and consumers. Up to 2030 cumulative upstream investment requirements are estimated at $2.3 trillion (in constant dollars of 2008). It remarks that costs have been sharply inflated since 2003 but by mid-2009 a slow reversal had been observed, factored into this estimate.

An alternative protracted recession scenario, both deeper and longer than that assumed in the reference case was explored in this *World Oil Outlook*. In the year or so since this was published in mid-2009 this seems to us still quite appropriate in mid-2010 on account of the concerns relating to sovereign debt in several Eurozone countries emerging during the second quarter of 2010, as well as uncertainties as to whether all bad bank debts have yet been revealed, continuing tightness in credit markets and deflation dangers – all these and other unfavourable influences could combine to induce a so-called double-dip or W-shaped recession. The currently different policy positions in mid-2010 of the US administration in favour of more fiscal stimulus contrasted with consolidation and deficit reduction measures in the leading European economies, led by Germany, are a somewhat unfavourable augury, also apparent at the G20 meeting in late June 2010. Some uneven economic growth has been seen since late 2009 but high unemployment and problems in the housing sector in several countries, such as the US and Spain, give some credence to this pessimistic case proposed by OPEC in mid-2009.

This protracted recession scenario of OPEC assumes that crude oil prices are significantly softer than in the reference case, but this has not really been realized over the period since mid-2009 to mid-2010 because of the combination of continuing strong growth of oil demand in developing countries (+1.2 million b/d in 2009, +1.5 million b/d foreseen in 2010) and modest but reasonable level of OPEC crude oil production. This protracted recession scenario shows worldwide demand at only 85.5 million b/d even in 2013, 2.4 million b/d less than in the reference case. From the standpoint of mid-2010 this looks too low a figure, given the continuing growth of oil demand in the developing countries, especially China, even if there was to be a double-dip recession in the OECD countries, possibly in Europe, given the current stance of policy.

In this context OPEC points out that in a climate of demand pessimism and low oil prices, there is a risk of investment in capacity that is not needed, or the difficulty of securing credit militating against investments in increasing capacity being made.

The projections in the reference case envisage an increase of 6 million b/d in crude oil distillation capacity to be added globally by 2015. Almost 50 per cent of this is foreseen for Asia, mainly China and India. Also, 5 million b/d of new conversion capacity is foreseen plus more than 6 million b/d of desulphurization capacity. All this implies a low level of refinery utilization and poor refinery economics because of a prospective surplus which becomes worse in the protracted recession scenario. Even in the reference case, global crude runs do not recover to the 2007 level until 2015 and increase by only 9.8 million b/d above this level by 2030.

A surge in ethanol supply is foreseen in the United States and Canada with a decline in gasoline demand as a consequence. Crude oil throughputs in the US and Canada are never expected to recover to 2007 levels. Increasing dieselization of the vehicle fleet is projected for Europe. OPEC goes on to suggest the need for closures of 10 million b/d of refinery capacity, mainly in the OECD countries, in order to restore utilization rates and refining margins to a reasonable level. Evidently, this marks a dramatic contrast with the prospect in developing countries, especially in the Asia/Pacific region where an increase in capacity of 10 million b/d is foreseen, 5 million b/d in China alone, and 3 million b/d in the Middle East, with the global total rising by only 9 million b/d by 2030 from 2007 levels.

OPEC's projections highlight a sustained need for incremental hydro cracking facilities of some additional 4.3 million b/d out of the 5.4 million b/d of global conversion capacity requirements to 2030. Conversely, additions to coking capacity only appear to be required after 2020 after recent substantial additions and the prospect of a decline in the supply of heavy sour crudes in the medium term. The requirements for catalytic cracking units are adversely affected by declining gasoline demand growth and rising ethanol supply, especially in the Atlantic basin. Substantial desulphurization capacity additions of some 14.5 million b/d are foreseen as being required through to 2030 which is above existing projects of 6.4 million b/d in order to meet sulphur content specifications. More than 70 per cent of the 21 million b/d total, or 15 million b/d, are for distillate desulphurization, with the bulk of the remainder being for gasoline sulphur reduction. To fund these changes investment of around $780 billion is needed in the global refining system to 2030 with the Asia/Pacific region being in the lead.

The global oil trade (all inclusive, crude oil, refined products, intermediates and non-crude-based products) is seen as rising by only 2 million b/d from 52.5 million b/d in 2007 to 54.6 million b/d in 2015. This disguises a shift in the expected structure of the trade: trade in crude oil is expected to decline by almost 1 million b/d and the trade in oil products increasing by 3 million b/d. In the period after 2015, inter-regional oil trade is expected to have stronger growth by almost 12 million b/d to more than 66 million b/d by 2030 in the reference case. The tanker market is expected to decline in the short term, with a relatively large increase in tanker capacity in the next few years as a result of record order books. However, in the longer term the global tanker fleet is expected to expand by 100 million dwt or 25 per cent by 2030 from 2008.

The OPEC *WOO* goes on to discuss the cyclicality of the world oil market with its ensuing challenges of making the appropriate investments in an uncertain environment and in an industry characterized by massive upfront capital requirements and long lead times. The financial and economic crisis of 2007 to 2009 has given added emphasis to the problems facing the industry and especially the need for counter-cyclical measures to support stability in the oil market, now recognized more than ever, OPEC states. This is something which has been recognized in the policies of the Kingdom of Saudi Arabia for at least the past thirty years.

The *World Oil Outlook* suggests that it is evident from the reference case and the protracted recession scenario that the overarching challenge facing the energy industry in general and OPEC in particular stems from the large uncertainties about future demand levels for energy and oil and the resulting difficulties in making appropriate and timely investment decisions. It then proceeds to discuss alternative Lower and Higher Growth scenarios in response to these uncertainties.

In the Lower Growth scenario downside demand risks from lower economic growth than in the reference case are coupled with a strong policy drive, over and above the reference case assumptions, to further improve oil use efficiency in the longer term. In the Higher Growth scenario the possibility of a swifter recovery from the economic recession than that assumed in the reference case is combined with a more positive outlook for longer term growth prospects. The authors of this book sympathize with these four approaches in trying to deal with the uncertainties in both the short–medium term and the longer term twenty-year horizon of 2030.

OPEC goes on to point out that even to 2013, a time frame over which investments are effectively locked in, investments could be as low as $70 billion or as high as $170 billion. By 2020 it estimates the figure could be as low as $180 billion in the Lower Growth Scenario but $430 in real terms (dollars of 2008) in the Higher Growth scenario. It points out that while recession-driven oil and energy demand destruction has demonstrated worries over security of demand, the current environment also clearly reveals the benefit of OPEC's counter-cyclical measures. For example OPEC's substantial supply increase between 2002 and 2006 had a strong mitigating effect on pro-cyclical developments, when world demand sharply increased and non-OPEC supply declined. Of course, we have already examined this phenomenon in Part II. The OPEC *World Oil Outlook* goes on to state that OPEC's supply adjustment (downwards) in the face of the deep economic recession in the OECD countries and fall in oil demand had the effect of making an important contribution to stabilizing world oil prices. These averaged something in the comparatively small range of $70 to $80 a barrel almost throughout the twelve months to June 2010 compared with fluctuations from less than $40 to more than $140 a barrel during the preceding twelve months.

The economic stimulus packages put in place in the leading economies are another example of the necessity of counter-cyclical policy measures, OPEC states. They demonstrate broad agreement on the requirement for sound regulation in financial markets. But the report goes on to assert that for oil there is a need to improve the functioning of futures and over-the-counter spot markets by upgrading the availability of and access to information on paper oil market participants and transactions and imposing a cap on speculative activity, together with the strengthening of regulations to close various loopholes.

The authors of this book believe this is very much the right approach and one which the G20 should be deliberating, along with inputs from the International Energy Forum, OPEC, the IEA and probably major professional participants in these markets as well, especially major international oil companies, but also major national oil companies, too.

OPEC is also exercised about fluctuations in both upstream and downstream costs in the oil industry, their relationship to economic activity and the investment cycle and the degree to which changes over time are structural or cyclical. Another concern is the quality and number of staff available to maintain and enhance the industry's skills base – one which has been repeatedly emphasized over many years by the present Saudi Arabian Minister of Petroleum and Mineral Resources, and even before that in his role as president and chairman of Saudi Aramco. This was discussed in Part I above.

The 2009 *World Oil Outlook* goes on to discuss the rising environmental challenges. It points out that with the world expected to rely on fossil fuels for many decades to come, it is vital to ensure the early and swift development, diffusion, deployment and transfer of cleaner fossil fuel technologies, for both local and global environmental protection. There is a need to adapt to a more carbon-constrained environment. Carbon capture and storage is a proven technology that has a high economic potential for mitigation, it states. It suggests that developed (OECD) countries, having the financial and technological capabilities and bearing the historical responsibility for the Earth's atmosphere, should take the lead in mitigation and adaptation in providing the necessary resources.

The OPEC report concludes its main text by recalling that poverty eradication is the very first UN Millennium Goal. Sound energy services should be available to all. A strengthening of the dialogue between energy producing and consuming countries is seen by OPEC as essential. The meetings of the G20 countries provide one obvious policy forum for this purpose, with countries in both categories being among the leading potential contributors to an international debate with the UN also necessarily being involved. Another institution which could surely play an important role in providing information as a basis for policy-making is the International Energy Forum. This was formed in 1991 and held its twelfth biennial meeting in late March 2010. It has a Secretariat in Riyadh, Saudi Arabia. It has members from both leading oil and energy producing and consuming countries as well as senior executives from leading oil companies around the world.

OPEC's *World Oil Outlook* has examined oil consumption by sector. It includes projections of passenger car ownership and populations in different regions of the world through to 2030. It makes the point that the developed countries of the OECD are approaching saturation levels in contrast to the extremely low levels of car ownership in many developing countries. It states that in 2006 there were 4.3 billion people living in countries with an average of fewer than 50 cars per 1,000 people compared with 484 cars per 1,000 people in the OECD countries as a group. Even more extreme, the number of cars in China increased by 25 per cent in 2006, yet the number of cars per 1,000 people was only 18 and in South Asia it was only 10 compared with 574 per 1,000 people in North America. The most extreme countries identified were Bangladesh and Ethiopia where there was just 1 car per 1,000 people. Even among OPEC members, the average was only 53 cars per 1,000 people, little more than 10 per cent of the average in the OECD countries. These remarkable differences illustrate the enormous potential growth for ownership in the developing countries. This begins to be realized to some extent over the years to 2030, as shown in Table IV.9.

Table IV.9. Projections of Passenger Cars per 1000 People

	Cars per 1000 People				Cars millions	Growth % p.a.
	2007	2010	2020	2030	in 2030	2007–30
North America	575	557	584	603	325	1.0
Western Europe	440	436	463	489	277	0.7
OECD Pacific	424	427	442	449	88	0.2
Total OECD	488	481	508	530	691	0.7
Latin America	115	122	141	162	85	2.5
Middle East and Africa	26	29	39	48	63	4.8
South Asia	11	14	32	69	143	9.6
Southeast Asia	44	48	67	91	71	4.2
China	20	26	62	115	167	8.4
OPEC	51	56	73	95	52	4.4
Developing countries	31	36	56	87	582	5.8
Russia	199	218	286	344	42	1.8
Other transitional economies	157	174	232	286	56	2.6
World	120	121	139	165	1372	2.4

Thus in spite of the narrowing of the gap over the next twenty years between the developed countries of the OECD and all developing countries in terms of the number of cars per 1,000 people, the density in the former is still projected to be more than six times the latter even in 2030. It can be seen that growth of motorization in OPEC is slower than in developing countries as a whole where annual growth is projected to be particularly high from very low starting levels in populous China and South Asia.

The OPEC *World Oil Outlook* points out that today road transportation is the largest oil consuming sector in the world, with a total share of over 40 per cent. In its reference case it needs an average of 0.3 million b/d per year of additional oil for the period 2008–30. This is on the basis of the above projection, but also taking account of economic, policy and technology dimensions, especially improvements in fuel efficiency, etc. It goes on to foresee that the diesel engine will remain the most efficient internal combustion engine and that liquid fuels will remain the preferred type by 2030, with the internal combustion engine maintaining its dominance in the industry, following a critical review of all the currently foreseen alternatives.

Worldwide an average annual change in oil use per vehicle of -1.6 per cent is projected for the period from 2007 to 2030, with the fall being greater at -2.1 per cent p.a. in the developing countries as a whole.

Oil demand in road transportation in the reference case is shown as being contrastingly different in the OECD countries compared with all developing countries, with the latter surpassing the former before 2030, as can be seen in Table IV.10.

Table IV.10. Oil Demand in Road Transportation in the Reference Case (million b/d)

	2007	2010	2020	2030	Changes 2007–30
OECD	21.7	19.8	19.5	18.4	-3.3
Developing countries	10.2	11.2	15.8	20.4	10.2
Transition economies	1.6	1.7	2.1	2.4	0.8
World	33.5	32.7	37.5	41.2	7.8

Another big difference between the OECD countries and all developing countries (where some 1.6 billion people lack access to electricity supply) is in terms of electricity consumption per capita. For example, in North America it exceeded 0.9 tonnes oil equivalent in 2006 compared with less than 0.2 tonnes o.e. in all developing countries and less than 0.1 tonnes o.e. in South Asia and Africa. These disparities remain wide. This is in spite of the fact of electricity demand growth having decelerated significantly during the forty years since 1970 in OECD countries to an average annual rate of 2.1 per cent from 1990 to 2006 while it has been much higher at 7.0 per cent annually in all developing countries over the same period.

The OPEC *World Oil Outlook* goes on to review the prospects for global oil product demand. It states that the continuing shift to middle distillates over the entire period remains the dominant feature of future demand. Out of the total increase of 20 million b/d by 2030 compared with 2008 more than 56 per cent is for middle distillates and less than 42 per cent for light products.

Table IV.11. Global Product Demand in Reference Case

	Global Demand in mn b/d				Growth Rates % p.a.		
	2008	2015	2020	2030	2008–15	2015–30	% Share 2030
Light Products							
Ethane/LPG	8.7	9.0	9.3	10.2	0.5	0.9	9.7
Naphtha	5.6	6.2	6.8	8.7	1.3	2.3	8.2
Gasoline	21.4	22.3	23.1	25.1	0.6	0.8	23.8
Middle Distillates							
Jet/Kerosene	6.5	6.8	7.3	8.1	0.7	1.2	7.7
Gasoil/Diesel	24.5	27.2	29.7	34.2	1.5	1.6	32.4

Heavy Products							
Residual fuel+	9.7	9.5	9.4	9.4	-0.2	-0.1	8.9
Other **	9.1	9.3	9.7	9.8	0.2	0.4	9.3
Total	**85.6**	**90.2**	**95.4**	**105.6**	**0.8**	**1.1**	**100.0**

+ Includes refinery use.

** Include bitumen, lubricants, waxes, still gas, coke, sulphur, direct use of crude oil etc.

The *World Oil Outlook* goes on to remark that it is the Asia/Pacific and Middle East regions that will host most of the foreseen petrochemicals expansion. The main reasons for this are the favourable feedstock availability, the fact that demand for basic petrochemical materials is anticipated to grow mainly in the Asia/Pacific, particularly China and India, and conversion of these materials into end products and consumer goods is enjoying a cost advantage all along the manufacturing chain in these regions.

The *WOO* discusses upstream costs attributed to finding, developing and producing oil, including those concerning human resources, a crucial component of any company's investment decisions. By mid-2008, upstream costs were clearly inflated. By then, the average worldwide unit capital cost of adding one new barrel of oil or gas had more than doubled since 2000, due mainly to higher finding and development costs. The cost to find and develop the marginal barrel had almost tripled. It pointed out that the oil sands projects and some of the deep and ultra deepwater projects are still considered to be the industry's benchmark for marginal costs. Nine months before the BP disaster with the Deepwater Horizon explosion on the Macondo Well in April 2010, the *WOO* had noted unexpected supply disruptions in the US Gulf of Mexico, Azerbaijan and Brazil. With the Macondo Well fully capped only after three months leakage, the hurricane season just having commenced as of end June 2010, and the ultimate costs of the disaster for BP being unknown at this point in time (in spite of $20 billion having been paid into an escrow account by BP under pressure from President Obama), it remains to be seen what effect this will have on government regulators' policy actions in the medium to longer term to control or even prevent deepwater drilling for oil (and gas) in very sensitive environments such as the Arctic. OPEC surely proved to be most perspicacious in 2009 in remarking that the projects most at risk are those with high costs and/or harsh environments.

The *WOO* discusses decline rates for oilfields once the maximum production capacity has been reached and passed. Even small changes or divergences can have a significant effect on future oil supply projections. Thus this is a subject followed closely by the OPEC Secretariat, both in terms of research and in the analysis of a number of studies recently released. Building from disaggregated data for individual countries, the production-weighted average annual observed decline rate for non-OPEC over the period since 2000 is estimated to be around 4.6 per cent p.a. This implies that the volumes of non-OPEC crude oil that have been replaced as a result of the observed decline rate have averaged around 1.8 million b/d p.a. so far this decade.

The decline rate is considerably greater in OECD Pacific and Western Europe estimated at averaging 9.3 per cent and 8.6 per cent p.a., but lower in the United States and Canada at 4.9 per cent and 4.3 per cent respectively, benefiting from the adoption of EOR techniques in the US lower forty-eight states. In Russia, Azerbaijan and Kazakhstan the two latter have become major producers, and Russian oil production has recovered strongly from its collapse during the 1990s, resuming investment in existing fields to help slow decline rates. The production-weighted observed decline rate there is around 3.1 per cent p.a. In China the use of infill drilling and the extensive development of EOR projects for some years past has helped to keep the country's observed decline rate to around 3 per cent p.a. For non-OPEC developing countries, the decline rates vary from 4.6 per cent in Latin America to 5.8 per cent in the Middle East (outside OPEC) with Asia at 5.1 per cent and Africa at 5.6 per cent.

Deepwater finds offshore Brazil have given rise to some optimism: the Tupi field is estimated to have between five and eight billion barrels of recoverable reserves of medium gravity low sulphur crude oil, albeit at depths of some 2km below the surface of the ocean and the salt layer which will make drilling particularly challenging and expensive. BP's disaster with the Macondo Well in the Gulf of Mexico gives added point to this caveat, in addition to the stance of governments and international regulatory authorities once the full report(s) of that catastrophe for BP are in the public domain. Nevertheless, as OPEC concludes in the *WOO*, for the oil industry as a whole, the Brazilian finds underline how reserves keep on expanding as technological and physical barriers are increasingly pushed back. It is a trend that has been with the industry since its very beginning and one that is expected to continue, it concluded in mid-2009, prior to the Macondo disaster.

Projections for non-OPEC crude oil and NGL supply over the period from 2008 to 2030 show the progression as flat to 2020 then declining by 0.5 per cent p.a. over the final decade, a net fall of 2.3 million b/d. OECD falls by -5.2 million b/d, involving declines in the US, Canada, Mexico and Western Europe. Declines are also projected for the Mid-East (non-OPEC), Africa, China and other Asia with partially offsetting rises in Russia, other transition economies (Kazakhstan, Azerbaijan) and Latin America. This takes total non-OPEC crude oil and NGL supply from 45.2 million b/d in 2008 down to 42.9 million b/d in 2030.

More than offsetting this net decline, there is an increase in non-conventional oil supply foreseen for non-OPEC sources of 4.2 million b/d from 2008 to 2030. This excludes bio fuels. The increase is from the low level of 1.8 million b/d in 2008 to 6.0 million b/d in 2030, 3.3 million b/d of the rise comes from the OECD, almost entirely from the US and Canada. China moves up from zero in 2008 to 0.7 million b/d in 2030.

In addition, bio-fuels supply from non-OPEC is projected to increase by 3.4 million b/d from 1.3 million b/d in 2008 to 4.7 million b/d in 2030 in the reference case; 2.0 million b/d of the increase comes from the OECD countries.

Thus aggregating the three non-OPEC sources of supply, an increase of 5.3 million b/d is projected over the twenty-two years to 2030 with almost all of it coming from countries/regions outside the OECD as the latter's fall in crude and NGL output is merely offset by projected increases in non-conventional oils and bio fuels.

The OPEC *World Oil Outlook* quotes both its Statute and its Long Term Strategy in particular on 'supporting security of supply to consumers', by expanding production capacity in such a way as to not only meet the increased demand for its oil, but also to 'offer an adequate level of spare capacity'.

Prior to the financial crisis and economic recession OPEC member countries had projects to increase gross crude and NGL capacity by 14 million b/d between 2009 and 2013. However, the change in the market prospects means that OPEC member countries have been reviewing their investment plans. Over 35 out of over 150 projects totalling around 5 million b/d were, by mid-2009, expected to be delayed or postponed until after 2013. The revision reflected the fact that the surge in investments plans in OPEC were aimed at addressing perceived market tightness, particularly as seen in 2007 and the first half of 2008.

We turn now to a consideration of the OPEC protracted recession scenario. One involves a 1 per cent reduction in annual economic growth below the reference case, 2009 to 2011 and the other a prolonged slowdown assuming a 2 per cent drop in annual growth compared to the baseline for all world regions over the years 2009 to 2013. OPEC stated that with some signs of a slowdown in the rate of contraction and an improvement in business and consumer confidence by mid-2009, the likelihood of these scenarios occurring had subsided. Nevertheless, banking system confidence remained low with no sign at that time (or even in mid-2010) of a return to pre-crisis normality.

Table IV.12. Main Components of Economic Growth Assumptions in the Protracted Recession Scenario (% p.a.)

	2009	2010	2011	2012	2013
OECD	-4.8	-1.6	0.1	1.2	1.7
All developing countries	1.9	2.6	3.6	4.2	4.8
China	6.0	5.3	6.2	6.7	7.2
OPEC	-0.1	1.5	2.1	2.6	3.2
Russia	-5.7	0.5	1.5	2.3	2.7

Other transitional economies	-4.7	-0.5	1.1	2.2	2.7
All transitional economies	-5.2	0.1	1.3	2.3	2.7
World	-2.3	0.1	1.5	2.5	3.0

This serves to emphasize the much sharper downturn envisaged in the OECD and Russia compared with the slowing of economic growth in the developing countries, particularly China, with annual economic growth there exceeding 5 per cent p.a. in all these five years.

As a consequence, OPEC sees world oil demand at 85.5 million b/d in 2013, almost the same as it was in 2008, and 2.4 million b/d lower than in the reference case. To summarize, we show the annual progression of the main features of supply and demand in the protracted recession scenario as foreseen by OPEC in mid-2009.

Table IV.13. Oil Supply and Demand in the Protracted Recession Scenario (million b/d)

	2009	2010	2011	2012	2013
World demand	83.9	83.8	84.3	85.1	85.4
Non-OPEC supply	50.2	49.9	49.5	49.0	48.3
OPEC crude	28.0	29.1	29.8	30.9	31.5

Note: No reference is made to OPEC NGLs or refinery gain, etc, in this abbreviated table.

Nevertheless, OPEC crude supply rises by 3.5 million b/d from 2009 to 2013, more than offsetting a fall of 1.9 million b/d projected for non-OPEC supply, given the rise projected of 1.5 million b/d in world oil demand even in this scenario.

The *World Oil Outlook* goes on to discuss the alternative Lower Growth and Higher Growth Scenarios for the medium and longer term for the period 2015 to 2030. In the Lower Growth scenario the downside demand risks that have been identified over the medium term from the threat of a protracted recession have been coupled with a strong policy drive, beyond the reference case assumptions, to further increase the efficiency of oil use in the longer term.

It features long term constraining effects upon the potential for economic growth associated with much lower productivity gains and the absence of a strong economic engine. Furthermore, there is a real threat of losing the benefits of trade liberalization if protectionism becomes an established feature of the future world economy. Percipiently, OPEC also warned of the additional threat of insolvency in some countries and this became a real possibility in the Eurozone during the second quarter of 2010. Beyond the protracted recession period the annual rates of economic growth are 0.5 per cent p.a. lower than in the reference case with the downside risks to demand being seen as more substantial than the upside potential.

Table IV.14. Oil Demand in the Lower Growth Scenario (million b/d)

	2015	2020	2025	2030
OECD	43.2	41.5	39.6	37.8
Developing countries	37.6	41.8	45.5	49.4
Transition economies	5.2	5.3	5.4	5.4
World	85.9	88.5	90.5	92.7

As compared with the reference case, world demand is 4.3 million b/d lower in 2015 rising to 6.9 million b/d lower in 2020 and 12.9 million b/d lower in 2030. In the horizon year OECD demand is 5.6 million b/d lower, developing countries are 6.7 million b/d lower and the transition economies are 0.7 million b/d lower.

Table IV.15. Oil Supply in the Lower Growth Scenario (million b/d)

	2015	2020	2025	2030
Non-OPEC	51.7	52.9	53.7	54.4
OPEC crude	28.7	29.2	29.8	30.6

On the supply side both non-OPEC crude and especially OPEC crudes are both lower than the reference case. As compared with the reference case, non-OPEC supply falls by 0.7 million b/d in 2015 with this rising to 1.9 million b/d in 2030, a comparatively modest difference as compared with OPEC. OPEC crude production in this Low Growth scenario is seen as being 3.3 million b/d below the reference case in 2015, rising to a difference of 5.1 million b/d in 2020, 7.7 million b/d in 2025 and 10.5 million b/d in 2030.

In the Higher Growth scenario economic growth is assumed to be 0.5 per cent p.a. higher than in the reference case. In this scenario world oil demand is almost 2 million b/d higher by 2015 than in the reference case and 8 million b/d higher by 2030. Slightly higher oil prices foreseen would provide support for additional non-OPEC conventional and non-conventional oil supply with output about 1 million b/d higher by 2015 compared to the reference case and 1.9 million b/d higher by 2030. As a result the amount of OPEC crude oil required is about 1 million b/d higher than in the reference case in 2015 and 7 million b/d higher by 2030.

Table IV.16. Oil Demand in the Higher Growth Scenario (million b/d)

	2015	**2020**	**2025**	**2030**
OECD	46.4	46.7	46.9	46.8
Developing countries	40.1	46.5	53.2	60.6
Transition economies	5.3	5.8	6.1	6.3
World	92.1	99.1	106.3	113.9

There is thus scarcely any change in OECD oil demand over the fifteen-year period. By contrast oil demand in all developing countries rises by over 20 million b/d and by just 1 million b/d in Russia and the other transitional countries. As compared with the reference case demand in the developing countries rises by more by 2030, 4.5 million b/d, than it does in the OECD countries, 2.4 million b/d.

Table IV.17. Oil Supply in the Higher Growth Scenario (million b/d)

	2015	**2020**	**2025**	**2030**
Non-OPEC	53.4	56.1	57.5	58.1
OPEC crude	33.1	36.6	41.7	48.1

Thus in spite of the rapid rise of 15 million b/d in OPEC crude oil supply over the fifteen-year period compared with a total increase of less than 5 million b/d in total non-OPEC crude supply, the OPEC supply needed to balance the world oil supply system in this scenario remains 10 million b/d less than that of non-OPEC.

The OPEC Secretariat points out that the uncertainty relating to world oil demand in these two scenarios is quite substantial, i.e. 89–99 million b/d in 2020 rising to 93–114 million b/d in 2030. Similarly, there is a wide range in the need for OPEC crude from a low of 29 million b/d in 2020 to a high of more than 36 million b/d in that year, increasing to a low of 31 million b/d in 2030 or a high of 48 million b/d. These differences imply significant uncertainty for investment needs in OPEC member countries. In the Lower Growth scenario, investment would only be necessary to compensate for production declines in existing facilities while the higher growth scenario requires additional new capacity over the projection period. In estimating the investment requirements adjustments are made to the decline rates and unit costs according to each scenario.

The OPEC *World Oil Outlook* makes a strong plea for the need to develop a sustainable energy future, to look carefully at where the financial crisis started, i.e. in the banking system, which should be made immune to excesses and over-leverage. Reform is needed to ensure the same problems never happen again with the focus being on reining in financial speculation everywhere and in a coordinated manner.

The report goes on to discuss the financial markets and oil prices in a way with which the authors of this book strongly agree. Oil price volatility in the recent past has been extreme (as we have shown elsewhere in this book). The OPEC Reference Basket Price of crudes rose to record levels in July 2008 reaching more than $140 a barrel, although there was no indication of a significant shortage of oil. The market was well supplied with crude oil and stock levels were high. Non-fundamental factors have clearly played a driving role in the extreme price volatility, OPEC states.

The emergence of oil as a financial asset class led to increased activity by non-oil industry operators with enhanced liquidity. In many respects the paper oil market exhibited prices characteristic of financial assets rather than simply reflecting oil market fundamentals. It is essential to find and sustain a stable and realistic price. It goes on to state that recent developments (i.e. in the 12+ months to June 2009) clearly point to the need for improving the functioning of futures and OTC (spot) markets, upgrading the availability of, and access to information on paper oil markets and transactions, better monitoring, imposing a cap on speculative activity and strengthening regulations to close various loopholes. International cooperation is also critical in this regard, OPEC concludes. It went on to recall the Third OPEC Summit call to 'strengthen and broaden the dialogue between energy producers and consumers through the International Energy Forum and other international and regional fora, for the benefit of all'.

The IEA's *World Energy Outlooks*
of 2009 and 2008

Our review concentrates on the IEA *World Energy Outlook* (*WEO*) published in November 2009 with some limited references to the earlier one published in 2008, having regard to the deep recession in the leading OECD countries. The impact of this was especially marked in the fourth quarter of 2008 and the first quarter of 2009. We have concentrated our attention on certain important points of difference between the two reports and the prominence given in the 2009 *WEO* to the threats relating to global warming and climate change associated with the use of fossil fuels provoking greenhouse gas emissions, especially CO_2.

In 2009, just prior to the UNFCCC summit in Copenhagen in that year, the International Energy Agency developed two scenarios as a basis for its projections through 2020 to 2030. These were a Reference scenario which provided a baseline picture of how global energy markets would evolve if governments made no changes in their existing policies and measures. A 450 Scenario depicted a world in which collective policy action is taken to limit the long-term concentration of greenhouse gases in the atmosphere to 450 parts per million of CO_2 equivalent, an objective which is gaining widespread support around the world – the IEA claimed. This is consistent with the aim of limiting the global temperature rise to 2° C.

We now proceed to a review of the points we consider worthy of note in the Foreword of the *World Energy Outlook* for 2009, followed by an extended treatment of the Executive Summary. The IEA points out that this latest *WEO* quantifies the impact of the financial crisis on energy investment. Paradoxically, it suggests that the sudden halt to new investment is an important opportunity; when it comes, new investment can make the most of the best available technologies, guided by any evidence from the Copenhagen Summit (of December 2009) that the international community is serious about climate change. In the event, the outcome of this event was disappointing. In another sense the effect of the financial and economic crisis represented a threat of consequential under-investment which, if prolonged, could constrain energy supply, pushing up the price of energy and even stifling the economic recovery.

Secondly, the IEA foresaw a possibility of a glut in natural gas supply in the short term with a boom in supplies of gas in the United States from unconventional sources. This report makes an in-depth study of natural gas in 2009 just as it did for oil in the *WEO* of 2008. It goes on to say that limiting the global average temperature rise to 2° C is the ultimate goal. This requires the wholesale transformation of the energy system. It suggests that it would require fossil fuel consumption to peak around 2020 and then decline, absolutely, by implication. SE Asia is the region selected for detailed study in this *WEO* of 2009. It says it has a growing influence in the global energy market.

The Executive Summary of IEA's *World Energy Outlook* 2009 justifies a rather comprehensive review with a few interspersed comments from ourselves. It starts by pointing out (before the end of 2009) that the global financial crisis and ensuing recession have had a dramatic impact on the outlook for energy markets over the next few years. However, primary energy use actually rose by 0.4 per cent between 2007 and 2009.

The coordinated fiscal and monetary stimuli in response to the threat of economic meltdown have included measures to promote clean energy with the aim of tackling an even bigger and just as real, long-term threat – that of disastrous climate change, the IEA states. The UNFCCC meeting in Copenhagen in December 2009 (after the *WEO* was published) represented a decisive opportunity in this context, but one not taken in the view of many commentators. The *WEO* 2009 quantified the challenge and shows what is required to overcome it. It emphasizes the need to concentrate investment on low-carbon technologies. It goes on to say that households and businesses are largely responsible for making the required investments but governments hold the key to changing the mix of energy investment.

The Reference Scenario

World primary energy demand is projected to grow at 1.5 per cent p.a. from more than 12 billion tonnes of oil equivalent in 2007 to 16.8 billion tonnes in 2030, an overall increase of 40 per cent. This is in spite of the modest rise we noted above between 2007 and 2009. The Asian countries are the main driver of the rise, followed by the Middle East. The rise in energy demand is expected by the IEA to rise by an average of 2.5 per cent p.a. from 2010 to 2015 but slackens progressively after this, as the emerging economies mature, the IEA expects, and global population growth slows.

Fossil fuels remain the dominant source of energy worldwide, accounting for 75 per cent of the increase from 2007 to 2030 in the IEA projections in the Reference scenario. Coal is by far the biggest increase, followed by gas and oil. Oil remains the largest energy source but falls from 34 per cent now to 30 per cent in 2030. Oil demand is projected to grow at 1 per cent p.a. on average from 85 million b/d in 2008 to 105 million b/d in 2030. All oil demand growth is in non-OECD countries. OECD demand for oil is projected to decline. The transport sector is seen as accounting for 97 per cent of the increase in oil use.

Conventional oil production outside OPEC is seen as peaking around 2010. It goes on to say most of the increase in output would need to come from OPEC members. Realistically it then remarks that these countries hold the bulk of recoverable conventional oil resources.

This *WEO* states that the main driver for coal and gas demand is input to electricity, projected to grow at 2.5 per cent p.a. to 2030. An additional total capacity of 4800 GW is foreseen as being required by 2030 worldwide. More than 80 per cent of demand growth for electricity is foreseen in non-OECD countries with China alone accounting for 28 per cent, i.e. 1344 GW. Coal's share in electricity generation rises to 44 per cent in 2030 in the Reference scenario. Nuclear is projected to grow everywhere except in Europe, but its share falls. Hydro drops from 16 per cent to 14 per cent in the horizon year. Other renewable energy is projected to increase from 2.7 per cent in 2007 to 8.6 per cent in 2030 with a combination of wind, solar, geothermal, tidal/wave and biomass energy. The use of bio fuels for transport is also seen as rising strongly but no quantities or growth rates are quoted.

Because of the financial crisis and economic recession, energy investment has plunged, the IEA states, along with weakening demand. There is a tougher financing environment and a lower cash flow in the sector. While existing projects have been slowed, planned ones have been postponed or cancelled. Capital expenditures have been reduced. Households too, are not buying more efficient energy using appliances. It reports a $90 billion fall (-19 per cent) cut in global upstream oil and gas investment budgets for 2009 compared with 2008. Oil sands projects in Canada account for the bulk of suspended oil capacity.

Government fiscal stimulus policies resulted in a fall of only 20 per cent in renewable investment, the IEA stated, as compared with a fall of 30 per cent which would have occurred from 2008 to 2009 without these actions.

Falling energy investment has consequences for energy security, climate change and energy poverty, the IEA says. A constraint on capacity growth, especially for long lead time projects, threatens a shortfall in supply. This could lead to a surge in prices in a few years as demand recovers, in turn acting as a constraint on global GDP growth. The concerns are most acute for oil and electricity.

The capital expenditure needed to meet energy demand growth to 2030 is estimated at $26 trillion dollars, in constant dollars of 2008, in the Reference scenario, i.e. $1.1 trillion p.a. or 1.4 per cent of global GDP. The power sector required 53 per cent of the total investment. The financing of energy investment is likely to be both more difficult and more costly than before the crisis.

The IEA goes on to warn that current policies put us on an alarming fossil energy path. There are serious consequences for climate change and energy security. In the Reference scenario there is a continued rapid rise in energy-related CO_2 emissions resulting from the increasing global demand for fossil energy. It estimates these emissions as shown in Table IV.18.

Table IV.18. Worldwide CO_2 Emissions

	1990	2007	2020	2030
Billion tonnes CO_2	20.9	28.8	34.5	40.2

However, these numbers imply growth of only 1.9 per cent p.a. over the seventeen years to 2007, falling to 1.4 per cent over the next thirteen years to 2020 and 1.5 per cent p.a. over the decade to 2030. Pointedly, the IEA states that non-OECD countries account for all the projected growth in CO_2 emissions to 2030. The 11.4 billion tonnes increase worldwide involves China at 6 billion tonnes, India at 2 billion tonnes and the Middle East at 1 billion tonnes. By contrast, OECD emissions are projected to fall slightly because of the decline in energy demand to 2009, followed by big improvements in energy efficiency in the longer term and increased reliance on nuclear power and renewables. To be fair the IEA does acknowledge that the non-OECD countries account for 52 per cent of world annual emissions of energy-related CO_2 today, though they are responsible for only 42 per cent of the world's cumulative emissions since 1890, according to the *WEO* of 2009.

However, we suggest this is a far from equitable analysis of the current position worldwide and the prospect over the next twenty years or so. We show later in this chapter and in the next one relating to comparable US data, how the problem of greenhouse gas/CO_2 emissions, based on data from these two sources, yields an entirely different perspective with important implications for policy when viewed on the basis of CO_2 emissions per capita. On this basis, the need for action over the next decade rests almost entirely with the OECD countries and Russia with only some of the developing countries needing to take action over the following ten to fifteen years because of the huge disparities in CO_2 emissions between countries/regions at present and still large ones beyond 2020 to 2030 on a per capita basis.

The IEA goes on to caution that the observed trends in the Reference scenario would lead to a rapid increase in the concentration of greenhouse gas emissions in the atmosphere. The rate of growth of fossil fuel consumption takes us towards a level of more than 1,000 parts per million of CO_2 equivalent, resulting in the global temperature rising by upwards of 6° C, leading to almost certain massive climate change and irreparable damage to the planet.

This rather alarmist picture portrayed by the IEA is then given another dimension by reference to this scenario heightening concerns about energy supplies. While the OECD countries as a group are projected to import less oil in 2030 than they do 'today' (supposedly in 2008), some non-OECD countries see big increases in their imports, notably China and India. However, for China at least, this is unlikely to be a problem, given their enormous value of foreign exchange reserves of $2.45 trillion reported in July 2010, continuing remarkable growth of the economy and exports in particular, with the OECD economy now recovering (mid-2010), though with some uncertainty.

Gas imports are projected to rise in Europe and developing Asia. The IEA goes on to discuss an increasingly high level of spending on energy imports as representing a major economic burden for importing countries. Not for China, though, in our view.

The *WEO* goes on to estimate the high level of oil prices at $97 a barrel in 2008 falling to around $60 in 2009 but then rebounding to $100 in 2020 with the economic recovery and to $115 a barrel in 2030, in terms of constant dollars of 2008. As a result, OECD countries as a group are projected to spend on average close to 2 per cent of their GDP on oil and gas imports to 2030. The IEA says the burden is higher in most importing non-OECD countries with China projected to overtake the United States soon after 2025 to become the world's biggest spender on oil and gas imports. It expects India's spending on oil and gas imports to surpass Japan soon after 2020 to become the world's third largest importer.

The IEA proceeds to discuss the increasing access to modern energy, i.e. electricity for the world's poor, which remains a pressing matter. It estimates that 1.5 billion people still lack access to electricity. In the Reference scenario the total drops by only 200 million by 2030. It says that with appropriate policies universal electricity access could be achieved with additional annual investment of \$35 billion (in dollars of 2008) through to 2030, or just 6 per cent of the power sector investment projected in the Reference scenario. The associated increase in primary energy demand and CO_2 emissions would be very modest.

The 450 Scenario

Limiting the temperature rise to 2° C requires a low carbon-energy revolution consensus on this emerging. To limit to 50 per cent the probability of the global average temperature rise in excess of 2° C, the concentration of greenhouse gas emissions needs to be stabilized at around 450 parts per million (ppm) of CO_2 equivalent. How this can be achieved in the 450 Scenario is by the coordination of policy, action across all regions, the IEA asserts. We believe this is not realistic if, by this, the IEA is implying big downward adjustments in CO_2 emissions for countries already and/or projected to emit less than 3 tonnes per capita in both 2007 and 2030, as is characteristic for almost 60 per cent of the world population living in developing countries, based on the IEA's own data.

The IEA 450 Scenario puts the worldwide emissions peaking at 30.9 billion tonnes just before 2020 and then declining to 26.4 billion tonnes in 2030. It says this is 2.4 billion tonnes below the 2007 level and 13.8 billion tonnes below that in the Reference scenario, or −34.3 per cent. It goes on to outline how this result could be achieved: a combination of carbon markets, sectoral agreements and national policies with appropriate measures. It says that only by taking advantage of mitigation potential in all sectors and regions can the necessary emissions reductions be achieved. The IEA states that the OECD and non-OECD Europe are assumed to take on emissions reduction commitments from 2013. All other countries are assumed to adopt domestic policies and measures and to generate and sell emissions credits. After 2020 commitments are extended to other major economies: China, Brazil, Russia, South Africa and the Middle East in the IEA plan. In our view this seems somewhat unrealistic because Brazil's emissions are currently low and at little more than 3 tonnes per capita will be low even in 2035, based on US projections to be discussed in the next chapter.

At 30.7 billion tonnes in 2020, worldwide emissions are 3.7 billion tonnes lower in this 450 Scenario than they are in the Reference scenario, or -11 per cent less. It goes on to remark that in non-OECD countries national policies currently under consideration yield 1.6 billion tonnes of emissions abatement, but will not happen unless there is an appropriate international framework. It says that China alone accounts for 1 billion tonnes of emissions reduction in this 450 Scenario. A reduction of 2.2 billion tonnes is delivered by OECD+ countries by means of an emissions cap in the power and industrial sectors, domestic policies and financing through the carbon market. In 2020 the OECD+ carbon price reaches $50 a tonne of CO_2. It is crucial to put in place an agreement providing clear economic signals to encourage the deployment of low carbon technologies. It says a low carbon revolution could put the world on to this 450ppm CO_2 trajectory. The IEA states that there is a need for energy to be used more efficiently and for the carbon content of energy we use to be switched to low or zero carbon sources.

The growth of primary energy demand averages only 0.8 per cent in the 450 Scenario compared with 1.5 per cent p.a. in the Reference scenario, or +23 per cent over twenty-three years from 2007 to 2030. Increased efficiency in buildings and industry reduces demand for electricity and to a lesser extent for fossil fuels, too. The IEA says the average emissions intensity of new cars is reduced by more than half. This seems to be a very ambitious target for a twenty-year-hence horizon, we can remark.

The share of non-fossil fuels in the overall primary energy mix increases from 19 per cent in 2007 to 32 per cent in 2030 in this 450 Scenario. Yet except for coal, demand for all fuels is higher in 2030 than in 2007 and fossil fuels remain the dominant energy source in 2030 (we infer 68 per cent).

Energy efficiency improvement offers the biggest scope for cutting emissions, the IEA says. End use efficiency accounts for more than half the total savings in the 450 Scenario compared with the Reference scenario. Investments in buildings, industry and transport usually have short payback periods and negative abatement costs as the fuel cost savings over the lifetime of the (new) capital stock often outweigh the additional capital costs of the efficiency

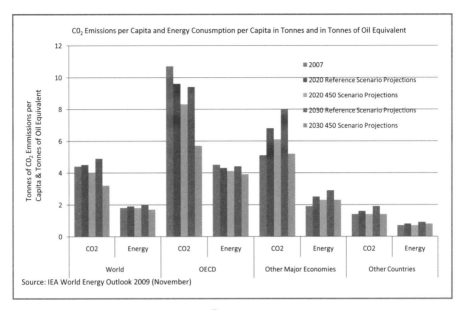

Figure IV.1

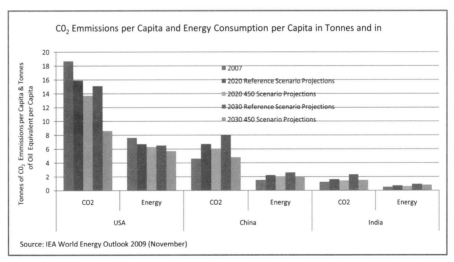

Figure IV.2

measure, even when future savings are discounted (over time). Decarbonization of the power sector accounts for more than two-thirds of the savings in the

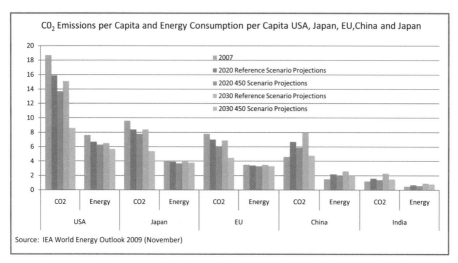

Figure IV.3

450 Scenario, of which 40 per cent results from lower electricity demand. A shift in the mix of fuels and technologies in power generation with coal-based electricity reduced by half compared with the Reference scenario is associated with nuclear and renewables making much bigger contributions.

The USA and China together contribute about half the reduction in global power sector emissions. Carbon capture and storage in the power sector and industry represents 10 per cent of total emissions savings in 2030 in the 450 Scenario as compared with the Reference scenario. By 2030 transport demand for oil is cut by 12 million b/d, i.e. more than 70 per cent of the oil savings in the 450 Scenario, with road transport being the major source of the saving.

The IEA suggests that by 2030 internal combustion-engined cars would represent only 40 per cent of sales in the 450 Scenario compared with 90 per cent in the Reference scenario. Hybrids and plug-in hybrids along with full electric cars are seen as the replacement new cars. This seems a very ambitious target for just twenty years hence. Also in the 450 Scenario, efficiency improvements in new aircraft and the use of bio fuels in aviation are seen as saving 1.6 million b/d of (conventional) oil demand by 2030.

This most recent *World Energy Outlook* from the IEA states that new financing mechanisms will be critical to achieving low carbon growth. The 450 Scenario entails $10.5 trillion more investment in energy related capital stock globally as compared with the Reference scenario through to 2030. Approximately 45 per cent of the increased investment, or $4.7 trillion dollars, are seen as being required in the transport sector with other additions as follows: $2.5 trillion in buildings and appliances; $1.7 trillion in power plants; $1.1 trillion in industry; and $0.4 trillion in bio fuels production, mostly second generation, and mainly after 2020. More than 75 per cent of the total is needed during the decade 2020 to 2030. The IEA goes on to suggest the total is almost equally divided between the OECD+ countries and the rest of the world. On an annual basis the IEA says investment needs reach $430 billion (0.5 per cent of GDP) in 2020 and $1.2 trillion (1.1 per cent of GDP) in 2030. Most of this would fall on private households, with most of the extra expenditure directed towards low-carbon vehicle expenditure. In the short term it acknowledges that the maintenance of government stimulus efforts is crucial to this investment.

We wish to point out here on the basis of the IEA's own statistics in this *World Energy Outlook* that the population outside the OECD+ countries is more than 5.1 times as great as in the OECD+, yet the total GDP of all of them, even in 2030, after taking account of faster growth in China, India etc, is only 1.3 times as much as in OECD+. Thus GDP per capita in 2030 in the OECD+ countries at $44,643 on average (in US dollars of 2008) is projected to be almost exactly four times greater than the average of $11,172 for all other countries worldwide. Thus a 50/50 split of the incremental burden of $10.5 billion for the 450 Scenario seems most unjust and unreasonable in our view. A more realistic and justifiable split would be for the OECD+ countries to meet 80 per cent and for all developing countries to meet just 20 per cent of the incremental burden, $8.4 and $2.1 trillion respectively, on the basis of the estimate quoted, particularly having regard to the starting point levels of 2007 in estimated CO_2 emissions per capita illustrated in our Figures IV.1, IV.2 and IV.3. At this point we can remind our readers that the IEA estimates US CO_2 emissions per capita at 18.7 tonnes per capita in 2007 (i.e. less than the 19.8 tpc estimated by the US DOE EIA for the same year). This is just over four times the estimated Chinese CO_2 emission of 4.6 tonnes per capita and 15.6 times the estimated CO_2 emissions for India in 2007, again based on the IEA's own numbers published in the *World Energy Outlook* of 2009.

The IEA goes on to assert that the additional investments needed to put the world onto a 450ppm path is at least partly offset by economic, health and energy security benefits. This latter suggests that memories are very long at the IEA, implicitly recalling the Arab oil embargo of thirty-seven years ago resulting in the formation of the IEA. It states that energy bills in transport, buildings and industry are reduced by $8.6 trillion globally over the period 2010 to 2030, with the fuel cost saving in the transport sector alone amounting to $6.2 trillion. It states that cumulative OPEC oil export revenues in 2008 to 2030 are 16 per cent less than in the Reference scenario, evidently a significant plus point for oil-importing IEA member countries in favour of the 450 Scenario. But then it goes on to say that in real terms they are still four times their level of the previous twenty-three years, i.e. 1985 to 2007 inclusive. It seems to us necessary to identify this as a red herring. Our analysis in this book shows that the real oil price was below its 1976 level (the mid-point during five years of relative stability in world oil prices) throughout this lengthy period, except for the final years. The IEA states that other implications include a big reduction in air pollutants, particularly in China and India, and in the cost of installing pollution control equipment – presumably in unit terms, because of the much greater scale of installation needed in the 450 Scenario compared with the Reference scenario.

The final paragraph devoted to this topic in the IEA's Executive Summary of this *WEO* 2009 states that it is widely agreed that developed countries (i.e. OECD countries) must provide more financial support to developing countries in reducing their emissions, but the level of support and the mechanisms for providing it and the relative burden across countries are matters for negotiation. It says that in the 450 Scenario $197 billion of additional investment is required in 2020 in non-OECD countries but this is a miniscule amount compared with the $5.25 trillion by 2030 implied by the IEA's proposed 50/50 split of $10.5 billion for the world as a whole in that year as between the OECD+ and the rest of the world. As we suggested above, a much more realistic way of analysing and reviewing what is reasonable to propose is to look at the problem on a per capita basis. This would exempt almost 60 per cent of the world population, all of them outside the OECD+ countries, from any need for CO_2 emissions abatement. This is because, on the basis of IEA WEO statistics, they are projected to be emitting about 3 tonnes of CO_2 per capita or less even in 2030, even in the Reference case.

Actually, our alternative and more selective approach to the problem results in a marginally lower level of per capita CO_2 emissions worldwide in the year 2030 at 3.08 tonnes, as compared with the IEA's 3.2 tonnes per capita in that year in the 450 Scenario. At this rate worldwide emissions would be less than 25.4 billion tonnes in 2030, but could be lower. This is on account of developing countries' comparatively fast-growing car fleets, for example, as noted in the OPEC *WOO*, importing more energy-efficient cars and/or hybrid/electric cars from OECD+ countries, or building their own more efficient, especially small cars, based on OECD countries' evolving technology, as indeed China, India and Brazil are doing already.

We summarize in Table IV.19 the key statistical estimates and projections of CO_2 emissions per capita for the world as a whole, for the key component groups of it and for the three most populous countries worldwide.

Table IV.19. CO_2 Emissions per Capita (tonnes)

	2007	2020		2030	
		RS	450	RS	450
World	4.4	4.5	4.0	4.9	3.2
OECD+	10.7	9.6	8.3	9.4	5.7
Other major economies (OMEs)	5.1	6.8	6.1	8.0	5.2
Other countries (OCs)	1.4	1.6	1.4	1.9	1.4
United States	18.7	15.9	13.7	15.1	8.6
China	4.6	6.7	5.9	8.0	4.8

India	1.2	1.6	1.4	2.3	1.5

Data for US are included in OECD+ averages. Data for China are included in OMEs averages. Data for India are included in OCs averages.

There is an enormous difference in average CO_2 emissions per capita even in the 450 Scenario in 2030 between the OECD+ countries and other countries, a factor of more than 4:1 difference, with the former accounting for 16 per cent of the worldwide population and the latter for 58 per cent. Our Figures IV.28 and IV.30 complement these statistics and projections.

Prior to, during and subsequent to the Copenhagen meeting, there was a major controversy relating to damaging revelations that the 2007 report by the International Panel on Climate Change, meant to be the infallible source for policy-makers, contained a number of errors. Scientists at the UK's University of East Anglia were involved. An inquiry published on 7 July 2010 was said to have cleared climate scientists of any allegations of dishonesty or corruption and has lifted the cloud of suspicion that has hung over the climate research community. A scientist from elsewhere was also reported as remarking that 'the whole of climate research had been tarnished by speculation that certain emails had been deleted'. The official inquiry concluded that the 'rigour and honesty' of scientists who sent the emails was 'not in doubt', that no evidence was found of behaviour that might undermine the conclusions of the Intergovernmental Panel on Climate Change. However, responses to reasonable requests for information were unhelpful and defensive; also, there was evidence that emails might have been deleted in order to make them unavailable should a subsequent request be made for them. While one blogger called the report a 'whitewash', the final item noted above from the official inquiry was widely seized upon by sceptics who seem to have agreed that widespread mistrust of climate change science would not be eased by the report.

Thus the absence of firm national commitments following the Copenhagen conference and the somewhat uneasy feelings about the seriousness of the global warming and climate change threat to the planet leave the matter of the implementation of the IEA's 450ppm scenario in an indeterminate and uncertain state at international level, at least as we see it in July 2010. An interesting editorial headed 'Climate Politics' in the *Financial Times* of 9 July 2010 discussed some of the problems in the following terms:

> There is dispute among climatologists about projections. Economists and scientists disagree honestly about mitigation strategies. But researchers in the field often see themselves as campaigners; and so try to stamp out dissent. This leads them to breach the rules of scientific discourse.

The Stern Review of 2006 into climate change concluded that: 'the average estimate for the cost of holding carbon at safe levels will cost one per cent of global output by 2050. This price is worth paying: a six degree rise in temperatures could reduce economic activity by more than 10 times that figure.' The editorial goes on: 'Even so, an insurance premium of one per cent of output is an enormous cost. Governments will struggle to impose this burden.' It concludes: 'As treasuries look for ways to raise more revenues, climate change activists should make the case for green taxes.'

Complementing the topical analysis of CO_2 emissions per capita, we show in Table IV.20 the analysis of primary energy consumption per capita for the same years and regions/countries as for CO_2 emissions.

Table IV.20. Primary Energy Demand per Capita (tonnes o.e.)

	2007	2020		2030	
		Ref	**450**	**Ref**	**450**
World	1.8	1.9	1.8	2.0	1.7
OECD+	4.5	4.3	4.1	4.4	3.9
OMEs	1.9	2.5	2.3	2.9	2.3
OCs	0.7	0.8	0.7	0.9	0.8
United States	7.6	6.7	6.3	6.5	5.7
China	1.5	2.2	2.0	2.6	2.0
India	0.5	0.7	0.6	0.9	0.8

Thus even in 2030 energy demand per capita in the other major economies is projected to be only some 66 per cent of the OECD's level in the Reference scenario and 59 per cent in the 450 case. Similarly, for all other countries representing a majority of the human race, the comparative numbers are barely 20 per cent of the OECD average in 2030.

For the three most populous countries worldwide the differences are considerably wider in 2030. China's energy demand per capita is projected to be 40 per cent of the US level in the Reference scenario and 35 per cent in the 450 scenario. India is down at only 14 per cent of the US projected demand in both scenarios, likewise in 2030.

We proceed now to make selective reference to certain other features of the IEA *World Energy Outlook* and to make a few comments where we consider these appropriate. This section is mainly concerned with the presentation of some statistics and projections included in the *World Energy Outlook* in the two scenarios mentioned above.

The population and the GDP growth assumptions are the same in both the Reference and the 450 Scenarios. The principal differences between them are that new policies are assumed in the 450 Scenario along with some differences in technology. Prices (of oil) are also assumed to be affected by these changes.

The *WEO* 2009 has a section (on p. 60) raising the question 'To what extent are high oil prices to blame for the economic crisis?' The three-paragraph discussion of this topic is really quite unsatisfactory because it fails to recognize the importance of a coinciding fall in OECD oil production, rising world demand and rising OPEC and Russian oil production such that the tightening of the world oil balance amounted to only some 0.2 million b/d. In our view, this should not have resulted in the dramatic rise in world oil prices to more than $140 a barrel in July 2008. We have discussed this phenomenon in other parts of this book, notably in Part II, but consider we are justified in pointing to speculation fuelled by the big credit expansion of some five years to 2008 for the unjustified rise in futures prices of high profile crudes such as West Texas Intermediate and Brent from the North Sea, as the proximate cause. In the *WEO* of 2008, the IEA reported that "The amount of money invested in commodity funds has certainly risen strongly in recent years – twentyfold since 2003 to more than $250 billion on some estimates. A growing number of analysts believe that this represents a speculative bubble rather than the outcome of market fundamentals' (p. 71).

In the 450 Scenario oil prices are the same as in the Reference scenario through until 2015, but then float until 2030 because of weaker demand in this case. The price is 10 per cent less than in the Reference scenario in 2020, then 22 per cent lower in 2030, the IEA estimates. Gas prices are higher in Europe and Asia/Pacific than in the US, thanks to shale gas drilling during recent years leading to a rise in supply in the latter.

In another passage on p. 65 of the *WEO* the discussion concerning the increase in oil prices over several years to July 2008 ignores the influence of speculators in pushing up the oil price to an unprecedented level. We do not accept that 'oil market fundamentals certainly played a central role in drawing prices up', as stated by the IEA. Again, we refer to our interpretation of events in Part II of this book and the quote above from the *WEO* of 2008.

The *WEO* discusses major new technologies that are approaching commercialization and which are assumed to be deployed at various points over the projection period. These include carbon capture and storage (CCS) which it says is a crucial but relatively costly form of emissions abatement in the 450 Scenario. It also mentions concentrating solar power; electric and plug-in hybrid vehicles; and advanced bio fuels. But it concludes that no new technologies are assumed to be deployed in either of the two scenarios. It remarks that there is no way of knowing when breakthroughs may occur – hope springs eternal.

Table IV.21. Oil Prices Assumed by the IEA

	2000	2008	2015	2020	2030
$ a barrel, real $ of 2008 in Ref case	34.30	97.19	86.67	100.00	115.00
Nominal	28.00	97.19	101.62	131.37	189.65
$ of 2008 450 case				90.00	90.00
The figure assumed for 2009 was approximately $60 a barrel.					

Oil prices assumed by the IEA are as shown in Table IV.21. These oil prices assumed by the IEA are slightly below those of the US DOE's Energy Information Administration but significantly higher than those of OPEC, respectively £130 a barrel in 2030 and $70 to $100 a barrel over the next decade for the OPEC reference basket of crudes.

Natural Gas

Natural gas is the subject of a detailed study in the *World Energy Outlook* of November 2009. It suggests that natural gas will play a key role whatever the policy landscape. Demand for natural gas worldwide is set to resume its long-term upward trend though the pace of change hinges critically on the strength of climate policy acting along with GDP growth and the relative competitiveness of the gas price. The low carbon content of gas *vis-à-vis* coal and oil means that gas demand will continue to expand in the 450 Scenario. In the Reference scenario gas demand rises from 3.0 trillion cubic metres to 4.3 trillion cubic metres (tcm) in 2030, an average rate of increase of 1.5 per cent p.a. However, the share of natural gas in the primary energy mix is seen as rising very marginally, by only 0.3 percentage points from 2007 to 21.2 per cent in 2030. Over 80 per cent of the increase in gas use occurs in non-OECD countries with the biggest rises being in the Middle East, India and China. The power sector is expected to remain the largest consumer of gas demand in all regions. The *BP Statistical Review of World Energy*, published in June 2010, estimated that gas demand worldwide fell 70 billion cubic metres or -2.1 per cent in 2009, less than expected in the *WEO*.

In the IEA's 450 Scenario world gas demand is seen as growing by 17 per cent from 2007 to 2030 (after the dip in 2009), but this still leaves it 17 per cent below the projection for gas in 2030 in the Reference scenario. Gas continues to grow in most non-OECD regions through 2020 but there are suggestions of a decline in demand after that.

Measures to encourage energy savings by improving the efficiency of gas use and encouraging low carbon technologies reduce gas demand, the IEA says. This is in spite of its advantage relative to oil and coal in terms of CO_2

emissions. Higher carbon prices and regulatory instruments are seen as more important effects, but this surely begs the question of both the comparative economics of new renewables technology and how quickly they will actually be introduced in the electricity generating sector, thus constraining growth of gas demand, potentially. The US sees higher gas use in the 450 Scenario between 2020 and 2030 than in the Reference scenario as gas becomes relatively more competitive against coal.

The world's remaining resources (note, not proven reserves) are easily large enough to cover any conceivable increase in demand through to 2030 and well beyond but the cost of developing new resources is set to rise over the long term. Proven gas reserves at end 2008 were estimated at more than 180 trillion cubic metres, over half of them in just three countries, Russia, Iran and Qatar. At current rates of production the proved reserves have an average worldwide lifespan of sixty years, but much longer in Iran and Qatar. Unconventional gas resources make up 45 per cent of a much bigger estimate of a total worldwide, comprising coal-bed methane, tight gas and shale gas.

Non-OECD countries account for almost all the projected increase in gas production from 2007 to 2030, with the Middle East accounting for the biggest increase in both gas production and exports. It has both the largest reserves (though Russia is actually no. 1) and the lowest production costs, especially when gas is produced in association with oil. Turkmenistan in Central Asia, some countries in Africa, notably Algeria and Nigeria, and Russia are all able to significantly increase their production volumes.

The inter-regional gas trade is projected to grow from 677 billion cubic metres in 2007 to 1,070 bcm in 2030 in the Reference scenario and to more than 900bcm in the 450 Scenario. Both OECD Europe and the Asia/Pacific region are seen as increasing their imports over this period.

The IEA goes on to say the rate of decline in production from existing fields is the prime factor in determining the amount of new capacity and investment needed to meet projected demand. Close to half the world's existing capacity will need to be replaced by 2030 as a result of depletion. This implies approximately double Russia's current production of about 600 bcm. By then approximately one-third of total output comes from currently producing fields in the Reference scenario, despite continuing investment in them. Decline rates in production for fields past their peak are lower for the largest fields and higher for offshore fields than for onshore fields of a similar size. For the world's largest gas fields, weighted by production, the decline rate is 5.3 per cent p.a. but for all fields worldwide, the rate is 7.5 per cent p.a., similar to oil fields.

Unconventional gas changes the game in North America and elsewhere, the IEA reports. Rapid development of unconventional gas, especially in the last three years to 2009, has transformed the gas market outlook. New technology, especially horizontal well-drilling combined with hydraulic fracturing, has increased productivity per well, notably for shale gas, and cut production costs.

Thus this supplement to supply, combined with weak demand following the economic crisis and higher than usual storage levels, has led to a steep drop in US gas prices from almost $9 per million BTUs in 2008 to less than $3 per million BTUs in early September 2009, cutting LNG import needs into the US and putting downward pressure on prices elsewhere. This has resulted in reduced drilling activity, but production has held up as marginal costs have fallen sharply. The *WEO* goes on to claim that unconventional sources of gas supply have the potential to increase overall North American production at a wellhead cost of between $3 and $5 per million BTUs (in 2008 dollars) for the coming several decades. But rising material costs and rig rates will exert upward pressure in unit costs over time. High decline rates for unconventional gas will require constant drilling and completion of new wells to maintain output, not to mention the capital costs involved.

The IEA says it is highly uncertain the extent to which the boom in unconventional gas production in North America can be replicated in other parts of the world endowed with such resources. Some regions, including China, India, and Europe, are thought to hold such resources but there are major potential obstacles to their development in some cases. In the Reference scenario unconventional gas production of 367bcm in 2007 rises to 639bcm in 2030, much of the increase being in the US and Canada, with its share in total US production of gas rising from 50 per cent in 2008 to 60 per cent in 2030.

Globally, the share rises from 12 per cent in 2007 to 15 per cent in 2030, though the IEA warns that this projection is subject to considerable uncertainly, especially after 2020, with the potential to increase much more.

The *WEO* summary on natural gas concludes on a rather pessimistic note for producers. It says a glut of gas is looming over the next few years as a result of the recession's effect on demand. There is a prospective big increase in spare inter-regional gas transportation capacity in both pipelines and LNG projects. Under-utilization is projected to rise from 60bcm in 2007 to nearly 200bcm in 2012 to 2015. Utilization drops from 88 per cent to 75 per cent, with the drop for pipelines being the most marked. Also, it foresees the looming gas glut leading to less connectivity between major regional markets, i.e. the US on the one side and Europe and Asia/Pacific on the other, with consequences for the structure of gas markets and the way gas is priced in the two latter. Low prices in North America are expected to discourage LNG imports. Assuming oil prices rise (as the IEA projects) gas prices will tend to rise in Europe and the Asia/ Pacific because of the prominence of oil indexation. It goes on to speculate on a possible moving away from this with falling spot prices for LNG increasing pressure on gas exporters, but if this happened there would be a boost for demand. It also speculates that, if prices were depressed for a period, wealthy Qatar might prefer to shut in its rapidly rising production for a while.

The IEA talks about a Clean Energy New Deal with a shift in investment to low carbon technologies to curb the growth of greenhouse gas emissions. It emphasizes that much more needs to be done to get anywhere near an emissions path consistent with stabilization of greenhouse gas emissions at 450ppm and limiting the rise in global temperature to 2° C. It remarks that the speed of governments' actions is regarded as a critical ingredient. It asserts that every year that passes the window of opportunity becomes narrower and the costs of transforming the energy sector increase. It estimates that each year of delay adds approximately $500 billion to global incremental investment costs of $10.5 trillion for 2010 to 2030. If this happens the additional adaptation costs would be many times this figure, the IEA says.

In view of the comparative failure of the Copenhagen Summit in December

2009, the IEA will obviously be disappointed that its considerable efforts to develop its 450ppm scenario have not borne more fruits in terms of international efforts to counter the threat of global warming and climate change.

Comparison of IEA World Energy Outlooks for 2009 and 2008

Finally in this chapter we show a comparison of the two *World Energy Outlooks* published by the IEA in November 2009 and a year earlier, by means of two tables of statistics, one for oil demand and another for oil supply. In the case of total world oil demand, it can be seen that there was a dramatic reduction in the projection for 2015 amounting to 291 million tonnes or 6 million b/d. However, by 2030 this narrows to only 100 million tonnes. The reduction is especially sharp for the OECD countries which have been much harder hit by the financial crisis and economic recession than the developing countries. In the OECD the gap between the consecutive *WEOs* is 4.5 million b/d in 2015 and narrows rather little to 3.8 million b/d in 2030. For all developing countries, the gap in projections between the *WEO* for 2009 and 2008 narrows to only 1.5 million b/d in 2030 with the gap for fast-growing China and India between the two consecutive *WEOs* being rather small in the horizon year.

As one would expect, there is a similar fall in world oil supply, particularly marked in 2015. Crude oil supply is 1.3 million b/d lower in 2015 than in 2008 but supplies of both NGLs and unconventional oils are projected to rise and continue to do so through to 2030. Also, crude oil production is projected to rise by 7.5 million b/d between 2015 and 2030 in this latest *WEO*.

The reader should note that the supply of both natural gas liquids and unconventional oils are projected to rise significantly by 13.7 million b/d worldwide with OPEC members accounting for 7.4 million b/d of the combined increase in supply over this twenty-three-year period.

Finally, we have to note that the IEA has reduced its projection for Saudi Arabia from 15.6 million b/d in the *WEO* of 2008 to 12.0 million b/d in the *WEO* of 2009. For crude oil alone this is consistent with what has been reported in the public media such as *Middle East Economic Survey* in June

2010 which made it clear that the number is 12 million b/d for the Kingdom's production of crude, as officially foreseen, with an additional 0.5 million b/d from the Neutral Zone shared with Kuwait. In addition to this, an increase in Saudi Arabia's output of NGLs is expected to be made within the total OPEC increment of 6.4 million b/d projected by the IEA in its Reference scenario over the twenty-two years to 2030. This is 1 million b/d less than a year earlier, as just mentioned.

Table IV.22. Comparison of IEA WEOs for 2008 and 2009: Oil Demand

Reference Scenario		2007*	2015	2030	% p.a. 2007–30
World oil demand	WEO m.t.o.e.				
	2009	4093	4234	5009	0.9
	2008	4093	4525	5109	1.0
	= mn b/d				
	2009	85.2	88.4	105.2	0.9
	2008	85.2	94.4	106.4	1.0
OECD	2009	43.2**	41.2	40.1	-0.3
	2008	46.5	45.7	43.9	-0.2
USA	2009	18.5	17.9	17.2	-0.3
	2008	20.2	19.3	19.0	-0.3
All non-OECD	2009	35.0	40.2	56.2	2.2
	2008	34.9	44.6	57.7	2.2
China	2009	7.7	10.4	16.3	3.5
	2008	7.5	11.3	16.6	3.5

India	2009	3.0	3.8	6.9	3.9
	2008	2.9	4.1	7.1	3.9

Data not shown but derived from implicit conversion from mn tonnes.

** Data in *WEO* 2009 show data for 2008 as the base year whereas the *WEO* 2008 showed data for 2007 as the base year, except for tonnage estimates which are for 2007 in both 2008 and 2009 *WEO*s.

Table IV.23. Comparison of IEA WEOs for 2008 and 2009: Oil Supply (mn b/d)

Reference Scenario		*2007***	*2015*	2030	% p.a. change 2007-30
World oil supply			WEO		
	2009	84.6	88.4	105.2	1.0
	2008	84.3	94.4	106.4	1.0
Crude oil	2009	70.5	69.2	76.7	0.4
NGLs		10.8	13.9	18.9	2.6
Unconventional		1.8	3.5	7.4	6.6
Total non-OPEC	2009	46.8	46.3	49.2	0.2
of which crude		39.3	36.6	35.3	-0.5
NGLs		5.8	6.6	7.6	1.2
Unconventional oil		1.7	3.2	6.3	6.2
Total non-OPEC	2008	46.3	47.6	50.9	0.4
OECD crude only	2009	13.5	10.5	9.5	-1.6
total	2008	19.3	18.6	20.8	0.3

Total OPEC:**	2009	36.3	40.3	53.8	1.8
	2008	35.9	44.4	52.9	1.7
crude only	2009	31.2	32.6	41.4	1.3
NGLs	2009	4.9	7.3	11.3	3.9
	2008	4.7	8.1	13.2	4.6
Unconventional oil	2009	0.1	0.3	1.1	10.7
	2008	0.1	0.4	0.9	10.0
Middle East crude only	2009	21.5	22.6	29.2	1.4
	2008	23.6	30.3	37.1	2.0
Saudi Arabia crude only	2009	9.2	10.9	12.0	1.2
.	2008	10.2	14.4	15.6	1.9

*Data in WEO 2009 show data for 2008 as the base year whereas the WEO 2008 shows data for 2007 as the base year, except in the table for world; growth rates take account of different base years.

Our numbers do not always add up because we have ignored processing gains in refineries.

**The numbers for Total OPEC include NGLs and unconventional oils.

In WEO 2009 the numbers for non-OPEC NGLs and unconventional oils have not been shown separately for OECD countries and all others. Thus a strict comparison between total OECD oil production between the WEOs for 2008 and 2009 is not possible. However, it is probable that a high proportion of NGLs and unconventional oils produced/projected to be produced outside OPEC are expected to come from OECD countries.

GDP Per Capita and Electricity Generation Per Capita

We now continue with a comparative review of GDP per capita and electricity generation per capita based on the IEA statistics published in the *World Energy Outlook* of November 2009. The statistical data and projections per capita are based on the aggregate data published by the IEA in the *WEO*.

Table IV.24. GDP per Capita ($ 2008, ppp basis)

	2007	2020	2030
World	10,160	13,420	16,634
OECD +	32,628	38,026	44,643
OMEs	7,575	14,403	20,327
OCs	3,645	5,340	7,048
USA	46,078	52,770	61,035
China	5,727	13,156	19,507
India	2,760	5,383	8,729

Table IV.25. Electricity Generation per Capita, GWH

		Ref	450	Ref	450
World	2,987	3,579	3,418	4,164	3,635
OECD +	8,786	9,177	8,849	9,972	9,185
OMEs	3,025	4,835	4,552	6,121	5,055
OCs	920	1,237	1,186	1,639	1,426
USA	14,124	13,843	13,328	14,379	13,150
China	2,500	4,683	4,353	6,055	4,806
India	705	1,251	1,202	1,911	1,672

Source: IEA *World Energy Outlook* 2009.

Table IV.26. Annual Average Growth Rate 2007 to 2030, per Capita

	GDP % p.a.	Electricity Ref Scenario	Electricity 450 Scenario	Proportion of World Total Population in 2030 %
World	2.2	1.5	0.9	100
OECD +	1.4	0.6	0.2	16

OMEs	4.4	3.1	2.3	26
OCs	2.9	2.5	1.9	58
USA	1.2	0.1	-0.3	4
China	5.5	3.9	2.9	18
India	5.1	4.4	3.8	17

Our principal purpose in showing these derived estimates and projections on a per capita basis is to reinforce the message already conveyed in comparable estimates for energy consumption and CO_2 emissions per capita discussed above. This is to the effect that there remain vast discrepancies in the world between the three major groups, as defined by the IEA, and between the three most populous countries worldwide, even after taking account of the very different annual average growth rates per capita over the period from 2007 to 2030 implicit in the IEA's estimates and projections. Even in 2030 the population of the advanced OECD+ countries and the United States amount to only 16 per cent and 4 per cent of humankind respectively. The other major economies and China account for 26 and 18 per cent respectively while all other countries worldwide account for 58 per cent of the total population and India within that category for just 17 per cent in 2030.

Table IV.27. Projected Relationships in 2030 on an Average per Capita Basis in Index Number Form (World = 100)

	GDP	PE		Electricity		CO_2 Emissions	
		RS	450	RS	450	RS	450
World	100	100	100	100	100	100	100
OECD+	268	220	229	240	253	192	178
OMEs	122	145	135	147	139	163	163
OCs	42	45	47	39	39	39	44
USA	367	325	335	345	362	308	269

China	117	130	118	145	132	163	150
India	53	45	47	47	46	47	47

From this we can see that on average 58 per cent of the world's population living in the other countries category will enjoy a per capita GDP of just over $7,000 p.a. in 2030, or just about 15 per cent of the average level projected for the OECD+ countries. Similarly, their energy consumption per capita will be just over 20 per cent of the OECD+ countries' average and electricity consumption lower, within this range. Their CO_2 emissions per capita are projected to be slightly higher at 20.3 per cent and 24.7 per cent of the average for the OECD+ countries in the Reference and 450 Scenario respectively, but below 2 tonnes per person in both of them and less than 20 per cent of the OECD average back in 1990.

For the other major economies GDP per capita is projected to be less than 50 per cent of the OECD+ average but energy consumption is expected to be higher at 59–66 per cent of the OECD average in the Reference and 450 Scenarios respectively, with electricity consumption at 55–61 per cent of the OECD average. Only in respect of CO_2 emissions per capita do the other major economies approach the OECD average in 2030, being at 85 per cent and 92 per cent of it in the Reference scenario and the 450 Scenario respectively.

China's GDP per capita is projected to be less than 32 per cent of that of the United States in 2030 with India at less than 15 per cent of the US GDP per capita. For primary energy consumption the projected numbers for China are rather higher at 35–40 per cent of the US average, but for India the numbers are rather lower at around 14 per cent of the US average. For electricity the numbers are similar for China at 36–42 per cent of US per capita consumption but for India the numbers are marginally lower at around 13 per cent of the average US consumption in 2030. For CO_2 emissions per capita the projected estimates for China in 2030 are 53–6 per cent of the US level and for India they are much lower at 15.3–17.5 per cent of US projected emissions in the Reference and 450 Scenarios respectively, still an enormous difference, with Indian emissions of CO_2 projected at the low level of 2.3 tonnes per capita in the Reference scenario and only 1.5 tonnes in the 450 Scenario.

US DOE/Energy Information Administration's

International Energy Outlook 2010

The *International Energy Outlook* published by the US Energy Information Administration (EIA), part of the Department of Energy, is a well presented and up-to-date document, the highlights of which and a great deal of statistical data and projections through to 2035 were published in late May 2010. The full report was scheduled for July 2010.

This interim review of it is based on what is available as of 1 July 2010. This consists of the following:

1. Highlights, eight pages of text, full of important data providing a worldwide perspective.

2. An International Energy Outlook 2010 with Projections to 2035: a professional style PowerPoint visual presentation of twenty pages from the Deputy Administrator of the EIA to the Center for Strategic and International Studies.

3. A set of sixteen pages of small visual aids and abbreviated statistical tables showing some principal features of the world energy market.

4. Ten appendices totalling 150 pages providing historical data and projections at five-year intervals from 2015 to 2035. These are listed below to give readers of this book an introduction to what is included.

1. Appendix A   Reference case

2. Appendix B   High Economic Growth case

3. Appendix C   Low Economic Growth case

4. Appendix D   High Oil Price case

5. Appendix E   Low Oil Price case

6. Appendix F   Reference case projections by end-use

7. Appendix G   Projections of petroleum and other liquids production in five cases

8. Appendix H   Reference case projections for electricity capacity and generation by fuel

9. Appendix I   Projections of natural gas production

10. Appendix J   Kaya identity components by region

Energy-Related CO_2 Emissions and Climate Change

We choose to start our analysis and review of this impressive and very professionally presented documentation with the topic of climate change and greenhouse gas emissions (or rather CO_2, explicitly), as shown in their figure 10, along with the statistics for the OECD countries, all non-OECD countries grouped together and the World as a whole for the period from 2007 to 2035.

Their bar chart shows energy-related carbon dioxide emissions in the OECD countries hardly changing over the twenty-year projection period, but actually falling between 2007 and 2015, attributable to the deep economic recession of

2008–9 and reduced fossil fuel usage at this time. Subsequently, there is a slight rise over the period of twenty years from 2015 to 2035 averaging less than 0.45 per cent p.a.

By contrast, the bar chart for all non-OECD countries appears to rise quite rapidly from just over 16 billion tonnes in 2007 to nearly 28.2 billion tonnes in 2035, though the actual average rate of increase is only 2.0 per cent p.a.

In spite of these differences, if one looks at the population statistics and projections likewise included in this US report and proceeds to a comparison of energy-related CO_2 emissions per capita one arrives at a very different conclusion. In 2007 CO_2 emissions in the OECD countries on average were 11.56 tonnes per capita compared with only 2.93 tonnes in the whole of the rest of the world. In other words, the CO_2 emissions per capita in the OECD countries were actually 3.9 times as great as the average in all non-OECD countries worldwide. The ratio falls to slightly less than 2.7 times by 2035. Nevertheless, this is still an enormous disparity, given the pressures to reduce greenhouse gas emissions articulated by individuals and institutions in the OECD countries because of the threat of climate change and global warming.

The OECD countries largely bear past responsibility for the historic build-up of energy-related CO_2 emissions in the global atmosphere, primarily related to the burning of fossil fuels. Also, they possess the wealth and technological expertise in renewable energy available in most advanced economies. Thus, we might suggest that they should bear the responsibility for bringing about dramatic change in their energy systems and structures in order to substantially reduce emissions of greenhouse gases worldwide.

Politically and environmentally, there can be no doubt that the responsibility for worldwide adjustment rests primarily with those countries already well advanced in terms of per capita incomes and living standards to make a fundamental adjustment and reduce their CO_2 emissions, over the next forty to fifty years, if not the next twenty. A start of 5 per cent from the high level reported for 2007 is already in prospect in the OECD countries from 2007 to 2015, thanks to the recent deep recession, based on the US data and projections with fossil fuel usage having fallen 7.5 per cent over two years from 2007 to 2009 in the OECD.

It so happens that these data and projections for the world as a whole yield an average of 5.01 tonnes of CO_2 per capita in the horizon year of 2035, based on 10.58 tonnes in the OECD countries and 3.96 tonnes on average in the rest of the world in that year.

Table IV.28. Per Capita CO2 Emissions in Reference Case: Actual for 2007 and Projections through to 2035 by US DOE/EIA

Tonnes per person	OECD	All Non-OECD Countries*	China	World
2007	11.56	2.93	4.76	4.47
2015	10.50	3.08	5.57	4.34
2020	10.38	3.26	6.73	4.44
2025	10.40	3.46	7.29	4.60
2030	10.46	3.69	8.23	4.78
2035	10.58	3.96	9.18	5.01

*Including China

It seems unrealistic to argue against the aspirations of developing countries to develop their economies over the next twenty to forty years towards the current levels of the existing average of the OECD countries. These levels of high GDP per capita have been achieved largely on the basis of fossil fuels providing the energy wherewithal for this purpose. Given the indigenous coal reserves of China, India and South Africa, for example, natural gas in Russia and Turkmenistan, as well as both oil and gas in OPEC countries in the Middle East and in other OPEC countries, too, it seems quite implausible for any international agreement to be drafted to deny or severely limit well-endowed developing countries the use of their own indigenous fossil fuels as an essential basis for economic development.

Our bar chart accompanying this text shows considerable differences in CO_2 emissions per capita, not only among OECD countries, but also among non-OECD countries and groups of countries across the world.

If all countries/regions exceeding 5 tonnes per capita of CO_2 emissions by 2035, twenty-five years from now, were to undertake to get their projected emissions down to this level in that year, then worldwide CO_2 emissions could be 12.1 per cent lower than they were in 2007 and 38.5 per cent lower on a per capita basis, given the projected rise of 27.4 per cent in the worldwide population over the twenty-five years to 2035. The statistics for this scenario, highly differentiated by country/region related to actual and potential CO_2 emissions per capita, are shown in Table IV.31. The average per capita emissions fall to only 3.08 tonnes per capita simply because 59.6 per cent of the projected world population in 2035 live in countries/regions where per capita emissions are close to that level (Brazil), or mostly projected to be significantly lower than that, with large populations involved in non-OECD Asia, including India, Africa and the rest of Central and South America.

Table IV.29. World CO2 Emissions in Reference Case in 2035 (metric tonnes)

	On Basis of US DOE/EIA Projections	On Basis of Emissions Reduced to Maximum of 5 Tonnes Per Capita in 2035	% Reduction Column 2 Compared to Column 1
USA	6320	1,955	-69.1
Canada	643	215	-66.6
Mexico	741	675	-8.9
OECD Europe	4,107	2,885	-29.8
OECD Asia/Pacific	2,389	980	-59.0
Total OECD	**14,200**	**6,710**	**-52.7**
Russia	1,811	625	-65.5
Other non-OECD Europe/Eurasia	1,361	990	-27.3
China	13,326	7,260	-45.5
India	2,296	2,296*	Nc

Other non-OECD Asia	3,362	3,362*	Nc
Middle East	2,692	1,525	-43.4
Africa	1,610	1,610*	Nc
Brazil	761	761*	Nc
Other C and S America	973	973*	Nc
Total non-OECD	**28,193**	**19,402**	**-31.2**
Total world	**42,392**	**26,112**	**-38.4**
Tonnes per capita	**5.01**	**3.08**	**-38.5**
Tonnes per capita in 2007	**4.47**		

* Projections as in Column 1, < 5 tonnes CO_2 per capita in these countries/regions.

Thus our proposal is that countries such as the United States, Canada, OECD Pacific and Russia with CO_2 emissions exceeding 10 tonnes per capita in 2007 should, in the context of the UN Framework Convention on Climate Change, agree to reduce their emissions to this level within the next ten years to 2020.

Among non-OECD developing countries China, with its continuing rapid economic development, is projected to account for 57.8 per cent of the rise in all CO_2 emissions projected for non-OECD developing countries in total over the years to 2035. Its per capita emissions of CO_2 are projected to rise from a modest 5.57 tonnes of CO_2 in 2015 to 9.18 tonnes in 2035. The rise in CO_2 emissions in the Middle East is much slower from 2007 to 2035 but nevertheless projected to increase to 8.83 tonnes per capita in the latter year. In addition to the countries/regions mentioned above, only OECD Europe and non-OECD Europe and Eurasia are projected to emit more than 5 tonnes of CO_2 per capita in 2035.

Thus we suggest that all of these – the United States, Canada, OECD Asia/Pacific, OECD Europe, Russia, China, the Middle East and other non-OECD Europe/Eurasia – should be involved in a follow-up conference under UN auspices to reduce their global emissions per capita to 5 tonnes per capita or less over the twenty-five years to 2035. Renewable forms of energy such as nuclear, hydro, geothermal, solar, biomass and wind etc., need to be investigated from both technological and economic standpoints in terms of large-scale applications.

As a notable past success we can quote the example of France which planned a big nuclear energy programme in the mid-1970s. Within some ten to fifteen years, this was fully implemented. It was able to meet the country's base load demand for electricity and supply some for export, too. With the development of its expertise in this sector, it has met with no major accidents and by 2000 it provided over 37 per cent of French primary energy needs and 38.4 per cent in 2009, with hydro-electricity providing another 5.4 per cent of the country's primary energy needs in that year.

Economic Growth and Energy Consumption

The summarized highlights concentrate on the Reference case, reflecting a scenario assuming that current laws and policies remain unchanged throughout the projection period to 2035. Thus unlike the IEA's *World Energy Outlook* published prior to the Copenhagen meeting of the UNFCCC in December 2009, this more up-to-date US *International Energy Outlook 2010* does not contain comparable projections to those shown in the IEA's 450 Scenario. It does show world CO_2 emissions by region in the Reference case in terms of world carbon dioxide emissions in millions of metric tonnes of carbon dioxide in appendix A10 (p. 141). Also, in appendix J4 (p. 308), it shows world carbon dioxide intensity of energy use by region in the Reference case expressed in metric tonnes per billion BTUs, its customary heat-value measurement. Data and projections are also shown for CO_2 emissions associated with the use of liquids, i.e. petroleum (A11), with the use of natural gas (A12) and with the use of coal (A13), so the fossil fuels are all covered. We can note here that natural gas usage results in 18.0 per cent less CO_2 emissions per unit consumed than liquids and coal gives rise to 46.2 per cent more CO_2

emissions per unit consumed than liquids (i.e. petroleum), all implicit in the US statistics for the year 2007.

Table IV.30. Growth Rates in GDP and Per Capita in Reference Case (% p.a.)

GDP in bn $ of 2005 in Reference Case (purchasing power parity basis)	2007 to 2015	2015 to 2035
All OECD countries	1.5	2.2
All non-OECD countries	5.3	4.1
Worldwide	3.2	3.3
GDP per capita		
All OECD countries	0.9	1.8
All non-OECD countries	4.1	3.3
Worldwide	2.1	2.5
GDP in three most populous countries		
USA	1.9	2.7
China	8.2	4.9
India	6.8	4.5
GDP per capita		
USA	0.8	1.7
China	7.6	4.7
India	5.4	3.9

Table IV.31. Primary Energy Consumption in Reference Case: Quadrillion BTUs and Annual Average Growth Rates

		2007		2015		2035
OECD	BTUs Quads	245.7		246.0		280.7
	Average % pa		Ø		0.7	

Non OECD		249.5		297.5		458.0
			2.2		2.2	
World		495.2		543.5		738.7
			1.2		1.6	
USA		101.7		101.6		114.5
			Ø		0.6	
China		78.0		101.4		181.9
			3.3		3.0	
India		20.3		24.3		37.6
			2.3		2.2	

Ø = less than 0.05%

Table IV.32. Energy Consumption Per Capita in the Reference Case: BTUs Millions and Annual Average Growth Rates

		2007		**2015**		**2035**
OECD	BTUs mn	207.7		198.7		209.2
	Average % p.a.		-0.6		0.3	
Non-OECD		45.6		49.4		64.3
			1.0		1.3	
World		74.5		74.9		87.2
			0.1		0.8	
USA		336.8		310.7		292.8
			-1.0		-0.3	
China		59.0		73.2		125.3
			2.7		2.7	
India		17.4		18.8		24.6
			1.0		1.4	

Growth Rates for GDP and PE Projected in Various Scenarios

Growth rates for gross domestic product (GDP) and primary energy consumption (PE) are shown in the Reference case for the period 2007 to 2035 with absolute values for these and for the intervening years. The same has been done for alternative scenarios, too: high and low economic growth and high and low oil prices. Scenario projections have been provided for twenty-four major countries/regions and the world as a whole in a useful standard presentation format.

In the Reference case which assumes no policy-induced charges to disturb trends we see that GDP growth in the OECD countries is seen as averaging 2.0 per cent p.a. over the twenty-eight-year period to 2035 compared with 4.4 per cent annually on average for all non-OECD countries/regions, yielding a worldwide average of 3.2 per cent p.a. This seems to us to be reasonable.

OECD North America (including Mexico) is projected to grow faster than OECD Europe which is seen as growing slightly faster than OECD Asia. The respective annual average percentage growth rates are 2.5, 1.7 and 1.4 per cent with Japan in the latter pulling the average down, at only 0.5 per cent p.a. compared with 2.9 per cent for South Korea and 2.6 per cent annually for Australia/New Zealand, also included in OECD Asia.

Among non-OECD countries the fastest growing region is Asia at 5.2 per cent p.a. led by China at an average of 5.8 per cent p.a. and India at 5.0 per cent p.a. It is worth noting that on the basis of this US source data, China's GDP is projected to almost match that of the United States in 2020 and to surpass that of the USA and of OECD Europe as whole by 2025, each projected at more than $19.8 trillion in terms of 2005 dollars, with China at more than $22.4 trillion. By 2035 China is projected to account for more than 21.3 per cent of worldwide GDP with the US trailing at 16.5 per cent and OECD Europe at 15.5 per cent. China's GDP is projected to grow by more than $10 trillion in just ten years to 2035, having accounted for 26.5 per cent of worldwide economic growth over this ten-year period, based on these US projections in the Reference case.

China and non-OECD Asia are the fastest growing country/region followed by the Middle East, where the economy is projected to grow at 3.7 per cent on average each year and Africa at an average of 3.6 per cent annually. Brazil is seen as the fastest growing economy in Latin America at 4.1 per cent on average with the region as a whole growing at 3.4 per cent p.a. over the twenty-eight-year period. Russia (with a declining population, like Japan) is projected to grow at 2.7 per cent on average each year, along with other countries in non-OECD Europe and Eurasia, i.e. a slower rate than other non-OECD countries/regions, but nevertheless faster than the average for the OECD countries as a whole.

Growth of primary energy consumption in the OECD countries is projected to be remarkably low at an average of only 0.5 per cent p.a. in this Reference case, or just one quarter of the rate of GDP growth projected. Although an OECD member now, Mexico has more the character of a developing country with its GDP growth projected to average 3.5 per cent annually and its primary

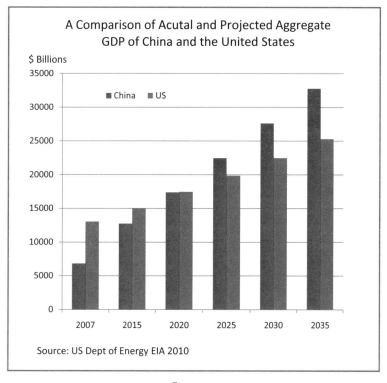

Figure IV.4

energy consumption growing at 2.0 per cent p.a., higher than any other OECD country. South Korea is somewhat similar with respective growth rates of 2.9 per cent for GDP and 1.5 per cent for energy.

Primary energy growth in all the non-OECD countries is projected to average 2.2 per cent annually with non-OECD Asia being the fastest growing region at 2.8 per cent p.a. led by China at 3.1 per cent p.a. Brazil and other non-OECD Asia (mainly ASEAN countries) are projected to increase their consumption of primary energy at 2.4 and 2.5 per cent p.a. respectively over the twenty-eight years to 2035 in this Reference case.

Unlike the OECD countries, the non-OECD countries/regions are projected to increase their consumption of primary energy at more than half the rate of their GDP growth, with their energy coefficients mostly above 0.50, as compared with 0.25 as an average for OECD countries.

In the high economic growth case worldwide GDP is projected to grow at 3.7 per cent p.a., i.e. 0.5 per cent p.a. more than in the Reference case, with the OECD averaging 2.5 per cent p.a. and all non-OECD countries averaging 4.9 per cent annually – both likewise 0.5 per cent higher than in the Reference case. Similarly, growth of primary energy consumption is higher in this case by 0.4 per cent at an average of 1.8 per cent p.a. at world level than in the Reference case and likewise higher in both OECD and developing countries too. The energy coefficient (growth in energy consumption relative to growth in GDP) is higher, too, at 0.49 at world level compared with 0.44 in the Reference case. A bigger difference between these two scenarios on this measure is seen for the OECD countries as a group than for all non-OECD countries.

The low economic growth case is almost a mirror image of the high economic growth projections, but on the downside. GDP growth at world level averages 2.7 per cent p.a. from 2007 to 2035, just 1.5 per cent on average each year in the OECD compared with 4.0 per cent p.a. for non-OECD countries. At world level, growth of primary energy consumption is somewhat less sensitive to the lower economic growth assumption, projected to grow at 1.1 per cent p.a., compared with 1.4 per cent on average in the Reference case. Again, the energy coefficient shows much greater sensitivity to the variation in GDP growth between scenarios in OECD countries where it is estimated at only 0.13 in this low economic growth case than in non-OECD countries where it is 0.49.

We can remark here that Japan is in an extreme position in that it is projected to have the lowest GDP growth rate among OECD countries/regions (or worldwide, for that matter), 0.5 per cent p.a. in the Reference case and a mere 0.1 per cent on average in the low economic growth case from 2007 to 2035. In fact, Japan is unique among all countries/regions shown in the *International Energy Outlook* 2010 projections with falling primary energy consumption in the Reference case averaging -0.1 per cent p.a., and -0.4 per cent annually in the low economic growth scenario. However, another source estimates Japanese consumption of primary energy did fall by -8.6 per cent in the exceptional year of 2009 and an average annual fall of -3.8 per cent annually from the peak reached in 2006.

The high and low oil price projections from the US DOE's Energy Information Administration are remarkable for two reasons. First, because the high oil price case indicates a price rising to $210 a barrel in 2035, almost 58 per cent higher than the $133 a barrel in the Reference case (expressed in constant US dollars of 2008 for light sweet crude). The low oil price case of $51 a barrel, on the same basis is almost 62 per cent below the Reference case price in the horizon year, having been virtually flat at about $51 to $52 a barrel over the twenty years from 2015 to 2035. This is a very different trajectory from that shown in the high oil price case, as shown in Figure IV.4. In the same year, 2015, the price on the graph is $145 a barrel and still rising sharply until 2020 with the rise decelerating considerably after that. Thus the range of oil prices shown in these two scenarios is very wide indeed on a constant, real dollar basis, albeit on a twenty-five-year horizon from the date of publication of this *International Energy Outlook* 2010.

Most surprising of all, however, is the fact of the virtual absence of feedback from such different oil price assumptions to GDP growth effects related to them. The 57.9 per cent increase in the real oil price in this high oil price case compared with the Reference case provokes an incredibly small difference of only -0.3 per cent in world GDP between the two. Similarly, the low oil price scenario, 61.7 per cent lower than in the Reference case, gives rise to a world GDP estimate in 2035 of only +0.5 per cent higher than in the Reference case, over the full period.

For those of us among analysts who estimated the short and longer term effects of the big oil price changes in 1973–4, and subsequently, on oil-importing and oil-exporting countries and the world economy more generally (volume and value of oil trade, prospective capital flows, etc) the outcomes discussed above seem remarkable if scarcely credible when manifest differences in real oil prices are projected for such a long period.

Table IV.33. US DOE/EIA Projections

Case Name	Description
Reference	Baseline economic growth (2.4% p.a. from 2008 through 2035), world oil price and technology assumptions
Low Economic Growth	Real GDP grows at an average annual rate of 1.8% from 2008 to 2035. Other energy market assumptions are the same as in the Reference case.
High Economic Growth	Real GDP grows at an average annual rate of 3.0% from 2008 to 2035. Other energy market assumptions are the same as in the Reference case.
Low Oil Price	More optimistic assumptions for economic access to non-OPEC resources and for OPEC behaviour than in the Reference case. World light, sweet crude oil prices are $51 per barrel in 2035, compared with $133 per barrel in the Reference case (2008 dollars). Other assumptions are the same as in the Reference case.
High Oil Price	More pessimistic assumptions for economic access to non-OPEC resources and for OPEC behaviour than in the Reference case. World light, sweet crude oil prices are about $210 per barrel (2008 dollars) in 2035. Other assumptions are the same as in the Reference case.

We show in Table IV.35 the US DOE/EIA brief descriptions of all five cases featured and discussed above. Growth rates for primary energy consumption are projected to average only very slightly more in the low oil price case than in the high oil price case through to 2035 in both the OECD countries and the rest of the world, as shown in Table IV.36. However, GDP growth rates are either identical or virtually identical in the two cases.

Table IV.34. Average Annual Percentage Growth Per Capita 2007–2035

		GDP	Primary Energy	PE/GDP Coefficient
OECD:	High oil price	2.0	0.4	0.20
	Low oil price	2.0	0.6	0.30
All other countries/regions:				
	High oil price	4.4	2.1	0.48
	Low oil price	4.5	2.3	0.51
World:	High oil price	3.2	1.4	0.44
	Low oil price	3.2	1.5	0.47

The analysis of projections of GDP growth and energy consumption per capita over the twenty-eight years to 2035 in the Reference case is quite revealing.

Mexico and South Korea appear to be more typical of non-OECD countries in having projected growth rates of GDP averaging over 2.5 per cent p.a. while all others in OECD are less than 2.0 per cent p.a., on average. All other countries/regions are projected to grow at a minimum of 1.8 per cent Central and South America (except Brazil), 1.9 per cent Africa, up to 5.4 per cent p.a. for China, 4.0 per cent for India and 3.2 per cent for both Brazil and Russia.

Worldwide growth of GDP per capita is projected to average 2.3 per cent p.a. with primary energy consumption per capita increasing at a rate of only 0.6 per cent on average each year, yielding an energy coefficient of only 0.25. The energy intensity of the world economy is projected to fall at an average rate of 1.7 per cent p.a., i.e. the difference in the rate of growth in GDP and primary energy consumption.

Energy consumption per capita is projected to fall between 2007 and 2035 in the heaviest consuming countries on this basis, i.e. the United States and Canada, with the latter having the highest per capita consumption in both 2007 and 2035. In contrast, Mexico's per capita energy consumption increases by 36.4 per cent but this is much less than the remarkable rise of 53.6 per cent projected for South Korea where the population is expected to be unchanged between the base and horizon years. Unsurprisingly, much of the largest rise per capita is foreseen for China, up 112.4 per cent over the twenty-eight years, with Brazil up 56 per cent, Russia up 32.2 per cent and India higher by 41.4 per cent, albeit from a very low base in 2007, even lower than the average for the African continent which rises only very marginally over this long period.

Projections for Oil

Production

The *International Energy Outlook* 2010 refers to projections of liquid fuels and other petroleum, the latter including all types of unconventional liquids: bio fuels, oil sands/bitumen, extra heavy oil, coal-to-liquids, gas to liquids and shale oil. We have shown below a separate analysis of the projections for these to 2035.

We show in Table IV.37 the volumes of production estimated at worldwide levels for total liquids, conventional and unconventional oil estimated for 2007 and projected for 2035. The numbers for that year are shown for each of the scenarios: the Reference case; the high and low oil price cases; and the high and low economic growth cases.

In the Reference case, total production worldwide is projected to rise from 84.8 million b/d in 2007 to 110.6 million b/d in 2035, an average annual rate of increase of just 1.0 per cent, or 25.8 million b/d over the twenty-eight years. Conventional crude oil production is projected to rise by only 16.3 million b/d as the unconventional oils in total rise by 9.5 million b/d with oil sands/ bitumen increasing by 3.8 million b/d and bio fuels up by 2.9 million b/d within this group.

In the high oil price scenario world oil production is projected at only 95.5 million b/d in 2035. This is 15.1 million b/d less than in the Reference case and 27.2 million b/d below the comparable figure projected for the same year in the low oil price scenario. This is a difference of only 22.2 per cent in volume response relative to a price difference of 61.4 per cent in the horizon year as between the high and low oil price cases.

The high economic growth scenario is projected to result in a production volume of 123.4 million b/d in 2035, marginally above that in the low oil price case. Nevertheless, the low economic growth case projection of 98.8 million b/d in the same year yields a difference of 24.6 million b/d between these two scenarios, rather less than the difference between the high and low oil price scenarios.

For Saudi Arabia, unsurprisingly, no figures are shown for unconventional oil production. A projection of 15.1 million b/d is shown for 2035 in the Reference case with, as usual in this report, no distinction being made between crude oil and natural gas liquids, though the latter, of course, are included in the total. In the high oil price scenario, Saudi production is projected at only 11.0 million b/d in 2035, only 0.8 million b/d above the estimate for 2007. This is 35 per cent less than the 16.8 million b/d projected by this US source for Saudi Arabian oil production in the low oil price scenario. Some well-placed analysts and commentators may be somewhat sceptical about the feasibility of such a high figure for twenty-five years hence from the time of our writing, given the conservative policy of the Kingdom in wishing to maximize ultimate recovery from its proven oil reserves and keep its capacity to produce crude on its plateau as long as possible. The high economic growth scenario projects Saudi production at 16.2 million b/d – again, a comparatively high figure and just 2.1 million b/d higher than in the low economic growth in the horizon year of 2035. Evidently, it would have been useful to distinguish between crude oil and NGLs in the long-term projections for Saudi Arabian oil production.

Table IV.35. World Liquid Production in Reference Case (mn b/d)

Scenario	Petroleum					
	Total		Conventional		Unconventional	
	2007	2035	2007	2035	2007	2035
Reference	84.8	110.6	81.4	97.7	3.4	12.9

High Oil Price		95.5		77.6		17.9
Low Oil Price		122.7		112.2		10.5
High Economic Growth		123.4		109.3		14.1
Low Economic Growth		98.8		85.8		13.0
*Split of Unconventional Oil in Reference Case:						
Bio fuels					1.2	4.1
Oil sands/bitumen					1.4	5.2
Extra heavy oil					0.6	1.5
Coal-to-liquids					0.2	1.4
Gas-to-liquids					0.1	0.4
Shale oil					0.0	0.4
Saudi Arabia						
Reference	10.2	15.1	10.2	15.1	nil	nil
High Oil Price		11.0		11.0		nil
Low Oil Price		16.8		16.8		nil
High Economic Growth		16.2		16.2		nil
Low Economic Growth		14.1		14.1		nil

We go on to compare the projections for OPEC and all non-OPEC countries in the various scenario cases.

Table IV.36. Projections for Saudi Arabian Oil Production (Total Liquids) in Various Scenarios (mn b/d)

	Reference Case	High Oil Price	Low Oil Price	Economic Growth – High	Economic Growth – Low
2007	10.2	10.2	10.2	10.2	10.2
2008	10.7	10.7	10.7	10.7	10.7
2015	10.7	9.3	11.5	10.8	10.5
2020	11.2	9.2	12.5	11.6	10.9
2025	12.1	9.6	13.6	12.7	11.5
2030	13.3	10.0	14.9	14.2	12.5
2035	15.1	11.0	16.8	16.2	14.1
Average % change p.a. 2007–35	1.4	0.3	1.8	1.5	1.0

Source: US DOE/Energy Information Administration; appendix G of *International Energy Outlook* 2010 with Projections to 2035

Table IV.37. Saudi Arabian Oil Production Crude and NGLs (mn b/d)

	WEO 2008	WEO 2009	
		Crude*	NGLs (total OPEC)
2000	9.3	8.1	2.8
2007/2008	10.2	9.2	4.9
2015	14.4	10.9	7.3

| 2030 | 15.6 | 12.0 | 11.3 |

Sources: IEA World Energy Outlook 2008 (November) T11.4 page 272, 2007 base year; IEA World Energy Outlook 2009 (November) T1.4 page 84, 2008 base year; NGL production in Saudi Arabia is not identified in the WEO.

* Includes condensates.

Consumption

Table IV.38. World Liquids (Petroleum) Consumption in the Reference Case

	2007		2035	
	Quad BTUs	% of World	Quad BTUs	% of World
OECD				
North America	49.4	28.3	52.5	23.5
Europe	31.6	18.1	28.3	12.7
Asia	16.9	9.7	17.0	7.6
Total	**97.9**	**56.0**	**97.7**	**43.7**
Non-OECD				
E Europe and Eurasia	10.4	6.0	11.0	4.9
Asia*	34.6	19.8	66.5	29.7
Middle East	13.3	7.6	22.7	10.2
Africa	6.4	3.7	9.4	4.2
C and S America	12.2	7.0	16.3	7.3
Total non-OECD	**76.8**	**44.0**	**125.9**	**56.3**
Total World	**174.7**	**100.0**	**223.6**	**100.0**

Total Liquids includes both conventional and non-conventional petroleum. Quadrillion = 10^{15}

* Includes both China and India + ASEAN countries, etc.

Between the estimated numbers for 2007 and the projections for 2035 in the Reference case of the *International Energy Outlook*, there is an almost complete reversal for liquids (petroleum including synthetics) consumption between the positions of the OECD countries and non-OECD countries in total over this twenty-eight-year period. Whereas in 2007 the OECD countries, as a whole, accounted for 56 per cent of the worldwide total, by 2035 all non-OECD countries together are projected to account for 56.3 per cent of the worldwide total. All three OECD regions, North America, Europe and Asia/Pacific (including Australia and New Zealand) see their percentage shares fall with an absolute decline projected for OECD Europe.

Among the non-OECD regions much the biggest rise is projected for Asia which includes China and India as well as the ASEAN countries. Collectively, these increase their share of world liquids consumption by almost 10 percentage points from just under 20 per cent to almost 30 per cent. The Middle East is projected to increase its share by 2.6 percentage points to more than 10 per cent of the worldwide total.

The average annual rate of growth in worldwide consumption is projected at 0.9 per cent. Non-OECD Asia accounts for more than 65 per cent of the aggregate increase worldwide and the Middle East for more than another 19 per cent.

In the Reference case total OPEC production is projected at 47.0 million b/d in 2035 compared with 63.6 million b/d in the non-OPEC countries. Of this latter total 11.2 million b/d are accounted for by unconventional oil which is seen as growing by 5.6 per cent on average each year from only 2.8 million b/d in 2007.

In the high oil price scenario total OPEC oil production is projected at only 33.0 million b/d in 2035 compared with 61.5 million b/d in the low price scenario. This is some 86 per cent lower in the high oil price case relative to a fourfold price difference between these two scenarios in 2035. This reflects the report's continuing implicit assumption of OPEC oil production being the swing energy supplier meeting the world's needs as non-OPEC production is projected to be 1.3 million b/d higher in the high oil price scenario than in the low oil price scenario in 2035.

In the high economic growth scenario total OPEC oil production at 52.2 million b/d in 2035 compares with 41.7 million b/d projected in the low economic growth case – a much narrower difference than that projected between the high and low oil price scenarios. The difference for non-OPEC oil producers between the high and low economic growth assumptions in this horizon year of 2035 is wider at 14.1 million b/d. Total production volume in the high economic growth case is projected at the remarkably high level of 71.2 million b/d for non-OPEC with conventional oil at 58.8 million b/d – only 16.5 million b/d of this is expected to come from OECD countries and 42.3 million b/d from countries outside both the membership of OECD and OPEC. The rise from the 2007 level is 17 million b/d with non-OECD Europe and Eurasia contributing more than 7 million b/d extra (with Russia at almost 5 million b/d more, still seen as the dominant supplier from this region) and Central and South America almost 7 million b/d more (here Brazil is projected to be the dominant incremental supplier, up 5.6 million b/d over the twenty-eight years to 2035).

Table IV.39. OPEC and Non-OPEC Production in the Various Scenarios (mn b/d)

	Petroleum					
	Total		Conventional		Unconventional	
OPEC Liquids Production	2007	2035	2007	2035	2007	2035
Reference Case	34.4	47.0	33.8	45.3	0.6	1.7
High Oil Price		33.0		32.4		0.6
Low Oil Price		61.5		57.5		3.9
High Economic Growth		52.2		50.5		1.7
Low Economic Growth		41.7		39.8		1.8
Non-OPEC Liquids Production						
Reference Case	50.4	63.6	47.7	52.5	2.8	11.2

High Oil Price		62.5		45.2		17.3
Low Oil Price		61.2		54.6		6.6
High Economic Growth		71.2		58.8		12.5
Low Economic Growth		57.1		46.0		11.1

We proceed now to analyse the oil (liquids) and gas projections in this *International Energy Outlook* 2010 in terms of the shares of each of them in the eight regions for which statistics are shown, plus the aggregates OECD, non-OECD and the world as a whole. The oil share of energy consumption can be seen to decline in all eight regions over the twenty-eight years from 2007 to 2035 and declines absolutely in OECD Europe, the region where total energy consumption is projected to grow least, at a meagre 0.2 per cent p.a. For the OECD as a whole, total liquids consumption is projected to be almost the same in 2035 as it was in 2007 in the Reference case after a projected recession-induced sharp drop of 6 per cent between 2007 and 2015. For the non-OECD regions as a whole, growth in consumption of liquids averages only 1.8 per cent annually but this means an increase of almost 64 per cent over the lengthy period to 2035. Non-OECD Asia accounts for 65 per cent of the total increase and the Middle East for 19 per cent in this large group of five regions. Total energy growth is faster in these two regions than elsewhere, averaging 2.8 and 2.2 per cent p.a. respectively.

We have compared the effect of projected oil price changes in three scenario cases (reference, high and low oil prices with the volume responses, as projected in the *International Energy Outlook* 2010). These projections were shown graphically in Figure IV.4. The key numbers on which this is based appear in Table IV.42. From this it can be see that there is a considerable difference between the relatively short-term effect over the eight years from 2007 to 2015 and the long-term effect over the fifteen years from 2020 to 2035. Of course, the earlier period includes both the unsustainable rise in oil prices which occurred in 2008 as well as the economic recession which saw a small fall in oil demand that year followed by a bigger one of -1.7 per cent in 2009.

Table IV.40. World Liquids Consumption: Sensitivity to Alternative Projected Prices

Case/Scenario	Price* ($ of 2008 per bbl)			Volume (mn b/d)		
	Ref.	High	Low	Ref.	High Price	Low Price
2007	73.89	73.89	73.89	86.1	86.1	86.1
2015	94.52	144.78	51.59	88.7	83.4	94.2
2020	108.28	185.63	51.86	92.1	82.1	100.2
2025	115.09	196.01	51.73	97.6	85.7	106.8
2030	123.50	203.91	51.63	103.9	90.4	114.6
2035	133.22	209.60	51.44	110.6	95.5	122.7
Average change % p.a. 2007–35	2.1	3.8	-1.3	0.9	0.4	1.3
2007–15 (first 8 years)	3.1	8.8	-4.4	0.4	-0.4	1.1
2020–35 (last 15 years)	1.4	0.8	-0.1	1.2	1.0	1.4

From this it can be seen that the average annual percentage price changes associated with each of the three scenarios vary much more during the first eight years (variation of 13.2 percentage points) than during the last fifteen years from 2020 to 2035 (variation of only 0.9 percentage points). Similarly, the volume response varies by only 1.5 percentage points in the first eight years (comparatively muted between the high and low oil price cases), to a mere 0.4 percentage points over the longer term trend period from 2020 to 2035 between the two extreme oil price cases. One might also question the credibility of the faster rate of increase of the oil price in the Reference case than in the high oil price case over the last fifteen years of the projection period since there is no obvious explanation for it.

It is worth noting the shares of both oil and gas in total energy consumption remain higher in 2035 among OECD countries than among all other countries worldwide (p. 82). This reflects the continuing dominance of coal in China and India within non-OECD Asia.

Natural Gas

Production

The US DOE/EIA projections for natural gas production to 2035 show the worldwide output rising by an average 1.4 per cent p.a in the Reference case from 106.6 trillion cubic feet in 2007 to 155.4 tcf in 2035, an increase of 48.8 tcf over the twenty-eight years. Growth in gas production in the leading countries is set out in Table IV.43.

Table IV.41. Growth in Gas Production

Country	Reference Case 2007–2035 trillion cubic feet
Qatar	+7.3
Russia	+7.2
Iran	+4.7
US	+4.2
China	+3.2
Australia/New Zealand	+2.8
Brazil	+2.2
India	+2.2
Saudi Arabia	+2.2

These countries account for almost 74 per cent of the projected worldwide increase. The principal rises elsewhere are projected to come from the following regions: North Africa, 4.5 tcf; other Central and South America 3.1 tcf; West Africa 2.7 tcf and Central Asia 2.1 tcf.

OECD countries as a whole account for a net increase of only 5.3 trillion cubic feet over the twenty-eight years with a fall foreseen in OECD Europe.

By contrast, non-OECD countries worldwide account for an increase of 43.6 trillion cubic feet, or 89 per cent of the total increase.

The variation in projections for the horizon year 2035 is not too great between the five scenarios shown in the *International Energy Outlook* 2010. The principal numbers are given in Table IV.44.

Table IV.42. World Natural Gas Production (trillion cubic feet)

	2007	2035	% p.a. Growth
	106.6		
Reference Case		155.4	1.4
High Economic Growth		162.5	1.5
Low Economic Growth		147.9	1.2
High Oil Price		160.9	1.5
Low Oil Price		153.3	1.3

There is a special analysis and projections for tight gas, shale gas and coal-bed methane production. The volume worldwide in the Reference scenario is projected to increase from 5.3 trillion cubic feet in 2007 to 21.9 tcf in 2035, an annual average growth rate of 5.2 per cent over the twenty-eight years. Unlike the overall prospect for world gas production, the OECD countries are projected to account for 57 per cent of the worldwide increase and all non-OECD for 43 per cent of the rise of 16.6 tcf in this category of increasing gas production.

Changes in projected trade in natural gas

An analysis and projections for net natural gas trade by region shows an increase of 5.8 trillion cubic feet into the OECD countries with a rise of 5.1 tcf into OECD Europe. The US is projected to reduce its imports by 2.3 tcf from 2007 to 2035 but more than offset by a 2.9 tcf rise of imports into Mexico. Exports of gas from Australia/New Zealand rise by 2 tcf.

Among all other countries worldwide Chinese gas imports are projected to rise 4.2 tcf by 2035 with those into both India and developed Asia up by 0.8 tcf each. Exports are projected to rise by 4.9 tcf from Qatar, 3.4 tcf from Russia and

2.9 tcf from North Africa. Smaller rises are projected for exports from Iran (1.7 tcf), for 1.4 tcf from West Africa and 1.3 tcf from Central Asia. It is of interest to note that this US source projects gas exports from Iraq starting in 2020 at 0.3 tcf rising to 0.8 tcf in 2035.

Consumption

Growth in natural gas consumption is projected to be stronger than for oil in all regions. It is also seen as being stronger than total energy in all regions, except, rather surprisingly, in non-OECD Europe and Eurasia. This is in spite of the considerable potential for gas growth in Russia and Turkmenistan, both of which have large reserves. Gas increases its share of the energy market in all the other seven regions. However, late in the projection period the share of gas falls quite sharply in the non-OECD countries in total and in the world as a whole. Thus by 2035 it is projected to be lower than in 2007, based on these US DOE/IEA numbers in the Reference case for countries outside the OECD. Coal, nuclear and other renewable energies are projected to rise at the expense of natural gas.

For natural gas there is a projected turnaround from 2007 to 2035, though all OECD regions are shown as increasing their consumption. However, their share of the worldwide total falls from just under 50 per cent to 41.2 per cent. Thus the non-OECD countries as a whole increase their share of world gas consumption by 8.4 percentage points with Asian consumption rising by 7.8 percentage points and the Middle East increasing by 3.3 percentage points. In spite of the Russian Federation being the largest holder of gas reserves in the world and ranking second behind the US in terms of gas consumption, Eastern Europe and Eurasia inclusive of the Russian Federation are projected to see their share of world consumption fall by 5.6 percentage points, although the volume rises by over 10 per cent over the twenty-eight years.

Over this period worldwide consumption of natural gas rises by 44.5 per cent, an annual average rate of growth of over 1.3 per cent.

Table IV.43. World Natural Gas Consumption in the Reference Case

| | 2007 | | 2035 | |
	Quad BTUs	% of World	Quad BTUs	% of World
OECD				
North America	29.2	26.0	35.8	22.1
Europe	19.8	17.7	22.6	14.0
Asia	6.7	6.0	8.5	5.2
Total	55.6	49.6	66.8	41.2
Non-OECD				
E Europe and Eurasia	26.3	23.5	29.0	17.9
Asia*	10.8	9.6	28.2	17.4
Middle East	11.2	10.0	21.5	13.3
Africa	3.3	2.9	7.4	4.6
C and S America	4.9	4.4	9.1	5.6
Total non-OECD	**56.5**	**50.4**	**95.2**	**58.8**
Total world	**112.1**	**100.0**	**162.0**	**100.0**

* Includes both China and India + ASEAN countries, etc.

Table IV.44. Growth Rates of GDP and Primary Energy Consumption in the Reference Case 2007–2035 (% p.a.)

	GDP	PE	PE/GDP Coefficient
OECD North America	2.5	0.6	0.24
USA	2.4	0.4	0.17
Canada	2.1	0.9	0.43
Mexico	3.5	2.0	0.57

OECD Europe	1.7	0.2	0.12
OECD Asia	1.4	0.5	0.36
Japan	0.5	-0.1	Nc
South Korea	2.9	1.5	0.52
Australia/New Zealand	2.6	0.9	0.35
Total OECD	2.0	0.5	0.25
Non-OECD Europe and Eurasia	2.7	0.6	0.22
Russia	2.7	0.5	0.19
Other	2.8	0.6	0.21
Non-OECD Asia	5.2	2.8	0.54
China	5.8	3.1	0.53
India	5.0	2.2	0.44
Other	4.3	2.5	0.58
Middle East	3.7	2.2	0.59
Africa	3.6	1.8	0.50
Central and South America	3.4	1.8	0.53
Brazil	4.1	2.4	0.59
Other	2.8	1.1	0.39
Total non-OECD	**4.4**	**2.2**	**0.50**
Total world	**3.2**	**1.4**	**0.44**

NC = not computable.

Table IV.45. Growth Rates of GDP and Primary Energy Consumption in the High Economic Growth Case 2007–2035 (% p.a.)

	GDP	PE	PE/GDP Coefficient
OECD North America	3.0	1.0	0.33
USA	2.9	0.8	0.28
Canada	2.5	1.2	0.48

Mexico	4.0	2.4	0.60
OECD Europe	2.2	0.5	0.23
OECD Asia	1.8	0.9	0.50
Japan	1.0	0.2	0.20
South Korea	3.4	1.9	0.56
Australia/New Zealand	3.0	1.2	0.40
Total OECD	**2.5**	**0.8**	**0.32**
Non-OECD Europe and Eurasia	3.2	0.8	0.25
Russia	3.2	0.8	0.25
Other	3.2	0.8	0.25
Non-OECD Asia	5.7	3.2	0.56
China	6.2	3.4	0.55
India	5.5	2.6	0.47
Other	4.7	2.9	0.62
Middle East	4.2	2.5	0.60
Africa	4.1	2.1	0.51
Central and South America	3.8	2.1	0.55
Brazil	4.5	2.8	0.62
Other	3.3	1.5	0.45
Total non-OECD	**4.9**	**2.5**	**0.51**
Total world	**3.7**	**1.8**	**0.49**

Table IV.46. Growth Rates of GDP and Primary Energy Consumption in the Low Economic Growth Case 2007–2035 (% p.a.)

	GDP	PE	PE/GDP Coefficient
OECD North America	1.9	0.3	0.16
USA	1.8	0.1	0.06

Canada	1.6	0.6	0.38
Mexico	3.0	1.7	0.57
OECD Europe	1.2	0.0	Nc
OECD Asia	0.9	0.2	0.22
Japan	0.1	-0.4	Nc
South Korea	2.4	1.2	0.50
Australia/New Zealand	2.1	0.6	0.29
Total OECD	**1.5**	**0.2**	**0.13**
Non-OECD Europe and Eurasia	2.3	0.3	0.13
Russia	2.3	0.4	0.17
Other	2.3	0.3	0.13
Non-OECD Asia	4.7	2.5	0.53
China	5.3	2.7	0.51
India	4.5	1.9	0.42
Other	3.8	2.2	0.58
Middle East	3.3	1.8	0.55
Africa	3.1	1.4	0.45
Central and South America	2.9	1.4	0.48
Brazil	3.6	2.0	0.56
Other	2.3	0.8	0.35
Total non-OECD	**4.0**	**1.9**	**0.48**
Total world	**2.7**	**1.1**	**0.41**

NC = Not computable.

Table IV.47. Growth Rates of GDP and Primary Energy Consumption in the High Oil Price Case 2007–2035 (% p.a.)

	GDP	PE	PE/GDP Coefficient
OECD North America	2.5	0.6	0.24

	GDP	PE	PE/GDP Coefficient
USA	2.4	0.4	0.17
Canada	2.1	0.8	0.38
Mexico	3.5	1.9	0.54
OECD Europe	1.7	0.1	0.06
OECD Asia	1.3	0.4	0.31
Japan	0.5	-0.2	NC
South Korea	2.9	1.4	0.48
Australia/New Zealand	2.6	0.8	0.31
Total OECD	**2.0**	**0.4**	**0.20**
Non-OECD Europe and Eurasia	2.7	0.5	0.19
Russia	2.8	0.5	0.18
Other	2.7	0.5	0.19
Non-OECD Asia	5.2	2.7	0.52
China	5.7	3.0	0.53
India	5.0	2.1	0.42
Other	4.3	2.4	0.56
Middle East	3.8	2.0	0.53
Africa	3.6	1.6	0.44
Central and South America	3.4	1.7	0.50
Brazil	4.1	2.4	0.59
Other	2.8	1.0	0.36
Total non-OECD	**4.4**	**2.1**	**0.48**
Total world	**3.2**	**1.4**	**0.44**

NC = Not computable.

Table IV.48. Growth Rates of GDP and Primary Energy Consumption in the Low Oil Price Case 2007–2035 (% p.a.)

OECD North America	2.5	0.7	0.28
USA	2.4	0.5	0.21
Canada	2.1	1.0	0.48
Mexico	3.5	2.1	0.60
OECD Europe	1.7	0.3	0.18
OECD Asia	1.4	0.7	0.50
Japan	0.6	0.0	NC
South Korea	2.9	1.7	0.59
Australia/New Zealand	2.6	0.9	0.35
Total OECD	**2.0**	**0.6**	**0.30**
Non-OECD Europe and Eurasia	2.7	0.6	0.22
Russia	2.7	0.6	0.22
Other	2.8	0.7	0.25
Non-OECD Asia	5.2	2.9	0.56
China	5.8	3.1	0.53
India	5.0	2.3	0.46
Other	4.3	2.6	0.60
Middle East	3.7	2.1	0.57
Africa	3.6	1.9	0.53
Central and South America	3.4	1.9	0.56
Brazil	4.1	2.5	0.61
Other	2.8	1.3	0.46
Total non-OECD	**4.5**	**2.3**	**0.51**
Total world	**3.2**	**1.5**	**0.47**

NC = Not computable.

Table IV.49. GDP and Primary Energy Consumption Per Capita in 2007 and 2035 in the Reference Case (GDP in US$ of 2005, in terms of purchasing power parity)

	GDP $ 000s		Primary Energy bns of BTUs	
	2007	2035	2007	2035
OECD North America	35,554	54,766	280.5	257.1
United States	43,076	64,700	336.8	292.8
Canada	37,423	50,529	443.3	423.3
Mexico	13,351	27,289	73.3	100.0
OECD Europe	27,427	41,234	152.1	152.9
OECD Asia	29.140	43,460	197.5	236.2
Japan	31,629	40,125	178.1	191.4
South Korea	20,560	45,211	202.0	310.4
Australia/New Zealand	32,873	53,044	288.0	287.5
Total OECD	**30,745**	**47,292**	**207.7**	**209.2**
Non-OECD Europe and Eurasia	10,227	22,978	151.5	185.8
Russia	13,967	33,671	214.8	284.0
Other	7,552	16,220	106.1	124.7
Non-OECD Asia	4,063	13,419	36.1	63.1
China	5,162	22,558	59.0	125.3
India	2,506	7,497	17.4	24.6
Other	4,413	10,443	27.7	40.8
Middle East	11,368	20,763	126.1	149.8
Africa	2,811	4,748	19.0	19.4
C and S America	8,757	16,998	60.3	75.4
Brazil	8,761	21,117	64.1	100.0
Other	8,755	14,242	57.7	59.0
Total non-OECD	**4,897**	**12,645**	**45.6**	**64.3**

World	9,494	18,144	74.5	87.2

Table IV.50. Annual Change Per Capita in GDP and Primary Energy Consumption: 2007–2035 Reference Case (% p.a.)

	GDP	PE	Energy Intensity %
OECD North America	1.6	-0.3	-1.8
United States	1.5	-0.5	-1.9
Canada	1.1	-0.1	-1.2
Mexico	2.6	+1.1	-1.4
OECD Europe	1.5	Ø	-1.4
OECD Asia	1.4	+0.6	-0.8
Japan	0.9	+0.3	-0.6
South Korea	2.9	+1.5	-1.3
Australia/New Zealand	1.7	Ø	-1.6
Total OECD	**1.5**	**Ø**	**-1.5**
Non-OECD Europe and Eurasia	2.9	+0.7	-2.1
Russia	3.2	+1.0	-2.1
Other	2.8	+0.6	-2.1
Non-OECD Asia	4.4	+2.0	-2.2
China	5.4	+2.7	-2.5
India	4.0	+1.2	-2.6
Other	3.1	+1.4	-1.7
Middle East	2.2	+0.6	-1.5
Africa	1.9	+0.1	-1.8
C and S America	2.4	+0.8	-1.6
Brazil	3.2	+1.6	-1.5
Other	1.8	+0.1	-1.6
Total non-OECD	**3.4**	**+1.2**	**-2.1**

| World | 2.3 | +0.6 | -1.7 |

Ø = less than 0.05

Table IV.51. World Population and Primary Energy Consumption in Total and Per Capita in the Reference Case

	Population millions		Primary Energy BTUs × quadrillions		PE Consumption per capita BTUs × billions	
	2007	2035	2007	2035	2007	2035
OECD North America	441	569	123.7	146.3	280.5	257.1
United States	302	391	101.7	114.5	336.8	292.8
Canada	33	43	14.3	18.2	433.3	423.3
Mexico	105	135	7.7	13.5	73.3	100.0
OECD Europe	541	577	82.3	88.2	152.1	152.9
OECD Asia	201	196	39.7	46.3	197.5	236.2
Japan	128	116	22.8	22.2	178.1	191.4
South Korea	48	48	9.7	14.9	202.1	310.4
Australia/New Zealand	25	32	7.2	9.2	288.0	287.5
Total OECD	**1,183**	**1,342**	**245.7**	**280.7**	**207.7**	**209.2**
Non-OECD Europe and Eurasia	340	324	51.5	60.2	151.5	185.8
Russia	142	125	30.5	35.5	214.8	284.0
Other	198	198	21.0	24.7	106.1	124.7
Non-OECD Asia	3,525	4,398	127.1	277.3	36.1	63.1
China	1,321	1,452	78.0	181.9	59.0	125.3

India	1,165	1,528	20.3	37.6	17.4	24.6
Other	1,039	1,418	28.8	57.8	27.7	40.8
Middle East	199	305	25.1	45.7	126.1	149.8
Africa	939	1,494	17.8	29.0	19.0	19.4
C and S America	464	606	28.0	45.7	60.3	75.4
Brazil	192	243	12.3	24.3	64.1	100.0
Other	272	363	15.7	21.4	57.7	59.0
Total non-OECD	**5,467**	**7,127**	**249.5**	**458.0**	**45.6**	**64.3**
World	6,650	8,469	495.2	738.7	74.5	87.2

Table IV.52. Projected Shares of Oil and Natural Gas in the Reference Case: % of Total Energy Consumption

		2007	2015	2025	2035	2007–35 Average Change % p.a.	Total Energy 2007–35 Average Change % p.a.
OECD North America							
	Oil	38.9	38.2	36.6	35.9	0.2	
	Gas	23.0	22.8	23.9	24.5	0.7	0.6
Europe							
	Oil	38.4	35.4	32.6	32.1	-0.4	
	Gas	24.1	25.4	26.0	25.6	0.5	0.2
Asia							
	Oil	42.6	39.3	38.1	36.7	0.0	
	Gas	16.9	18.6	18.9	18.4	0.8	0.5

Total OECD							
	Oil	39.8	37.4	35.5	35.6	0.0	
	Gas	22.6	23.0	23.8	23.8	0.7	0.5
Non-OECD Europe and Eurasia							
	Oil	20.2	19.3	18.1	18.3	0.2	
	Gas	51.1	52.1	50.9	48.2	0.3	0.6
Asia							
	Oil	27.2	26.1	24.6	24.0	2.4	
	Gas	8.5	10.8	11.1	10.2	3.5	2.8
Middle East							
	Oil	53.0	45.6	45.3	49.7	1.9	
	Gas	44.6	51.7	51.7	47.0	2.4	2.2
Africa							
	Oil	36.0	34.6	32.5	32.4	1.4	
	Gas	18.5	24.5	28.0	25.5	2.9	1.8
C and S America							
	Oil	43.6	41.7	37.2	35.7	1.0	
	Gas	17.5	18.7	20.7	19.9	2.3	1.8
Total non-OECD							
	Oil	**30.8**	**29.3**	**27.6**	**27.5**	**1.8**	
	Gas	**22.6**	**24.4**	**23.4**	**20.8**	**1.9**	**2.2**
Total world							
	Oil	**35.3**	**33.0**	**30.9**	**30.3**	**0.9**	
	Gas	**22.6**	**23.8**	**23.5**	**21.9**	**1.3**	**1.4**

A Comparison of Projections from OPEC, IEA and US DOE/EIA

This chapter draws on some of the projections just discussed in more detail and compares some key indicators.

Carbon Dioxide and Greenhouse Gas Emissions

This topic has been discussed in all three of the source documents. It is a major feature of the IEA projections as it is one of two scenarios in the *World Energy Outlook* published in November 2009. OPEC's *World Oil Outlook* 2009 is the only one of the three not to include projections for changes in emissions through to 2030. Both the IEA and US DOE/EIA have what we can call a perspective on the problem based on the advanced countries/OECD aggregate level of emissions, already high, but growth of emissions over the coming twenty to twenty-five years coming mainly from the developing countries.

For the reasons already discussed we suggest the problem must be analysed on the basis of emissions based on a per capita basis if any international agreement is to be reached that is likely to be politically acceptable to developing countries generally. On the basis of projections from both the IEA and the US DOE/EIA almost 60 per cent of the world population live in countries where the level of emissions in 2030 or 2035 is projected to be at about or less than 3 tonnes per capita per annum. This is less than the 3.2 tonnes projected in the IEA's 450

Scenario projected for 2030 and designed to limit the world's global warming to 2° C. This would mean countries such as India and many others would not need to participate in international negotiations under UNFCCC auspices, which should concentrate on the big changes required to be made in those countries with already high per capita emissions such as the advanced OECD economies and Russia and those with fast-growing per capita emissions such as China.

The responsibility for making big changes in their energy consumption and reducing their dependence on fossil fuels surely rests on these countries already well-equipped to do so, given their economic and technological resources and their historical responsibility for emissions generated in the past.

The Middle East region is one where per capita emissions are comparatively high but less than in the OECD countries and Russia, and relatively slow growing. Also, it seems quite relevant to point out that over the period 1977 to 1982, the Kingdom of Saudi Arabia constructed its Master Gas System which enabled large quantities of gas produced in association with rapidly rising oil production over the preceding twenty to thirty years to be put to economic use rather than being flared, thus minimizing emissions long before greenhouse gases became a major policy concern on the world stage. This topic has been discussed in more detail elsewhere in Part I above.

The numbers in Tables IV.55 and IV.56 bring out the big differences in terms of per capita projected emissions between the OECD and all other countries (in the US source), with the latter significantly subdivided by the IEA between other major economies (e.g. Russia, China and South Africa) and all other countries where 57.7 per cent of the total world population is projected to be living in 2030, India being the most populous in this large group.

Table IV.53. CO2 Emissions Per Capita

		IEA					US DOE/EIA		
		OECD	OMEs	OCs	World		OECD	Non-OECD	World
2007		10.7	5.1	1.4	4.4		11.56	2.93	4.47

							Reference Case:		
2015							10.50	3.08	4.34
2020	Ref	9.6	6.8	1.6	4.5		10.38	3.26	4.44
	450	8.3	6.1	1.4	4.0				
2025							10.40	3.46	4.60
2030	Ref	9.4	8.0	1.9	4.9		10.46	3.69	4.78
	450	5.7	5.2	1.4	3.2				
2035							10.58	3.96	5.01
		USA	**China**	**India**		**Other Scenarios in 2035**			
2007		18.7	4.6	1.2		High Econ. Growth	11.64	4.41	5.56
2020	Ref	15.9	6.7	1.6		Low Econ. Growth	9.63	3.55	4.51
	450	13.7	5.9	1.4		High Oil Price	10.18	3.85	4.85
2030	Ref	15.1	8.0	2.3		Low Oil Price	11.08	4.02	5.14
	450	8.6	4.8	1.5					

Table IV.54. GDP Growth Rates: World

	OPEC	IEA		US DOE/EIA
Constant $	(2008 base)	(2007 base)		(2005 base)
				Reference Case
Reference Case		2007-2030		2007-2035
	3.0% pa	3.15% p.a.		3.2% p.a.
		2007-2020		2007-2015

		3.3% p.a.		3.2% p.a.
		2020-2030		2015-2035
		3.0% p.a.		3.3% p.a.
	2008–30			2007-2035
	2.2% p.a.		Reference	3.2% p.a.
Protracted Recession followed by Low Growth	2008–15	No difference for GDP growth between scenarios, i.e. Reference and 450	High Ec. Growth	3.7% p.a.
	1.5% p.a.		Low Ec. Growth	2.7% p.a.
	2015–30		High Oil Price	3.2% p.a.
	2.5% p.a.		Low Oil Price	3.2% p.a.
High Economic Growth	2015–30			
	3.5% p.a.			

There are negligible differences in the Reference case between the three sources at 3.0 per cent p.a. assumed on average over the period to 2030 or 2035 for the world as a whole. OPEC has a precautionary protracted recession case followed by low GDP growth averaging 2.2 per cent over the full period to 2030. A more optimistic high economic growth case shows 3.5 per cent average annual rise. By contrast the IEA has GDP growth averaging 3.3 per cent annually from 2007 to 2020 in spite of the severe downturn in 2008–9 in the OECD followed by 3.0 per cent p.a. over the decade to 2030. The US DOE/EIA has a Reference case averaging 3.2 per cent p.a. for the world economy with high and low growth cases averaging 0.5 per cent p.a. above and below this projected level respectively.

Table IV.55. Primary Energy Consumption Growth: World

	OPEC	IEA	US DOE/EIA

Reference Case	2007–30	2007–30	2007–20	2020–30		2007–35	2007–15	2015–35
1.5% p.a.	1.5	1.4	1.5			1.4	1.2	1.6
450 Scen.	0.8	1.0	0.6	High Economic Growth	1.8	1.4	1.9
					Low Economic Growth	1.1	1.0	1.2
					High Oil Price	1.4	0.9	1.5
					Low Oil Price	1.5	1.4	1.6

There are virtually no differences in the Reference case between the three sources at 1.5 per cent to 2030 or 1.4 per cent p.a. to 2035 on average. The IEA 450 Scenario has a very low estimate of only 0.8 per cent on average over the twenty-three-year projection period, falling to 0.6 per cent annually over the last decade to 2030, lower than anything in the five scenarios in the US source, either over the full period or the later part of it. The one percentage point difference in GDP growth between the high and low scenarios is associated with a marginally smaller difference of 0.7 per cent p.a. in primary energy consumption growth between the two cases.

Projections of Primary Energy Balances in the Reference Case – World

The numbers are expressed in terms of millions of tonnes of oil equivalent by both OPEC and the IEA but in quadrillions of Btus by the US DOE/EIA. We show below the estimates for annual average growth rates for each type of energy from 2007 to 2030 and their percentage shares for each of these and for the intermediate year of 2020.

The growth rates for oil are almost identical. For gas OPEC projects higher growth at an average of 1.9 per cent p.a. than the other two sources. For coal, the IEA is higher than the other two in the Reference case, also 1.9 per cent annually. For nuclear the projections are low and comparatively similar ranging from 1.6 per cent p.a. from OPEC down to 1.3 per cent annually from the IEA. For all forms of renewable energy there is more diversity between the sources, with OPEC projecting an annual rise of 3.5 per cent on average from 2007 to 2030, the IEA the lowest at only 2.0 per cent p.a. and the US DOE/EIA in between at 2.8 per cent p.a. It is interesting to see the OPEC projections for renewables broken down between hydro, growing at 2.3 per cent, biomass at 3.4 per cent and other renewables at 7.4 per cent on average each year.

Over the twenty-three years from 2007 to 2030 the oil share is seen as declining in all sources but by slightly different amounts: 5.4 percentage points by OPEC, 4.3 by the IEA and by 4.7 percentage points by the US DOE/EIA. Similarly, natural gas increases its share of world primary energy consumption: by 1.8 percentage points in the OPEC projections, but by only 0.3 and 0.1 percentage points in the IEA and US DOE/EIA cases respectively. For coal, the IEA sees the biggest gain, by 2.6 percentage points with the US DOE/EIA projecting a rise of 0.3 and OPEC a loss of 0.1 percentage points to 2030 after a gain of 0.6 percentage points from 2007 to 2020. The US DOE/EIA is the most optimistic about nuclear seeing it rise by 0.9 percentage points between 2007 and 2030 with OPEC projecting a rise of only 0.1 and the IEA a loss of 0.2 percentage points in its share of world primary energy over the same period.

For the fastest growing energy sector, all renewables, OPEC shows its share growing by 3.6 percentage points, the US DOE/EIA by only slightly less at 3.4 and the IEA a gain of only 1.6 percentage points from 2007 to 2030. OPEC sees the gains for renewables being only 0.4 percentage points attributable to hydro-electricity, 1.8 percentage points for biomass and 1.4 percentage points for all other forms of renewable energy. This latter remains the smallest component of the three elements, even in 2030.

Table IV.56. World Energy Forecasts

Type of Energy	Growth % p.a.			Fuel Changes					
	2007–30			% in 2007			% in 2030		
	OPEC	IEA	US	OPEC	IEA	US	OPEC	IEA	US
Oil	0.8	0.9	0.8	36.4	34.1	35.3	31.0	29.8	30.6
Gas	1.9	1.5	1.4	22.3	20.9	22.6	24.1	21.2	22.7
Coal	1.5	1.9	1.5	28.2	26.5	26.7	28.1	29.1	27.0
Nuclear	1.6	1.3	1.4	6.6	5.9	5.5	6.7	5.7	6.4
All renewables	3.5	2.0	2.8	6.5	12.6	9.9	10.1	14.2	13.3

Note: It seems probable that OPEC has estimated hydro on the basis of electricity output (so-called Low Factor) rather than on the conventional high factor, alternative fossil fuel input basis.

Table IV.57. Energy Coefficients – Primary Energy Growth – World GDP Growth

	OPEC		IEA		US DOE/EIA
Reference Case	2008–30 0.50		2007–30 0.48		2007–35 0.44
			2007–20 0.42		2007–15 0.38
			2020–30 0.50		2015–35 0.48
			2007–30		2007–35
		450 Case	0.27	High Oil Price	0.44
				Low Oil Price	0.47

At world level, there is not too much difference between the three sources in the Reference case energy coefficients over the full period with the US DOE/EIA numbers implying slightly more efficient use of energy than those implicit in the IEA numbers. The big differences are those already identified between the OECD and developing countries, and between the worldwide 450 Scenario proposed by the IEA compared with its Reference case involving no difference in GDP growth but a significant difference in growth in primary energy consumption between the two cases.

Table IV.58. Oil Demand Projections, Reference Case

Source	Category	2008	2015	2030		% p.a. change 2007/08–2030/5
		mn b/d				
OPEC	OECD	47.5	45.5	43.4		- 0.4
	China	8.0	10.4	15.9		3.2
	OPEC	7.7	9.0	11.5		1.8
	Non-OECD	38.1	44.7	62.2		2.3
	Total World	85.6	90.2	105.6		1.0
IEA		2007	2020	2030		
		m.t.o.e.				
	OECD	2135	1923	1880		-0.6
	China	358	557	758		3.3
	OMEs	888	1238	1544		2.4
	OCs	740	897	1138		1.9
	World	4093	4440	5009		0.9
US OE/ EIA		2007	2015	2030	2035	
		mn b/d				
	OECD	48.8	46.3	48.3	49.5	0.1
	China	7.6	10.0	15.3	16.9	2.9

	Non-OECD	37.3	42.4	55.6	61.1	1.8
	World	86.1	88.7	103.9	110.6	0.9

OPEC and the IEA both see OECD oil demand falling over the projection period to 2030, but so too does the US DOE/EIA to this year, with a slight rise of 2.5 per cent over the following five years to its 2035 horizon.

We have featured China in these comparisons because it is clearly projected to be the fastest growing oil consuming country worldwide over the period. However we consider Chinese oil demand may grow faster than projected here if its economy continues to grow more rapidly than foreseen in these projections, if the supply of other forms of energy slips below projected rates and the efficiency of energy use in China fails to live up to projected improvements and the rate of vehicle ownership/use increases more quickly than projected.

As might be expected, less positive rates of change for oil demand characterize some of the alternative scenarios. From OPEC, the oil demand in OECD countries is projected to decline at an average rate of -1.0 per cent p.a. but to rise slightly in the world as a whole at 0.4 per cent on average each year in the low growth case. In IEA's 450 Scenario the annual fall in the OECD is greater at an average rte of -1.4 per cent and for the world as a whole the rise is a mere 0.2 per cent p.a. In US DOE/EIA Reference case oil demand in the OECD is projected to be virtually the same in 2035 as it was in 2007, while in all non-OECD countries it is projected to rise at an average rate of 1.8 per cent annually. Among the other scenarios in this source, growth over the twenty-eight-year period is projected at 1.3 per cent annually in both the high economic growth and low oil price cases, but only 0.5 per cent p.a. in the low economic growth case and a mere 0.3 per cent annually on average in the high oil price case. This oil price rises by 4.5 per cent annually in real, constant dollar terms over this lengthy horizon, but much of the increase occurs in the next few years to 2015 in this case.

World Oil Supply

Total world oil supply is projected to rise at almost identical rates of some 1 per cent annually in each of the three sources but there is a marked difference in the composition of growth foreseen by the US DOE/IEA and the other two as between conventional and non-conventional oil supply.

Table IV.59. World Oil Supply Growth in Reference Case (% p.a.)

	OPEC	IEA	US DOE/EIA
Conventional	0.4	0.4	0.7
Non-conventional	6.0	6.6	4.9
Total	**1.1**	**1.0**	**1.0**

Also, the balance of oil supply varies between the different projection sources and between OPEC and non-OPEC over the projection period. OPEC itself projects crude supply from its members at only 30.6 million b/d in 2030 compared with 54.4 million b/d from non-OPEC sources in the low economic growth scenario. In contrast, the call on OPEC rises to 48.1 million b/d in the high economic growth case whereas supplies from non-OPEC sources are seen as rising only 3.7 million b/d to 58.1 million b/d in this case, as it is relatively constrained without the capacity to increase very much. This makes it quite different from the period some thirty years ago when oil production from non-OPEC sources was rising quite significantly.

Table IV.60. World Oil Supply Sources

	IEA				US DOE/EIA		
	2007	2015	2030		2007	2020	2035
Non-OPEC				mn b/d			
Total	46.8	46.3	49.2	Total	50.4	53.3	63.6
Crude	39.3	36.6	35.3	Conv.	47.7	47.0	52.5
NGL	5.8	6.6	7.6				
Non-conv.	1.7	3.2	6.3	Non-conv.	2.8	6.3	11.2
OPEC							
Total	36.3	40.3	53.8	Total	34.4	38.8	47.0

Crude	31.2	32.6	41.4	Conv.	33.8	37.5	45.3
NGL	4.9	7.3	11.3				
Non-conv.	0.1	0.3	1.1	Non-conv.	0.6	1.3	1.7

Reference case projections from the other two sources are compared in Table IV.62. From the OPEC Secretariat projections, we can see that crude oil as a proportion of total oil supply falls over the period as in Table IV.63.

Table IV.61. Crude as % of Total Oil Supply

2008	2015	2030
85.0	80.9	75.1

Also, from this source in the Reference case, total non-OPEC supply rises by 6.0 million b/d from 2008 to 2030 while OPEC supplies increase by 13.1 million b/d to 41.1 million b/d. For the world outside OPEC a fall of more than 3 million b/d in crude oil production is offset by rises of more than 9.3 million b/d in non-conventional oil and NGLs.

For Saudi Arabia, the IEA *WEO* 2009 projects a rise in crude oil production alone from 9.2 million b/d in 2007 through 10.9 million b/d in 2015 to 12.0 million b/d in 2030. The US DOE/EIA projects a bigger rise for total Saudi Arabian production inclusive of NGLs in the Reference case, as in Table IV.64.

Table IV.62. Total Saudi Arabian Oil Production (mn b/d)

2007	2015	2020	2030	2035
10.2	10.7	11.2	13.3	15.1

Oil Price (in Dollars of 2008)

The OPEC Secretarial is working on the assumption of oil prices in nominal dollars remaining in the range of $70 to $100 a barrel (p. 7 of the *World Oil Outlook*, 2009) with no reference as to what it expects this to mean in real, constant dollar terms over the period to 2030. It pointed out that the price of the OPEC Reference basket of crudes started 2008 at $92 a barrel, rose to a record $141 in early July before falling to $33 a barrel by the end of that year. Other remarks made in its *WOO* suggest OPEC is very chary of indicating an expected trend in oil prices.

In the light of these unprecedentedly sharp fluctuations we have analysed and discussed previously, the IEA has nevertheless projected oil prices in constant dollars of 2008, as in Table IV.65.

Table IV.63. IEA Projections for Oil Prices (in $ of 2008)

	$ bbl	
IEA	Reference Case	450 Scenario
2008	97.19	
2015	86.67	(implied)
2020	100.00	90.00
2030	115.00	90.00

Maybe in the light of what happened in 2008, as reported by OPEC, the US DOE/EIA has produced a very wide range of numbers for its high and low oil price cases around its Reference case with much of the variation projected to occur by 2015 in the latter.

Table IV.64. US DOE/EIA Projections for Light Sweet Crude Price in Constant Dollars of 2008

	Reference Case	High Oil Price	Low Oil Price
2007	73.89		
2008	101.45		
2010	70.30		
2015	94.52	144.78	51.59
2020	108.28	185.63	51.86

| 2030 | 123.50 | 203.91 | 51.63 |
| 2035 | 133.22 | 209.60 | 51.44 |

Natural Gas Demand

OPEC projects world gas demand to rise at an average rate of 1.9 per cent annually from 2007 to 2030 with the IEA projections coming in lower at 1.5 per cent p.a. over the same period in the Reference case. In its 450 Scenario the growth in gas demand projected by the IEA is only 0.7 per cent annually in spite of its being the lowest greenhouse gas emitter of the three fossil fuels. The US DOE/EIA projects growth of gas demand at an average 1.3 per cent p.a. from 2007 to 2035 in the Reference case.

Natural Gas Supply

OPEC seems to carry no projections for gas production in its *World Oil Outlook* of 2009. By contrast, the IEA has an in-depth study of natural gas in its *World Energy Outlook* published in November 2009. Of the twelve prospectively leading gas producing countries in 2030 four of them are shown as increasing production by more than 100 billion cubic metres. In rank order these are as shown in Table IV.67.

Table IV.65. Increase in Projected Production of Gas, 2007–2030 (bcm)

Qatar	159
Iran	140
Russia	124
Nigeria	111

Some of these countries and others among the top twelve, as varied as Australia and Turkmenistan, might be expecting to export gas to China over this period (by LNG or pipeline) but China itself is projected to increase its production by 56 billion cubic metres and there have been reports of China developing gas from shale (July 2010) as has occurred in the United States during recent years.

Coal in Reference Case – World

Table IV.66. Coal in Reference Case: World

	OPEC		IEA				US DOE/EIA	
	m.t.o.e.	% share	m.t.o.e.		% PE share		Quads Btu	% share
2007	3129	28.2	3184		26.5		132.4	26.7
2020	3871	28.8	Ref	450	Ref	450	152.4	25.8
2030	4438	28.1	4125	3507	28.5	25.8	185.6	27.0
			4887	2614	29.1	18.2	2035 206.3	2035 27.9
Growth rate			% p.a.				% p.a.	
2007– 30	1.5% p.a.		1.9	-0.9			2007–30	1.6

In the Reference case world coal consumption is projected to rise at similar average rates, 1.5 per cent on average each year by OPEC, by 1.9 per cent by the IEA and by 1.6 per cent by the US DOE/EIA. As a result, coal's share of world primary energy consumption grows fastest in the IEA's projections from 26.5 per cent of the total in 2007 to 29.1 per cent in 2030. The US DOE/EIA projects a fall in coal's share between 2007 and 2020 followed by a sharper rise from 2020 to 2035 when growth in its consumption is projected to average 2.0 per cent p.a. In contrast, OPEC projects faster growth for coal consumption from 2007 to 2020 at more than 1.6 per cent p.a. followed by slower growth of less than 1.4 per cent p.a. over the next ten years to 2030.

Nuclear and All Renewable Forms of Energy

Nuclear energy is projected to grow rather slowly in the Reference case for the world at large: by an average of 1.6 per cent by OPEC, by only 1.3 per cent annually by the IEA and by 2.0 per cent by the US DOE/EIA. Comparatively little change is foreseen in the nuclear share of total primary energy consumption, though the IEA projects a slight fall and the US DOE/EIA shows a slight rise. For all forms of renewable energy, the IEA projects a modest rise averaging 2.0 per cent annually to 2030 with the US DOE rather higher at 2.6 per cent p.a. to 2035. In its 450 Scenario, the IEA projects growth for nuclear averaging 3.1 per cent p.a. and 3.3 per cent p.a. for all renewable forms of energy, both thus increase their shares significantly in world primary energy. Consumption of total primary energy is projected to grow only 0.8 per cent p.a. to 2030 in this case.

OPEC has separate categories for renewable types of energy with hydro growing at an average rate of only 2.3 per cent p.a., biomass at 3.4 per cent and all other renewables significantly faster at 7.4 per cent annually from a low base of only 0.5 per cent of the world's commercial energy in 2007.

Table IV.67. Nuclear and All Renewables: World – Reference Case

		OPEC		IEA		US DOE/EIA	
		m.t.o.e.	% share	m.t.o.e.	% share	Quads	% share
World nuclear	2007	736	6.6	709	5.9	27.1	5.5
	2020	873	6.5	851	5.9	37.4	6.3
	2030	1065	6.7	956	5.7	43.9	6.4
						2035	
						47.1	6.4
Growth			1.6%		1.3%		2.0%
2007–30			p.a.		p.a.		p.a.
Hydro	2007	268	2.4				
	2020	366	2.7				
	2030	448	2.8				

Growth 2007–30			2.3% p.a.				
Biomass	2007	394	3.5	1514	12.6	48.8	9.9
	2020	618	4.6	1999	13.8	73.4	12.4
	2030	840	5.3	2376	14.2	91.2	13.3
						2035 99.8	13.5
Growth 2007–30			3.4% p.a.				2.6% p.a.
Other renewables	2007	59	0.5				
	2020	151	1.1				
	2030	303	1.9				
Growth 2007–30			7.4% p.a.				
Total PE	2007	11,109	100.0	12,013		495.2	
	2020	13,461	100.0	14,450		590.5	
	2030	15,804	100.0	16,790		686.5	
						2035 738.7	
Growth 2007–30			1.5% p.a.		1.5% p.a.		1.4% p.a.
All renewables	2007	721					
	2020	1135					
	2030	1591					
Growth 2007–30	3.5% p.a.						

China Compared with the Rest of the World

From 1965 to 2008 Chinese GDP growth (now inclusive of Hong Kong) averaged almost 9.0 per cent p.a., growing by a multiple of 36.3 times over the forty-three years. By comparison, worldwide growth (inclusive of China), averaged 3.4 per cent p.a. and grew by a multiple of 4.3 times over the same period. Just as Japan had a period of unprecedented economic growth starting some fifty years ago, today the world's focus must be on China. Because it is the world's most populous country with a huge potential domestic market to satisfy, as well as being the workshop of the world, generating an enormous surplus on its external trade, China has become quite unique in the modern world. A comparison between China and the United States is quite salutary, together with India, as can be noted in Table IV.70.

Table IV.68. GDP and Energy Consumption in the Three Most Populous Countries

	GDP Per Capita $ in 2008	Energy Consumption Per Capita in 2008 m.t.o.e.
USA	46,648	7.55
China	3,423	1.53
India	1,059	0.38

From this it can be seen that in 2008 US GDP per capita was still more than thirteen times that of China and forty-four times that of India, on average. In terms of primary energy consumption per capita the differences were somewhat less with the US at five times that of China but almost twenty times that of India. Thus the world's two most populous countries still have a great deal of catching up to do if they are to approach the US levels of the recent past, the world's third most populous country.

A comparison of total Chinese and US primary energy consumption in 2008 split by type is revealing to an extent, but much more so is a comparison between them in terms of growth rates over the eight years from 2000 to 2008.

459

Table IV.69. Proportions of World Consumption of Energy in 2008 and Contrast in Growth Rates between China and the USA 2000–2008

	% of World Primary Energy Consumption in 2008		Contrast in Growth in Primary Energy Consumption 2000–8 % p.a.	
	China	USA	China	USA
Oil	9.8	23.0	6.6	-0.2
Gas	2.8	21.8	14.9	-0.1
Coal	42.8	17.1	9.8	-0.1
Hydro	18.5	7.9	12.9	-1.3
Nuclear	2.5	31.0	19.2	0.8
Total PE				
2008	17.9	20.4	9.5	-0.1
2009	19.7	19.5	8.4	-5.2

This shows that Chinese total energy consumption was only 2.5 percentage points less than that of the United States in 2008 after a period of high annual compound growth only slightly below 10 per cent p.a. with virtual stability in the United States over the same eight years. We have added in the estimates for the exceptional year 2009 (recession in the US) to show China, inclusive of Hong Kong, surpassing the United States in terms of primary energy consumption by more than 18 million tonnes of oil equivalent in that year. Chinese energy consumption would have to rise by only 7.3 per cent in 2010 to be greater than the highest total yet recorded in any one year by the US – in 2007.

The dramatic differences in the energy consumption mixes is apparent in the comparison between the first two columns of Table IV.71, already discussed in more detail and shown in terms of statistics in Part II above.

Table IV.70. Energy Consumption

	1965–73	1973–9	1979–85	1985–90	1990–2000	2000–8
Primary energy	6.3	6.9	3.2	5.2	3.5	9.5
GDP	6.7	6.0	10.2	7.9	10.4	9.6
PE coefficient	0.94	1.15	0.31	0.66	0.34	0.99

A further analysis of the progress of Chinese primary energy consumption over the long period of forty-three years from 1965 until 2008, along with growth of the Chinese economy, is instructive to an extent. Thus in the cheap oil era up to 1973, the energy coefficient was high, as it was worldwide, generally. But then, insulated as it was with its dependence on domestically produced coal from higher real oil prices after 1973, the Chinese energy coefficient rose further. However, the oil price shock of 1979–80 induced by market forces seems to have had a major impact in dramatically reducing the growth of Chinese energy consumption relative to GDP growth from 1979 to 1985, following the economic reforms introduced in 1978, as the energy coefficient fell to only 0.31 during this six-year period. The following five years to 1990 associated with much lower prices for oil entering world trade saw a rise in the Chinese energy coefficient.

Though world oil prices continued to be quite modest over the decade to 2000 the Chinese energy coefficient fell sharply again as high economic growth was associated with comparatively low average growth in energy usage. During the eight years to 2008, the Chinese economy continued to grow rapidly, with its energy consumption growing at a similar rate in spite of world oil prices rising in most years through this period leading to an energy coefficient close to 1.0. However, by this time the combination of the strength of the Chinese export sector, and the enormous build-up in its foreign exchange reserves, its surplus on its external trade account, meant it was well equipped to absorb rising oil prices, along with its heavy dependence on still fast growing indigenous coal production meeting close to 70 per cent of its primary energy needs. In spite of the remarkable growth of its energy consumption, China's energy self-sufficiency fell only from 91.3 per cent in 2000 to 89.8 per cent in 2008.

If the remarkable growth rate of 9.5 per cent in Chinese primary energy actually recorded from 2000 until 2008 continued through the coming years it could reach the following totals:

1. 3.83 billion tonnes oil equivalent

2. > 6 billion tonnes oil equivalent

3. 2030 > 14.9 billion tonnes oil equivalent

The latter figure represents more than 32 per cent above the worldwide total in 2008.

Coal as the main source of Chinese energy increased its production by an average rate of 10.1 per cent p.a. from 2000 until 2008. In that year Chinese coal production and consumption were almost the same at 1.41 billion metric tonnes o.e. Relative to even this high level of coal production, Chinese proved coal reserves had a lifespan of forty-one years but the high rate of growth noted above indicates that this number would fall to only 13.6 years in 2015 if this rate of increase continued and if no additional reserves were found in the meantime. Though Chinese coal production in 2009 continued to outpace consumption, perhaps significantly there was reportedly strong growth in Chinese coal imports in that year, with Asian coal prices falling less sharply for that reason than those in North America and Western Europe.

All sorts of questions could arise by 2015 regarding the feasibility of continuing high growth in Chinese energy consumption and how it might conceivably be satisfied by some combination of imported oil and gas, coal from domestic sources as well as imports and further fast growth in nuclear capacity, hydro-electricity and renewable sources of energy. Improvements in the efficiency of energy use in terms of a fall in the PE/GDP relationship is another potentially important contributor, given past experience in China, together with a possible reduction in the growth rate of the Chinese economy.

A potentially critical element in the Chinese energy mix is the extent to which growth in oil production lags far behind growth in Chinese oil consumption. Over the eight years to 2008 the respective annual average growth numbers were 1.9 per cent for oil production and 6.8 per cent for oil consumption, with the gap between the two being 3.32 million b/d in 2008. If the gap between Chinese oil production and consumption continued to increase at the rate of 12.3 per cent p.a. as it did between 2000 and 2008, then the potential demand for Chinese oil imports in terms of this gap would be 10.42 million b/d in 2015, 18.99 million b/d in 2020 and 63 million b/d in 2030, clearly likely to be not feasible, even though China is likely to be the world's leading economy around 2020, in spite of its growth rate projected to slow down in the external sources quoted in the earlier chapters in Part IV of this book.

Even in 2009 Chinese oil imports exceeded 5.1 million b/d, having grown by 734,000 b/d or 16.7 per cent from less than 4.4 million b/d in 2008. There can be little doubt that the future size and shape of the Chinese energy balance remains the biggest uncertainty in the evolution of the worldwide energy picture. This is in spite of the fact that even in 2009 China remained 89.7 per cent self-sufficient in terms of its energy needs.

Relative Dependence on Nuclear and Hydro in Leading Energy Consuming Countries

We start our analysis here with a comparison of some of the principal economies worldwide for their relative dependence not on fossil fuels but on the leading forms of nuclear and renewable commercial energy, i.e. hydro-electricity.

We suggest it is of interest to analyse the G7 countries and so-called BRIC countries within the G20 in terms of the proportion of nuclear and hydro-electricity (renewable energy[12]) in their total primary energy needs in 2009. This reveals vast differences between France at the top, followed by Brazil and Canada (mainly because of their hydro-electricity contribution), and followed by Japan, Russia, Germany and the United States in the range of 17 per cent down to below 12 per cent for the latter. The others, the UK, China, Italy and India all rely on nuclear and hydro-electricity for less than 10 per cent of their primary energy needs in 2009. The comparative data are shown in Table IV.73 and also in Figure IV.5 on a percentage basis in the latter. It is of interest to note that not only did China become the world's biggest consumer of primary energy in 2009, just ahead of the United States, but its hydro-electricity production was much the largest in the world, ahead of Canada and Brazil, having grown at an average rate of 11.7 per cent p.a. over the ten years to 2009 with its nuclear electricity having increased even faster (from an admittedly low base) at 16.7 per cent p.a. – both significantly faster than its remarkably fast-growing GDP over the same period. Thus China has become 'greener' in its energy usage in spite of coal still being dominant in its energy mix. Economically China is well-equipped to continue its increasing dependence on nuclear and all forms of renewable energy. Peer group pressure within the G20 is likely to be brought to bear on China to do just this in order to alleviate the growth of its energy-related greenhouse gas emissions over the next twenty to twenty-five years.

Table IV.71. Nuclear and Hydro Contributions to Primary Energy Needs of Leading Economies in 2009

	Nuclear	Hydro	Total Primary Energy	Non-Fossil Fuel % of Total Primary Energy
	Mn tonnes oil equivalent			
France	92.9	13.1	241.9	43.8
Brazil	2.9	88.5	225.7	40.5
Canada	20.3	90.2	319.2	34.6
Japan	62.1	16.7	463.9	17.0
Russia	37.0	39.8	635.3	12.1
Germany	30.5	4.2	289.9	12.0
USA	190.2	64.2	2182.0	11.6
UK	15.7	1.2	198.9	8.5
China	15.9	139.3	2200.1	7.1
Italy	Nil	10.5	163.4	6.4
India	3.8	24.0	468.9	5.9

Source: BP *Statistical Review of World Energy* (June 2010).

This analysis suggests that all eight countries below the top three need to set an example, as leading G20 members, for the rest of the world to move in the direction of more dependence on renewable energy, whatever form they decide it should take. With the economic recovery, the proportion of coal, natural gas and oil in their national energy balances seems bound to increase again in the short term from the comparatively low levels generally recorded in 2009.

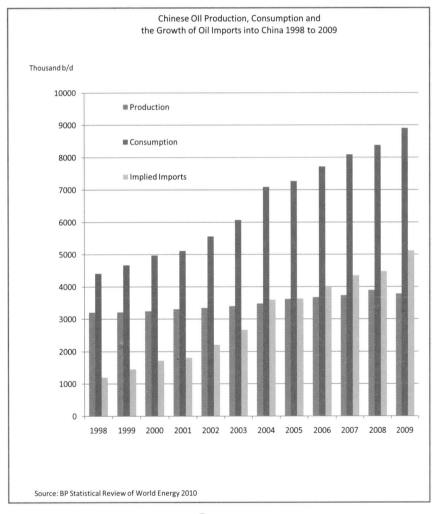

Figure IV.5

Part v

Conclusion

1. Saudi Arabia had unique advantages in two respects: (a) an outstanding personality in King Abd Aziz al Saud, 1902–53, who unified the country and recognized the importance of development for the future of his country; (b) much the largest and unique oilfield worldwide, Ghawar, with proven reserves initially estimated at 80 billion barrels, subsequently 140 billion barrels, plus other giant oilfields.

2. The Arabian American Oil Company (Aramco) was formed in 1948 from among the four large American partner companies Socal (now Chevron), Texaco, Exxon and Mobil, able to deploy the great experience and technological expertise in the development of the Saudi oil industry in partnership with Saudi nationals.

3. The formation of OPEC in September 1960 led to fundamental change in the world oil industry (1970 to 1975), with effective power over their indigenous natural resources passing from the major transnational oil companies to OPEC member countries.

4. Continuity and stability have been the hallmark of Saudi Arabian politics since 1953. The Kingdom has been governed over a period of nearly sixty years by just five monarchs (all sons of the Kingdom's founder) with four oil ministers responsible for the coordination of oil policy.

5. Given the historical importance of the foundation of Islam in Saudi Arabia with the two Holy Places, Makkah and Madinah as its focus, the religious establishment has always formed an integral part of the machinery of government in the Kingdom.

6. Large losses of hydrocarbons occurred in Saudi Arabia as a result of the flaring of associated natural gas produced with crude oil over twenty years or more until the inauguration of the Government Master Gas System in 1977. The amount of greenhouse gases emitted will have been equivalent to almost 30 per cent of those associated with worldwide consumption of natural gas in that year, 1977, or 719 million tonnes of CO_2 with no economic benefit. To put the loss in a contemporary perspective we can say the loss from the flaring of associated gas in Saudi Arabia amounted to 574 times as much as BP lost from its unrecovered oil from the Macondo oil-spill in the Gulf of Mexico over ninety days between April and July 2010. Saudi Arabia's loss was 7.2 times as much as BP's loss on the same timeframe. Saudi Arabian Government invested more than $13 billion in the recovery and economic use of a hydrocarbon resource formerly wasted. A recent announcement was made of an additional $2 billion as an expansion of the Government's Master Gas System to use additional non-flared natural gas for industrial purposes.

7. Saudi Arabia has benefited from a system of planning over five-year periods since 1970. This has enabled it to integrate very large capital projects in a systematic way – Master Gas System (MGS), Jubail and Yanbu industrial cities, trans-Arabian pipeline, other refineries, shipping, gas oil separation plants, Sabic petroleum chemicals, Exploration and Petroleum Engineering Centre and Computer Centre etc – in spite of fluctuations in petroleum export earnings on account of big changes in both prices and volumes over the years.

8. Saudi Aramco developed from 1988 to 2008. Saudi nationals now form the great majority of its workforce. PIW ranked it as top oil company for

many years. Sustainable production capacity for crude oil increased to 12 million barrels per day by end 2009. But in the interests of maximizing the recovery from proven oil reserves in place and the needs of future generations too, it is not expected to go above this level. Additional to this is the production of natural gas liquids.

9. This means there are evidently limits as to what Saudi Arabia can do to stabilize the world oil market when there are either upward or downward pressures from time to time on both prices and volumes of oil entering world trade, as we saw in 1979–80, 1981–6 and 2003–2008 (up, down and up respectively).

10. During recent years, foreign participation has been actively sought and utilized in the search for natural gas in relatively unexplored areas of the Kingdom. The continuing development of Saudi Arabia's industrialization programme is based on growing needs for natural gas, preferably that not associated with oil production.

11. Political considerations continue to play an important role in the determination of Saudi Arabian oil policy, as they have done throughout the last sixty years or so. Most notable among these is the Israeli–Palestinian issue, still unresolved throughout this period; relations with Iran, the United States, China, the Russian Federation and the European Union, as well as with other Arab countries are all important features.

12. As one who has been actively involved on the international stage since 1975 as chairman of the Energy Commission on behalf of the Group of 19 at the Conference on International Economic Co-operation, I Abdulhadi H. Taher welcomed the initiative to create the Group of Twenty (G20). This seems a more appropriate forum in a multi-polar world, supplanting the former more narrowly defined G7 and G8 which tended to create an 'us and them' set of opposed factions. As a member of the G20, Saudi Arabia believes this should prove a more appropriate way of exposing and debating leading international issues, whether

on the political or economic plane or within the critically important energy sector, as well as topical issues such as climate change. The fact of a preponderance of the world population, gross domestic product and world energy production and consumption being accounted for by these G20 countries should facilitate resolution of problems between them more effectively than in the past. While the relatively faster growth of populous developing countries such as China and India made the formation of the G20 more obviously desirable, the financial crisis followed by a severe economic recession from 2007 through 2008 and 2009 in the former G7 countries gave a particular impetus to the formation of the G20.

13. In Part II of this book, we analysed the leading countries in the world economy and their patterns or mix in their consumption of primary energy and changes over time in the past. Primarily, these are G20 member countries, but an important distinguishing feature among them is their variability on criteria such as GDP per capita and differences in their dependence on different forms of energy such as oil, gas, coal, nuclear and hydro-electricity to meet their needs. Big differences also exist among the leading countries in terms of the extent of their energy self-sufficiency and their dependence on international trade to meet their needs.

14. A major proportion of the world's hydrocarbon reserves are concentrated in relatively few countries. For oil, the top three countries, Saudi Arabia, Iran and Iraq, account for 41.0 per cent of the world's proved reserves. The top ten countries inclusive of these three account for 80.7 per cent of the worldwide total. For natural gas, the top three account for a higher proportion, 53.2 per cent, these being the Russian Federation, Iran (again) and Qatar. The top ten holders of gas reserves account for 76.4 per cent of the world total. Perhaps surprisingly for some, the world's coal reserves are even more concentrated with the top three, USA, Russian Federation and

China, accounting for 61.7 per cent of the global total with the top ten accounting for 91.4 per cent.

15. The ranking of Iran as the world's second largest holder of proved reserves of both oil and gas with a very long lifespan for both at rates of production in 2008 implies that it has no need for nuclear energy for peaceful purposes for decades to come. Any requirement it may have for medical isotopes etc, can be purchased from other countries.

16. Just as for the three fossil fuels, there is a high degree of concentration of economic activity among the leading economies. The top five, US, China, Japan, Germany and the UK accounted for 52.5 per cent of the worldwide total with the United States alone amounting to 26.4 per cent in 2007. The top twenty-two economies inclusive of Saudi Arabia had a combined GDP amounting to 83.5 per cent of the global total with the top ten alone accounting for 68.1 per cent.

17. All these data, together with the G20 initiative, point to the need to concentrate one's attention on these leading groups of countries. Then, among them, one needs to be able to discriminate between the fast-growing countries such as China, currently, those progressing closer to the worldwide average and the laggards such as the former Soviet Union became during the 1990s, in order to monitor changes accurately.

18. Other factors of great significance are variations through time such as the economic cycle. This is important in individual economies such as the United States but normally even more important for variations in the volume and value of merchandise trade, perhaps especially for energy products such as oil, natural gas and coal. As we have seen, as between 1978 and 1979–80, unusual changes in stock levels can exacerbate swings in the trade cycle for oil. Cyclical fluctuations have important implications for national policy decisions.

19. High and rising taxes on petroleum in the leading European countries have clearly acted both as a revenue source for their governments and demand depressant in these countries. But arguably they have damaged the export competitiveness of these countries *vis-à-vis* the United States and Japan and arguably, too, relative to others such as South Korea and Taiwan, and China and India, as well.

20. All these differences between countries and variations through time together with important political and economic events can have an important influence on the progression of the world economy and relationships both between and within individual countries. Fundamental changes in prices, both absolute and relative, can have a profound effect on relationships worldwide and vary through time. In the energy sector this includes the change in the growth of consumption of primary energy relative to the growth of gross domestic product (GDP). Thus both increases and decreases in the price of oil entering world trade have impacted on the PE/GDP measure of improvements in the efficiency of energy use, albeit somewhat disturbed through time by comparatively abrupt price changes: up in 1973–4, 1979–80 and 2004–2008 and down from 1981 to 1986.

21. To put the changes in primary energy consumption and its components in perspective, it is necessary to look at China and the rest of the world separately in terms of percentage changes over the two years, 2007–9, affected by the economic recession in the OECD countries and Russia, but hardly at all in China.

Table v.1. Changes in Energy Demand 2007–2009 (%)

	China	Rest of World	World
Oil	+10.0	-3.5	-2.2
Gas	+27.1	-0.6	Ø
Coal	+16.9	-7.0	+3.0

Hydro	+26.9	+2.5	+6.3
Nuclear	+12.8	-2.2	-1.9
Total Primary Energy	+16.5	-2.9	+0.4

Source: BP *Statistical Review of World Energy* (June 2010).
Ø = less than 0.05.

22. Thus China is now so big and relatively unaffected by the deep recession in the OECD countries and Russia, that it must be analysed and monitored separately henceforth. This is so even if the two years from 2007 to 2009 were quite exceptional and probably unique in terms of the comparative table. However, there have been other years, 2003 and 2004, when annual growth of Chinese energy consumption has exceeded 15 per cent, i.e. much more than it did in either 2008 or 2009 when the annual rises were below 10 per cent.

23. One other consequence of the changes noted above was that China, inclusive of Hong Kong, became the world's biggest energy consumer in 2009, ahead of the United States. Looking at growth in Chinese consumption of total primary energy over a longer period back to 1999 compared with the whole of the rest of the world, we can see the differences in terms of percentage points started to be quite significant in 2001 and became quite remarkable in 2003 and 2004. Since then, the differences have remained in excess of 6 percentage points over each of the five years from 2005 to 2009 inclusive. The data are shown in graphical form in Figure iv.6. While Chinese consumption of primary energy accounted for only 10.5 per cent of the worldwide total in 1999 by 2009 it had risen to 19.7 per cent.

Table v.2. Chinese Growth in Primary Energy Consumption Above that in the Rest of the World by the Following Margins in % Points

| 1999 | 0.3 | 2005 | .5 |
| 2000 | 0.7 | 2006 | 10.0 |

2001	3.5	2007	6.4
2002	4.5	2008	6.9
2003	14.1	2009	11.8
2004	13.3		

Source: BP *Statistical Review of World Energy*.

24. New oil finds over the past thirty years have been much greater than we had expected during 1980–1 when preparing *Energy: A Global Outlook*, particularly during the 1985–90 period in OPEC member countries. This reflects not merely the discovery of new oil fields but also a very significant increase in the recovery factor for oil in place. For example, in the United States, the US Geological Survey estimated that the recovery factor in that oldest-established oil province was only 22 per cent in 1979, 120 years after Drakes Well was found, but given the long-established technology available in the US oil industry and the economic incentive related to higher oil prices, the recovery factor rose to an estimated 35 per cent just twenty years later in 1999, a very significant improvement.

25. The other major shortcoming in our projections in *Energy: A Global Outlook* was the changes in the real oil price which have actually occurred since 1980–1. However, if one now reviews the prices in this base period as being unrealistic in terms of subsequent events, as we did in Part II above, one can instead suggest that the comparatively stable oil prices of 1974 to 1978 provide a more realistic alternative base period price. Though prices over a five-year period do not provide a secure foundation for projections more than thirty years ahead, particularly given the ups and downs during this lengthy intervening period, the data available do suggest that a price in the $70 to $80 a barrel range (which it has been mostly between mid-2009 and mid-2010) is consistent with an average growth in real terms of about 1.5 per cent p.a., albeit highly variable since 1978, for a depleting natural resource.

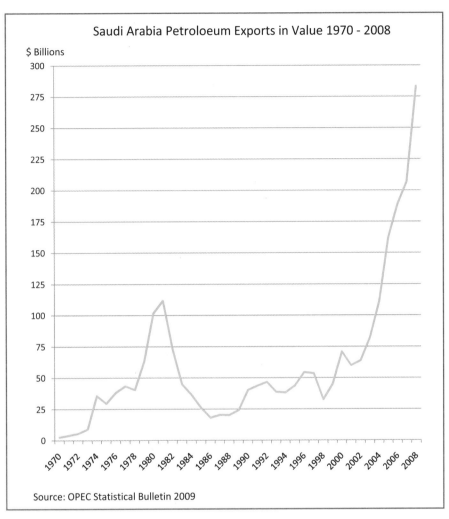

Figure v.i

26. The combination of shortcomings in the two paragraphs discussed above meant that the tighter oil market and rising real oil prices envisaged in *Energy: A Global Outlook* thirty years ago did not come to fruition during this period to 2000. Furthermore, worldwide production at 74.8 million b/d in the year 2000 was in fact much higher

than projected in any of our scenarios of thirty years ago. However, given the limiting constraint of a rather low reserves to production ratio for most countries outside OPEC, it is quite instructive to note the much more even progression of OPEC production volumes over the years since 1985 than the changes which have occurred in the former Soviet Union or in the rest of the world.

Table v.3. Changes in Oil Production (mn b/d)

	World	OPEC	Former Soviet Union	Rest of World
1985 to 2000	+17.3	+14.1	-4.0	+7.2
2000 to 2008	+7.2	+4.5	+4.8	-2.1

27. OPEC production continued rising from 2000 to 2008 along with the recovery in volume of 4.8 million b/d from the former Soviet Union as its production recovered from the lows in the late 1990s. In contrast, there were significant offsetting falls of 1 million b/d in the US and 1.1 million b/d in the UK and 0.9 million b/d in the Norwegian sectors of the North Sea over these eight years. Falls in production in all three are likely to continue, especially in the North Sea, barring significant new discoveries. Additionally, falls in production were also recorded in Mexico and Australia over this eight-year period, too.

28. Volatility of oil prices in real terms over thirty-one years to 2008 can be summarized as in Table v.4. In other words, oil price fluctuations in real terms exceeding 10 per cent in consecutive years occurred in almost two years in every three while fluctuations exceeding 20 per cent in consecutive years occurred in almost one year in every three.

Table v.4. Number of Years in the 31 Years to 2008 When Prices Moved Significantly

Real oil price fell more than 10% in consecutive years	9
Real oil price rose more than 10% in consecutive years	11
Annual fluctuations of more than 10%	20
Real oil prices fell more than 20% in consecutive years	3
Real oil prices rose more than 20% in consecutive years	7
Annual fluctuations of more than 20%	10

29. There seems little doubt that such pronounced fluctuations can be attributed largely to the growth of spot and futures trading of both crude oil and refined products. These formerly marginal markets have been the driver of prices for virtually the whole of the market for oil entering world trade for almost the whole of the last thirty years, supplanting contract prices which provided an element of stability for both oil exporters and importers in earlier periods.

30. These pronounced oil price fluctuations have happened in spite of the fact that OPEC production in general and that of Saudi Arabia in particular has fallen in soft or softening markets and risen when oil prices have been increasing in an attempt to dampen these price fluctuations and meet fluctuations in demand, as well as protecting their export volumes and export earnings.

31. What it seems most desirable to try and eliminate are freak bubbles in the oil price for the bulk of oil volumes entering world trade unsupported by supply and demand fundamentals: the price rose to more than $140 a barrel in July 2008 then fell to less than $40 a barrel within seven to eight months, overshooting on both the up and down sides, as illustrated in Part II. Comparatively sharp fluctuations have characterized some other commodity markets, too, with speculative activity probably exacerbating price changes.

32. The variability of oil prices entering world trade over the last thirty years or so is a feature which we believe has led to disturbances if not disruptions in the evolution of the world economy and has been inimical to investment plans in production of energy. Thus there is evidently a role for possible regulation to limit the wilder swings in oil prices in both directions such as those seen in 2008.

33. The relative positions of oil and gas in the world market for energy remain quite finely poised, with the two together accounting for almost 60 per cent of world primary energy consumption. However, there are marked differences between them: 67 per cent of worldwide production in oil went into international trade in 2008 whereas only 27 per cent of global gas production did so, via pipelines or as LNG.

34. Although world proved oil reserves are larger than reserves of natural gas, the prospective lifespan of gas reserves is much longer than for oil, both among OPEC countries and other countries worldwide, and thus for the world as a whole. The reserves to production ratios for each group in 2008 were as shown in Table v.5.

Table v.5. Reserves to Production Ratios in Years

	OPEC	Rest of World	World as a Whole
Oil	72.7	17.9	41.6
Gas	171.2	35.5	60.3

35. These comparative estimates serve to emphasize the world's almost inevitably increasing reliance on OPEC source supplies of both oil and gas in the medium to longer term, given the rather limited scope for increasing conventional oil supplies from sources outside OPEC, barring big new discoveries and/or significant further increases in the recovery factor of oil in place. Russian gas is the one external source capable of

making a large incremental contribution to world hydrocarbon supplies outside OPEC on the basis of current estimates for proved reserves.

36. If all countries with reserves to production ratios exceeding 60:1 (prospective lifespan in years) were to invest to increase their sustainable production to this level for both oil and gas, then incremental world oil supplies could increase by some 11.2 million b/d but supplies of natural gas could increase by a significantly higher amount of some 21.1 million b/d of oil equivalent. Thus together these two hydrocarbon sources could add some 32 million b/d to the volume of supply reported for 2008 consistent with a reserves to production ratio being maintained at 60:1 for a theoretically discretionary group of producers of both oil and gas. Some of these may feel they may have no need to make the necessary investments to increase production and export earnings merely to set up or add to sovereign wealth funds in the absence of international financial markets providing absolute guarantees for the maintenance of capital values in real terms.

37. A comparison between OPEC and the rest of the world reveals a remarkable difference between net additions to proved reserves over the twenty-eight years to end year 2007 compared with their levels of production over this same period.

Table v.6. Production and Additions to Oil Reserves 1979–2007 (bn barrels)

	Net Additions to Proved Reserves	Oil Production
OPEC	497	290
Rest of World	96	438

38. Thus OPEC's net additions to its proved oil reserves amounted to 71 per cent more than its production over the period while the net additions in the rest of the world amounted to just 22 per cent of its production volume. Figures 11.11, 11.12 and 11.13 illustrate the key differences

between OPEC and the rest of the world. Discussion of them is to be found in Part II above.

39. OPEC production volume fell by 14.5 million b/d from a peak of 31.4 million b/d in 1979 to a low of only 16.9 million b/d in 1985. Over the same period oil production in the rest of the world rose by 5.9 million b/d. In the twenty-three years subsequently OPEC production increased by 19.8 million b/d to a new peak of 36.7 million b/d in 2008. During this same period oil production in the whole of the rest of the world rose by a mere 4.75 million b/d. The comparative annual average changes over these six- and twenty-three-year periods were as in Table v.7.

Table v.7. Comparative Average Annual Changes in Oil Production

	1979 to 1985	1985 to 2008
	% p.a	
OPEC	-9.8	3.4
Rest of World	2.7	0.6

40. Thus to restore its production and export volumes in 1986 OPEC was obliged to restore its competitiveness. Saudi Arabia's technique for doing this was the introduction of netback pricing. However, the consequence of this sort of initiative was that the average world spot price of crude oil fell by 52.4 per cent from 1985 to only $13.10 a barrel in 1986, almost the same level it had been in 1978. Tables II.38 and II.43 above provide the detail.

41. There is a certain rationale for OPEC. Had world oil production continued to rise at the rate of 7.6 per cent p.a. which it did over the eight years to 1973, then the world's proved oil reserves would have been completely depleted in the year 2000. Thus had OPEC not existed, market forces alone would brought about a fundamental upward change in the real price of oil entering world trade during the last quarter of

the twentieth century, anyway. The OPEC price initiatives of 1973–4 were intended to be a once and for all fundamental change for oil entering world trade. The further big changes in the oil price induced by speculative market forces in 1979–80 and 2004–8 proved unsustainable. On the contrary, the prices prevailing over the period 1974 to 1978 appeared quite sustainable. Given the inflation recorded in the export unit value of industrial countries to 2008, a real price increase for oil averaging 1.5 per cent p.a. from 1976 would have led to a price in the $70 to $80 a barrel range in 2008. For a depletable and non-renewable form of energy this seems reasonable and likely to be achievable over the twelve months from mid-2009 to mid-2010.

42. In a worldwide context OPEC member countries present a series of characteristics. In 2008 their population, at 613 million, was 9.1 per cent of the world population; their GDP was 4.75 per cent of world GDP $2.88 trillion. Their GDP per capita was 52 per cent of the world average: $4,699 compared with $9,036 worldwide. 69 per cent of the population in four OPEC member countries had a GDP per capita below the OPEC average. Only 1.4 per cent of the population in three OPEC countries had a GDP capita above $50,000, i.e. higher than the US average. OPEC petroleum exports hit an unprecedented high in value in 2008 of just above $1 trillion but this represented just 35 per cent of their combined GDP and less than 1.7 per cent of the worldwide aggregate GDP.

43. In the circumstances outlined in this book, having regard to both the volume of proved reserves held by some OPEC countries and their prospective lifespan, it is not difficult to envisage that the OPEC share of world oil production could once again exceed 50 per cent as it did in six of the seven years from 1971 to 1977. This period was followed by strong growth in supplies from the North Sea, Alaskan North Slope and elsewhere, with no comparable high growth in oil production now envisaged within three to five years from mid-2010.

44. The combination of rising OPEC oil production from 2002 until 2008 and rapidly increasing spot (and futures) prices for crude oil, culminating in the unsustainable peak in the latter year, meant that the value of OPEC's oil production increased almost 4.9 times over just these six years. Of course, this leaves out of account comparatively fast-rising oil consumption in OPEC countries over this period.

45. The deep economic recession which started to affect worldwide oil consumption in 2008, but much more so in 2009, meant that OPEC oil production fell by 7 per cent in the latter year while the spot price of Dubai crude (as a proxy for OPEC) was 35 per cent lower than the year before. This meant that the value of OPEC production was almost 40 per cent lower in 2009 than it had been in 2008. Nevertheless, this was still 18.5 per cent higher than it had been as recently as just four years previously in 2005. Thus given that 2008 was an exceptional year in terms of the world oil price being determined by speculative market forces, the adverse effect of the financial crisis and economic recession on the value of OPEC oil production was comparatively modest given the inevitable fluctuations associated with the trade cycle.

46. Given the very long lifespan of both the reserves of oil and gas in Iraq and the prospect of the world running short of these hydrocarbons over the coming decades, there should be worldwide interest in preserving peace among the three populations native to this country. In spite of ongoing problems since 2003, the domestic development and redevelopment of the Iraqi oil and gas sector could make an enormous contribution to restoring the Iraqi economy, increasing the depressed incomes of Iraqi citizens and increasing supplies of both oil and gas to the world market, given its obvious potential to do so.

47. In 2008 total Middle East oil exports were very similar in volume to what they had been in 1979, just over 20 million b/d, in spite of the dramatic drop through to 1985. The distribution of these exports had changed

dramatically, however, with the East and Far East destinations becoming dominant, accounting for more than 69 per cent of Middle East oil exports in 2008, up from less than 35 per cent of the total in 1979. US imports from the Middle East were up marginally to nearly 12 per cent of the total in 2008. Europe was not quite the mirror image of the East/Far East, though its share of Middle East exports of oil declined by 30 percentage points over the twenty-nine years to only 12.7 per cent in 2008. European oil imports were marginally higher by 0.7 million b/d in 2008 at 13.75 million than in 1979 but in 2008 the former Soviet Union accounted for 46.7 per cent of European oil imports compared with only 8.5 per cent in 1979, a rise of 38 percentage points. Assuming oil demand remains buoyant in China, India, Japan and South Korea etc, Middle Eastern oil exports are likely to find markets in those countries with Europe perhaps losing access to the world's major supply source in the event of a tightening in world supplies, with the oil reserves to production ratio in the Russian Federation being much lower than in the Middle East.

48. As shown in Parts II and III of this book, the demise of the Soviet Union had a dramatic effect on the economy of its constituent members and its very important energy sector over the decade from 1990 to 2000. Figure 11.24 encapsulated the principal measures of decline and contrasted them with the growth prevailing over the same period in the rest of the world.

49. The low point in oil exports from the former Soviet Union was reached in 1998, but then started to recover and by 2007 they had risen by almost 4.8 million b/d. This served to enable European oil imports to rise by more than 2.9 million b/d from this source over the same nine years, making up for a fall in North Sea production in Norway and the UK, together having fallen by 1.75 million b/d.

50. Also, as a result of natural gas consumption in the former Soviet Union falling by more than production of it over this decade, increases in gas availability for export were a feature of the 1990s too. This has continued

during the period from 2000 to 2008.

51. However, by 2008, as the biggest holder of world gas reserves, Russia's gas production at 10.85 million b/d oil equivalent almost exactly equalled Saudi Arabia's oil production in the same year.

52. Following the oil price increases of 1973/74, France took the initiative to reduce its relative dependence on oil to meet its growing energy needs as a medium- to long-term objective. This has been discussed and illustrated in an international comparative context in Part IV, Chapter 6, above. In Table V.8 we show simply how that policy and its effect worked out over the following decades.

Table V.8. Nuclear as % of Total Primary Energy Consumption in France

1975	1980	1985	1990	1995	2000	2005	2009
3.8	7.3	25.6	32.5	36.2	37.1	39.4	38.4

53. It is in the context of global warming and the threat of climate change that we show this progression. France is quite unique in having demonstrated that a firm policy decision implemented by successive governments can lead to important progress over just a twenty-year time-frame, the length of time which the OPEC and IEA projections cover. It is perhaps remarkable that these, along with those from the US DOE/EIA, in their reference cases, show no significant rises in the nuclear contribution to the world energy balance. This is in spite of its potential contribution to reducing greenhouse gas emissions from the burning of fossil fuels, given the widespread concerns about global warming and climate change.

54. Even in the IEA's 450 Scenario with very low growth of primary energy consumption, its projection for the year 2030 shows nuclear as representing only 9.9 per cent of worldwide primary energy demand and renewable energies of all types accounting for another 22 per cent,

making 31.9 per cent together. This looks to us to be optimistic, given the lack of progress in Copenhagen in December 2009. This compares with 43.8 per cent for just nuclear and hydro-electricity together in France, already in 2009.

55. Much of our analysis in Part IV involved looking at greenhouse gas/ CO_2 emissions on a per capita basis for various countries and groups of countries. Almost 60 per cent of the worldwide population live in countries where energy related emissions, even in 2030/2035, are projected to be less than 3.2 tonnes per capita featured in the IEA's 450 Scenario. Thus leaving this large percentage out of account should facilitate negotiations among other mainly advanced countries, especially G20 members. In these, emissions per capita are already far higher and/ or where growth of emissions is projected to be greatest, e.g. China, should be the priority for the medium term, entailing action over the next twenty to twenty-five years.

56. The advanced OECD countries and Russia have been primarily responsible for the historical growth of greenhouse gas emissions. They are economically and technologically best equipped to make fundamentally important changes in their energy balances in favour of clean energy with less greenhouse gas emissions. Purposeful policy action among them could result in reducing global emissions to the 450 parts per million consistent with limiting the temperature rise to 2° C. The UN Framework Convention on Climate Change, probably in association with G20, provides a ready-made institution to promote the necessary initiative.

57. The central message of this book is that, even with the enhanced base of proven oil reserves compared with thirty to forty years ago, with some 75 per cent of them concentrated in OPEC member countries, there needs to be a constructive international dialogue to seek a generally acceptable way forward over the years to 2020 and 2030, taking account of the

threat from global warming and climate change.

58. The formation of the G20 represents one institution which might usefully debate this issue. Others include possible cooperation between OPEC and the IEA (but this would exclude China) or, perhaps more appropriately, a series of annual meetings between the world's ten leading oil-exporting countries and the ten leading oil-importing countries. Chinese participation seems essential. Another existing institution capable of providing a potentially worthwhile input is the International Energy Forum founded in 1991. Its Secretariat is a neutral one, involving both oil producing and consuming countries.

59. Both periods of oil prices overshooting then undershooting a long-term trend based on market fundamentals have jeopardized long-term comparative stability in a more gradual evolution of the world economy. This phenomenon should be studied in depth for its implications for market coordination and possible regulatory action. These periods are 1979 to 1986 and 2004 to 2008. The financial crisis of 2007–8, followed by the economic recession of 2008–9, should be considered as part of the latter, too, having regard to links between the financial and energy sectors of the world economy and the speculative activities which seem to have characterized both of them during this most recent period, not to mention other commodities, too.

60. The insistence in April 2010 of Israeli Prime Minister Benjamin Netanyhu in extending Jewish settlements in East Jerusalem, could have unfortunate consequences. This is in spite of such action being against international law and in violation of the wishes of the US Administration, the Arab community of nations and even more reasonable elements within Israel itself. It promises to exacerbate the poisonous relationship between Israel and many of its neighbours. The probability is that only stronger political and economic pressure against Israel by President Barack Obama will be able to turn the tide, notwithstanding the power

of the Jewish lobby in Washington, DC, especially if the current mission of US representative George Mitchell concerned with the so-called peace process proves unsuccessful. Perhaps the United Nations itself should make a serious effort to ensure not simply a peaceful solution but a just one, too, on behalf of dispossessed Palestinians. Following the visit of the UN Secretary General to Gaza in 2010 conceivably the UN could be seen as more detached, dispassionate and objective than the US in its consideration of this intractable problem, with the whole of the UN General Assembly being able to call Israel to account, if necessary.

Notes

1. Even in 2007, this figure of 719 million tonnes of CO_2 represented 12.1 per cent of global emissions attributed to worldwide consumption of natural gas estimated by the US DOE/EIA in its *International Energy Outlook* 2010.
2. This implies a recovery factor of 35 per cent.
3. Excluding renewable energy other than hydro-electricity.
4. This represented some 4.6 per cent of worldwide GDP in 2008.
5. Initially it had been intended to make this analysis for natural gas on the same criteria as for oil, i.e. 6.6 billion cubic metres of gas reserves, approximately equivalent to 10 billion barrels of oil reserves. However, it was found that only five countries qualified on this basis, so qualification for inclusion in this analysis was reduced to 3 trillion cubic metres of gas reserves, i.e. less than 5 billion barrels of oil equivalent. This resulted in the inclusion of a further six countries, all of which were OPEC members in 2008.
6. Between 2007 and 2008 Turkmenistan increased its gas reserves by almost 3.3 times putting its R:P ratio up to 120.1, i.e. above both Saudi Arabia and the Russian Federation in terms of lifespan, based on estimates in the *BP Statistical Review* published in June 2009. However, the estimates published in the *Oil and Gas Journal* in December 2008 showed Turkmenistan's gas reserves falling by 6,000 billion cubic feet (i.e. $168 \times 10^9 m^3$) through the year 2008, as indicated in Table 11.47.
7. Chinese reserves of sub-bituminous coal and lignite, 52.3 billion tonnes at the end of 2008, is equal to approximately 17.4 billion tonnes of oil equivalent, i.e. 42% of its reserves of anthracite and bituminous coal in terms of oil equivalent. Thus total Chinese coal reserves amount to 58.9 billion tonnes of oil equivalent. Even this represents only forty-one years lifespan at the very high and fast-rising coal production as of 2008.
8. 7.5 per cent is based on current US dollar estimate for 2008; the figure is 7.1 per cent

based on constant dollars of the year 2000 for 2008.

9. To bring this analysis up to date we can refer to a comparison between the big increase in the crude oil cif price averaging about $60 a barrel in the leading G7 advanced countries from 2004 to 2008 compared with the increases in taxes over the same period levied by these same countries. The bar chart in Figure 11.27 shows that, unlike the similarity of the crude oil price increase between these countries, there was a remarkable difference between these countries in the extent of the tax increase over the same period. These ranged from less than $20 a barrel in the United States to tax increases per barrel which exceeded the crude oil price increase by a significant margin in both the UK and Germany.

10. Now Commonwealth of Independent States comprising the Russian Federation, Armenia, Azerbaijan, Belarus, Estonia, Georgia, Kazakhstan, Kyrgyzstan, Latvia, Lithuania, Moldova, Tajikistan, Turkmenistan, Ukraine, Uzbekistan.

11. i.e. the nominal price adjusted for the export unit values of industrial countries expressed in US dollars (sometimes downward but more usually up, as reported by the IMF.

12. Other forms of renewable energy were not yet very significant in 2009 and not documented in the source used.

Index